SOME RECOLLECTIONS OF OUR ANTISLAVERY CONFLICT.

BY

SAMUEL J. MAY.

BOSTON:
FIELDS, OSGOOD, & CO.
1869.

UNIVERSITY PRESS: WELCH, BIGELOW, & CO.,
CAMBRIDGE.

PREFACE.

MANY of these Recollections were published at intervals, during the years 1867 and 1868, in *The Christian Register.* They were written at the special request of the editor of that paper; and without the slightest expectation that they would ever be put to any further use. But so many persons have requested me to republish them in a volume, that I have gathered them here, together with several more recollections of events and transactions, illustrative of the temper of the times as late as the winter of 1861, when our guilty nation was left "to be saved so as by the fire" of civil war.

My readers must not expect to find in this book anything like a complete history of the times to which it relates. The articles of which it is composed are fragmentary and sketchy. I expect and hope they will not satisfy. If they whet the appetites of those who read them for a more thorough history of the conflict with slavery in our country and in Great Britain, they will have accomplished their purpose. That in the two freest, most enlightened, most Christian nations on earth there should have been, during more than half of the nineteenth century, so stout a defence of "the worst system of iniquity the world has ever known," is a marvel that cannot be fully studied and explained, without discovering that the mightiest nation, as well as the humblest individual, may not with impunity consent to any sin, nor persist in unrighteousness without ruin.

I am happy to announce that in due time a somewhat elaborate history of the rise and fall of the slave power in America may be expected from the Hon. Henry Wilson. He is competent to the undertaking. He is cautious and candid as well as brave and explicit. He was an Abolitionist before he became a politician. He has never ignored the rights of humanity, for the sake of partisan success or personal aggrandizement. Mr. Wilson, I believe, did as much as any one of our prominent statesmen to procure the abolition of slavery in the District of Columbia, and to effect its subversion throughout the country.

My brief sketches have been taken, I presume, from a point of sight different somewhat from his. Many of my readers may wish that I had not reported so many of the evil words and deeds of ministers and churches. I have done so with regret and mortification. But it has seemed to me that the most important lesson taught in the history of the last forty years — the influence of slavery upon the religion of our country — ought least of all to be withheld from the generations that are coming on to fill our places in the Church and in the State.

My book, I fear, will be displeasing to many because they will not find in it much that they expect. I can only beg such to bear in mind what I have proposed to give my readers, — not a history of the antislavery conflict, only some of my recollections of the events and actors in it. I have merely mentioned the names of our indefatigable and able fellow-laborers, Henry C. Wright, Stephen S. Foster, and Parker Pillsbury. A due account of their valuable services in this country and Great Britain would fill a volume as large as this. But, for the most part, these became known to me through *The Liberator* and *Antislavery Standard.*

My sphere of operation and observation was confined almost entirely to Massachusetts and Connecticut, until I removed to Central New York in 1845. My travels as an antislavery agent and lecturer were restricted to New England, and to the years from 1832 to 1836, before many who have since become distinguished had given themselves to the work. The field has been coextensive with our vast country. It cannot be supposed that I have personally known a tenth part of the individuals who have done good services, much less that I have been a witness of their words and deeds. Often have I been encouraged and delighted by unexpected tidings of noble words uttered and brave deeds done, in one part and another of the land, by individuals whom I never saw before nor since. Almost everywhere there was some one who promptly responded to the demand for the liberation of the enslaved, and dared to advocate their right to freedom. Could a perfect history be written of the antislavery labors of the last forty years, hundreds would be named as having rendered valuable services, of whom I have never heard ; whose good word or work perhaps was not known beyond the immediate circle that was affected by it. But the memory thereof will not be lost. Every righteous act, every heroic, generous, true utterance in the cause of the outraged, crushed, despised bondmen, will be had in everlasting remembrance, and He who seeth in secret will hereafter, if not here, openly reward the faithful.

S. J. M.

CONTENTS.

RISE OF ABOLITIONISM.

EVER and anon in the world's history there has been some one who has broken out as a living fountain of the *free spirit* of humanity, has given bold utterance to the pent-up thought of wrongs, too long endured, and has made the demand for some God-given right, until then withheld, — a demand so obviously just, that the tyrants of earth have trembled as if called to judgment, and the oppressed have rejoiced as at the voice of their deliverer. "It is thus the spirit of a single mind makes that of multitudes take one direction."

Such, as the subsequent history of our country has shown, such was the spirit of the mind of that man who will be honored through all coming time, as the leader of the most glorious movement ever made in humanity's behalf, — the movement for *perfect, impartial liberty*, which for the last thirty-nine years has rocked our Republic from centre to circumference, and will continue to agitate it until every vestige of slavery is shaken out of our civil fabric.

"When the tourist of Europe has descended from the Black Forest into Suabia, his guide asks him if he does not wish to see the source of the Danube. Only one answer can be given to such a question. So he is conducted into the garden of an obscure nobleman of Baden; and there, within a small stone enclosure, he is shown the highest spring of that river, which has worn its channel deeper and wider for sixteen hundred miles, and, receiving on its way the contributions of thirty navigable streams, enters the Black Sea by five mouths, thus opening a communication between the interior of Europe and the Mediterranean, bearing on its bosom the commerce of fifty millions of people, and bringing them into the community of nations."

Soon after Mr. Garrison's assault upon the institution of American slavery began to be felt, (and that was almost as soon as it began,) a Southern governor wrote to the mayor of Boston, demanding to know what was to be expected, what to be feared, from this attack upon "the peculiar institution of the South." In due time the gentleman who was then the high official addressed replied to his Southern excellency, that there was no occasion for uneasiness. "He had made diligent search for the would-be 'Liberator.' The city officers had ferreted out the paper and its editor. His office was an obscure hole, his only visible auxiliary a negro boy, and his supporters a few very insignificant persons of all colors."

Undoubtedly to that dainty gentleman the rise of the antislavery enterprise in our country did seem insignificant, — quite as insignificant as the little spring of water in the garden at Baden. He may never have learnt among his nursery rhymes, that

"Large streams from little fountains flow,
Tall oaks from little acorns grow,"

and he must have forgotten that Christianity began in a stable, — "that not many wise men after the flesh, not many mighty, not many noble were called. But that God chose the *foolish* things of the world to confound the wise, and the *weak* things of the world to confound the things which are mighty." Our poet, Lowell, estimated more justly "the would-be Liberator," his office and his humble assistant.

"In a small chamber, friendless and unseen,
Toiled o'er his types one poor, unlearned young man;
The place was dark, unfurnitured, and mean;
Yet there *the freedom of a race* began.

"Help came but slowly; sure no man yet
Put lever to the heavy world with less.
What need of help? He knew how types to set;
He had a dauntless spirit and a press.

"Such dauntless natures are the fiery pith,
The compact nucleus round which systems grow;
Mass after mass becomes inspired therewith,
And whirls impregnate with the central glow."

It cannot be denied that the spirit of Mr. Garrison's mind has made the minds of multitudes — yes, of the majority of the people of our country — take a new direction in favor of impartial liberty. Of course, I do not claim that this new love of liberty originated with him. He was no more the creator of this moral power, which has taken our nation in its grasp, and is remoulding all our civil and religious institutions, than the fountain in the garden at Baden is the originator of the mighty Danube. Mr. Garrison, no less than that spring, is but a medium, through which the Father of all mercies pours from the hollow of his hand the waters that refresh the earth, and, from the fulness of his heart, the streams that purify the souls, making glad the children of God on earth and in heaven. But although to God we must ultimately ascribe all our blessings, yet do we naturally, and with great reason, revere and love as our *benefactors* those persons who have been the means and instruments by which personal, political, or religious blessings have been conferred upon us. Especially do we acknowledge our indebtedness to them, if they have suffered reproach, persecution, loss, death, for the sake of the good which we enjoy. The time, therefore, is coming, if it be not now, when the people of our re-united Republic will gratefully own William Lloyd Garrison among the greatest benefactors of our nation and our race.

However much our gratitude to the fathers of our Revolution may dispose us to hide their shortcomings of the goal of impartial liberty, however much we may find or devise to excuse or extenuate their infidelity to the cause of down-trodden humanity, there the shameful facts stand, and never can be effaced from the record; — the *fact* that (notwithstanding their glorious Declaration) the American revolutionists did not intend the deliverance of *all* men from oppression; no, not of all the men who heroically fought for it side by side with themselves; no, not of the men who, of all others, needed that deliverance the most;—the *fact* that the Constitution of this Republic (notwithstanding its avowed purpose) did not mean to secure liberty to *all* the dwellers in the land over which it was to preside; nor did it provide that those might depart from under it who were not to have any share in its blessings, nor allow the spirit of liberty in them to assert its claims; — the shameful *fact* that the aim, the tendency, and the result of that great struggle for freedom were partial, restricted, selfish; — the terrible fact that the American revolutionists of 1776 left more firmly established in our country a system of bondage, a slavery, "one hour of which" was known and acknowledged by them to be "more intolerable than whole ages of that from which they had revolted."

To complete, *by moral and religious means and instruments*, the great work which the American revolutionists commenced; to do what they left undone; to exterminate from our land the worst form of oppression, the tremendous sin of slavery, was the sole purpose of the enterprise of the Abolitionists, commenced in January, 1831. In this great work Mr. Garrison has been the leader from the beginning. Of him, therefore, I shall have the most to say. But of many other noble men and women I shall have occasion to make most grateful mention.

Although I claim that Mr. Garrison has done more than any one else for the liberation of the immense slave population of America, I am not ignorant or forgetful of those who, before his day, made some attempts for their deliverance. Not to mention the many eminent divines and statesmen of England and the Colonies, before the Revolution, who utterly condemned slavery,—the prominent leaders in that momentous conflict with Great Britain, and in the institution of our Republic, felt and acknowledged its glaring inconsistency with a democratic government. Some of that day predicted, with almost prophetic foresight, the evils, the ruin, which it would bring upon our nation, if slavery should be permitted to abide in our midst. Many protested against the Constitution, because of those articles in it which favored the continuance and indefinite extension of "the great iniquity." But their objections were too generally overruled by plausible expositions of the potency of other parts of our Magna Charta; and they acquiesced, in the vain hope that the *spirit* of the Constitution would prove to be better than the letter.

For twenty years after the re-formation of our General Government in 1787, true-hearted men and women spoke and wrote in terms of strong condemnation of slavery, as well as the slave-trade. They spoke and wrote and published what the spirit of liberty dictated, in Maryland, Virginia, and North Carolina, not less than in Pennsylvania, New York, and the New England

States. Nay, more, they instituted "societies for the amelioration of the condition of the enslaved, and their *gradual* emancipation." Headed by no less a man than Dr. Franklin, they besieged Congress with petitions for the suppression of the African slave-trade, and the *gradual* abolition of slavery. But after, in 1808, they had obtained the prohibition of the trade, they subsided, as did the abolitionists of Great Britain, into the belief that the subversion of the whole evil of slavery would soon follow as a consequence; not foreseeing that, so long as the *market* for slaves should be kept open, the commodity demanded there would be forthcoming, let the hazard of procuring it be ever so great. It is now notorious that the traffic in human beings has never been carried on so briskly as since its nominal abolition, while the sufferings of the victims, and the destruction of their lives, have been threefold greater than before.

Owing to this mistaken expectation of the effect of the Act of 1808 abolishing the slave-trade, the attention of philanthropists was in a great measure withdrawn from the subject of slavery for ten years or more. Meanwhile, the friends of "the peculiar institution" were busily engaged in extending its borders and strengthening its defences. The purchase of the Louisiana and Florida territories threw open countless acres of *virgin* soil, on which the labor of slaves was more profitable than elsewhere. The invention of the "cotton-gin" rendered the preparation of that staple so easy, that our Southern planters could compete with any producers of it the world over. Cotton plantations, therefore, multiplied apace. The value of slaves was more than doubled. The spirit of private manumission, which in Virginia alone, between 1798 and 1808, had set free more than a thousand bondmen annually, was checked by avarice, and then forbidden by law. And the "Ancient Dominion," proud Virginia, rapidly became the home of slave-breeders; and from that American Guinea was carried on a traffic in human beings as brisk and horrible as ever desolated the coast of Africa.

The free colored population at the South were subjected to new disabilities, were exposed to most vexatious annoyances, and were denied the protection of law against encroachments or personal injuries by the "whites"; and very many of them, on slight pretexts, were reduced to slavery again.

Social intercourse between the Northern and the Southern States was then infrequent. It was kept up mainly by the wealthy and pleasure-seeking, who, in their enjoyment of the hospitality of the planters, could learn little of the condition and character of their bondmen, and were easily led to take "South-side views of slavery."

Whatsoever we gathered from these sources of information led us too readily to acquiesce in the common assumption, that the negroes were a thick-skulled, stupid, kind-hearted, jolly people, not much if any worse off in slavery at the South than most of the free people of color, and some other poor folks were at the North. So, when we were disquieted at all on their account, it was but for a little time, and we relieved ourselves of the burden by a sigh or two over the misery that everywhere "flesh is heir to."

The first event that fixed the attention of Northern men seriously upon the subject of slavery, over which they had slumbered since 1808, was the dispute that arose in 1819, upon the proposal to admit Missouri into the Union as a slave State. The contest was a vehement one. Mr. Webster was *then* upon the side of liberty. He led the van of the opposition that arrayed itself in New England, and would have averted the catastrophe, but for the cry "dissolution of the Union," then first raised at the South, and the necromancy of Henry Clay, who, with his wand of compromise, conjured the people into acquiescence. Words, however, significant words, touching the evil and the awful wrong of slavery, were uttered in that controversy which were not to be forgotten. And feelings of compassion for the bondmen were awakened which were not allayed by the result.

Shortly before the Missouri controversy a movement had commenced in the slave States, which was pregnant with effects very different from those intended by the projectors of it. Often was it roughly demanded of us Abolitionists, "Why we espoused so zealously the cause of the enslaved?" "why we meddled so with the civil and domestic institutions of the Southern States?" Our first answer always was, in the memorable words of old Terence, "Because we are men, and, therefore, cannot be indifferent to anything that concerns humanity." Liberty cannot be enjoyed, nor long preserved, at the North, if slavery be tolerated at the South. But to those who felt so slightly the cords of love and the bonds of a common humanity that they could not appreciate these reasons, we gave another reason for our interference with the slavery in our Southern States, even this: *we were solicited, we were urged, entreated by the slaveholders themselves to interfere.*

About the year 1816, while intent upon their projects for perpetuating and extending their "peculiar institution," the slaveholders were alarmed by symptoms of discontent among the free colored people, imagined that they were promoting insubordination amongst the slaves, and so conceived the project of colonizing them in Africa. To insure the accomplishment of so mighty an undertaking, it was obviously necessary to obtain the aid of the general government. In order to sustain that government in making such a large appropriation of the public money as would be needed, the people of the North, as well as of the South, were to be conciliated to the plan; and to conciliate them it was necessary to make it appear to be a philanthropic enterprise, conferring great benefits immediately upon the free colored people, and tending certainly, though indirectly, to the entire abolition of slavery. Accordingly, agents, eloquent and cunning men, were sent into all the free States, especially into Pennsylvania, New York, and New England, to press the claims of the oppressed people of the South upon the compassion and generosity of the Northern philanthropists. Never did agents do their work better. Never were more exciting appeals made to the humane than were pressed home upon us by such men as Mr. Gurley, Mr. Cresson, and their fellow-laborers. They kept out of sight the real design, the primal object, the animus of the founders and Southern patrons of the American Colonization Society. They presented to us views of the debasing, dehumanizing effects of slavery upon its victims; the need of a far-distant removal from its overshadowing presence of those who had been blighted by it, that they might revive, unfold their humanity, exhibit their capacities, command the respect of those who had known them only in degradation, and, by their new-born activities, not only secure comfort and plenty for themselves on the shores of their fatherland, but prepare homes there for the reception of millions still pining in slavery, who, we were assured, would be gladly released whenever it should be known that the bestowment of freedom would be a blessing and not a curse to them. Such appeals were not made to our hearts in vain. Suffice it to say that Mr. Garrison,

Gerrit Smith, Arthur Tappan, William Goodell, and all the early Abolitionists, were induced to espouse the cause of our oppressed and enslaved countrymen, by the speeches and tracts of Southern Colonizationists.

If I were intending to write a complete history of the conflict with slavery in our country, gratitude would impel me to give some account of a number of philanthropists who, in different parts of the Union, some of them in the midst of slaveholding communities, before Mr. Garrison's day, had fully exposed and faithfully denounced "the great iniquity," I should make especial mention of

REV. JOHN RANKIN AND REV. JOHN D. PAXTON.

The former was a Presbyterian minister in Kentucky, where, in 1825, having heard that his brother, Mr. Thomas Rankin, of Virginia, had become a slaveholder, he addressed to him a series of very earnest and impressive letters in remonstrance. They were published first in a periodical called the *Castigator*, and afterwards went through several editions in pamphlet form. He denounced "slavery as a never-failing fountain of the grossest immoralities, and one of the deepest sources of human misery." He insisted that "the safety of our government and the happiness of its subjects depended upon the extermination of this evil." We New England Abolitionists, in the early days of our warfare, made great use of Mr. Rankin's volume as a depository of well-attested facts, justifying the strongest condemnation, we could utter, of the system of oppression that had become established in our country and sanctioned by our government.

Mr. Paxton was the pastor of a Presbyterian church in Cumberland, Virginia. He was a member of the

Presbyterian General Assembly, which in 1818 denounced "the voluntary enslaving of one part of the human race as a gross violation of the most precious and sacred rights of human nature, — *utterly inconsistent with the law of God.*" Believing what that grave body had declared, he set about endeavoring to convince the church to which he ministered of the exceeding sinfulness of slaveholding; and that "they ought to set their bondmen free so soon as it could be done with advantage to them." His preaching to this effect gave offence to many of his parishioners, and led to his dismission. In justice to himself, and to the cause of humanity, for espousing which he had been persecuted, Mr. Paxton also published a volume of letters, which were of great service to us. In these letters he faithfully exposed the abject, debased, suffering condition of our American slaves, — incomparably worse than that which was permitted under the Mosaic dispensation, — and pretty effectually demolished the Bible argument in support of the abomination. However, the labors of these good men, and of those whom they roused, were erelong diverted into the seductive channel of the Colonization scheme.

But there was another of the early antislavery reformers, of whom I may write much more fully in accordance with my plan, which is to give, for the most part, only my *personal recollections* of the prominent actors, and the most significant incidents, in our conflict with the giant wrong of our nation and age.

BENJAMIN LUNDY.

In the month of June, 1828, there came to the town of Brooklyn, Connecticut, where I then resided, and to the house of my friend, the venerable philanthropist, George Benson, a man of small stature, of feeble health, partially deaf, asking for a public hearing upon the subject of American slavery. It was *Benjamin Lundy.* We gathered for him a large congregation, and his address made a deep impression on many of his hearers. He exhibited the wrong of slavery and the sufferings of its victims in a graphic, affecting manner. But the relief which he proposed was to be found in removing them to some of the unoccupied territory of Texas or Mexico, rather than in recognizing their rights as men here, in the country where so many of them had been born; and in making all the amends possible for the injuries so long inflicted upon them by giving them here the blessings of education, and every opportunity and assistance to become all that God has made them capable of being. Nevertheless, Mr. Lundy had done then, and he continued afterwards, until his death in 1839, to do excellent service in the cause of the enslaved. Indeed, his labors were so abundant, his sacrifices so many, and his trials so severe, that no one will stand before the God of the oppressed with a better record than he.

Benjamin Lundy was born in New Jersey, of Quaker parents, in 1789, and was educated in the sentiments and under the influence of the society of Friends. He was, therefore, from his earliest days, taught to regard slaveholding as a great iniquity. At the age of nineteen he went to reside in Wheeling, Virginia, and there learnt the saddler's trade. This he afterwards carried on, with great success for a number of years, in the village of St. Clairville, Ohio, about ten miles from Wheeling. But he could not banish from his memory the sights he had seen at Wheeling, which was the great thoroughfare of the slave-trade between Virginia and the Southern and Southwestern States; nor efface from his heart the impression that he ought "to attempt to do something for the relief of that most injured portion of the human race."

As early as 1815, when twenty-six years of age, he formed an antislavery society, which at first consisted of only six members, but in a few months increased to nearly five hundred, among whom were many of the influential ministers, lawyers, and other prominent citizens of several of the counties in that part of Ohio. Although unused to composition, he wrote an appeal to the philanthropists of the United States, which was published and extensively circulated, and led to the formation, in different parts of the State, of societies similar in spirit and purpose to the one he had instituted. He then engaged in the publication of an antislavery paper; and to promote its circulation, and to gather materials for its columns, he commenced his travels in the slave States. These were performed for the most part on foot. Thus he journeyed thousands of miles, through Virginia, Missouri, Kentucky, Tennessee, and North Carolina. In most places where he lectured publicly, or privately, he obtained subscribers to his paper. In some places he succeeded in forming associations similar to his own. Not unfrequently he met with angry rebuffs and violent threats of personal injury. But he was a man of the most quiet courage, as well as indomitable perseverance. He disconcerted his assailants by letting them see that they could not frighten him; that the threat of assassination would not deter him from prosecuting his object. Several slaveholders were so much affected by his exposition of their iniquity that they manumitted their bondmen, on condition that he would take them to a place where they would be free. Twice or thrice he went to Hayti, conducting such freed ones thither, and finding homes for others whom he hoped to send there. Afterwards he explored large portions of Mexico and Texas; and made strenuous endeavors to obtain by grant or purchase sections of lands, upon which he might found colonies of emancipated people from this country. In this attempt he was unsuccessful; but while prosecuting it he gathered much valuable information respecting the state of that country, of which afterwards important use was made by the Hon. J. Q. Adams, in his strenuous opposition in 1836 to the audacious plot by which Texas was annexed to our Republic.

Mr. Lundy was indefatigable in laboring for whatever he undertook to accomplish. He learnt the printer's art, that he might communicate to the public whatever he discovered by his diligent inquiries of the condition of the enslaved, and enkindle in others that sympathy for them which glowed in his own bosom. He was not stationary for a long while in any one place. His paper, *The Genius of Universal Emancipation*, was published successively in Ohio, Missouri, Tennessee, and in Philadelphia, Washington, and Baltimore. For a considerable time his lecturing excursions were so frequent, diverse, and distant, that it was most convenient to him to get his paper printed, wherever he happened to be, from month to month. So he carried along with him the type, "heading," the "column-rules," and his "direction-book," and issued "the Genius," &c., from any office that was accessible to him. He often had to pay for the publication of it by working as a journeyman printer, and at other times had to support himself by working at his saddler's trade. Nothing discouraged, nothing daunted Benjamin Lundy. He possessed, in an eminent degree, the faith, patience, self-denial, courage, and endurance necessary to a pioneer. He was frequently threatened, repeatedly assaulted, and once brutally beaten. But he could not be deterred from prosecuting the work to which he was called. He was a rare specimen of perfect fidelity to duty, a conscientious, meek, but fearless, determined man, a soldier of the cross, a moral hero.

WILLIAM LLOYD GARRISON.

William Lloyd Garrison commenced his literary and philanthropic labors when a young journeyman printer, in his native place, Newburyport, Mass. In 1825 he removed to Boston, and labored for a while in the office of the *Recorder*. In 1827 he united with Rev. William Collier in editing and publishing the *National Philanthropist*, the only paper then devoted to the Temperance cause. And soon after he engaged in conducting *The Journal of the Times*, at Bennington, Vt. In each of these papers, especially the last, he took strong ground against slavery. Believing the plan of the Colonization Society to be intended to remove the great evil from our country, he espoused it with ardor, and advocated it with such signal ability, that he was recalled to Boston to deliver, in Park Street church, the annual address to the Massachusetts Colonization Society, on the 4th of July, 1828.

Mr. Garrison's writings attracted the attention of that devoted, self-sacrificing friend of the enslaved, Benjamin Lundy, of whom I have just now given some account. He urged him in 1828, and persuaded him in the autumn of 1829, to remove to Baltimore, and assist in editing *The Genius of Universal Emancipation.* There Mr. G. soon saw, with his own eyes, the atrocities of slavery and the inter-state slave-trade; there he discovered the real design and spirit of the Colonization scheme; there the radical doctrine of *immediate, unconditional* emancipation was revealed to him. He soon made himself obnoxious to slaveholders by his faithful exposure of their cruelties; and his unsparing condemnation of their atrocious system of oppression.

After he had been in Baltimore a few months, a Northern captain came there in a ship owned and freighted by a gentleman of Newburyport, Mr. Garrison's birthplace. Failing to obtain another cargo, said captain, with the consent of his owner, took on board a load of slaves to be transported to New Orleans. Such an outrage on humanity, perpetrated by Massachusetts men, enkindled Mr. G.'s hottest indignation, and drew from his pen a scathing rebuke. He was forthwith arrested as both a civil and criminal offender. He was prosecuted for a libel upon the captain and owner of the ship "Francis," and for disturbing the peace by attempting to excite the slaves to insurrection.

It would be needless to spend time in proving that, in the presence of a slaveholding judge, before a slaveholding jury, surrounded by a community of incensed slaveholders, the young reformer did not have a fair trial. He was found guilty under both indictments. He was fined and sentenced to imprisonment a certain time, as the punishment for his alleged crime, and afterward, until the fine imposed for "the libel" should be paid. It was then and there that his free, undaunted spirit inscribed upon the walls of his cell that joyous, jubilant sonnet, which could have been written only by one conscious of innocence in the sight of the Holy God, of a great purpose and a sacred mission yet to be accomplished.

"High walls and huge the body may confine,
And iron grates obstruct the prisoner's gaze,
And massive bolts may baffle his design,
And watchful keepers eye his devious ways;
Yet scorns the immortal *mind* this base control!
No chain can bind *it*, and no cell enclose.
Swifter than light it flies from pole to pole,
And in a flash from earth to heaven it goes.
It leaps from mount to mount. From vale to vale
It wanders, plucking honeyed fruits and flowers.

It visits home to hear the fireside tale,
Or in sweet converse pass the joyous hours.
'T is up before the sun, roaming afar,
And in its watches, wearies every star."

After seven weeks of close confinement Mr. Garrison was liberated by the noble, discriminating generosity of the late Arthur Tappan, then in the height of his affluence, who, so long as he had wealth, felt that he was an almoner of God's bounty, and gave his money gladly, in many ways, to the relief of suffering humanity. The spirit of freedom, — the true American eagle, — thus uncaged, flew back to his native New England, and thence sent forth that cry which disturbed the repose of every slaveholder in the land, and has resounded throughout the world.

It so happened, in the good Providence "which shapes our ends," that I was on a visit in Boston at that time, — October, 1830. An advertisement appeared in the newspapers, that during the following week W. Lloyd Garrison would deliver to the public three lectures, in which he would exhibit the awful sinfulness of slaveholding; expose the duplicity of the Colonization Society, revealing its true character; and, in opposition to it, would announce and maintain the doctrine, that immediate, unconditional emancipation is the right of every slave and the duty of every master. The advertisement announced that his lectures would be delivered on the Common, unless some church or commodious hall should be proffered to him gratuitously. If I remember correctly, it was intimated in the newspapers, or currently reported at the time, that Mr. G. had applied for several of the Boston churches, and been refused, because it was known that he had become an opponent of the Colonization Society. A day or two after the first I saw a second advertisement, informing the public that the free use of "Julien Hall," occupied by Rev. Abner Kneel-

and's church, having been generously tendered to Mr. Garrison, he would deliver his lectures there instead of the Common. I had not then seen this resolute young man. I had been much impressed by some of his writings, knew of his connection with Mr. Lundy, and had heard of his imprisonment. Of course I was eager to see and hear him, and went to Julien Hall in due season on the appointed evening. My brother-in-law, A. Bronson Alcott, and my cousin, Samuel E. Sewall, accompanied me. Truer men could not easily have been found.

The hall was pretty well filled. Among some persons whom I did, and many whom I did not know, I saw there Rev. Dr. Beecher, Rev. Mr. (now Dr.) Gannett, Deacon Moses Grant, and John Tappan, Esq.

Presently the young man arose, modestly, but with an air of calm determination, and delivered such a lecture as he only, I believe, at that time, could have written; for he only had had his eyes so anointed that he could see that outrages perpetrated upon Africans were wrongs done to our common humanity; he only, I believe, had had his ears so completely unstopped of "prejudice against color" that the cries of enslaved black men and black women sounded to him as if they came from brothers and sisters.

He began with expressing deep regret and shame for the zeal he had lately manifested in the Colonization cause. It was, he confessed, a zeal without knowledge. He had been deceived by the misrepresentations so diligently given, throughout the free States by Southern agents, of the design and tendency of the Colonization scheme. During his few months' residence in Maryland he had been completely undeceived. He had there found out that the design of those who originated, and the especial intentions of those in the Southern States that engaged in the plan, were to remove from the country, as "a disturbing element" in slaveholding communities, all the free colored people, so that the bondmen might the more easily be held in subjection. He exhibited in graphic sketches and glowing colors the suffering of the enslaved, and denounced the plan of Colonization as devised and adapted to perpetuate the system, and intensify the wrongs of American slavery, and therefore utterly undeserving of the patronage of lovers of liberty and friends of humanity.

Never before was I so affected by the speech of man. When he had ceased speaking I said to those around me: "That is a providential man; he is a prophet; he will shake our nation to its centre, but he will shake slavery out of it. We ought to know him, we ought to help him. Come, let us go and give him our hands." Mr. Sewall and Mr. Alcott went up with me, and we introduced each other. I said to him: "Mr. Garrison, I am not sure that I can indorse all you have said this evening. Much of it requires careful consideration. But I am prepared to embrace you. I am sure you are called to a great work, and I mean to help you." Mr. Sewall cordially assured him of his readiness also to coöperate with him. Mr. Alcott invited him to his home. He went, and we sat with him until twelve that night, listening to his discourse, in which he showed plainly that *immediate, unconditional emancipation, without expatriation, was the right of every slave, and could not be withheld by his master an hour without sin.* That night my soul was baptized in his spirit, and ever since I have been a disciple and fellow-laborer of William Lloyd Garrison.

The next morning, immediately after breakfast, I went to his boarding-house and stayed until two P. M. I learned that he was poor, dependent upon his daily labor for his daily bread, and intending to return to the printing business. But, before he could devote himself to his own support, he felt that he must deliver his message, must communicate to persons of prominent influence what he had learned of the sad condition of the enslaved, and the institutions and spirit of the slaveholders; trusting that all true and good men would discharge the obligation pressing upon them to espouse the cause of the poor, the oppressed, the down-trodden. He read to me letters he had addressed to Dr. Channing, Dr. Beecher, Dr. Edwards, the Hon. Jeremiah Mason, and Hon. Daniel Webster, holding up to their view the tremendous iniquity of the land, and begging them, ere it should be too late, to interpose their great power in the Church and State to save our country from the terrible calamities which the sin of slavery was bringing upon us. Those letters were eloquent, solemn, impressive. I wonder they did not produce a greater effect. It was because none to whom he appealed, in public or private, would espouse the cause, that Mr. Garrison found himself left and impelled to become the leader of the great antislavery reform, which must be *thoroughly accomplished* before our Republic can stand upon a sure foundation.

The hearing of Mr. Garrison's lectures was a great epoch in my own life. The impression which they made upon my soul has never been effaced; indeed, they moulded it anew. They gave a new direction to my thoughts, a new purpose to my ministry. I had become a convert to the doctrine of "immediate, unconditional emancipation, — liberation from slavery without expatriation."

I was engaged to preach on the following Sunday for Brother Young, in Summer Street Church. Of course I could not again speak to a congregation, as a Christian minister, and be silent respecting the *great iniquity* of our nation. The only sermon I had brought from my home in Connecticut, that could be made to bear on the subject, was one on Prejudice, — the sermon about to be published as one of the Tracts of the American Unitarian Association. So I touched it up as well as I could, interlining here and there words and sentences which pointed in the new direction to which my thoughts and feelings so strongly tended, and writing at its close what used to be called an *improvement*. Thus: "The subject of my discourse bears most pertinently upon a matter of the greatest national as well as personal importance. There are more than two millions of our fellow-beings, children of the Heavenly Father, who are held in our country in the most abject slavery, — regarded and treated like domesticated animals, their rights as men trampled under foot, their conjugal, parental, fraternal relations and affections utterly set at naught. It is our *prejudice* against the color of these poor people that makes us consent to the tremendous wrongs they are suffering. If they were white, — ay, if only two thousand or two hundred *white* men, women, and children in the Southern States were treated as these millions of colored ones are, we of the North should make such a stir of indignation, we should so agitate the country, with our appeals and remonstrances, that the oppressors would be compelled to set their bondmen free. But will our *prejudice* be accepted by the Almighty, the impartial Judge of all, as a valid excuse for our indifference to the wrongs and outrages inflicted upon these millions of our countrymen? O no! O no! He will say, "Inasmuch as ye did not what ye could for the relief of these, the least of the brethren, ye did it not to me." Tell me not that we are forbidden by the Constitution of our country to interfere in behalf of the enslaved. No compact our fathers may have made for us, no agreement we could ourselves make, would annul our obligations to suffering fellow-men. "Yes, yes," I said, with an emphasis that seemed to startle everybody in the house, "if need be, the very foundations of our Republic must be broken up; and if this stone of stumbling, this rock of offence, cannot be removed from under it, the proud superstructure must fall. It cannot stand, it ought not to stand, it will not stand, on the necks of millions of men." For "God is just, and his justice will not sleep forever." I then offered such a prayer as my kindled spirit moved me to, and gave out the hymn commencing,

> "Awake, my soul, stretch every nerve,
> And press with vigor on."

When I rose to pronounce the benediction I said: "Every one present must be conscious that the closing remarks of my sermon have caused an unusual emotion throughout the church. I am glad. Would to God that a deeper emotion could be sent throughout our land, until all the people thereof shall be roused from their wicked insensibility to the most tremendous sin of which any nation was ever guilty, and be impelled to do that righteousness which alone can avert the just displeasure of God. I have been prompted to speak thus by the words I have heard during the past week from a young man hitherto unknown, but who is, I believe, called of God to do a greater work for the good of our country than has been done by any one since the Revolution. I mean William Lloyd Garrison. He is going to repeat his lectures the coming week. I advise, I exhort, I entreat — would that I could compel! — you to go and hear him."

On turning to Brother Young after the benediction I found that he was very much displeased. He sharply reproved me, and gave me to understand that I should never have an opportunity so to violate the propriety of his pulpit again. And never since then have I lifted up my voice within that beautiful church, which has lately been taken down.

The excited audience gathered in clusters, evidently talking about what had happened. I found the porch full of persons conversing in very earnest tones. Presently a lady of fine person, her countenance suffused with emotion, tears coursing down her cheeks, pressed through the crowd, seized my hand, and said audibly, with deep feeling: "Mr. May, I thank you. What a shame it is that I, who have been a constant attendant from my childhood in this or some other Christian church, am obliged to confess that to-day, for the first time, I have heard from the pulpit a plea for the oppressed, the enslaved millions in our land!" All within hearing of her voice were evidently moved in sympathy with her, or were awed by her emotion. For myself I could only acknowledge in a word my gratitude for her generous testimony.

The next day I perceived, on his return from his place of business in State Street, that my revered father was much disturbed by the reports he had heard of my preaching. Some of the "gentlemen of property and standing" who had been my auditors said it was fanatical, others that it was incendiary, others that it was treasonable, and begged him to "arrest me in my mad career." The only one, as he soon afterwards informed me, who had spoken in any other than terms of censure was the great and good Dr. Bowditch, who said, "Depend upon it, the young man is more than half right." My father tried to dissuade me from engaging in the attempt to overthrow the system of slavery which Mr. Garrison proposed. He had come, with most others, to regard it as an unavoidable evil, one that the fathers of our Republic had not ventured to suppress, but had rather given to its protection something like a guaranty. He thought, with most others at that day, that slavery must be left to be gradually removed by the progress of civilization, the growth of higher ideas of human nature, and the manifest superiority and better economy of free labor. He admonished me that, in assailing the institution of American slavery, I should only be "kicking against the pricks," that I should lose my standing in the ministry and my usefulness in the church. I need not add that he failed to convince me that "the foolishness of preaching" would not yet be "mighty to the pulling down of the stronghold of Satan." In less than ten years he was reconciled to my course.

A few days afterwards I gave my sermon on Prejudice to my most excellent friend, Rev. Henry Ware, Jr., who was then the purveyor of tracts for the American Unitarian Association. He accepted the discourse as originally written, but insisted that the interlineations and the additions respecting slavery should be omitted. He would not have done this, nor should I have consented to it, a few years later. But we were all in bondage then. Unconsciously to ourselves, the hand of the slaveholding power lay *heavily* upon the mind and heart of the people in our Northern as well as Southern States.

What a pity that my words in that sermon, respecting slavery, were not published in the tract! They might have helped a little to commit our Unitarian denomination much earlier to the cause of impartial liberty, in earnest protest against the great oppression, the unparalleled iniquity of our land. Of whom should opposition to slavery of every kind have been expected so soon as from Unitarian Christians?

The insensibility of the people of our country to the wrongs, the outrages, we were directly and indirectly inflicting upon our colored brethren, when Mr. Garrison commenced the antislavery reform, — the insensibility of the Northern people, scarcely less than that of the Southern, — of New England as well as of the Carolinas and Georgia, of the professing Christians, almost as much as of the political partisans, — that insensibility, not yet wholly overpast, even in Massachusetts, is a *moral phenomenon.* A more glaring inconsistency does not appear in the whole history of mankind.

The love of liberty was an American passion. We gloried in our Revolution. We thought our fathers were to be honored above all men for throwing off the British yoke. Taxation without representation was not to be submitted to. "Resistance to tyrants was obedience to God." We regarded the "Declaration of Independence" as the most momentous document ever penned by mortal man, the herald note of deliverance to the race. The first sentence of the second paragraph of it was as familiar to everybody as the Lord's Prayer; and almost as sacred as that prayer did we hold the words "All men were created equal, endowed by their Creator with certain unalienable rights, among which are life, liberty, and the pursuit of happiness." And yet few had given a thought to the fact that there were millions of men, women, and children in our land who were held under a heavier bondage than that to which the Israelites were subjected in the land of Egypt, were denied all the rights of humanity, were herded together like brutes, — bought, sold, worked, whipped like cattle.

All in our country who were descendants from the Puritans, especially those of us who claimed descent from the fathers of New England, were imbued with the spirit of *religious* liberty, had much to say about the rights of conscience; but we gave no heed to the awful fact that there were millions in the land who were not allowed to exercise any of those rights, were not permitted to read the Bible or any other book, and were taught little else about God, but that He was an invisible, ever-present, almighty overseer of the plantations upon which they were worked like cattle, standing ready at all times, everywhere, to inflict upon them, if they neglected their unrequited tasks, a thousand-fold more dreadful punishment than their earthly tormentors were able even to conceive.

We Americans, especially we New-Englanders, were, or thought we were, all alive to the cause of human freedom. We were quick to hear the cry of the oppressed, that came to us from distant lands. We stopped not to ask the language, character, or complexion of the sufferers. It was enough for us to know that they were human beings, and that they were deprived of liberty. We hesitated not to denounce their tyrants.

The call for succor which came to us from Greece was quickly heard and promptly answered in almost all parts of our country. And why? Not because the Greeks were a more virtuous or more intelligent people than their enemies. No; we had little reason to think them better than the Turks. But they were the *injured* party, and therefore we roused ourselves to aid them. How much soever our orators and poets gathered up the hallowed associations which cluster around that classic land, they all were but the decorations, not the point, of their appeals. It was the story of the *wrongs* of the Grecians which found the way to our hearts, and stirred us up to encourage and succor them in their conflict for *liberty*. Dr. Howe will tell you that it was not their admiration of Greece in her ancient glory, but their sympathy for Greece in her modern degradation, that impelled him and his chivalrous companions to fly thither, and peril their lives in her cause.

Coming to us from any other land, the cry for freedom sent through American bosoms a thrilling emotion. We stopped not to inquire who they were that would be free. If they were men, we knew they had a right to liberty. No matter how the yoke had been fastened on them, — whether by inheritance, or conquest, or political compromise, — we felt that it ought to be broken. And although to break it the whole social fabric of their oppressors must be overturned, still we said, *Let the yoke be broken!*

Thus we quickly felt, thus we reasoned and acted, in all cases of oppression excepting one, — the one *at home*, the one in which we were implicated with the oppressors. We were blind, we were deaf, we were dumb, to the wrongs and outrages inflicted upon one sixth part of the population of our own country. In the Southern States the colored people were held as property, chattels personal, liable to all the incidents of the estates of their owners, could be seized to pay their debts, or mortgaged, or given away, or bequeathed by them. To all intents and purposes, they were regarded by the laws of those States, and might be legally disposed of, and otherwise treated, just like domesticated brute animals. In most of the Northern States they were not admitted to the prerogatives of citizens. In none of them were they allowed to enjoy equal social, educational, or religious privileges; nor were they permitted to engage in any of the lucrative professions, trades, or handicrafts. They were condemned to all the menial offices. It was impossible not to respect and value many of them as servants and nurses, but they were not suffered to come nearer to white people in any domestic or social relations. Intermarriages with them were illegal, and punishable by heavy penalties. They were not allowed to travel (unless as servants) in any public conveyances. Their children were excluded from the schools which white children attended, and they were set apart in one corner of the places of public worship called the houses of God, — *the impartial Father* of all men. A certain shade of complexion, though much lighter than some brunettes, consigned any one guilty of it to the grade of the blacks, which was de-gradation. We were educated to regard negroes as an inferior race of beings, not entitled to the distinctive rights and privileges of white men. Ignorance, poverty, and servitude came to be considered the birthright, the inheritance, of all Africans and their descendants; and therefore we did not feel the pressure of their bonds, nor the smart of the wounds that were continually given them.

Prejudice against color had become universal. The most elevated were not superior to it; the humblest white men were not below it. *Colorphobia* was a disease that infected all white Americans. Let me give my readers one instance of its virulence.

In 1834, being on a visit to my father in Boston, I was requested to call upon one of his old friends, that he might dissuade me from co-operating any further with "that wrong-headed, fanatical Garrison." The honorable gentleman was very prominent in the fashionable, professional, and political society of that city. He had always expressed a kind regard for me, and had shown his confidence by committing to my care the education of two of his sons.

I did not doubt that he had been moved to send for me by his sincere concern for what he deemed my welfare. He received me with elegant courtesy, as he was wont to do, but entered at once upon the subject of "Mr. Garrison's misdirected, mischievous enterprise."

He insisted that, while the negroes ought to be treated humanely, the thought of their ever being elevated to an equality with white men was preposterous, and he wondered that a man of common sense should entertain the thought an hour. He said: "Why, they are evidently an inferior race of beings, intended to be the servants of those on whom the Creator has conferred a higher nature," and adduced the arguments which were then becoming, and have since been, so common with those who would maintain this position. At length I said to him: "Sir, we Abolitionists are not so foolish as to require or wish that ignorant negroes should be considered wise men, or that vicious negroes should be considered virtuous men, or poor negroes be considered rich men. All we demand for them is that negroes shall be permitted, encouraged, assisted to become as wise, as virtuous, and as rich as they can, and be acknowledged to be just what they have become, and be treated accordingly." He replied, with great emphasis: "Mr. M., if you should bring me negroes who had become the wisest of the wise, the best of the good, the richest of the rich, I would not acknowledge them to be my equals." "Then," said I, "you might be laughed at; for, if there be any meaning in your words, such men would be your superiors. Think, sir, a moment of your presuming to contemn the wisest of the wise, the best of the good, the richest of the rich, because of their complexion. This would be the insanity of prejudice. Why, sir," I continued, "Rammohun Roy is soon coming to this country; and he is of a darker hue than many American persons who are proscribed and degraded because of their color." "Well, sir," he angrily replied, "I am not one who will show him any respect." "What," I cried, "not take pains to know and treat with respect Rammohun Roy?" "No," he rejoined,—"no, not even

Rammohun Roy!" "Then," I retorted, "you will lose the honor of taking by the hand the most remarkable man of our age." He was much offended, and, as I afterwards learnt, chose that our acquaintance should end with that interview.

Such was the prejudice that Mr. Garrison found confronting him everywhere, and it still is the greatest obstacle in our country to the progress of liberty and the establishment of peace.

> "Truths would you teach to save a sinking land?
> All fear, none aid you, and few understand."

Never, since the days of our Saviour, have these lines of Pope been more fully verified than in the experience of Mr. Garrison. So soon as it was known that he opposed the Colonization plan, and demanded for the enslaved immediate emancipation, without expatriation, he was at once generally denounced as a very dangerous person. Very few of those who were convinced by his facts and his appeals that something should be done forthwith for the relief of our oppressed millions ventured, during the first twelve months of his labors, to help him. Even the excellent Deacon Grant would not trust him for paper on which to print his *Liberator* a month. And most of those who assisted him to get audiences wherever he went, and who subscribed for the *Liberator*, and who expressed their best wishes, were intimidated by his boldness, frequently half acknowledged that he demanded too much for our bondmen, and could not be made to understand his fundamental doctrine of "immediate unconditional emancipation," often and clearly as he expounded it.

In November, 1831, I happened again to be in Boston on a visit, when it was proposed to attempt the formation of an antislavery society. A meeting was called at the office of Samuel E. Sewall, Esq. Fifteen gentlemen assembled there. We agreed in the outset that, if the apostolic number of twelve should be found ready to unite upon the principles that should be thought vital, and in a plan of operations deemed wise and expedient, we would then and there organize an association. Mr. Garrison announced the doctrine of "immediate emancipation" as being essential to the great reform that was needed in our land, the extirpation of slavery, and the establishment of the human rights of the millions who were groaning under a worse than Egyptian bondage. We discussed the point two hours. But though we were the earliest and most earnest friends of the young reformer, only *nine* of us were brought to see, eye to eye with him, as to the right of the slave and the duty of the master. Only nine of us were brought to see that a man was a man, let his complexion be what it might be; and that no other man, not the most exalted in the land, could regard and hold him a moment as his property, his chattel, *without sin.* Only nine of us were brought to understand that the first thing to be done for those men held in the condition of domesticated brutes, was to recognize, acknowledge their *humanity*, and secure to them their God-given rights, — those rights of all men set forth as inalienable in the immortal Declaration of American Independence. Only nine of us were brought to see that the *first* thing to be done for the improvement of the condition of the slave is to break his yoke, to set him free, and that what needs to be done first ought to be done without delay, immediately. The rest of the company partook of the fear, common at that day, that it would be very dangerous to set millions of slaves free at once. Although liberty was announced to the world, in our American Declaration, as the *birthright* of all the children of men, yet were the people of our country so blinded and besotted by the influence of our slave system, that it was almost universally pronounced unsafe to give liberty to adult men, who were slaves, until they should be prepared for freedom, and deemed qualified to exercise it aright. Mr. Garrison had had to meet and combat this senseless fear everywhere, from the commencement of his enterprise. He had shown to all who could see that slavery was not a school in which men could be educated for liberty; that they could no more be trained to feel and act as freemen should, so long as they were kept in bondage, than children could be taught to walk so long as they were held in the arms of nurses. Moreover, he argued, that if those only should be intrusted with liberty who knew how to use it, slaveholders were of all men the last that should be left free, seeing that they habitually outraged liberty,—indeed, had been educated to trample upon human rights. Still, his doctrine was generally misunderstood, egregiously misrepresented, and violently opposed. And, as I have stated, only nine out of fifteen of his elect followers, after he had been preaching and publishing the doctrine a year, fully believed or dared to unite with him in announcing it to the world as their faith. We therefore separated in November, 1831, without having organized. I returned disappointed to my home in Connecticut, eighty miles from Boston; too far at that day, ere railroads were lain, to come, in the depth of winter, to assist in the formation of the New England Antislavery Society, which took place in January, 1832. So I lost the honor of being one of the actual founders of the first society based upon the true principle,— *immediate emancipation.*

That there was point, vitality, power, in this doctrine was proved by the commotion which was everywhere caused by the promulgation of it. From one end of the country to the other the cry went forth against the editor of the *Liberator*, Fanatic! Incendiary! Madman! The slaveholders raved, and their Northern apologists confessed that they had too much cause to be offended. Grave statesmen and solemn divines pronounced the doctrines of the New England Abolitionists unwise, dangerous, false, unconstitutional, revolutionary. Encouraged by these responses, the slaveholding aristocrats grew so bold as to demand that "this fanatical assault upon one of their domestic institutions should be quelled at once," that the publications of the Abolitionists should be suppressed, our meetings dispersed, our lecturers and agents arrested. And scarcely had the *Liberator* entered upon its second year before a reward was offered by a Southern Legislature for the abduction of the person, or for the life of its editor. And no Northern Legislature expressed its alarm or surprise. No Northern paper, secular or religious, reproved these assaults upon the liberty of the press and the freedom of speech. Thus was the viper *cherished* that has since stung so deeply the bosom of our Republic, has inflicted a wound that is still open and festering.

The grossest abuse was heaped upon Mr. Garrison; the vilest aspersions cast upon his character by those who knew nothing of his private life; the worst designs imputed to his great enterprise by those who were interested directly or indirectly in upholding the system of iniquity which he had resolved to overthrow.

One of the charges brought against him, the one which probably hindered his success more than any other, was that he was an enemy of religion, an infidel, and that his covert but real purpose was to subvert the institutions of Christianity.

Now Mr. Garrison is, and ever has been since I knew him, a profoundly religious man, one of the most so I have ever known. No one really acquainted with him will say the contrary, unless it be under the impulse of a sectarian prejudice, personal resentment, or a sinister purpose. True, his doctrinal opinions and his regard for rites and forms have come to differ from those of the popular religionists of our day, as much as did the opinions of Jesus Christ differ from those of the temple and synagogue worshippers of his day. It would have been *politic* in him not to have incurred, as he did, the opposition and hatred of so many of the ministers and churches of our country. But Mr. Garrison knew not how to counsel with the wisdom of this world. He surely had as much cause and as frequent occasions to expose the inhumanity and hypocrisy of our country as Jesus had to denounce the scribes, Pharisees, and priests of Judea. He soon discovered, to his astonishment, that the American Church was the bulwark of American slaveholders. The truth of this accusation was afterwards elaborately proved by the Hon. J. G. Birney. It was emphatically acknowledged by the Rev. Dr. Albert Barnes, and has since been repeatedly declared by Rev. Henry Ward Beecher and Rev. Dr. Cheever, all honorable, orthodox men. Now, pray, how ought a great captain, though his army be a small one, — how ought he to treat the *bulwark* of the enemy he means to subdue? how but to assail and demolish it if he can? God be praised, Christianity and the American Church were not then, and are not now, identical. The religion of Jesus Christ is dearer to Mr. Garrison than his own life. It was only the hollow-hearted pretenders to piety whom he exposed, censured, ridiculed. He never uttered from his pen or his lips a word that I have read or heard, or that has been reported to me, — not a word but in reverence and love of the truth and the spirit, the doctrines and the precepts, of Jesus Christ.

Many of those who were interested in Mr. Garrison's holy purpose, and wished him success, thought him too severe; many more thought him indiscreet. He was remonstrated with often earnestly. But he could not be persuaded that it was not right and wise to blame those persons *most* for our national sin who had the most influence on the government, the policy, the prevailing sentiments, the customs, and, above all, the *religion* of the nation. Mr. Garrison would sometimes argue, and argue powerfully, convincingly, with those who found fault with his words of fiery indignation, and show that tamer language would be inapt, unfelt. At other times he would say, "Do the poor, hunted, hounded, down-trodden slaves think my language too severe or misapplied? Do that wretched husband and wife who have just now been separated from each other forever by that respectable gentleman in Virginia, — the one sold to be taken to New Orleans, the other kept at home to pine in the hovel made desolate, — do that husband and wife think my denunciation of their master too severe, because he is a judge, or a governor, or a minister, or because he is a member of a Christian church, or even because he has been hitherto, and in other respects, a kind master to them? Until I hear such ones complain of my severity, I shall not doubt its propriety." "If those who deserve the lash feel it and wince at it, I shall be assured I am striking the right persons in the right place." "I will be," are his memorable words that rung through the land, — "I will be as harsh as truth, and as uncompromising as justice. On the subject of slavery I do not wish to think or speak or write with moderation. No! No! Tell a man whose house is on fire to give a moderate alarm; tell him to moderately rescue his wife from the hands of the ravisher; tell the mother to gradually extricate her babe from the fire; but urge me not to use moderation in a cause like the present. I am in earnest. I will not equivocate; I will not excuse; I will not retreat an inch; and *I will be heard*."

Mr. Garrison will perhaps remember that, a few months after he commenced the *Liberator*, when almost everybody was finding fault with him, or wishing that he would be more temperate, I was one of the friends that came to remonstrate and entreat. He and his faithful partner, Isaac Knapp, were at work in the little upper chamber, No. 6 Merchants' Hall, where they lived, as well as they could, with their printing-press and types, all within an enclosure sixteen or eighteen feet square. I requested him to walk out with me, that we might confer on an important matter. He at once laid aside his pen, and we descended to the street. I informed him how much troubled I had become for fear he was damaging the cause he had so much at heart by the undue severity of his style. He listened to me patiently, tenderly. I told him what many of the wise and prudent, who professed an interest in his object, said about his manner of pursuing it. He replied somewhat in the way I have described above. "But," said I, "some of the epithets you use, though not perhaps too severe, are not precisely applicable to the sin you denounce, and so may seem abusive." "Ah!" he rejoined, "until the term 'slaveholder' sends as deep a feeling of horror to the hearts of those who hear it applied to any one as the terms 'robber,' 'pirate,' 'murderer' do, we must use and multiply epithets when condemning the sin of him who is guilty of the '*sum of all villanies*.'" "O," cried I, "my friend, do try to moderate your indignation, and keep more cool; why, you are all on fire." He stopped, laid his hand upon my shoulder with a kind but emphatic pressure, that I have felt ever since, and said slowly, with deep emotion, "Brother May, I have need to be *all on fire*, for I have mountains of ice about me to melt." From that hour to this I have never said a word to Mr. Garrison, in complaint of his style. I am more than half satisfied now that he was right then, and we who objected were mistaken.

A year or two afterwards I was in the study of Dr. Channing, who, from the rise of the antislavery movement, watched it with deep and increasing emotion, and often sent for me, and oftener for the heroic Dr. Follen, to converse with us about it. I was in the Doctor's study, and had been endeavoring to explain and reconcile him to some measures of the Abolitionists which I found had troubled him, when he said, with great gravity and earnestness, "But, Mr. May, your friend Garrison's style is excessively severe. The epithets he uses are harsh, abusive, exasperating." I replied, "Dr. Channing, I thought so once myself. But you have furnished me with a sufficient apology, if not justification, of Mr. Garrison's severity." And taking from his bookcase the octavo volume of the Doctor's Discourses, Reviews, and Miscellanies, published in 1830, I read parts of the passage commencing on the twenty-second and closing on the twenty-fourth page, in which he replies to the charge, brought against the great Milton's prose writings, of "party-spirit, coarse invective, and controversial asperity." I wish there were room here for me to quote the whole of it, it is all so applicable to Mr. Garrison; but I will give only the close: "Men of natural softness and timidity, of a sincere but effeminate virtue, will be apt to look on these bolder, hardier spirits as violent, perturbed, uncharitable; and the charge will not be wholly groundless. But that deep feeling of evils, which is necessary to effectual conflict with them, and which marks God's most powerful messengers to mankind, cannot breathe itself in soft and tender accents. The deeply moved soul will speak strongly, and ought to speak so as to move and shake nations. We must not mistake Christian benevolence as if it had but one voice, — that of soft entreaty. It can speak in piercing and awful tones. There is constantly going on in our world a conflict between good and evil. The cause of human nature has always to wrestle with foes. All improvement is a victory won by struggles. It is especially true of those great periods which have been distinguished by revolutions in government and religion, and from which we date the most rapid movements of the human mind, that they have been signalized by conflict. At such periods men gifted with great power of thought and loftiness of sentiment are especially summoned to the conflict with evil. They hear, as it were, in their own magnanimity and generous aspirations the voice of a divinity; and thus commissioned, and burning with a passionate devotion to truth and freedom, they must and will speak with an indignant energy, and they ought not to be measured by the standard of ordinary minds in ordinary times.

"Milton reverenced and loved human nature, and attached himself to its great interests with a fervor of which only such a mind was capable. He lived in one of those solemn periods which determine the character of ages to come. His spirit was stirred to its very centre by the presence of danger. He lived in the midst of battle. That the ardor of his spirit sometimes passed the bounds of wisdom and charity, and poured forth unwarrantable invective, we see and lament. But the purity and loftiness of his mind break forth amidst his bitterest invectives. We see a noble nature still. We see that no feigned love of truth and freedom was a covering for selfishness and malignity. He did indeed love and adore uncorrupted religion and intellectual liberty, and let his name be enrolled among their truest champions."

The Doctor bowed and smiled blandly, saying, "I confess the quotation is not inapt nor unfairly made."

MISS PRUDENCE CRANDALL AND THE CANTERBURY SCHOOL.

Often, during the last thirty, and more often during the last ten years, you must have seen in the newspapers, or heard from speakers in Antislavery and Republican meetings, high commendations of the *County of Windham* in Connecticut, as bearing the banner of equal human and political rights far above all the rest of that State. In the great election of the year 1866 the people of that county gave a large majority of votes in favor of *negro suffrage*.

This moral and political elevation of the public sentiment there is undoubtedly owing to the distinct presentation and thorough discussion, throughout that region, of the most vital antislavery questions in 1833 and 1834, called out by the shameful, cruel persecution of Miss Prudence Crandall for attempting to establish in Canterbury a boarding-school for "colored young ladies and little misses."

I was then living in Brooklyn, the shire town of the county, six miles from the immediate scene of the violent conflict, and so was fully drawn into it. I regret that, in the following account of it, allusions to myself and my acts must so often appear. But as Æneas said to Queen Dido, in telling his story of the Trojan War, so may I say, respecting the contest about the Canterbury school, "All of which I saw, and part of which I was."

In the summer or fall of 1832 I heard that Miss Prudence Crandall, an excellent, well-educated Quaker young lady, who had gained considerable reputation as a teacher in the neighboring town of Plainfield, had been induced by a number of ladies and gentlemen of Canterbury to purchase a commodious, large house in their pretty village, and establish her boarding and day school there, that their daughters might receive instruction in several higher branches of education not taught in the public district schools, without being obliged to live far away from their homes.

For a while the school answered the expectations of its patrons, and enjoyed their favor; but early in the following year a trouble arose. It was in this wise. Not far from the village of Canterbury there lived a worthy colored man named Harris. He was the owner of a good farm, and was otherwise in comfortable circumstances. He had a daughter, Sarah, a bright girl about seventeen years of age. She had passed, with good repute as a scholar, though the school of the district in which she lived, and was hungering and thirsting for more education. This she desired not only for her own sake, but that she might go forth qualified to be a teacher of the colored people of our country, to whose wrongs and oppression she had become very sensitive. Her father encouraged her, and gladly offered to defray the expense of the advantages she might be able to obtain. Sarah applied for admission into this new Canterbury school. Miss Crandall confessed to me that at first she hesitated and almost refused, lest admitting her might offend the parents of her pupils, several of whom were Colonizationists, and none of them Abolitionists. But Sarah urged her request with no little force of argument and depth of feeling. Then she was a young lady of pleasing appearance and manners, well known to many of Miss Crandall's pupils, having been their class-mate in the district school. Moreover, she was accounted a virtuous, pious girl, and had been for some time a member of the church of Canterbury. There could not, therefore, have been a more unexceptionable case. No objection could be made to her admission into the school, excepting only her dark (and not very dark) complexion. Miss Crandall soon saw that she was unexpectedly called to take some part (how important she could not foresee) in the great contest for impartial liberty that was then beginning to agitate violently our nation. She was called to act either in accordance with, or in opposition to, the unreasonable, cruel, wicked prejudice against the *color* of their victims, by which the oppressors of millions in our land were everywhere extenuating, if not justifying, their tremendous system of iniquity. She bowed to the claim of humanity, and admitted Sarah Harris to her school.

Her pupils, I believe, made no objection. But in a few days the parents of some of them called and remonstrated. Miss Crandall pressed upon their consideration Sarah's eager desire for more knowledge and culture, the good use she intended to make of her acquirements, her excellent character and lady-like deportment, and, more than all, that she was an accepted member of the same Christian church to which many of them belonged. Her arguments, her entreaties, however, were of no avail. Prejudice blinds the eyes, closes the ears, hardens the heart. "Sarah belonged to the proscribed, despised class, and therefore must not be admitted into a private school with their daughters." This was the gist of all they had to say. Reasons were thrown away, appeals to their sense of right, to their compassion for injured fellow-beings, made no impression. "They would not have it said that their daughters went to school with a nigger girl." Miss Crandall was assured that, if she did not dismiss Sarah Harris, her white pupils would be withdrawn from her.

She could not make up her mind to comply with such a demand, even to save the institution she had so recently established with such fond hopes, and in which she had invested all her property, and a debt of several hundred dollars more. It was, indeed, a severe trial, but she was strengthened to bear it. She determined to act right, and leave the event with God. Accordingly, she gave notice to her neighbors, and, on the 2d day of March, advertised in the *Liberator*, that at the commencement of her next term, on the first Monday of April, her school would be opened for "young ladies and little misses of color."

Only a few days before, on the 27th of February, I was informed of her generous, disinterested determination, and heard that, in consequence, the whole town was in a flame of indignation, kindled and fanned by the influence of the prominent people of the village, her immediate neighbors and her late patrons. Without delay, therefore, although a stranger, I addressed a letter to her, assuring her of my sympathy, and of my readiness to help her all in my power. On the 4th of March her reply came, begging me to come to her so soon as my engagements would permit. Accompanied by my friend, Mr. George W. Benson, I went to Canterbury on the afternoon of that day. On entering the village we were warned that we should be in personal danger if we appeared there as Miss Crandall's friends; and when arrived at her house we learnt that the excitement against her had become furious. She had been grossly insulted, and threatened with various kinds of violence, if she persisted in her purpose, and the most egregious falsehoods had been put in circulation respecting her intentions, the characters of her expected pupils, and of the future supporters of her school. Moreover, we were informed that a town-meeting was to be held on the 9th instant, to devise and adopt such measures as "would effectually avert the nuisance, or speedily abate it, if it should be brought into the village."

Though beat upon by such a storm, we found Miss Crandall resolved and tranquil. The effect of her Quaker discipline appeared in every word she spoke, and in every expression of her countenance. But, as she said, it would not do for her to go into the town-meeting; and there was not a man in Canterbury who would dare, if he were disposed, to appear there in her behalf. "Will not you, Friend May, be my attorney?" "Certainly," I replied, "come what will." We then agreed that I should explain to the people how unexpectedly she had been led to take the step which had given so much offence, and show them how she could not have consented to the demand made by her former patrons without wounding deeply the feelings of an excellent girl, known to most of them, and adding to the mountain load of injuries and insults already heaped upon the colored people of our country. With this arrangement, we left her, to await the coming of the ominous meeting of the town.

On the 9th of March I repaired again to Miss Crandall's house, accompanied by my faithful friend, Mr. Benson. There, to our surprise and joy, we found Friend Arnold Buffum, a most worthy man, an able speaker, and then the principal lecturing agent of the New England Antislavery Society. Miss Crandall gave to each of us a respectful letter of introduction to the Moderator of the meeting, in which she requested that we might be heard as her attorneys, and promised to be bound by any agreement we might see fit to make with the citizens of Canterbury. Miss Crandall concurred with us in the opinion that, as her house was one of the most conspicuous in the village, and not wholly paid for, if her opponents would take it off her hands, repaying what she had given for it, cease from molesting her, and allow her time to procure another house for her school, it would be better that she should move to some more retired part of the town or neighborhood.

Thus commissioned and instructed, Friend Buffum and I proceeded to the town-meeting. It was held in the "Meeting-House," one of the old New England pattern, — galleries on three sides, with room below and above for a thousand persons, sitting and standing. We found it nearly filled to its utmost capacity; and, not without difficulty, we passed up the side aisle into the wall-pew next to the deacon's seat, in which sat the Moderator. Very soon the business commenced. After the "Warning" had been read a series of Resolutions were laid before the meeting, in which were set forth the disgrace and damage that would be brought upon the town if a school for colored girls should be set up there, protesting emphatically against the impending evil, and appointing the civil authority and selectmen a committee to wait upon "the person contemplating the establishment of said school, ... point out to her the injurious effects, the incalculable evils, resulting from such an establishment within this town, and persuade her, if possible, to abandon the project." The mover of the resolutions, Rufus Adams, Esq., labored to enforce them by a speech, in which he grossly misrepresented what Miss Crandall had done, her sentiments and purposes, and threw out several mean and low insinuations against the motives of those who were encouraging her enterprise.

As soon as he sat down the Hon. Andrew T. Judson rose. This gentleman was undoubtedly the chief of

Miss Crandall's persecutors. He was the great man of the town, a leading politician in the State, much talked of by the Democrats as soon to be governor, and a few years afterwards was appointed Judge of the United States District Court. His house on Canterbury Green stood next to Miss Crandall's. The idea of having "a school of nigger girls so near him was insupportable." He vented himself in a strain of reckless hostility to his neighbor, her benevolent, self-sacrificing undertaking, and its patrons, and declared his determination to thwart the enterprise. He twanged every chord that could stir the coarser passions of the human heart, and with such sad success that his hearers seemed to be filled with the apprehension that a dire calamity was impending over them, that Miss Crandall was the author or instrument of it, that there were powerful conspirators engaged with her in the plot, and that the people of Canterbury should be roused, by every consideration of self-preservation, as well as self-respect, to prevent the accomplishment of the design, defying the wealth and influence of all who were abetting it.

When he had ended his philippic Mr. Buffum and I silently presented to the Moderator Miss Crandall's letters, requesting that we might be heard on her behalf. He handed them over to Mr. Judson, who instantly broke forth with greater violence than before; accused us of insulting the town by coming there to interfere with its local concerns. Other gentlemen sprang to their feet in hot displeasure; poured out their tirades upon Miss Crandall and her accomplices, and, with fists doubled in our faces, roughly admonished us that, if we opened our lips there, they would inflict upon us the utmost penalty of the law, if not a more immediate vengeance.

Thus forbidden to speak, we of course sat in silence,

and let the waves of invective and abuse dash over us. But we sat thus only until we heard from the Moderator the words, "This meeting is adjourned!" Knowing that now we should violate no law by speaking, I sprang to the seat on which I had been sitting, and cried out, "Men of Canterbury, I have a word for you! Hear me!" More than half the crowd turned to listen. I went rapidly over my replies to the misstatements that had been made as to the purposes of Miss Crandall and her friends, the characters of her expected pupils, and the spirit in which the enterprise had been conceived and would be carried on. As soon as possible I gave place to Friend Buffum. But he had spoken in his impressive manner hardly five minutes, before the trustees of the church to which the house belonged came in and ordered all out, that the doors might be shut. Here again the hand of the law constrained us. So we obeyed with the rest, and having lingered awhile upon the Green to answer questions and explain to those who were willing "to understand the matter," we departed to our homes, musing in our own hearts "what would come of this day's uproar."

Before my espousal of Miss Crandall's cause I had had a pleasant acquaintance with Hon. Andrew T. Judson, which had led almost to a personal friendship. Unwilling, perhaps, to break our connection so abruptly, and conscious, no doubt, that he had treated me rudely, not to say abusively, at the town-meeting on the 9th, he called to see me two days afterwards. He assured me that he had not become unfriendly to me personally, and regretted that he had used some expressions and applied certain epithets to me, in the warmth of his feelings and the excitement of the public indignation of his neighbors and fellow-townsmen, roused as they were to the utmost in opposition to Miss Crandall's project, which he thought I was inconsiderately and unjustly promoting. He went on enlarging upon the disastrous effects the establishment of "a school for nigger girls" in the centre of their village would have upon its desirableness as a place of residence, the value of real estate there, and the general prosperity of the town.

I replied: "If, sir, you had permitted Mr. Buffum and myself to speak at your town-meeting, you would have found that we had come there, not in a contentious spirit, but that we were ready, with Miss Crandall's consent, to settle the difficulty with you and your neighbors peaceably. We should have agreed, if you would repay to Miss Crandall what you had advised her to give for her house, and allow her time quietly to find and purchase a suitable house for her school in some more retired part of the town or vicinity, that she should remove to that place." The honorable gentleman hardly gave me time to finish my sentences ere he said, with great emphasis: —

"Mr. May, we are not merely opposed to the establishment of that school in Canterbury; we mean there shall not be such a school set up anywhere in our State. The colored people never can rise from their menial condition in our country; they ought not to be permitted to rise here. They are an inferior race of beings, and never can or ought to be recognized as the equals of the whites. Africa is the place for them. I am in favor of the Colonization scheme. Let the niggers and their descendants be sent back to their fatherland; and there improve themselves as much as they may, and civilize and Christianize the natives, if they can. I am a Colonizationist. You and your friend Garrison have undertaken what you cannot accomplish. The condition of the colored population of our country can never be essentially improved on this continent.

You are fanatical about them. You are violating the Constitution of our Republic, which settled forever the status of the black men in this land. They belong to Africa. Let them be sent back there, or kept as they are here. The sooner you Abolitionists abandon your project the better for our country, for the niggers, and yourselves."

I replied: "Mr. Judson, there never will be fewer colored people in this country than there are now. Of the vast majority of them this is the native land, as much as it is ours. It will be unjust, inhuman, in us to drive them out, or to make them willing to go by our cruel treatment of them. And, if they should all become willing to depart, it would not be practicable to transport across the Atlantic Ocean and settle properly on the shores of Africa, from year to year, half so many of them as would be born here in the same time, according to the known rate of their natural increase. No, sir, there will never be fewer colored people in our country than there are this day; and the only question is, whether we will recognize the rights which God gave them as men, and encourage and assist them to become all he has made them capable of being, or whether we will continue wickedly to deny them the privileges we enjoy, condemn them to degradation, enslave and imbrute them; and so bring upon ourselves the condemnation of the Almighty Impartial Father of all men, and the terrible visitation of the God of the oppressed. I trust, sir, you will erelong come to see that we must accord to these men their rights, or incur justly the loss of our own. Education is one of the primal, fundamental rights of all the children of men. Connecticut is the last place where this should be denied. But as, in the providence of God, that right has been denied in a place so near me, I feel that I am summoned to its defence. If you and your neighbors in Canterbury had quietly consented that Sarah Harris, whom you knew to be a bright, good girl, should enjoy the privilege she so eagerly sought, this momentous conflict would not have arisen in your village. But as it has arisen there, we may as well meet it there as elsewhere."

"That nigger school," he rejoined with great warmth, "shall never be allowed in Canterbury, nor in any town of this State."

"How can you prevent it legally?" I inquired; "how but by Lynch law, by violence, which you surely will not countenance?"

"We can expel her pupils from abroad," he replied, "under the provisions of our old pauper and vagrant laws."

"But we will guard against them," I said, "by giving your town ample bonds."

"Then," said he, "we will get a law passed by our Legislature, now in session, forbidding the institution of such a school as Miss Crandall proposes, in any part of Connecticut."

"It would be an unconstitutional law, and I will contend against it as such to the last," I rejoined. "If you, sir, pursue the course you have now indicated, I will dispute every step you take, from the lowest court in Canterbury up to the highest court of the United States."

"You talk big," he cried; "it will cost more than you are aware of to do all that you threaten. Where will you get the means to carry on such a contest at law?"

This defiant question inspired me to say, "Mr. Judson, I had not foreseen all that this conversation has opened to my view. True, I do not possess the pecuniary ability to do what you have made me promise. I have not consulted any one. But I am sure the lovers of impartial liberty, the friends of humanity in our land, the enemies of slavery, will so justly appreciate the importance of sustaining Miss Crandall in her benevolent, pious undertaking, that I shall receive from one quarter and another all the funds I may need to withstand your attempt to crush, by legal means, the Canterbury school." The sequel of my story will show that I did not misjudge the significance of my case, nor put my confidence in those who were not worthy of it. Mr. Judson left me in high displeasure, and I never met him afterwards but as an opponent.

Undismayed by the opposition of her neighbors and the violence of their threats, Miss Crandall received early in April fifteen or twenty colored young ladies and misses from Philadelphia, New York, Providence, and Boston. At once her persecutors commenced operations. All accommodations at the stores in Canterbury were denied her; so that she was obliged to send to neighboring villages for her needful supplies. She and her pupils were insulted whenever they appeared in the streets. The doors and door-steps of her house were besmeared, and her well was filled with filth. Had it not been for the assistance of her father and another Quaker friend who lived in the town, she might have been compelled to abandon "her castle" for the want of water and food. But she was enabled to "hold out," and Miss Crandall and her little band behaved somewhat like the besieged in the immortal Fort Sumter. The spirit that is in the children of men is usually roused by persecution. I visited them repeatedly, and always found teacher and pupils calm and resolute. They evidently felt that it was given them to maintain one of the fundamental, inalienable rights of man.

Before the close of the month, an attempt was made

to frighten and drive away these innocent girls, by a process under the obsolete vagrant law, which provided that the selectmen of any town might warn any person, not an inhabitant of the State, to depart forthwith from said town; demand of him or her *one dollar and sixty-seven cents* for every week he or she remained in said town after having received such warning, and in case such fine should not be paid, and the person so warned should not have departed before the expiration of ten days after being sentenced, then he or she should *be whipped on the naked body not exceeding ten stripes.*

A warrant to this effect was actually served upon Eliza Ann Hammond, a fine girl from Providence, aged seventeen years. Although I had protected Miss Crandall's pupils against the operation of this old law, by giving to the treasurer of Canterbury a bond in the sum of $10,000, signed by responsible gentlemen of Brooklyn, to save the town from the vagrancy of any of these pupils, I feared they would be intimidated by the actual appearance of the constable, and the imposition of a writ. So, on hearing of the above transaction, I went down to Canterbury to explain the matter if necessary; to assure Miss Hammond that the persecutors would hardly dare proceed to such an extremity, and strengthen her to bear meekly the punishment, if they should in their madness inflict it; knowing that every blow they should strike her would resound throughout the land, if not over the whole civilized world, and call out an expression of indignation before which Mr. Judson and his associates would quail. But I found her ready for the emergency, animated by the spirit of a martyr.

Of course this process was abandoned. But another was resorted to, most disgraceful to the State as well as the town. That shall be the subject of my next.

THE BLACK LAW OF CONNECTICUT.

Foiled in their attempts to frighten away Miss Crandall's pupils by their proceedings under the provisions of the obsolete "Pauper and Vagrant Law," Mr. Judson and his fellow-persecutors urgently pressed upon the Legislature of Connecticut, then in session, a demand for the enactment of a law, by which they should be enabled to effect their purpose. To the lasting shame of the State, be it said, they succeeded. On the 24th of May, 1833, the *Black Law* was enacted as follows :—

"SECTION 1. Be it enacted by the Senate and House of Representatives, in General Assembly convened, that no person shall set up or establish in this State any school, academy, or literary institution for the instruction or education of colored persons who are not inhabitants of this State; nor instruct or teach in any school, or other literary institution whatsoever, in this State; nor harbor or board, for the purpose of attending or being taught or instructed in any such school, academy, or literary institution, any colored person who is not an inhabitant of any town in this State, without the consent in writing, first obtained, of a majority of the civil authority, and also of the Selectmen of the town, in which such school, academy, or literary institution is situated," &c.

I need not copy any more of this infamous Act. The penalties denounced against the violation of it, you may be sure, were severe enough. That the persecutors of Miss Crandall were determined to visit them upon her, if they might, the sequel of my story will show.

On the receipt of the tidings that the Legislature had passed the law, joy and exultation ran wild in Canterbury. The bells were rung and a cannon fired, until all the inhabitants for miles around were informed of the triumph. So soon as was practicable, on the 27th of June, Miss Crandall was arrested by the sheriff of the county, or the constable of the town, and arraigned before Justices Adams and Bacon, two of the leaders of the conspiracy against her and her humane enterprise. The trial of course was a brief one; the result was predetermined. Before noon of that day a messenger came to let me know that Miss Crandall had been "committed" by the above-named justices, to take her trial at the next session of the Superior Court at Brooklyn in August; that she was in the hands of the sheriff and would be put into jail, unless I or some of her friends would come and "give bonds" for her in the sum of $ 300 or $ 500, I forget which. I calmly told the messenger that there were gentlemen enough in Canterbury whose bond for that amount would be as good or better than mine; and I should leave it for them to do Miss Crandall that favor. "But," said the young man, "are you not her friend?" "Certainly," I replied, "too sincerely her friend to give relief to her enemies in their present embarrassment; and I trust you will not find any one of her friends, or the patrons of her school, who will step forward to help them any more than myself." "But, sir," he cried, "do you mean to allow her to be put into jail?" "Most certainly," was my answer, "if her persecutors are unwise enough to let such an outrage be committed." He turned from me in blank surprise, and hurried back to tell Mr. Judson and the justices of his ill success.

A few days before, when I first heard of the passage of the law, I had visited Miss Crandall with my friend Mr. George W. Benson, and advised with her as to the course she and her friends ought to pursue, when she should be brought to trial. She appreciated at once and fully the importance of leaving her persecutors to show to the world how base they were, and how atrocious was the law they had induced the Legislature to enact, — a law, by the force of which a woman might be fined and imprisoned as a felon, in the State of Connecticut, for giving instruction to colored girls. She agreed that it would be best for us to leave her in the hands of those with whom the law originated, hoping that, in their madness, they would show forth all its hideous features.

Mr. Benson and I therefore went diligently around to all whom we knew were friendly to Miss Crandall and her school, and counselled them by no means to give bonds to keep her from imprisonment, because nothing would expose so fully to the public the egregious wickedness of the law, and the virulence of her persecutors, as the fact that they had thrust her into jail.

When I found that her resolution was equal to the trial which seemed to be impending, that she was ready to brave and to bear meekly the worst treatment that her enemies would venture to subject her to, I made all the arrangements for her comfort that were practicable in our prison. It fortunately so happened that the most suitable room, not occupied, was the one in which a man named Watkins had recently been confined for the murder of his wife, and out of which he had been taken and executed. This circumstance, we foresaw, would add not a little to the public detestation of the *Black Law.*

The jailer, at my request, readily put the room in as nice order as was possible, and permitted me to substitute, for the bedstead and mattress on which the murderer had slept, fresh and clean ones from my own house and Mr. Benson's.

About two o'clock P. M. another messenger came to inform me that the sheriff was on the way from Canterbury to the jail with Miss Crandall, and would imprison her, unless her friends would give him the required bail.

Although in sympathy with Miss Crandall's persecutors, he clearly saw the disgrace that was about to be brought upon the State, and begged me and Mr. Benson to avert it. Of course we refused. I went to the jailer's house and met Miss Crandall on her arrival. We stepped aside. I said :—

"If now you hesitate, if you dread the gloomy place so much as to wish to be saved from it, I will give bonds for you even now."

"O no," she promptly replied; "I am only afraid they will not put me into jail. Their evident hesitation and embarrassment show plainly how much they deprecate the effect of this part of their folly; and therefore I am the more anxious that they should be exposed, if not caught in their own wicked devices."

We therefore returned with her to the sheriff and the company that surrounded him to await his final act. He was ashamed to do it. He knew it would cover the persecutors of Miss Crandall and the State of Connecticut with disgrace. He conferred with several about him, and delayed yet longer. Two gentlemen came and remonstrated with me in not very seemly terms :—

"It would be a —— shame, an eternal disgrace to the State, to have her put into jail,—into the very room that Watkins had last occupied."

"Certainly, gentlemen," I replied, "and you may prevent this if you please."

"O," they cried, "we are not her friends; we are not in favor of her school; we don't want any more —— niggers coming among us. It is your place to stand by Miss Crandall and help her now. You and your —— abolition brethren have encouraged her to bring this nuisance into Canterbury, and it is —— mean in you to desert her now."

I rejoined: "She knows we have not deserted her,

and do not intend to desert her. The law which her persecutors have persuaded our legislators to enact is an infamous one, worthy of the Dark Ages. It would be just as bad as it is, whether we should give bonds for her or not. But the people generally will not so soon realize how bad, how wicked, how cruel a law it is, unless we suffer her persecutors to inflict upon her all the penalties it prescribes. She is willing to bear them for the sake of the cause she has so nobly espoused. And it is easy to foresee that Miss Crandall will be glorified, as much as her persecutors and our State will be disgraced, by the transactions of this day and this hour. If you see fit to keep her from imprisonment in the cell of a murderer for having proffered the blessing of a good education to those who, in our country, need it most, you may do so; *we shall not.*"

They turned from us in great wrath, words falling from their lips which I shall not repeat.

The sun had descended nearly to the horizon; the shadows of night were beginning to fall around us. The sheriff could defer the dark deed no longer. With no little emotion, and with words of earnest deprecation, he gave that excellent, heroic, Christian young lady into the hands of the jailer, and she was led into the cell of Watkins. So soon as I had heard the bolts of her prison-door turned in the lock, and saw the key taken out, I bowed and said, "The deed is done, completely done. It cannot be recalled. It has passed into the history of our nation and our age." I went away with my steadfast friend, George W. Benson, assured that the legislators of the State had been guilty of a most unrighteous act; and that Miss Crandall's persecutors had also committed a great blunder; that they all would have much more reason to be ashamed of her imprisonment than she or her friends could ever have.

The next day we gave the required bonds. Miss Crandall was released from the cell of the murderer, returned home, and quietly resumed the duties of her school, until she should be summoned as a culprit into court, there to be tried by the infamous "Black Law of Connecticut." And, as we expected, so soon as the evil tidings could be carried in that day, before Professor Morse had given to Rumor her telegraphic wings, it was known all over the country and the civilized world that an excellent young lady had been imprisoned as a criminal, — yes, put into a murderer's cell, — in the State of Connecticut, for opening a school for the instruction of colored girls. The comments that were made upon the deed in almost all the newspapers were far from grateful to the feelings of her persecutors. Even many who, under the same circumstances, would probably have acted as badly as Messrs. A. T. Judson and Company, denounced their procedure as unchristian, inhuman, antidemocratic, base, mean.

ARTHUR TAPPAN.

The words and manner of Mr. Judson in the interview I had with him on the 11th of March, of which I have given a pretty full report, convinced me that he would do all that could be done by legal and political devices, to *abolish* Miss Crandall's school. His success in obtaining from the Legislature the enactment of the infamous "Black Law" showed too plainly that the majority of the people of the State were on the side of the oppressor. But I felt sure that God and good men would be our helpers in the contest to which we were committed. Assurances of approval and of sympathy came from many; and erelong a proffer of all the pecuniary assistance we could need was made by one who was then himself a host. At that time Mr. Arthur Tappan was one of the wealthiest merchants in the country, and was wont to give to religious and philanthropic objects as much, in proportion to his means, as any benefactor who has lived in the land before or since his day. I was not then personally acquainted with him, but he had become deeply interested in the cause of the poor, despised, enslaved millions in our country, and alive to whatever affected them.

Much to my surprise, and much more to my joy, a few weeks after the commencement of the contest, and just after the enactment of the Black Law and the imprisonment of Miss Crandall, I received from Mr. Tappan a most cordial letter. He expressed his entire approbation of the position I had taken in defence of Miss Crandall's benevolent enterprise, and his high appreciation of the importance of maintaining, in Connecticut especially, the right of colored people, not less than of white, to any amount of education they might wish to obtain, and the respect and encouragement due to any teacher who would devote himself or herself to their instruction. He added: "This contest, in which you have been providentially called to engage, will be a serious, perhaps a violent one. It may be prolonged and very expensive. Nevertheless, it ought to be persisted in to the last. I venture to presume, sir, that you cannot well afford what it may cost. You ought not to be left, even if you are willing, to bear alone the pecuniary burden. I shall be most happy to give you all the help of this sort that you may need. Consider me your banker. Spare no necessary expense. Command the services of the ablest lawyers. See to it that this great case shall be thoroughly tried, cost what it may. I will cheerfully honor your drafts to enable you to defray that cost." Thus upheld, you will not wonder that I was somewhat elated. At Mr. Tappan's suggestion I immediately "retained" the Hon. William W. Ellsworth, the Hon. Calvin Goddard, and the Hon. Henry Strong, the three most distinguished members of the Connecticut bar. They all confirmed me in the opinion that the "Black Law" was unconstitutional, and would probably be so pronounced, if we should carry it up to the United States Court. They moreover instructed me that, as the act for which Miss Crandall was to be tried was denounced as *criminal*, it would be within the province of the jury of our State court to decide upon the character of the law, as well as the conduct of the accused; and that therefore it would be allowable and proper for them to urge the *wickedness* of the law, in bar of Miss Crandall's condemnation under it. But, before we get to the trials of Miss Crandall under Mr. Judson's law, I have more to tell about Mr. Arthur Tappan.

He requested me to keep him fully informed of the doings of Miss Crandall's persecutors. And I assure you I had too many evil things to report of them. They insulted and annoyed her and her pupils in every way their malice could devise. The storekeepers, the butchers, the milk-pédlers of the town, all refused to supply their wants; and whenever her father, brother, or other relatives, who happily lived but a few miles off, were seen coming to bring her and her pupils the necessaries of life, they were insulted and threatened. Her well was defiled with the most offensive filth, and her neighbors refused her and the thirsty ones about her even a cup of cold water, leaving them to depend for that essential element upon the scanty supplies that could be brought from her father's farm. Nor was this all; the physician of the village refused to minister to any who were sick in Miss Crandall's family, and the trustees of the church forbade her to come, with any of her pupils, into the House of the Lord.

In addition to the insults and annoyances mentioned above, the newspapers of the county and other parts of the State frequently gave currency to the most egregious misrepresentations of the conduct of Miss Crandall and her pupils, and the basest insinuations against her friends and patrons. Yet our corrections and replies were persistently refused a place in their columns. The publisher of one of the county papers, who was personally friendly to me, and whom I had assisted to establish in business, confessed to me that he dared not admit into his paper an article in defence of the Canterbury school. It would be, he said, the destruction of his establishment. Thus situated, we were continually made to feel the great disadvantage at which we were contending with the hosts of our enemies.

In one of my letters to Mr. Tappan, when thus sorely pressed, I let fall from my pen, "O that I could only leave home long enough to visit you! For I could tell you in an hour more things, that I wish you to know, than I can write in a week."

A day or two afterwards, about as quickly as he could then get to me after the receipt of my letter, the door of my study was opened, and in walked Arthur Tappan. I sprang to my feet, and gave him a pressure of the hand which told him more emphatically than words could have done how overjoyed I was to see him. In his usual quiet manner and undertone he said, "Your last letter implied that you were in so much trouble I thought it best to come and see, and consider with you what it will be advisable for us to do." I soon spread before him the circumstances of the case, — the peculiar difficulties by which we were beset, the increased and increasing malignity of Miss Crandall's persecutors, provoked, and almost justified in the public opinion, by the false reports that were diligently circulated, and which we had no means of correcting. "Let me go," said he, "and see for myself Miss Crandall and her school, and learn more of the particulars of the sore trials to which her benevolence and her fortitude seem to be subjected." As soon as possible the horse and chaise were brought to the door, and the good man went to Canterbury. In a few hours he returned. He had been delighted, nay, deeply affected, by the calm determination which Miss Crandall evinced, and the quiet courage with which she had inspired her pupils. He had learned that the treatment to which they were subjected by their neighbors was in some respects worse even than I had represented it to him; and he said in a low, firm tone of voice, which showed how thoroughly in earnest he was, she must be protected and sustained. "The cause of the whole oppressed, despised colored population of our country is to be much affected by the decision of this question."

After some further consultation he rose to his feet and said, "You are almost helpless without the press. You must issue a paper, publish it largely, send it to all the persons whom you know in the county and State, and to all the principal newspapers throughout the country. Many will subscribe for it and contribute otherwise to its support, and I will pay whatever more it may cost." No sooner said than done. We went without delay to the village, where fortunately there was a pretty-well-furnished printing-office that had been lately shut up for want of patronage. We found the proprietor, examined the premises, satisfied ourselves that there were materials enough to begin with, and Mr. Tappan engaged for my use for a year the office, press, types, and whatever else was necessary to commence at once the publication of a newspaper, to be devoted to the advocacy of all human rights in general, and to the defence of the Canterbury school, and its heroic teacher in particular.

We walked back to my house communing together about the great conflict for liberty to which we were committed, the spirit in which it ought to be conducted on our part, and especially the course to be pursued in the further defence of Miss Crandall. Soon after the stage-coach came along. Mr. Tappan, after renewed assurances of support, gave me a hearty farewell and stepped on board to return to New York. He left me the proprietor of a printing-office, and with ample means to maintain, as far as might be necessary, the defence of the Canterbury school against the unrighteous and unconstitutional law of the State of Connecticut. I need now only add that the trials at law were protracted until August, 1834, and that they, together with the conduct of the newspaper, cost me more than six hundred dollars, all of which amount was most promptly and kindly paid by that true philanthropist, —Arthur Tappan.

CHARLES C. BURLEIGH.

The excitement caused by Mr. Tappan's unexpected visit, the hearty encouragement he had given me, and the great addition he had made to my means of defence, altogether were so grateful to me that I did not at first fully realize how much I had undertaken to do. But a night's rest brought me to my senses, and I clearly saw that I must have some other help than even Mr. Tappan's pecuniary generosity could give me. I was at that time publishing a religious paper, — *The Christian Monitor*, — which, together with my pulpit and parochial duties, filled quite full the measure of my ability. Unfortunately the prospectus of *The Monitor*, issued a year before the beginning of the Canterbury difficulty, precluded from its columns all articles relating to personal or neighborhood quarrels. Therefore, though the editor of a paper, I could not, in that paper, repel the most injurious attacks that were made upon my character. Had it been otherwise, there would have been no need of starting another paper. But, as Mr. Tappan promptly allowed, another paper must be issued, and to edit two papers at the same time was wholly beyond my power. What should I do?

Soon after the enactment of the "Black Law" an admirable article, faithfully criticising it, had appeared in *The Genius of Temperance*, and been copied into *The Emancipator*. It was attributed to Mr. Charles C. Burleigh, living in the adjoining town of Plainfield. I had heard him commended as a young man of great promise, and had once listened to an able speech from him at a Colonization meeting. To him, therefore, in the need of help, my thoughts soon turned. And the morning after Mr. Tappan's visit I drove over to Plainfield. Mr. Burleigh was living with his parents, and helping them carry on their farm, while pursuing as he could his studies preparatory to the profession of a lawyer. It was Friday of the week, in the midst of haying time. I was told at the house that he was in the field as busy as he could be. Nevertheless, I insisted that my business with him was more important than haying. So he was sent for, and in due time appeared. Like other sensible men, at the hard, hot work of haying, he was not attired in his Sunday clothes, but in his shirt-sleeves, with pants the worse for wear; and, although he then *believed* in shaving, no razor had touched his beard since the first day of the week. Nevertheless, I do not believe that Samuel of old saw, in the ruddy son of Jesse, as he came up from the sheepfold, the man whom the Lord would have him anoint, more clearly than I saw in C. C. Burleigh the man whom I should choose to be my assistant in that emergency. So soon as I had told him what I wanted of him his eye kindled as if eager for the conflict. We made an arrangement to supply his place on his father's farm, and he engaged to come to me early the following week. On Monday, the 14th of July, 1833, according to promise, he came to Brooklyn. He then put on the harness of a soldier in the good fight for equal, impartial liberty, and he has not yet laid it aside, nor are there many, if indeed any, of the antislavery warriors who have done more or better service than Mr. Burleigh.

On the 25th of July, 1833, appeared the first number of our paper, called *The Unionist.* After the first two or three numbers most of the articles were written or selected by Mr. Burleigh, and it was soon acknowledged by the public that the young editor wielded a powerful weapon. The paper was continued, if I remember correctly, about two years, and it helped us mightily in our controversy with the persecutors of Miss Crandall. After a few months C. C. Burleigh associated with him, in the management of *The Unionist,* his brother, Mr. William H. Burleigh, who also, at the same time, assisted Miss Crandall in the instruction of her school; and for so doing suffered not a little obloquy, insult, and abuse.

It was still the cherished intention of C. C. Burleigh to devote himself to the law, and without neglecting his duties to *The Unionist* he so diligently and successfully pursued his preparatory studies, that in January, 1835, he was examined and admitted to the bar. The committee of examination were surprised at his proficiency. He was pronounced the best prepared candidate that had been admitted to the Windham County Bar within the memory of those who were then practising there; and confident predictions were uttered by the most knowing ones of his rapid rise to eminence in the profession. Scarcely did Wendell Phillips awaken higher expectations of success as a lawyer in Boston, than C. C. Burleigh had awakened in Brooklyn. But just at the time of his admission I received a letter from Dr. Farnsworth, of Groton, Massachusetts, then President of the Middlesex Antislavery Society, inquiring urgently for some able lecturer, whose services could be obtained as the general agent of that Society. I knew of no one so able as C. C. Burleigh. So I called upon him, told him of the many high compliments I had heard bestowed upon his appearance on the examination, and then said, "Now I have already a most important case, in which to engage your services," and showed him Dr. Farnsworth's letter. For a few minutes he hesitated, and his countenance fell. The bright prospect of professional eminence was suddenly overcast. He more than suspected that, if he accepted the invitation, he should get so engaged in the antislavery cause as to be unable to leave the field until after its triumph. He would have to renounce all hope of wealth or political preferment, and lead a life of continual conflict with ungenerous opponents; be poorly requited for his labors, and suffer contumely, hatred, persecution. I saw what was passing in his mind, and that the struggle was severe. But it lasted only a little while, — less than an hour. A bright and beautiful expression illuminated his countenance when he replied, "This is not what I expected or intended, but it is what I ought to do. I will accept the invitation." He did so. Before the close of the week he departed for his field of labor. And I believe he ceased not a day to be the agent of one antislavery society or another, until after the lamented President Lincoln had proclaimed emancipation to all who were in bondage in our land.

When, in April, 1835, I became the General Agent of the Massachusetts Antislavery Society, I was brought into more intimate relations with Mr. Burleigh. We were indeed fellow-laborers. Repeatedly did we go forth together on lecturing excursions, and never was I better sustained. With him as my companion I felt sure our course would be successful. I always insisted upon speaking first; for, if I failed to do my best, he would make ample amends, covering the whole ground, exhausting the subject, leaving nothing essential unsaid. And if I did better than ever, Mr. Burleigh would come after me, and fill twelve baskets full of precious fragments. He is a single-minded, pure-hearted, conscientious, self-sacrificing man. He is not blessed with a fine voice nor a graceful manner. And the peculiar dress of his hair and beard has given offence to many, and may have lessened his usefulness. But he has a great command of language. He has a singularly acute and logical intellect. His reasoning, argumentative powers are remarkable. And he often has delighted and astonished his hearers by the brilliancy of his rhetoric, and the surpassing beauty of his imagery, and aptness of his illustrations. The millions of the emancipated in our country are indebted to the labors of few more than to those of Charles C. Burleigh. But to return.

MISS CRANDALL'S TRIAL.

On the 23d of August, 1833, the first trial of Prudence Crandall for the *crime* of keeping a boarding-school for colored girls in the State of Connecticut, and endeavoring to give them a good education, — the first trial for *this crime*, — was had in Brooklyn, the seat of the county of Windham, within a stone's throw of the house where lived and died General Israel Putnam, who, with his compatriots of 1776, perilled his life in defence of the self-evident truth that "all men were created *equal*, and endowed by their Creator with the inalienable right to life, liberty, and the pursuit of happiness." It was had at the County Court, Hon. Joseph Eaton presiding.

The prosecution was conducted by Hon. A. T. Judson, Jonathan A. Welch, Esq., and I. Bulkley, Esq. Miss Crandall's counsel were Hon. Calvin Goddard, Hon. W. W. Ellsworth, and Henry Strong, Esq.

The indictment of Miss Crandall consisted of two counts, which amounted to the same thing. The first set forth, in the technical terms of the law, that "with force and arms" she had received into her school; and the second, that, "with force and arms," she had instructed certain colored girls, who were not inhabitants of the State, without having first obtained, in writing, permission to do so from the majority of the civil authority and selectmen of the town of Canterbury, as required by the law under which she was prosecuted.

Mr. Judson opened the case. He, of course, endeavored to keep out of sight the most odious features of the law which had been disobeyed by Miss Crandall. He insisted that it was only a wise precaution to keep out of the State an injurious kind of population. He urged that the public provisions for the education of all the children of the inhabitants of Connecticut were ample, generous, and that colored children belonging to the State, not less than others, might enjoy the advantages of the common schools, which were under the supervision and control of proper officials in every town. He argued that it was not fair nor safe to allow any person, without the permission of such officials, to come into the State and open a school for any class of pupils she might please to invite from other States. He alleged that other States of the Union, Northern as well as Southern, regarded colored persons as a kind of population respecting which there should be some special legislation. If it were not for such protection as the law in question had provided, the Southerners might free all their slaves, and send them to Connecticut instead of Liberia, which would be overwhelming. Mr. Judson denied that colored persons were citizens in those States, where they were not enfranchised. He claimed that the privilege of being a freeman was higher than the right of being educated, and asked this remarkable question: "Why should a man be educated who could not be a freeman?" He denied, however, that he was opposed to the improvement of any class of the inhabitants of the land, if their improvement could be effected without violating any of the provisions of our Constitution, or endangering the union of the States. His associates labored to maintain the same positions.

These positions were vigorously assailed by Mr. Ellsworth and Mr. Strong, and shown to be untenable by a great array of facts adduced from the history of our own country, of the opinions of some of the most illustrious lawyers and civilians of England and America, and of arguments, the force of which was palpable.

Nevertheless, the Judge saw fit, though somewhat timidly, in his charge to the Jury, to give it as his opinion that "the law was constitutional and obligatory on the people of the State."

The Jury, after an absence of several hours, returned into court, not having agreed upon a verdict. They were instructed on some points, and sent out a second, and again a third time, but with no better success. They stated to the Court that there was no probability they should ever agree. Seven of them were for conviction, and five for acquittal. So they were discharged.

Supposing that this result operated as a continuance of the case to the next term of the County Court, to be held the following December, a few days after the trial I went with my family to spend several weeks with my friends in Boston and the neighborhood. But much to my surprise and discomfort, the last week in September, just as I was starting off to deliver an antislavery lecture, at a distance from Boston, I received the information that the persecutors of Miss Crandall, too impatient to wait until December for the regular course of law, had got up a new prosecution of her, to be tried on the 3d of October, before Judge Daggett of the Supreme Court, who was known to be hostile to the colored people, and a strenuous advocate of the Black Law. It was impossible for me so to dispose of my engagements that I could get back to Brooklyn in time to attend the trial. I could only write and instruct the counsel of Miss Crandall, in case a verdict should be obtained against her, to carry the cause up to the Court of Errors.

The second trial was had on the 3d of October; the same defence as before was set up, and ably maintained. But Chief Justice Daggett's influence with the Jury was overpowering. He delivered an elaborate and able charge, insisting upon the constitutionality of the law; and, without much hesitation, the verdict was given against Miss Crandall. Her counsel at once filed a bill of exceptions, and an appeal to the Court of Errors, which was granted. Before that — the highest legal tribunal in the State — the cause was argued on the 22d of July, 1834. The Hon. W. W. Ellsworth and the Hon. Calvin Goddard argued against the constitutionality of the Black Law, with very great ability and eloquence. The Hon. A. T. Judson and the Hon. C. F. Cleaveland said all that perhaps could be said to prove such a law to be consistent with the Magna Charta of our Republic. All who attended the trial seemed to be deeply interested, and were made to acknowledge the vital importance of the question at issue. Most persons, I believe, were persuaded that the Court ought to and would decide against the law. But they reserved the decision until some future time. And that decision, I am sorry to say, was never given. The Court evaded it the next week by finding that the defects in the information prepared by the State's Attorney were such that it ought to be quashed; thus rendering it "unnecessary for the Court to come to any decision upon the question as to the constitutionality of the law."

Whether her persecutors were or were not in despair of breaking down Miss Crandall's school by legal process, I am unable to say, but they soon resorted to other means, which were effectual.

HOUSE SET ON FIRE.

Soon after their failure to get a decision from the Court of Errors, an attempt was made to set her house on fire. Fortunately the match was applied to combustibles tucked under a corner where the sills were somewhat decayed. They burnt like a slow match. Some time before daylight the inmates perceived the smell of fire, but not until nearly nine o'clock did any blaze appear. It was quickly quenched; and I was sent for to advise whether, if her enemies were so malignant as this attempt showed them to be, it was safe and right for her to expose her pupils' and her own life any longer to their wicked devices. It was concluded that she should hold on and bear yet a little longer. Perhaps the atrocity of this attempt to fire her house, and at the same time endanger the dwellings of her neighbors would frighten the leaders and instigators of the persecution to put more restraint upon "the baser sort." But a few nights afterwards it was made only too plain that the enemies of the school were bent upon its destruction. About twelve o'clock, on the night of the 9th of September, Miss Crandall's house was assaulted by a number of persons with heavy clubs and iron bars; five window-sashes were demolished and ninety panes of glass dashed to pieces.

I was summoned next morning to the scene of destruction and the terror-stricken family. Never before had Miss Crandall seemed to quail, and her pupils had become afraid to remain another night under her roof. The front rooms of the house were hardly tenantable; and it seemed foolish to repair them only to be destroyed again. After due consideration, therefore, it was determined that the school should be abandoned. The pupils were called together, and I was requested to announce to them our decision. Never before had I felt so deeply sensible of the cruelty of the persecution which had been carried on for eighteen months, in that New England village against a family of defenceless females. Twenty harmless, well-behaved girls, whose only offence against the peace of the community was that they had come together there to obtain useful knowledge and moral culture, were to be told that they had better go away, because, forsooth, the house in which they dwelt would not be protected by the guardians of the town, the conservators of the peace, the officers of justice, the men of influence in the village where it was situated. The words almost blistered my lips. My bosom glowed with indignation. I felt ashamed of Canterbury, ashamed of Connecticut, ashamed of my country, ashamed of my color. Thus ended the generous, disinterested, philanthropic, Christian enterprise of Prudence Crandall.

This was the second attempt made in Connecticut to establish a school for the education of colored youth. The other was in New Haven, two years before. So prevalent and malignant was our national prejudice against the most injured of our fellow-men!

MR. GARRISON'S MISSION TO ENGLAND. — NEW YORK MOBS.

The subject of this article is very opportune at the present time.* While the roar of the cannon, fired in honor of Mr. Garrison at the moment of his late departure from England, is still reverberating through the land, it will be interesting and instructive to recall the purpose of his mission to that country just thirty-four years ago; and how he was vilified when he went, and denounced, hunted, mobbed, on his return. He went there to undeceive the philanthropists of Great Britain as to a gigantic fraud which had been practised upon them, as well as the antislavery people of the United States. He has gone now to the World's Antislavery Convention as a delegate from our *National Association* for the education, and individual, domestic, and civil elevation of our colored population, whose condition thirty years ago, and until a much more recent period, it was confidently maintained, and pretty generally conceded, could not be essentially improved within the borders of our Republic, if, indeed, on the same continent with our *superior Anglo-Saxon race.*

The conscience of our country was never at peace concerning the enslavement of the colored people. It was denounced by Jefferson in his original draft of the Declaration of Independence, and afterwards in his "Notes on Virginia." An effort to abolish slavery was

* This chapter was written in June, 1867, and I give it here as it first came from my pen.

made in the Convention that framed our Constitution; and strenuous opposition to that Magna Charta was made in several of the State Conventions called to ratify it, because the abominable wrong was indirectly and covertly sanctioned therein. Soon after we became a nation plans were proposed and associations formed for the improvement of the condition of the colored population; and the General Government was earnestly entreated, in a petition headed by Dr. Franklin, "to go to the utmost limits of its power" to eradicate the great evil from the land. But the doctrine was industriously taught by our statesmen that the status of that class of the people was left, in the Constitution of the Union, to be determined by the government of each of the States in which they may be found. And still greater pains were taken, by those who were bent on the perpetuation of slavery, to make it generally believed throughout the country that negroes were naturally a very inferior race of men; utterly incapable of much mental or moral culture, and better off in domestic servitude on our continent than in their native state in Africa. Notwithstanding this disparagement of them, and the other inducements pressed upon the white people everywhere to acquiesce in their enslavement, many colored persons emancipated themselves, especially in Maryland, Virginia, Kentucky, and Louisiana; and many more were set free by the workings of the consciences of their owners, or in gratitude for their services to individuals or the public. Thus, considerable bodies of freedmen were found almost everywhere in the midst of the slaves. Not without reason, these persons became objects of distrust to slaveholders. Devices were therefore sought to get rid of their disturbing influence, and to prevent the increase of the number of such persons.

In 1816 the grand scheme was proposed, and readily

adopted in most of the slaveholding States, for colonizing on the coast of Africa the free colored people of the United States, and prohibiting the emancipation of any more of the enslaved, excepting upon the condition of their removal to Liberia.

To carry this great undertaking into complete effect it was necessary to secure the patronage of the Federal Government. This obviously could not be done, without first conciliating to the project the approval and coöperation of the people of the non-slaveholding States. Accordingly, agents, eloquent and cunning, were sent north, east, and west, to summon the benevolent and patriotic everywhere to aid in an enterprise which, it was claimed, would result in the safe but entire abolition of American slavery.

The dreadful wrongs and cruelties inflicted upon our bondmen were not kept out of sight by these agents, but sometimes glowingly depicted. The participation of the Northern States in the original sin of the enslavement of Africans was pertinently urged. The utter impracticability and danger of setting free such hordes of ignorant, degraded people were insisted on with particular emphasis. The immense good that would be done to benighted Africa was eloquently portrayed, — how the slave-trade might be stopped, and the knowledge of the arts of civilized America, and the blessings of our Christian religion, might be spread throughout that dark region of the earth, from the basis of colonies planted at Liberia and elsewhere along those coasts, hitherto visited only by mercenary and cruel white men. All these considerations were so pressed upon the churches and ministers and kind-hearted people of the Northern States, that erelong an enthusiasm was awakened everywhere in favor of colonizing the colored people of our country "in their native land," and thus, at the same time, evangelizing Africa and wiping out the shame of the American Republic. Without stopping to consider the glaring inconsistencies of the scheme, it was taken for granted to be the only feasible way of doing what we all longed to have done, — abolishing slavery. So the colonization of our colored population became the favorite enterprise at the North, even more than at the South. Thousands who were so prejudiced against them that they would never consent to admit them to the enjoyment of the rights, and the exercise of the prerogatives, of men in our country were ready to give liberally to have them transported across the Atlantic, and were deluded into the belief that it was a benevolent, yes, a Christian enterprise. The very elect were deceived. The men who have since been most distinguished among the Abolitionists — Mr. Garrison, Arthur Tappan, Gerrit Smith, James G. Birney, and hundreds more — were for a while zealous Colonizationists.

Not until Mr. Garrison had been some time resident in Baltimore as co-editor, with Benjamin Lundy, of the *Genius of Universal Emancipation*, were the true purpose and spirit of Colonization discovered. He there found out, as he afterwards made it plainly appear, that the *intention* of the originators, and of the Southern promoters of the scheme, really was, "to rivet still closer the fetters of the slaves, and to deepen the prejudice against the free people of color."

So different had been the representations of its purpose by the agents of the Colonization Society who had labored in its behalf throughout the free States, and so utterly unconscious were most of the Colonizationists on this side of Mason and Dixon's line of harboring any such designs, that Mr. Garrison's accusations fired them with indignation and wrath. They would not give heed to his incontrovertible evidence. Though his witnesses were numerous and could not be impeached, yet were they spurned by most of the persons in the free States who had espoused the cause. It was enough that Mr. Garrison had come out in opposition to the plan of Colonization. He was denounced as an infidel, set upon as an enemy of his country. The churches were all closed against him. Few ministers ventured to give him any countenance, and the politicians heaped upon him unmeasured abuse. All this made the more plain to the young Reformer and his co-laborers how thoroughly the virus of slavery had poisoned the American body ecclesiastic, as well as the body politic. It was seen that the church was becoming the bulwark of slaveholders. Mr. Garrison felt that the first thing to be done, therefore, was to batter down the confidence of the humane in the Colonization plan. Against this he drove his sharpest points, at this he aimed his heaviest artillery. So when it became known to us that the agents of that plan had labored, with sad effect, in Great Britain; that they had suborned to their purpose the aid of the English philanthropists, we all felt, with Mr. Garrison, that those friends of the oppressed must be undeceived without delay. No one was competent to do this work so thoroughly as Mr. Garrison himself. Accordingly, it was determined, in the spring of 1833, that he must see personally the prominent Abolitionists of Great Britain.

In pursuance of this object he sailed from New York on the first day of this month, thirty-four years ago. He went with the execrations of the leading Colonizationists, and all the proslavery partisans of our country upon his head. He was received in England with the utmost cordiality and respectful confidence by all the friends of liberty; for although, as he found, many of them had been persuaded by the agents of the Colonization Society to give their approval and aid to that scheme, they had done so because they had been made to believe that it was intended and adapted to effect the entire abolition of slavery in the United States.

Nothing could have been more opportune than was his arrival in London. He found there most of the leading Abolitionists of the United Kingdom watching and aiding the measures in Parliament about to issue in the emancipation of the enslaved in the British West India Islands. He was invited to their councils, and interchanged opinions freely and fully with them on the great questions, which were essentially the same in that country and our own. It was especially his privilege to become acquainted with William Wilberforce and Thomas Clarkson and Fowell Buxton and George Thompson, to name no more of the noble host that had fought the battles and won the victory of freedom for eight hundred thousand slaves. He was there when William Wilberforce was summoned to lay aside his earthly life, with his antislavery armor, and ascend, we trust, to the right hand of God. How appropriate that the young leader of the Abolitionists of America, whose work had just begun, should be present, as he was, at the obsequies of the veteran leader of the British Abolitionists just as their work was done!

Mr. Garrison remained in England three or four months, long enough to accomplish fully the object of his mission. He reached New York on the 30th of the following September, bringing with him this emphatic protest, signed by the most distinguished philanthropists, and several of the most distinguished statesmen of Great Britain: —

"We, the undersigned, having observed with regret that the American Colonization Society appears to be gaining some adherents in this country, are desirous to express our opinions respecting it. Our motive and excuse for thus coming forward are the claims which that Society has put forth to *Antislavery* support. These claims are, in our opinion, wholly groundless; and we feel bound to affirm that our deliberate judgment and conviction are that the professions made by the Colonization Society of promoting the abolition of slavery are delusive. . . . .

"While we believe its precepts to be delusive we are convinced that its *real* effects are of the most dangerous nature. It takes its root from a cruel prejudice and alienation in the whites of America against the colored people, slave or free. This being its source, its effects are what might be expected. . . . . .

"On these grounds, therefore, and while we acknowledge the colony of Liberia, or any other colony on the coast of Africa, to be *in itself* a good thing, we must be understood utterly to repudiate the principles of the American Colonization Society. That Society is, in our estimation, not deserving of the countenance of the British public.

(Signed)

"Wm. Wilberforce,
Zachary Macaulay,
William Evans, M. P.,
Samuel Gurney,
S. Lushington, M. P.,
T. Fowell Buxton, M. P.,
James Cropper,
Daniel O'Connell, M. P.,"
and others.

Nothing could have maddened the slaveholders and their Northern abettors more than Mr. Garrison's success in England, and their malignant, ferocious hatred of him broke out on his return. It so happened that, without any expectation of his arrival at the time, a meeting of those desirous of the abolition of slavery was called, on the evening of October 2, in Clinton Hall, to organize a city society. When it was known that Mr. Garrison would be present, most of the New York newspapers teemed with exciting articles, and an advertisement, signed "Many Southerners," summoned "all persons interested in the subject" to be present at the same time and place. The Abolitionists, aware that a meeting at

Clinton Hall would be broken up, quietly withdrew to Chatham Street Chapel, and had nearly completed the organization of the "New York City Antislavery Society," when the mob of *slaveholding patriots*, disappointed of their prey at Clinton Hall, and finding out the retreat of the Abolitionists, rushed upon and dispersed them from Chatham Street Chapel, with horrid cries of detestation and threats of utmost violence, especially aimed at Mr. Garrison, of whom they went in search from place to place, declaring their determination to wreak upon him their utmost vengeance. Mr. Garrison, secure in their ignorance of his person, and curious to learn all he might of the mistaken notions and corrupt principles by which they were misled and driven to such excesses, went around with them in their bootless pursuit until he was tired, and the fire of their fury had cooled.

The New York newspapers, especially the *Courier and Inquirer*, the *Gazette*, *Evening Post*, and *Commercial Advertiser*, by their half-way condemnation of this outrage, and their gross misrepresentations of the sentiments and purposes of Mr. Garrison and his fellow-laborers, virtually justified that fearful assault upon "the liberty of speech," and inauguration of "the Reign of Terror," of which I shall hereafter give my readers some account.

THE CONVENTION AT PHILADELPHIA.

The publication of Mr. Garrison's "Thoughts on Colonization" had arrested the attention of philanthropists in all parts of our country. Everywhere, public as well as private discussions were had respecting the professed and the real purpose and tendency of the Colonization plan. Converts to the great doctrine of the young Reformer — "Immediate emancipation *without expatriation*, the right of the slave and the duty of the master" —

were added daily. Tidings came to us that many town and several county antislavery societies had been formed in several States of the Union, and the circulation of the *Liberator* had greatly increased. There was a growing feeling that Abolitionists of the whole country ought to know each other, devise some plan of co-operation, and make their influence more manifest. Repeatedly during the spring of 1833 Mr. Garrison expressed his opinion that the time had come for the formation of a National Antislavery Society.

After his departure on his mission to England the need of such an organization became more and more apparent, and before Mr. Garrison's return, on the 30th of September, the call was issued for the Convention to be held in Philadelphia on the fourth, fifth, and sixth days of the ensuing December. Had we foreseen the peculiarly excited state of the public mind at that time, the important meeting might have been deferred. The success of Mr. Garrison's labors in England, in opening the eyes of the British philanthropists to the egregious imposition which had been put upon them by the Colonization Society, the protest of the sainted Wilberforce and his most illustrious fellow-laborers, the stinging sarcasms of O'Connell, the champion of Ireland and of universal freedom, were working like moral blisters. More than all, the report of the great Exeter Hall meeting in London, by which colonization was denounced, and the doctrine of "immediate emancipation" fully indorsed, had lashed into fury all the proslavery-colonization-pseudo patriotism throughout the land. The storm had burst upon us in the mobs at New York; and whether it would ever subside until it had overwhelmed us, was a question which many answered in tones of fearful foreboding to our little band. But, the Convention had been called before the outbreak, and we were not "wise and prudent" enough to relinquish our purpose of holding it.

On my way to the "City of Brotherly Love" I joined, at New York, a number of the brethren going thither, whom I had never seen before. I studied anxiously their countenances and bearing, and caught most thirstily every word that dropped from their lips, until I was satisfied that most of them were men ready to die, if need be, in the pass of Thermopylæ.

There was a large company on the steamer that took us from New York to Elizabethtown, and again from Bordentown to Philadelphia. There was much earnest talking by other parties beside our own. Presently a gentleman turned from one of them to me and said, "What, sir, are the Abolitionists going to do in Philadelphia?" I informed him that we intended to form a National Antislavery Society. This brought from him an outpouring of the commonplace objections to our enterprise, which I replied to as well as I was able. Mr. Garrison drew near, and I soon shifted my part of the discussion into his hands, and listened with delight to the admirable manner in which he expounded and maintained the doctrines and purposes of those who believed with him that the slaves — the blackest of them — were men, entitled as much as the whitest and most exalted men in the land to their liberty, to a residence here, if they choose, and to acquire as much wisdom, as much property, and as high a position as they may.

After a long conversation, which attracted as many as could get within hearing, the gentleman said, courteously: "I have been much interested, sir, in what you have said, and in the exceedingly frank and temperate manner in which you have treated the subject. If all Abolitionists were like you, there would be much less opposition to your enterprise. But, sir, depend upon it, that hair-brained, reckless, violent fanatic, Garrison will damage, if he does not shipwreck, any cause." Stepping forward, I replied, "Allow me, sir, to introduce you to Mr. Garrison, of whom you entertain so bad an opinion. The gentleman you have been talking with is he." I need not describe, you can easily imagine, the incredulous surprise with which this announcement was received. And so it has been from the beginning until now. Those who have only heard of Mr. Garrison, and have believed the misrepresentations of his enemies, have supposed him to be "a roaring lion, seeking whom he may devour." But those who have become most intimately acquainted with him have found him to be "as harmless as a dove," though indeed "as wise as a serpent."

When we arrived in Philadelphia on the afternoon of the 3d of December, 1833, we learnt that a goodly number were already there; and the newspapers of the day were seeking to make our coming a formidable affair, worthy the especial attention of those patriotic conservators of the peace who dealt in brickbats, rotten eggs, and tar and feathers. The Police of the city had given notice to our Philadelphia associates that they could not protect us in the evening, and therefore our meetings must be held by daylight.

A previous gathering was had that evening at the house of Evan Lewis, a man who was afraid of nothing but doing or being wrong. Between thirty and forty were there, and we made such arrangements as we could for the ensuing day. One thing we did, which we were not careful to report, so you may never have heard of it. It was a weak, a servile act. We were ashamed of it ourselves, and you shall have a laugh at our expense if you like.

Some one suggested that, as we were strangers in Philadelphia, our characters and manner of life not known there, the populace might the more easily be made to believe that we had come for an incendiary purpose, and be roused to prevent the accomplishment of it; that, in order to avert the opposition which seemed preparing to thwart us, it would be well to get some one of the distinguished philanthropists of that city to preside over our deliberations, and thus be, as it were, a voucher to the public for our harmlessness. There was no one proposed of whom we could hope such patronage, save only Robert Vaux, a prominent and wealthy Quaker. To him it was resolved we should apply. Five or seven of us were delegated to wait upon the great man, and solicit his acceptance of the Presidency of the Convention. Of this committee I had the honor to be one. Just for this once I wish I had some wit, that I might be able to do justice to the scene. But I need not help you to see it in all its ludicrousness. There were at least six of us — Beriah Green, Evan Lewis, Eppingham L. Capron, Lewis Tappan, John G. Whittier, and myself — sitting around a richly furnished parlor, gravely arguing, by turns, with the wealthy occupant, to persuade him that it was his duty to come and be the most prominent one in a meeting of men already denounced as "fanatics, amalgamationists, disorganizers, disturbers of the peace, and dangerous enemies of the country." Of course our suit was unsuccessful. We came away mortified much more because we had made such a request, than because it had been denied. As we left the door Beriah Green said in his most sarcastic tone, "If there is not timber amongst ourselves big enough to make a president of, let us get along without one, or go home and stay there until we have grown up to be men."

The next morning as we passed along the streets leading to the place of meeting, the Adelphi Buildings, we were repeatedly assailed with most insulting words.

On arriving at the hall we found the entrance guarded by police officers, placed there, I suppose, at the suggestion of some friends by order of the Mayor. These incidents helped us to realize how we and the cause we had espoused, were regarded in that City of Brotherly Love and Quakers.

At the hour appointed, on the morning of the 4th, nearly all the members were in their seats, — fifty-six in all, representing ten different States. No time was lost. A fervent prayer was offered for the divine guidance. If there was ever a praying assembly I believe that was one.

Beriah Green, then President of Oneida Institute, was chosen President of our Convention. Lewis Tappan, one of the earliest and most untiring laborers in the cause of the oppressed, a well-known merchant of New York, and John G. Whittier, one of Liberty's choicest poets, were chosen Secretaries.

The first forenoon was spent in a free but somewhat desultory interchange of thought upon the topics of prominent interest, and in listening to a number of cheering letters from individuals in different parts of the United States, assuring us of their hearty sympathy and co-operation, though they were unable to be with us in person.

Discussion and argument were not found necessary to bring us to the resolution to institute an American Anti-slavery Society, for that was the especial purpose for which we had come together. Committees were chosen to draft a constitution and to nominate a list of officers. When the dining hour arrived, with one consent it was agreed that it was better than meat to remain in the hall, and commune with one another upon the interests of the cause we had espoused. And there and thus did we spend the dinner-time on that and each of the succeeding days. Baskets of crackers and pitchers of cold water supplied all the bodily refreshment that we needed.

The reports of the committees occupied us through the afternoon. We then came unanimously to the conclusion that it was needful to give, to our country and the world, a fuller declaration of the sentiments and purposes of the American Antislavery Society than could be embodied in its Constitution. It was therefore resolved "that Messrs. Atlee, Wright, Garrison, Joselyn, Thurston, Sterling, William Green, Jr., Whittier, Goodell, and May be a committee to draft a Declaration of the Principles of the American Antislavery Society for publication, to which the signatures of the members of this Convention shall be affixed."

In my next article I will give my readers a particular account of the conception and production of our Magna Charta.

THE PHILADELPHIA CONVENTION.

The committee of ten, appointed at the close of the first day to prepare a declaration of the sentiments and purposes of the American Antislavery Society, felt that the work assigned them ought to be most carefully and thoroughly done, embodying, as far as possible, the best thoughts of the whole Convention. Accordingly, about half of the members were invited to meet, and did meet, the committee early at the house of our chairman, Dr. Edwin P. Atlee.

After an hour's general conversation upon the importance of the document to be prepared, and the character it ought to possess, we agreed that each one present should, in his turn, utter the sentiment or announce the purpose which he thought ought to be given in the declaration. This was done, and revealed great unanimity, and at the same time not a little individuality of opinion among the members. I cannot now recall many of the suggestions thrown out. One, however, was so pregnant that it contained the text and the substance of several of my lectures afterwards. "I wish," said Elizur Wright, "that the difference between our purpose and that of the Colonization Society should be explicitly stated. We mean to exterminate *slavery* from our country with its accursed influences. The Colonizationists aim only to *get rid of the slaves* so soon as they become free. Their plan is unrighteous, cruel, and impracticable withal. Our plan needs but a good will, a right spirit amongst the white people, to accomplish it."

After a session of more than two hours thus spent a sub-committee of three was appointed to prepare a draft of the proposed declaration, to be reported next morning at nine o'clock to the whole committee, in the room adjoining the hall of the Convention. William L. Garrison, John G. Whittier, and myself composed that sub-committee. We immediately repaired to the house of Mr. James McCrummel, a colored gentleman, with whom Mr. Garrison was at home; and there, after a half-hour's consultation, it was of course determined that Mr. Garrison, our Coryphæus, should write the document, in which were to be set before our country and the world "the sentiments and purposes of the American Anti-slavery Society." We left him about ten o'clock, agreeing to come to him again next morning at eight.

On our return at the appointed hour we found him, with shutters closed and lamps burning, just writing the last paragraph of his admirable draft. We read it over together two or three times very carefully, agreed to a few slight alterations, and at nine went to lay it before the whole committee. By them it was subjected to the severest examination. Nearly three hours of intense application were given to it, notwithstanding repeated and urgent calls from the Convention for our report. All the while Mr. Garrison evinced the most unruffled patience. Very few alterations were proposed, and only once did he offer any resistance. He had introduced into his draft more than a page in condemnation of the Colonization scheme. It was the concentrated essence of all he had written or thought upon that egregious imposition. It was as finished and powerful in expression as any part of that Magna Charta. We commented upon it as a whole and in all its parts. We writhed somewhat under its severity, but were obliged to acknowledge its exact, its singular justice, and were about to accept it, when I ventured to propose that all of it, excepting only the first comprehensive paragraph, be stricken from the document, giving as my reason for this large erasure, that the Colonization Society could not long survive the deadly blows it had received; and it was not worth while for us to perpetuate the memory of it, in this Declaration of the Rights of Man, which will live a perpetual, impressive protest against every form of oppression, until it shall have given place to that brotherly kindness, which all the children of the common Father owe to one another. At first, Mr. Garrison rose up to save a portion of his work that had doubtless cost him as much mental effort as any other part of it. But so soon as he found that a large majority of the committee concurred in favor of the erasure, he submitted very graciously, saying, "Brethren, it is your report, not mine."

With this exception, the alterations and amendments which were made, after all our criticisms, were surprisingly few and unessential; and we cordially agreed to report it to the Convention very much as it came from his pen.

Between twelve and one o'clock we repaired with it to the hall. Edwin P. Atlee, the Chairman, read the Declaration to the Convention. Never in my life have I seen a deeper impression made by words than was made by that admirable document upon all who were there present. After the voice of the reader had ceased there was a profound silence for several minutes. Our hearts were in perfect unison. There was but one thought with us all. Either of the members could have told what the whole Convention felt. We felt that the word had just been uttered which would be mighty, through God, to the pulling down of the strongholds of slavery.

The solemn silence was broken by a Quaker brother, Evan Lewis, or Thomas Shipley, who moved that we adopt the Declaration, and proceed at once to append to it our signatures. He said, "We have already given it our assent; every heart here has responded to it; and there is a doctrine of the 'Friends' which impelled me to make the motion I have done: '*First impressions are from heaven.*' I fear, if we go about criticising and amending this Declaration, we shall qualify its truthfulness and impair its strength."

The majority of the Convention, however, thought it best, in a matter so momentous, to be deliberate; to weigh well every word and act by which our countrymen and the world would be called to justify or condemn us and our enterprise. Accordingly, we adjusted ourselves to hear the Declaration read again, paragraph by paragraph, sentence by sentence, and to pass judgment upon it in every particular. The whole afternoon, from one o'clock until five, was assiduously and patiently devoted to this review. Discussion arose on several points; but no one spoke who had not something to say. Never had I heard in a public assembly so much pertinent speech, never so little that was unimportant. The result of the afternoon's deliberations was a deeper satisfaction with the Declaration. Some expressions in it were called in question, but few were changed. And just as the darkness of night had shut down upon us we resolved unanimously to adopt it. On motion of Lewis Tappan we voted that Abraham L. Cox, M. D., whom the mover knew to be an excellent penman, be requested to procure a suitable sheet of parchment, and engross thereon our magna charta before the following morning, that it might then receive the signatures of each one of the members.

At the opening of the meeting next morning the Doctor was there, with the work assigned him beautifully executed. He read the Declaration once and again. Another hour was expended in the consideration of certain expressions in it. But no changes were made. It was then submitted for signatures; and Thomas Whitson, of Chester County, Pennsylvania, being obliged to leave the city immediately, came forward and had the honor of signing it first. Sixty-one others subscribed their names on the 6th day of December, 1833.

If I ever boast of anything it is this: that I was a member of the Convention that instituted the American Antislavery Society. That assembly, gathered from eleven different States of our Republic, was composed of devout men of every sect and of no sect in religion, of each political party and of neither; but they were all of one mind. They evidently felt that they had come together for a purpose higher and better than that of any religious sect or political party. Never have I seen men so ready, so anxious to rid themselves of whatsoever was narrow, selfish, or merely denominational. I was all the more affected by the manifestation of this spirit, because I had been living for ten years in Connecticut, where every one who did not profess a faith essentially "Orthodox" was peremptorily proscribed. In the Philadelphia Convention there were but two or three of my sect, which you know at that time had but few avowed adherents anywhere except in the eastern half of Massachusetts, and was then, much more than now, especially obnoxious to all other religionists in the land. Yet we were cordially treated as brethren, admitted freely, without reserve or qualification, into that goodly fellowship. They were indeed a company of the Lord's freemen, a truly devout company. And the scrupulous regard for the rights of the human mind, no less than for the other natural rights of man, was shown from the beginning to the end of the Convention.

Much the largest number of any sect present were what were then, and are now, called Orthodox, or Evangelical. There were ten or twelve ministers of one or the other of those denominations that claim to be Orthodox; yet I distinctly remember that some of them were the most forward and eager to lay aside sectarianism, and their generous example was gladly followed by all others. At the suggestion of an Orthodox brother, and without a vote of the Convention, our President himself, then an Orthodox minister, readily condescended to the scruples of our Quaker brethren, so far as not to *call upon* any individual to offer prayer; but at the opening of our sessions each day he gave notice that a portion of time would be spent in prayer. Any one prayed aloud who was moved so to do.

It was at the suggestion also of an Orthodox member that we agreed to dispense with all titles, civil or ecclesiastical. Accordingly, you will not find in the published minutes of the Convention appendages to any names, — neither D. D., nor Rev., nor Hon., nor Esq., — no, not even plain Mr. We met as fellow-men, in the cause of suffering fellow-men.

When the resolution was read recommending the institution of a monthly "concert of prayer" for the abolition of slavery, a Quaker objected to its passage, on the ground that he believed not in stated times and seasons for prayers, but that then only can we truly pray when we are moved to do so by the Holy Spirit. Effingham L. Capron, a member of the "Society of Friends," immediately and earnestly expressed regret that his brother had interposed such an objection. "For," said he, "this measure is only to be recommended by the Convention, not insisted on, much less to be incorporated into the constitution of the society we have formed; and such is the liberal, catholic spirit of all here present," he added, "that I do not suspect any one wishes to urge the measure upon those who would have conscientious scruples against it." "Certainly not, certainly not," said the mover of the resolution. "Certainly not, certainly not," was responded from all parts of the hall. On this explanation the brother withdrew his opposition, and the resolution passed, *nem. con.*

LUCRETIA MOTT.

A number of excellent women, most of them of the "Society of Friends," were in constant attendance upon the meetings of the Convention, which continued three days successively, without adjournment for dinner. On the afternoon of the second day, in the midst of a very interesting debate (I think it was on the use of the productions of slave-labor), a sweet female voice was heard. It was Lucretia Mott's. She had risen and commenced speaking, but was hesitating, because she feared the larger part of the Convention not being Quakers might think it "a shame for a woman to speak in a church," and she was unwilling to give them offence. Her beautiful countenance was radiant with the thoughts that had moved her to speak; and the expression was made all the more engaging by the emotion of deference to the supposed prejudices of her auditors, with which it was suffused.

Our President, Beriah Green, conferred not with flesh and blood, but, filled as he was with the liberal spirit of the apostle who wrote, "There is neither Jew nor Greek, there is neither male nor female; for ye are all one in Christ Jesus," at once, without waiting for the formal sanction of the Convention, cried out in the most encouraging, cordial tone, "Go on, ma'am, we shall all be glad to hear you." "Go on," "Go on," was responded by many voices. She did go on; and no man who was there will dissent from me when I add that she made a more impressive and effective speech than any other that was made in the Convention, excepting only our President's closing address.

Lucretia Mott afterwards spoke repeatedly; and one or two graceful amendments of the language of our Declaration were made at her suggestion. Two other excellent women also took part in our discussions, — Esther Moore and Lydia White, — and they spoke to good purpose. Now, that no brother was scandalized by this procedure (and there were several there who afterwards opposed us on the "woman question,") we have evidence enough in the following resolution, which was passed near the close of the third day, without dissent or a word to qualify or limit its application: "*Resolved*, that the thanks of the Convention be presented to our female friends for the deep interest they have manifested in the cause of antislavery, during the long and fatiguing session of the Convention." Was not the fact that three of our female friends had taken an active part in our meetings, had repeatedly "spoken in the church"

— must not this fact have been prominent to the view of every one who was called to vote on the above resolution? And yet I do aver that I heard not a word, either in or out of the hall, censuring their course, or expressing regret that they had been allowed to take part in our discussions. Far otherwise. It seemed to be regarded as another of the many indications we had seen of the deep hold which the antislavery cause had taken of the public heart. We remembered in the history of our race that, (although women had ordinarily kept themselves in the retirement of domestic life,) in the great emergencies of humanity, — in those imminent crises which have tried men's souls, and from which we date the signal advances of civilization, — women have always been conspicuous at the martyr's stake, in the councils of Church and State, and even in the conduct of armies. We therefore hailed the deep interest manifested by them in the cause of our oppressed countrymen, as an omen that another triumph of humanity was at hand. No one suggested that it would be well to invite the women to enroll their names as members of the Convention and sign the Declaration. It was not thought of in season. But I have not a doubt, such was the spirit of that assembly, that, if the proposal had been made, it would have been acceded to joyfully by a large majority, if not by all. We had not convened there to shape our enterprise to the received opinions or usages of any sect or party. We were not careful to do what might please "the scribes and pharisees and rulers of the people." We had come together at the cry of suffering, wronged, outraged millions. We had come to say and do what, we hoped, would rouse the nation to a sense of her tremendous iniquity. We were willing, we were anxious, that all who had ears to hear should hear "the truth which only tyrants dread." And I have no doubt, that at that time all immediate Abolitionists would have readily consented that every one (man or woman) who had the *power* had also the *right* to utter that truth; to utter it with the pen or with the living voice; to utter it at the fireside in the private circle, or to the largest congregation from the pulpit, or, if need be, from the house-top. It was not then in our hearts to bid any one be silent, who might be moved to plead for the down-trodden millions in our country who were not permitted to speak for themselves. We were willing "that the very stones should cry out," if they would.

The subjects that elicited most discussion in the Convention were Colonization; the use of the productions of slave-labor; the doctrine of compensation; and the duty of relying wholly on moral power. The results to which we came are expressed in the Constitution, the Declaration, or the Resolutions that were passed.

No one can read the published minutes of our proceedings, and not perceive how emphatically and solemnly we avowed the determination not to commit the cause we had espoused in any way to an arm of flesh, but to trust wholly to the power of truth and the influence of the Holy Spirit to change the hearts of slaveholders and their abettors. This principle, which was repudiated by a portion of the American Antislavery Society under the excitement caused by the murder of Lovejoy in 1837, was accounted by a large majority of the Convention as *the principle* upon which our enterprise should be prosecuted, or could be brought to a peaceful triumph. Those only who were ready to take up the cross, to suffer loss, shame, and even death, seemed to us then fit to engage in the work we proposed. The third article of the Constitution was as follows: "This Society will never, in any way, countenance the oppressed in vindicating their rights by physical force." And the pacific spirit and intentions of the Society were still more distinctively and emphatically set forth in the Declaration, in exposition of the third article above quoted. That document begins with an allusion to the Magna Charta of the American Revolution, which was prepared and signed fifty-seven years before in the very city where we were assembled. It exhibits clearly the contrast between our philanthropic enterprise and that of our fathers. It says: "*Their* principles led them to *wage war* against their oppressors, and to spill human blood like water in order to be free. *Ours* forbid the doing of evil that good may come, and lead us to reject, and entreat the oppressed to reject, the use of any carnal weapons for deliverance from bondage; relying solely upon those which are spiritual and 'mighty through God' to the pulling down of strongholds. *Their* measures were physical,—the marshalling in arms, the hostile array, the mortal encounter. *Ours* shall be such only as the opposition of moral purity to moral corruption, the destruction of error by the potency of truth, the overthrow of prejudice by the power of love, the abolition of slavery by the spirit of repentance."

This language was not adopted hastily or inconsiderately. Its import was duly weighed. A few of the members hesitated. They were not non-resistants. They were not, at first, ready to say they would not fight, if they should be roughly used by the opposers of our cause. But it was strenuously urged in reply that, whatever might be true as to the right of self-defence, in the prosecution of our great undertaking, *violent* resistance to the injurious treatment we might receive would have a disastrous effect. It was insisted that we ought to go forth to labor for the abolition of slavery, in the spirit of *Christian* reformers, expecting to be persecuted, and resolved never to return evil for evil. The result of our discussion was that all the members of the Convention signed the Declaration, thereby pledging themselves, and all who should thereafter sign the Constitution — "Come what may to our persons, our interests, or our reputations; whether we live to witness the triumph of liberty, justice, and humanity, or perish untimely as martyrs in this great, benevolent, and holy cause."

Such was the spirit that at last pervaded the whole body. I cannot describe the holy enthusiasm which lighted up every face as we gathered around the table on which the Declaration lay, to put our names to that sacred instrument. It seemed to me that every man's heart was in his hand, — as if every one felt that he was about to offer himself a living sacrifice in the cause of *freedom*, and to do it cheerfully. There are moments when heart touches heart, and souls flow into one another. That was such a moment. I was in them and they in me; we were all one. There was no need that each should tell the other how he felt and what he thought, for we were in each other's bosoms. I am sure there was not, in all our hearts, the thought of ever making violent, much less mortal, defence of the liberty of speech, or the freedom of the press, or of our own persons, though we foresaw that they all would be grievously outraged. Our President, Beriah Green, in his admirable closing speech, gave utterance to what we all felt and intended should be our course of conduct. He distinctly foretold the obloquy, the despiteful treatment, the bitter persecution, perhaps even the cruel deaths we were going to encounter in the prosecution of the undertaking to which we had bound ourselves. Not an intimation fell from his lips that, in any extremity, we were to resort to carnal weapons and fight rather than die in the cause. Much less did he intimate that it might ever be proper for us to defend, by deadly weapons, the liberty of speech and the press. O no! The words which came glowing from his lips were of a very different import. He exhorted us most solemnly, most tenderly, to cherish the Holy Spirit which he felt was then in all our hearts, and go forth to our several places of labor willing to suffer shame, loss of property, and, if need be, even of life, in the cause of human rights; but not intending to hurt a hair of the heads of our opposers, whom we ought to regard in pity more than in anger. Would that every syllable which he uttered had been engraven upon some imperishable tablet! Would that the spirit which then inspired him had been infused into the bosom of every one who has since engaged in the antislavery cause!

MRS. L. MARIA CHILD.

The account I have given above of the valuable services rendered in the Philadelphia Convention by Lucretia Mott, Esther Moore, and Lydia White, doubtless reminded my readers of many other excellent women, whose names stand high among the early antislavery reformers. The memories of them are most precious to me. If I live to write out half of my Recollections, and you do not weary of them, I shall make most grateful mention of our female fellow-laborers in general, of several of them in particular, though I cannot do ample justice to any.

There is one of whom I must speak now, because I have already passed the time, at which her inestimable services commenced. In July, 1833, when the number, the variety, and the malignity of our opponents had become manifest, we were not much more delighted than surprised by the publication of a thoroughgoing antislavery volume, from the pen of Mrs. Lydia Maria Child. She was at that time, perhaps, the most popular as well as useful of our female writers. None certainly, excepting Miss Sedgwick, rivalled her. The *North American Review*, then, if not now, the highest authority on matters of literary criticism, said at the time: "We are not sure that any woman in our country would outrank Mrs. Child. This lady has long been before the public as an author with much success. And she well deserves it, for in all her works we think that nothing can be found which does not commend itself by its tone of healthy morality and good sense. Few female writers, if any, have done more or better things for our literature, in its lighter or graver departments." That such an author — ay, such an *authority*— should espouse our cause just at that crisis, I do assure you, was a matter of no small joy, yes, exultation. She was extensively known in the Southern as well as the Northern States, and her books commanded a ready sale there not less than here. We had seen her often at our meetings. We knew that she sympathized with her brave husband in his abhorrence of our American system of slavery; but we did not know that she had so carefully studied and thoroughly mastered the subject. Nor did we suspect that she possessed the power, if she had the courage, to strike so heavy a blow. Why, the very title-page was pregnant with the gist of the whole matters under dispute between us, — "Immediate Abolitionists," and the slaveholders on the one hand, and the Colonizationists on the other, — "*An Appeal in Favor of that Class of Americans* CALLED *Africans.*" The volume, still prominent in the literature of our conflict, is replete with facts showing, not only the horrible cruelties that had been perpetrated by individual slaveholders or their overseers, but the essential barbarity of the *system of slavery*, its dehumanizing influences upon those who enforced it scarcely less than upon those who were crushed under it. Her book did us an especially valuable service in showing, to those who had paid little attention to the subject, that the Africans are not by *nature* inferior to other — even the *white* — races of men; but that "Ethiopia held a conspicuous place among the nations of ancient times. Her princes were wealthy and powerful, and her people distinguished for integrity and wisdom. Even the proud Grecians evinced respect for Ethiopia, almost amounting to reverence, and derived thence the sublimest portions of their mythology. And the popular belief, that all the gods made an annual visit to feast with the excellent Ethiopians, shows the high estimation in which they were then held, for we are not told that such an honor was bestowed on any other nation." Mrs. Child's exposure of the fallacy of the Colonization scheme, as well as the falsity of the pretensions put forth by its advocates, amply sustained all Mr. Garrison's accusations. And her *exposé* of the principles of the "Immediate Abolitionists" was clear, and her defence of them was impregnable.

This "Appeal" reached thousands who had given no heed to us before, and made many converts to the doctrines of Mr. Garrison.

Of course, what pleased and helped us so much gave proportionate offence to slaveholders, Colonizationists, and their Northern abettors. Mrs. Child was denounced. Her effeminate admirers, both male and female, said there were "some very indelicate things in her book," though there was nothing narrated in it that had not been allowed, if not perpetrated, by "the refined, hospitable, chivalric gentlemen and ladies" on their Southern plantations. The politicians and statesmen scouted the woman who "presumed to criticise so freely the constitution and government of her country. Women had better let politics alone." And certain ministers gravely foreboded "evil and ruin to our country, if the women generally should follow Mrs. Child's bad example, and neglect their domestic duties to attend to the affairs of state."

Mrs. Child's popularity was reversed. Her writings on other subjects were no longer sought after with the avidity that was shown for them before the publication of her "Appeal." Most of them were sent back to their publishers from the Southern bookstores, with the notice that the demand for her books had ceased. The sale of them at the North was also greatly diminished. It was said at the time that her income from the productions of her pen was lessened six or eight hundred dollars a year. But this did not daunt her. On the contrary, it roused her to greater exertion, as it revealed to her more fully the moral corruption which slavery had diffused throughout our country, and summoned her patriotism as well as her benevolence to more determined conflict with our nation's deadliest enemy. Indeed, she consecrated herself to the cause of the enslaved. Many of her publications since then have related to the great subject, viz.: The Oasis, Antislavery Catechism, Authentic Anecdotes, Evils and Cure of Slavery, Other Tracts, Life of Isaac T. Hopper, and, more than all, her letters to Governor Wise, of Virginia, and to Mrs. Mason, respecting John Brown. Those letters had an immense circulation throughout the free States, and were blazoned by all manner of anathemas in the Southern papers. Her letter to Mrs. Mason especially was copied by hundreds of thousands, and was doubtless one of the efficient agencies that prepared the mind of the North for the final great crisis.

For several years, assisted by her husband, Mrs. Child edited the *Antislavery Standard,* elevated its literary character, extended its circulation, and increased its efficiency.

But, in a more private way, this admirable woman rendered the early Abolitionists most important services. She, together with Mrs. Maria W. Chapman and Eliza Lee Follen, and others, of whom I shall write hereafter, were presiding genuises in all our councils and more public meetings, often proposing the wisest measures, and suggesting to those who were "allowed to speak in the assembly" the most weighty thoughts, pertinent facts, apt illustrations, which they could not be persuaded to utter aloud. Repeatedly in those early days, before Angelina and Sarah Grimke had taught others besides Quaker women "to *speak* in meeting," if they had anything to say that was worth hearing, — repeatedly did I spring to the platform, crying, "Hear me as the mouthpiece of Mrs. Child, or Mrs. Chapman, or Mrs. Follen," and convulsed the audience with a stroke of wit, or electrified them with a flash of eloquence, caught from the lips of one or the other of our antislavery prophetesses.

N. B. — That Mrs. Child, when she became an Abolitionist, did not become a woman "of one idea" is evinced, not only by her two volumes of enchanting "Letters from New York," "Memoirs of Madame de Staël" and "Madame Roland," "Biographies of Good Wives," and several exquisite books for children, but still more by her three octavo volumes, entitled "Progress of Religious Ideas," which must have been the result of a vast amount of reading and profound thought on all the subjects of theology and religion. Her later work, "Looking towards Sunset," is full of beautiful ideas about that future life, for which her untiring devotion to all the humanities in this life must have so fully prepared her.

ERUPTION OF LANE SEMINARY.

Lane Seminary was an institution established by our orthodox fellow-Christians, mainly for the preparation of young men for the ministry. It attained so much importance in the estimation of its patrons, that, in 1832, they claimed for it the services and the reputation of Rev. Dr. Beecher, who left Boston at that time and became its president. There he found, or was soon after joined by, Prof. Calvin E. Stowe, another distinguished teacher of Calvinistic theology. This school of the prophets was placed on Walnut Hill, in the vicinity of Cincinnati, that it might be near to the Southwestern States, and was separated from Kentucky only by the river Ohio. It had attracted, by the reputation of its Faculty, from all parts of the country, quite a number of remarkably able, earnest, conscientious, and, as they proved to be, eloquent young men.

At the time when the signal event occurred of which I am now to give some account, there were in the literary and theological departments of Lane Seminary more than a hundred students. Eleven of these were from different slave States; seven of them sons of slaveholders, one himself a slaveholder when he entered the institution, and one of the number — James Bradley — had emancipated himself from the cruel bondage by the payment of a large sum, that he had earned by extra labor. Besides these, there were ten of the students who had resided more or less in the slave States, and were well acquainted with the condition of the people, and the influence of their "peculiar institution" of domestic servitude. Moreover, that you may appreciate fully the importance of the event I am going to narrate to you, and know that it was not (as some at the time represented it to be) a boyish prank, or mere college rebellion, — "a tempest in a teapot," — let me tell you that the youngest student in the seminary was nineteen years of age, most of the students were more than twenty-six years old, and several of them were over thirty. They were sober, Christian men, who were preparing themselves, in good earnest, to preach the Gospel; and they believed that one of its proclamations was "liberty to the captives, let the oppressed go free, break every yoke."

Soon after the seminary was opened, a Colonization Society was formed among the students. At the time of which I speak most of them were members of that Society, and were encouraged by the Faculty so to be. But the publication of Mr. Garrison's "Thoughts on Colonization," and the formation of the "American Antislavery Society," attracted the attention of some of their number. Conversations arose on the subject between them and their fellows. An anxious inquiry was awakened as to the truth of the allegations brought against the Colonization scheme, and as to the justice of the new demand made by Mr. Garrison and his associates for the "immediate abolition of slavery." At length, in February, 1834, it was proposed that there should be a thorough public discussion of two questions: —

1st. Whether the people of the slaveholding States ought to abolish slavery at once, and without prescribing, as a condition, that the emancipated should be sent to Liberia, or elsewhere, out of our country?

2d. Whether the doctrines, tendencies, measures, spirit of the Colonization Society were such as to render it worthy of the patronage of Christian people?

We were informed at the time, by several who were cognizant of the fact, that the Faculty, fearing the effect of such a discussion upon the prosperity of the seminary, officially and earnestly advised that it should be indefinitely postponed. But many of the students had become too deeply interested in these questions to consent that they should remain unsettled. They were therefore discussed, — each one through nine evenings, — in the presence of the President and most of the Faculty, fully, faithfully, earnestly, but courteously debated. The results were, on the first question, an almost unanimous vote to this effect: that "Immediate emancipation from slavery was the right of every slave and the duty of every slaveholder." And on the second question it was voted, by a large majority, "That the American Colonization Society and its scheme were not deserving of the approbation and aid of Christians." This was the purport, if not the exact language, of the resolutions at the close of the debate of eighteen evenings.

The report of the proceeding and the result went speedily through the land; and, as speedily, there came back, from certain quarters, no stinted measure of condemnation, warning, threats. These so alarmed the Faculty that, as soon as was practicable, they formally prohibited the continued existence of an Antislavery Society among the students of Lane Seminary; and required that the Colonization Society, which they had cherished hitherto, should be also disbanded and abolished.

At the next meeting of the Overseers, or Corporation of the Seminary, this high-handed measure of the Faculty was approved and confirmed. The remonstrance of the students (all but one of them adult men, thirty of them more than twenty-six years of age) availed not to procure a reconsideration of this oppressive decree. Accordingly, nearly all of them — seventy or eighty in number — withdrew from the Seminary, refusing to be the pupils of theological professors who showed so plainly that their sympathies were with the oppressors, rather than with the oppressed; or that they had not courage enough to denounce so egregious a wrong, so tremendous a sin, as the enslavement of millions of human beings.

Like the disciples after the martyrdom of Stephen, these faithful young men were scattered abroad throughout the land, and went everywhere, preaching the word which they were forbidden to utter within the enclosure of a school, dedicated to the promulgation of the religion of Jesus of Nazareth.

Antislavery truth was disseminated far and wide by their agency. Those who were the sons of slaveholders returned to the homes of their parents, and besought them and their neighbors to repent of their great unrighteousness and flee from the wrath to come. These entreaties were not all lost. Several slaveholders were converted, and gave liberty to their bondmen. If I mistake not, the attention of that admirable man, Hon. James G. Birney, of Kentucky, was fixed by the discussions in Lane Seminary, and by conversations with the students upon the really evil tendency of the Colonization plan, which, with the best intentions, he had done so much to promote. At any rate, his conversion about that time to the doctrine of "immediate emancipation" was an event of signal importance, as I hope to show you in a future article.

It was not my privilege to become personally acquainted with many of these young men, whose conscientious, courteous, dignified, yet determined course of conduct awakened our admiration, and whose subsequent labors helped mightily the great work projected by the American Antislavery Society. Several of them were called to announce and advocate their principles in communities where it was especially dangerous "to speak those truths which tyrants dread." We were delighted from time to time by the accounts that came to us of their unflinching fidelity. And undoubtedly there were some cases of peculiar trial and suffering endured by them, which are treasured among the secret things that are to be made known, when He "who seeth in secret will reward men openly."

Amos Dresser, eager to raise the funds he needed to enable him to pursue his studies and complete his preparation for the ministry, took of the publishers an agency for the sale of the "Cottage Bible" in Tennessee. For the transportation of himself and his load he procured a horse and barouche. He had proceeded without molestation as far as Nashville. There it was discovered that he was an Abolitionist, — one of the students that had left Lane Seminary on account of his principles. He was arrested by order of the Mayor, and brought before the Committee of Vigilance. By them his trunk was searched, his journal, private papers, and letters were examined. These showed plainly enough, and he promptly acknowledged, that he was opposed to slavery; that he pitied his fellow-men who were in bondage, and regarded those who held them in chains as guilty of great wickedness.

Therefore, although there was not the slightest proofs that, thus far, he had done or said anything that did not pertain to his business, he was condemned by the Committee to be taken out immediately, to receive twenty lashes upon his bare back, and to depart from the city within twenty-four hours. Accordingly, that American citizen, for the crime of believing "the Declaration of Independence," was taken by the excited populace to a public square in Nashville, and there on his knees received upon his naked back twenty lashes, laid on by a city officer with a heavy cowhide. He was then hurried away, leaving behind him five hundred dollars' worth of property, which was never restored.

James A. Thome, the son of a Kentucky slaveholder, was so thoroughly converted to Abolitionism that, during the pendency of the infamous decree of the Faculty and Trustees of the Seminary, he was sent as a delegate from the Antislavery Society which the students had formed to attend the annual meetings of the Abolitionists in May, 1834. He came and addressed the public in New York, Boston, and elsewhere. His heartfelt sincerity, his tender, fervid eloquence, made a peculiarly deep impression upon his audiences. And having been born and brought up in the midst of slavery, his testimony to its cruelties, its licentiousness, and its depraving influences was received without distrust, though it sustained the worst allegations that had ever been brought against the domestic servitude in our Southern States.

Henry B. Stanton came with Mr. Thome as another delegate from the Lane Seminary Antislavery Society to the May meetings of 1834. This then young man also evinced so much zeal in the cause, so much power as a speaker and skill in debate, that soon after the dissolution of his connection with the seminary, in the month of October of that year, he was appointed an agent of the American Antislavery Society, and, for ten years or more afterwards, Mr. Stanton continued to do us most valuable service by his eloquent lectures, his pertinent contributions to our antislavery papers, and his diligence and fidelity as one of the secretaries of the National Society.

But Theodore D. Weld was the master-spirit among the Lane Seminary students. Indeed, he was accused by the Trustees of being the instigator of all the fanaticism and incendiary movements that had given them so much trouble and threatened the ruin of the institution. Accordingly, it was moved that Mr. Weld be expelled. No breach of law was charged upon this gentleman; no disrespect to the Faculty, nor anything implicating in the least his moral character, only that he was the leader of the Abolitionists. Still, the proposition to expel him was favored by the majority of the Trustees. When, therefore, the final action of the Board had determined the students to ask for a dismission from the seminary, Theodore D. Weld, with becoming self-respect, chose to remain until he should be cleared by the Faculty of all charges of misconduct. As soon as the Board had had a meeting and withdrawn their accusation, he applied for and received an honorable dismission.

Then he accepted an appointment as an agent of the Antislavery Society, at a salary less by half than was offered him by another benevolent association. And throughout the Western and Middle States, and occasionally in New England, he lectured with a frequency, a fervor, and an effect that justify me in saying that no one, excepting only Mr. Garrison and Mr. Phillips, has done more than Mr. Weld for the abolition of American slavery.

What a loss it would have been to the cause of liberty, if the Faculty and Trustees of Lane Seminary had been wiser men!

GEORGE THOMPSON, M. P., LL. D.

I AM careful to affix his *titles* to the name of this distinguished friend of humanity, because they indicate, in some measure, the estimation to which George Thompson has risen both in England and in the United States. The former title was conferred upon him in his own country, the latter in ours. But both nations owe him much more than *titles*. By each he should be placed high on the list of its public benefactors, and the two should unite to give him every comfort that he may need in his old age, and enable him to provide well for all who are dependent upon him.

George Thompson was born in 1804, the same year that gave birth to William Lloyd Garrison, and, like our illustrious countryman, has risen to his high elevation from a lowly estate of life. His native place was Liverpool, not far from the residence of William Roscoe, his father being, at the time of his birth, in the service of that distinguished scholar and philanthropist. He never attended school a day, but, like Garrison, was indebted to his mother for all elementary instruction. For the rest of his acquisitions he was left to depend upon himself.

While he was quite young his parents removed to London, and so soon as he could be made serviceable he was employed as an errand-boy. Quickened and guided by his excellent mother's love of knowledge, he early acquired the habit of reading, and greedily devoured all books adapted to his age that she could procure for him.

He was so fortunate as to attract the kind regard of the Rev. Richard Watson, the distinguished writer and preacher in defence of the doctrines of Methodism. He was taken as a chore-boy into that good man's family, and was with him, as his humble assistant in indoor and outdoor work, during most of the time that Mr. Watson was preparing his most famous publications. Owing to the influence of this divine, but more to his mother, at the age of fifteen George Thompson became the subject of deep, religious convictions, and consecrated himself, by public profession, to the service of God and the redemption of man. When sixteen years old he was appointed a Tract-distributor, and joined a society for visiting and nursing the destitute sick. About the same time he was apprenticed to a grocer, and continued in his employment a number of years, having in due time become his accountant.

At the age of twenty George Thompson was admitted

a member of a large debating-club. In this connection, he soon disclosed to those about him the value of the acquisitions he had made by reading, under the direction of his mother and Mr. Watson; and sometimes gave off more than sparks of that eloquence which since then has so often electrified and fired his large audiences, throughout Great Britain and our Northern and Western States.

In the course of the years 1825, 1826, and 1827, the benevolent people of England were pretty thoroughly roused by Clarkson, Wilberforce, Macaulay, and their brother philanthropists, to a consciousness of their nation's wickedness, in consenting to the system of West India slavery under the dominion of the British Crown. The question of immediate emancipation was agitated everywhere throughout the realm. It was introduced into the debating-club which George Thompson had joined. His sympathy for the slaves had been awakened very early in life. His father, when a young man, ran away from home, and enlisted as captain's clerk on board a slave-ship, not knowing what he did. But so soon as he witnessed the embarkation of the victims of that accursed traffic, and the treatment of them on the "middle passage," he was too much horrified to remain an hour longer, than he was obliged to, in any way connected with "a business too bad for demons to do." Immediately, therefore, on the arrival of his ship in the West Indies, he fled to an officer of a British man-of-war, and begged that he might be impressed into the naval service, and so escape the repetition of the horrors he had seen and unwillingly helped to perpetrate. Often had George heard his father narrate the cruelties which were inflicted on board the ship with which he was connected, — cruelties inseparable from the forcible transportation of human beings, without the least regard to their personal comfort, from the freedom of their native wilds to the hell of slavery in

America. Thus was his young heart and soul fired with indignation at the sin of his nation, and baptized into the love of impartial liberty. He, of course, welcomed the introduction of the question into the club, and entered upon the debate with holy zeal. The discussion was continued through twelve evenings. It attracted much attention; resulted in a resolution, passed almost unanimously, in favor of *immediate emancipation;* and was deemed of sufficient importance to be reported to the government. Especial mention was made of "the heartfelt, impassioned eloquence of a young man, named George Thompson"; and our friend became the cherished associate of several gentlemen who have since been widely known among the active friends of all the reforms and social improvements that have blessed Great Britian and Ireland within the last forty years.

In 1828 Mr. Thompson was especially invited to join "The London Literary and Scientific Association," comprising about a thousand young men. "Here, too, the question of West India emancipation came up for consideration, was earnestly and ably debated through three long evenings, and resulted in favor of the *immediate abolition* of slavery. This result was attributed mainly to "the masterly logic, as well as fervid eloquence, of young Thompson." The newspapers commented on his success, as an augury of what might be expected from him in *a more august debating-club*, which in England means Parliament.

And here I must tell you a family secret. The lady who afterwards became his wife, whose position in society was much higher than his own (a circumstance of far greater importance in England than in our country), was present at these debates. She was fired with such admiration of his powers, and of his consecration of them to the cause of suffering humanity, that it lighted a kindred flame in his bosom ; or, to speak in plain American English, they there fell in love with each other, and were soon after married.

About this time the London Antislavery Society was formed. The directors, or executive committee thereof, advertised for a suitable man, who was willing to become their lecturing agent. This opened the door to what has since been the business of his life. He hesitated several weeks, distrusting his ability. But, encouraged and urged by his young wife, he at length consented that the Secretary, Mr. Thomas Pringle, should be informed of his wish to receive an appointment. By that gentleman he was invited to an interview with Sir George Stevens and Rev. Zachary Macaulay, who, after satisfying themselves of his qualifications, commended him to Lord Brougham, Lord Denham, and Sir George Bunting, the committee that was to decide the question of appointment. These gentlemen, after an extended conversation with him, gave him a commission for three months, and sent him forth to agitate the community on the question of West India emancipation.

Could you but turn to the English papers of that day, you would see for yourself how rapidly, and to what an unexampled height, rose his reputation as a lecturer. At the end of three months, the demands that came from all parts of the kingdom for the services of Mr. Thompson settled the question with the committee. They gave him an appointment until "the warfare should be accomplished." And for three or four years he was the principal, if not the only, agent of that Society, performing an amount of labor which seems almost superhuman. In all parts of the United Kingdom his voice was heard, either in speeches to the crowds that everywhere thronged to listen to him, or in debates with Mr. Bostwick and other agents hired by the West

India slaveholders to oppose him. And when, in 1833, the victory was achieved; when, overpowered by the outward pressure, both Houses of Parliament were compelled to make a virtue of necessity, and to magnify the glory of England by that Act which gave liberty to eight hundred thousand slaves, Lord Brougham rose in the House of Lords and said: "I rise to take the crown of this most glorious victory from every other head, and place it upon George Thompson's. He has done more than any other man to achieve it." This tribute was most justly deserved.

Yet for all his labors, his inestimable services, Mr. Thompson received only pecuniary compensation enough to pay his expenses and support his small family. He asked no more. He had consecrated himself to the cause of suffering humanity for its own sake, not expecting to be enriched thereby. But the friends of that cause which he had served so well, so nobly, could not be indifferent to his future career. Lord Brougham, Lord Denham, and others, confident that he would become an ornament and an honor to the legal profession, offered him all the assistance he could need to defray his own and his family's expenses for five years, while he should be pursuing his preparatory studies, and getting established as a member of the English bar. The prospect thus opened was most inviting to him; the proposed profession was congenial to his taste. Indeed, if I have been correctly informed, the preliminary arrangements were made, when the claims of the most oppressed of all men,—the enslaved in the United States,—were forcibly urged upon him.

Mr. Garrison had been in England several weeks, laboring successfully to undeceive the philanthropists and people of Great Britain as to the real design and tendency of the American Colonization Society. Their kindred spirits had met and mingled. He had heard Mr. Garrison's exposition, and had become, with Clarkson, Wilberforce, Buxton, and others, fully satisfied that the expatriation of the free colored people, their removal from this country, if practicable, would only perpetuate the bondage of the enslaved, and aggravate their wrongs. Mr. Garrison, on the other hand, had repeatedly witnessed the surpassing power of Mr. Thompson's eloquence on the audiences he addressed, had heard the tributes everywhere paid to the importance of his services, and was present at the consummation of his unsparing labors, — the passage by the British Parliament of the bill for the abolition of West India slavery. It was manifest to him that the man, who had done so much for the overthrow of British slavery, could help mightily to accomplish the far greater work needed to be done in this country; and his heart was set on enlisting Mr. Thompson in the service of the American Antislavery Society. He pressed his wish, his demand, upon him just as Mr. Thompson was about to agree to the above-named arrangement for the study of the law. Mr. Garrison's invitation was not to be accepted hastily, nor could he reject it without consideration. He revolved it anxiously in his mind, as he went from city to city with his now beloved brother, hearing him portray the peculiarities of the American system of slavery, the far greater difficulties against which Abolitionists here had to contend, the need we felt of a living voice, potent enough to wake up thousands who were *dead* in this iniquity.

On the eve of Mr. Garrison's departure from England in the fall of 1833 Mr. Thompson, with deep emotion, said to him: "I have thought much of the bright professional prospects opened to me here. I have thought yet more of the dark, dismal, desperate condition of millions of my fellow-beings in your country. They are no farther from me than are the eight hundred thousand whom I have been laboring to emancipate, and their claims upon me for the help God may enable me to give them are just as strong. I cannot withhold myself from their service. If, on your return to Boston, you shall still think I can render you much assistance, and your fellow-laborers concur with you in that opinion, command me, and I will hasten to you."

Mr. Thompson, however, remained in England almost a year after Mr. Garrison left him, that he might reorganize the antislavery hosts who had triumphed so gloriously in the conflict for British West India emancipation, and induce them to engage as heartily in the enterprise for the emancipation of the millions held in the most abject bondage in these United States, and for the abolition of slavery throughout the world.

GEORGE THOMPSON'S FIRST YEAR IN AMERICA.

When, on his return from England in October, 1833, Mr. Garrison informed us that he had obtained from George Thompson — the champion of the triumphant conflict for West India emancipation — the promise to "come over and help us," if we concurred in the invitation Mr. Garrison had given him, our hearts were encouraged, our hands strengthened, our purpose confirmed. Our own great antislavery orators, male and female, who since then have done so much to convict and convert the nation, had not yet appeared. Theodore D. Weld and Henry B. Stanton were studying theology in Lane Seminary; Parker Pillsbury, Stephen S. Foster, and John A. Collins were doing likewise somewhere in Vermont; Henry C. Wright had not plucked up quite courage enough to justify Mr. Garrison's terrible denunciations of slaveholders and their abettors; James G. Birney was the Secretary of the Kentucky Colonization Society; Gerrit Smith had not got wholly out of the toils of that fraudulent scheme which had deceived "the very elect"; Charles C. Burleigh was an unknown youth in Plainfield Academy; Wendell Phillips, our Apollo, was just preparing to leap into his place at the head of the Massachusetts bar; and Angelina Grimke, Lucy Stone, Abby Kelly Foster, Susan B. Anthony, Antoinette L. Brown, Sallie Holley, and other excellent women, who have since rendered such signal services, had not then left "the appropriate sphere of women."

That George Thompson would come to our aid, the orator to whose relentless logic and surpassing eloquence, more than to any other instrumentality, Lord Brougham had just attributed the triumph of the antislavery cause in England, — that he was about coming to help us did seem at that time a godsend indeed. But, as was stated in my last, his coming was deferred a year, that the Abolitionists of Great Britain and Ireland might not lay aside their well-used weapons, nor cease from their warfare, while so many millions of human beings remained in the most abject slavery, especially in the United States, where the horrid institution was established by the authority of England. Having re-enlisted his fellow-laborers throughout the United Kingdom to co-operate with us, he came to Boston in the fall of 1834.

At that time I was devoting a few weeks of permitted absence from my church in Connecticut to a lecturing tour in the antislavery cause, and came to Mr. Garrison's house in Roxbury an hour after the arrival of Mr. Thompson. He readily consented to go with us the next day to Groton, there to attend a county convention. We gladly spent the remainder of that day together, in earnest and prayerful communion over the great work in which we had engaged; and at night repaired to lodge at the Earl Hotel in Hanover Street, that we might not fail to be off for Groton the next morning at four o'clock, in the first stage-coach, no conveyance thither by railroad being extant then.

At the appointed hour, the house being well filled, the meeting was called to order, and business commenced. As all were eager to see and hear the great English orator, preliminary matters were disposed of as soon as practicable. Then Mr. Thompson was called up by a resolution enthusiastically passed, declaring our appreciation of the inestimable value of his antislavery labors in England, our joy that he had come to aid us to deliver our country from the dominion of slaveholders, and our wish that he would occupy as much of the time of the convention as his inclination might prompt and his strength would enable him to do. He rose, and soon enchained the attention of all present. He set forth the essential, immitigable sin of holding human beings as slaves in a light, if possible, more vivid, more intense, than even Mr. Garrison had thrown upon that "sum of all villanies." He illustrated and sustained his assertions by the most pertinent facts in the history of West India slavery. He inculcated the spirit in which we ought to prosecute our endeavor to emancipate the bondmen, — a spirit of compassion for the masters as well as their slaves, — a compassion too considerate of the harm which the slaveholder suffers, as well as inflicts, to consent to any continuance of the iniquity. He most solemnly enjoined the use of only moral and political means and instrumentalities to effect the subversion and extermination of the gigantic system of iniquity, although it seemed to tower above and overshadow the civil and religious institutions of our country. He showed us that he justly appreciated the greater difficulties of the work to be done in our land, than of that which had just been so gloriously accomplished in England, but exhorted us to trust undoubtingly in "the might of the right," — the mercy, the justice, the power of God, — and to go forward in the full assurance that He, who had crowned the labors of the British Abolitionists with such a triumph, would enable us in like manner to accomplish the greater work he had given us to do.

Mr. Thompson then went on to give us a graphic, glowing account of the long and fierce conflict they had had in England for the abolition of slavery in the British West Indies. His eloquence rose to a still higher order. His narrative became *a continuous metaphor*, admirably sustained. He represented the antislavery enterprise in which he had been so long engaged as a stout, well-built ship, manned by a noble-hearted crew, launched upon a stormy ocean, bound to carry inestimable relief to 800,000 sufferers in a far-distant land. He clothed all the kinds of opposition they had met, all the difficulties they had contended with, in imagery suggested by the observation and experience of the voyager across the Atlantic in the most tempestuous season of the year. In the height of his descriptions, my attention was withdrawn from the emotions enkindled in my own bosom sufficiently to observe the effect of his eloquence upon half a dozen boys, of twelve or fourteen years of age, sitting together not far from the platform. They were completely possessed by it. When the ship reeled or plunged or staggered in the storms, they unconsciously went through the same motions. When the enemy attacked her, the boys took the liveliest part in battle, — manning the guns, or handing shot and shell, or pressing forward to repulse the boarders. When the ship struck upon an iceberg, the boys almost fell from their seats in the recoil. When the sails and topmasts were wellnigh carried away by the gale, they seemed to be straining themselves to prevent the damage; and when at length the ship triumphantly sailed into her destined port with colors flying and signals of glad tidings floating from her topmast, and the shout of welcome rose from thousands of expectant freedmen on the shore, the boys gave three loud cheers, "Hurrah! Hurrah!! Hurrah!!!" This irrepressible explosion of their feelings brought them at once to themselves. They blushed, covered their faces, sank down on their seats, one of them upon the floor. It was an ingenuous, thrilling tribute to the surpassing power of the orator, and only added to the zest and heartiness with which the whole audience applauded (to use the words of another at the time) "the persuasive reasonings, the earnest appeals, the melting pathos, the delightful but caustic irony and enrapturing eloquence of Mr. Thompson."

Thus commenced his brilliant career in this country. The Groton Convention lasted two days, the 1st and 2d of October. Mr. Thompson went thence immediately to Lowell, where he spoke to a delighted crowd on the 5th. Four days after, on the 9th of October, he gave his first address in Boston. It was at an adjourned meeting of the Massachusetts Antislavery Society. All the prominent Abolitionists, who could be, were there to see and hear "the almost inspired apostle of negro emancipation," who had "come over to help us." Every one that heard him then felt that his signal gifts had not been overrated, and joined in thanksgiving to the God of the oppressed, whose Holy Spirit, we believed, had moved him to consecrate those gifts to the abolition of slavery.

Reports of Mr. Thompson's eloquence spread rapidly, and invitations came to him from all quarters. The day after the meeting in Boston he went into the State of Maine, and lectured on the 12th in Portland, on the 13th in Brunswick, on the 15th in Augusta. Everywhere he was heard with delight, and made many converts. At Augusta, it is true, he received an angry letter from five "gentlemen of property and standing," informing him that his "coming to their city had given great offence," and admonishing him not to presume to address the public there again. But his engagements elsewhere, rather than their threats, obliged him to leave immediately. The next evening he lectured in the neighboring city of Hallowell, where the people heard him gladly. On the 17th he delivered an address in Waterville, which was listened to by most of the students and several of the faculty of the College, and made deep impressions upon a large number. On the 20th he spoke again to a crowded audience in Brunswick, with like effect upon the students and faculty of Bowdoin College. Returning, he lectured at Portland in six different churches, to large and delighted audiences, before the close of the month; and then came into New Hampshire and gave lectures in Plymouth, Concord, and other places, on his way back to Boston. After a few days' repose, he went forth again, in answer to many urgent invitations, and lifted up his voice for the enslaved in Rhode Island, Connecticut, New York, Pennsylvania, and Ohio. Whoever will turn over the leaves of the *Liberator* for 1834 and 1835 will find on almost every page some admiring mention of Mr. Thompson's lectures or speeches, and grateful acknowledgments of the deep impressions his words had made.

It is true that in the same paper will be found, under the appropriate head "*Refuge of Oppression*," extracts from newspapers and letters from all parts of the country, denouncing, execrating him, and calling upon the patriotic to put a stop to his incendiary career. He was a foreign intruder, who had come here to "meddle with a delicate matter about which he could know nothing." He was "a British emissary, sent to embroil the Northern with the Southern States, and break up our glorious Union." He was "the paid agent of the enemies of republican institutions, supported in our midst, that he might do all in his power to prevent the success of the grandest experiment in national government ever tried on earth." The changes were rung on these and similar charges until those, who could be deceived thereby, were maddened in their fear and hatred of Mr. Thompson. He was threatened with all kinds of ill-treatment; yet he went fearlessly wherever he was invited to speak, and not unfrequently disarmed and converted some who had come to the meetings intending to do him harm.

In several of his lecturing tours I was his companion; and I wondered how any persons who heard him speak, in public or in private, could suspect or be persuaded that he was an enemy of our country. I was continually surprised, as well as delighted, by the evidences he gave of his just appreciation of the principles of our government, and the admiration of them that he always cordially expressed. Having hitherto contemplated our Republic from a distance, he seemed to have taken a more comprehensive view of it than too many of our own citizens, even statesmen, had done, whose regard for the whole nation had been warped by their concern for the supposed interests of a section or a State. Mr. Thompson's detestation of slavery was intensified by his clear perception of the corruption it had diffused throughout our body politic and body ecclesiastic; and, if not abolished, the ruin it would inevitably bring upon our country, called, in the providence of God, to be "the land of the free and the asylum of the oppressed." No American patriot ever felt, for no human heart could feel, a deeper, more sincere, or more intelligent concern for the honor, glory, perpetuity of our Republic than Mr. Thompson felt and evinced in his every word and act. Few home-born lovers of our country have done a tithe as much as he did to save her from the ruin she was bringing upon herself by her recreancy to the fundamental principles, upon which she professed to stand. Not a dozen names, of those who have lived within the last forty years, deserve to stand higher on the list of our public benefactors than the name of George Thompson.

Yet was he maligned, hated, hunted, driven from our shores. The story of the treatment he received is too shameful to be told. During the last six months of his stay here the persecution of him was continuous. The newspapers, from Maine to Georgia, with a few most honorable exceptions, denounced him daily, and called for his punishment as an enemy, or his expulsion from the country. Those few who dared to tell the truth testified, not only to his enrapturing eloquence and his friendliness to our nation, but to his eminently Christian deportment and spirit. But the tide of persecution could not be stayed. He was often insulted in the streets. Meetings to which he spoke, or at which he was expected to speak, were broken up by mobs. Rewards were offered for his person or his life. Twice I assisted to help his escape from the hands of hired ruffians.

All this he bore, for the most part, with fortitude and sweet serenity. He seemed less apprehensive of his danger than his friends were. Sometimes he overawed the men who were sent to take him by his dignified, heroic bearing, and at other times dispelled their evil intentions by his pertinent wit. I will give a single instance. At one of the last meetings he addressed in Boston, some Southerners cried out : —

" We wish we had you at the South. We would cut your ears off, if not your head."

Mr. Thompson promptly replied : " Would you ? Then should I cry out all the louder, ' He that *hath* ears to hear let him hear.' " It was irresistible. I believe the Southerners themselves joined in the rapturous applause.

On the 27th of September, 1835, we left Boston together in a private conveyance, — he to lecture at Abington, one of the most antislavery towns in the State, and I at Halifax, a few miles beyond. On my return the next morning I learnt that there had been a fearful onslaught upon Mr. Thompson; and, when I called to take him back to the city, I found him more subdued than I had ever seen him. He had not expected ill-usage there. As we passed the meeting-house, from which he and his audience had been routed the night before, he was overcome by his emotions. There lay strewn upon the ground fragments of windows, blinds, and doors, and some of the heavy missiles with which they had been broken down. He fell back in the chaise, and for several minutes gave way to his feelings. When able to command himself he said : —

" What does it mean ? Am I indeed an enemy of your country ? Do I deserve this at your hands ? Testify against me if you can, Mr. May. You know, if any one does, what sentiments I have uttered, what spirit I have evinced. You have been with me in private and in public. Have you ever suspected me ? Have you ever heard a word from my lips unfriendly to your country, — your magnificent, your might-be-glorious, but your awfully guilty country ? What have I said, what have I done, that I should be treated as an enemy ? Have not all my words and all my acts tended to the removal of an evil which is your nation's disgrace, and, if permitted to continue, must be your ruin?"

We rode on in silence, for he knew my answers without hearing them from my lips. But the outrage at Abington assured us that the spirit of persecution was rife in the land, and might manifest itself anywhere.

Nevertheless, Mr. Thompson accepted an invitation to lecture a few days afterwards in the afternoon, by daylight, at East Abington. Accordingly, on the 15th of October, I went with him to the appointed place. We had been credibly informed that a number of men were going thither to take him, if they could do so without harm to themselves. But the good men and women of the town and neighborhood were up to the occasion. The meeting-house was crowded, so that, though the evil intenders were there in force, they soon saw that the capture could not be made there. And then the wit, the wisdom, the pathos, the eloquence of the speaker disarmed them, took them captive, and, for the hour, at least, made them delighted hearers.

This was Mr. Thompson's last public appearance during his first year in America. All his friends insisted that he must keep out of sight, and as soon as practicable return to England. It was well known that his life was in danger. That we had not attributed too great malignity to our countrymen — even to the citizens of Boston — was soon made apparent by their own acts.

It was announced in the *Liberator*, and so became publicly known, that a regular meeting of the "Boston Female Antislavery Society" would be held in the Hall, 46 Washington Street, on the 21st of October, 1835. Without authority, it was reported by other papers that Mr. Thompson was to address them; and it was more than intimated that then and there would be the time and place to seize him. On the morning of that day the following placard was posted in all parts of the city: —

"THOMPSON THE ABOLITIONIST.

"That infamous foreign scoundrel, Thompson, will hold forth this afternoon at 46 Washington Street. The present is a fair opportunity for the friends of the Union to *snake* Thompson out! It will be a contest between the Abolitionists and the friends of the Union. A purse of *one hundred dollars* has been raised by a number of patriotic citizens, to reward the individual who shall first lay violent hands on Thompson, so that he may be brought to the Tar Kettle before dark. Friends of the Union, be vigilant!"

The sequel of the infamous proceedings thus inaugurated will be given hereafter. Mr. Thompson was not there, and so the mob vented itself upon another. Mr. Thompson was, and had been for several days, secreted by his friends in Boston, and afterwards in Brookline, Lynn, Salem, Phillips Beach, and elsewhere, until his enemies were baffled in their pursuit of him, and arrangements were made to take him safely out of the country.

On or about the 20th of November he was conveyed in a small boat, rowed by two of his friends, from one of the Boston wharves to a small English brig, that had fortunately been consigned to Henry G. Chapman, one of our earliest and best antislavery brothers; and in that vessel he was carried to St. Johns. From that port he sailed for England on the 28th of the same month. Would that all my countrymen could read the letter that he wrote to Mr. Garrison on the eve of his departure. If words can truly express a man's thoughts and feelings, the words of that letter were written by a lover of our country, a true philanthropist, a Christian hero.

ANTISLAVERY CONFLICT.

THERE were many noble confessors of the antislavery gospel, and many self-sacrificing sufferers in the cause, in various parts of our country, to whom I should be doing great injustice not to speak particularly of their services, if I were writing a complete history of our protracted conflict for impartial liberty. But I must confine myself, for the most part, to my personal recollections of prominent events and the individuals who were most conspicuous within my own limited view.

It is to be hoped that a complete history of this second American Revolution will, erelong, be written by Mr. Garrison, the man of all others best qualified to write it, — except that he will not give that prominence to himself in his narrative which he took in the beginning and occupied until emancipation was proclaimed for all in bondage throughout our borders. He has been the coryphæus of our antislavery band. He uttered the first note that thrilled the heart of the nation. He, more than any one, has corrected the national discord. And he has led the grand symphony in which so many millions of our countrymen at last have gladly, exultingly joined.

But so many have, at different periods and in various ways, contributed to the glorious result that it will not be possible even for Mr. Garrison to do ample justice to all his fellow-laborers. Indeed, many of them cannot be known to him, or to any one but the Omniscient. As in every other war, the fate of many a battle was decided by the indomitable will and heroic self-sacrifice of some nameless private soldier, who happened to be at the point of imminent peril, so, no doubt, has a favorable turn sometimes been given to our great enterprise by the undaunted moral courage and persistent fidelity of one and another, who are unknown but to Him who seeth in secret.

In my last article I gave an account of the bitter persecution of Mr. Thompson. The fact that he was a foreigner was used with great effect to exasperate the mobocratic spirit against him; but the real gist of his offence was the same that every one was guilty of, who insisted upon the abolition of slavery.

At the annual meeting of the American Antislavery Society in May, 1835, I was sitting upon the platform of the Houston Street Presbyterian Church in New York, when I was surprised to see a gentleman enter and take his seat who, I knew, was a partner in one of the most prominent mercantile houses in the city. He had not been seated long before he beckoned me to meet him at the door. I did so. "Please walk out with me, sir," said he; "I have something of great importance to communicate." When we had reached the sidewalk he said, with considerable emotion and emphasis, "Mr. May, we are not such fools as not to know that slavery is a great evil, a great wrong. But it was consented to by the founders of our Republic. It was provided for in the Constitution of our Union. A great portion of the property of the Southerners is invested under its sanction; and the business of the North, as well as the South, has become adjusted to it. There are millions upon millions of dollars due from Southerners to the merchants and mechanics of this city alone, the payment of which would be jeopardized by any rupture between the North and the South. We cannot afford, sir, to let you and your associates succeed in your endeavor to overthrow slavery. It is not a matter of principle with us. It is a matter of business necessity. We cannot afford to let you succeed. And I have called you out to let you know, and to let your fellow-laborers know, that we do not mean to allow you to succeed. We mean, sir," said he, with increased emphasis, — "we mean, sir, to put you Abolitionists down, — by fair means if we can, by foul means if we must."

After a minute's pause I replied: "Then, sir, the gain of gold must be better than that of godliness. Error must be mightier than truth; wrong stronger than right. The Devil must preside over the affairs of the universe, and not God. Now, sir, I believe neither of these propositions. If holding men in slavery be wrong, it will be abolished. We shall succeed, your pecuniary interests to the contrary notwithstanding." He turned hastily away; but he has lived long enough to find that he was mistaken, and to rejoice in the abolition of slavery.

We were soon made to realize that the words of the New York merchant were not an unmeaning threat. He had not spoken for himself, or any number of the moving spirits of that commercial metropolis alone. He was warranted in saying what he did by the pretty general intention of the "gentlemen of property and standing" throughout the country to put a stop to the antislavery reform. The storm-clouds of persecution had gathered heavily upon our Southern horizon. Fiery flashes of wrath had often darted thence towards us. But we were slow to believe that our Northern sky would ever become so surcharged with hatred for those, who were only contending for "the inalienable rights of man," as to break upon us in any serious harm. The summer and fall of

1835 dispelled our misplaced confidence We found, to our shame and dismay, that even New England had leagued with the slaveholding oligarchy to quench the spirit of impartial liberty, and uphold in our country the most cruel system of domestic servitude the world has ever known. The denunciations of the South were reverberated throughout the North. The public ear was filled with most wanton, cruel misrepresentations of our sentiments and purposes, and closed, as far as possible, against all our replies in contradiction, explanation, or defence. The political newspapers, with scarcely an exception, teemed with false accusations, the grossest abuse, and the most alarming predictions of the ultimate effects of our measures. The religious papers and periodicals were no better. The churches in Boston, not less than elsewhere, were closed against us. Not a minister* — excepting Dr. Channing, and the one in Pine Street Church — would even venture to read a notice of an anti-slavery meeting. Dr. Henry Ware, Jr., was denounced and vilified for having done so from Dr. Channing's pulpit. All the public halls, too, of any tolerable size, were one after the other refused us. Even Faneuil Hall, the so-called cradle of American liberty, was denied to our use, though asked for in a respectful petition signed by the names of a hundred and twenty-five gentlemen of Boston, whose characters were as irreproachable as any in the city. But a few weeks afterwards, on the 21st of August, at the request of fifteen hundred of the "gentlemen of property and standing," that hall, in which had been cradled the independence of the United States, was turned into the Refuge of Slavery. There as large a multitude as could crowd within its spacious walls, with feelings of alarm for the safety of our country,

* Rev. Mr. Pierpont, who afterwards did good service, was absent in Europe during 1835.

and of indignation at the Abolitionists as disturbers of the peace, already excited by the grossest misrepresentations of our sentiments, purposes, and acts, industriously disseminated by newspapers and in reports of public speeches throughout the Southern States,—there, in Faneuil Hall, thousands of our fellow-citizens were infuriated yet more against us by harangues from no less distinguished civilians than the Hon. Harrison Gray Otis, Peleg Sprague, and Richard Fletcher. These gentlemen reiterated all the common unproved charges against us, and solemnly, eloquently, passionately argued and urged that the enslavement of millions of the people in our country was a matter with which we of the Northern States had no right to meddle. It was a concern, they insisted, of the Southern States alone, found there when these portions of our Republic were about to emerge from their colonial dependence upon Great Britain, and left there by the framers of the Constitution, which was meant to be the fundamental law of our glorious Union. They harped upon the guaranties given to the slaveholders, that they should be sustained and undisturbed in *enforcing* their claim of *property* in the persons and services of their laborers. And those gentlemen insisted that the endeavors of Abolitionists to convince their fellow-citizens of the heinous wickedness of holding human beings in slavery gave just offence to those who were guilty of the sin; violated the compact by which these United States were held together, and, if they were permitted to be prosecuted, would cause the dissolution of the Union.

Meetings of a similar character, in the same or a more violent spirit of denunciation, were held in New York, Philadelphia, Baltimore, and most of the cities of the nation. What were the immediate effects of this general outcry against us I shall narrate as briefly as I may.

REIGN OF TERROR.

The nearly simultaneous uprising of the proslavery hosts in 1835, and the almost universal outbreak of violence upon our antislavery heads in all parts of the country, from Louisiana to Maine, showed plainly enough that Mr. Garrison's demand for the immediate emancipation of the enslaved had entered into the ear of the whole nation. All the people had heard it, or heard of it. It had received a heartfelt response from not a few of the purest and best men and women in the land. This was manifest at the Convention in Philadelphia, in December, 1833, where were delegates from ten of the States of our Union, all of whom seemed ready to do, to dare, and to suffer whatever the cause of the oppressed millions might require. It waked at once the lyre of our Whittier, which has never slumbered since, and inspired him to utter those thrilling strains which all but tyrants and their minions love to hear. It drew from Elizur Wright, Jr., Professor in Western Reserve College, Ohio, in 1833, a thorough searching pamphlet on "the sin of slavery." It called out from Hon. Judge William Jay, of New York, that "Inquiry," which brought so many to the conclusion that the Colonization plan tended, if it were not *intended,* to perpetuate slavery, and satisfied them that "the class of Americans called Africans" (to use the pregnant title of Mrs. Child's impressive Appeal) had as much right to live in this country and enjoy liberty here as any other Americans. Mr. Garrison's word gave rise to that memorable discussion in Lane Seminary, of which I have heretofore given some account, and which resulted in the departure, from that narrow enclosure, of eighty preachers of the doctrine of "immediate emancipation," to repeat and urge their deep convictions upon the willing and the unwilling in almost every part of the land, which sent out Theodore D. Weld and Henry B. Stanton and James A. Thome, sons of thunder, whose voices reverberated throughout our Middle, Western, and Southern States. Mr. Garrison's word came to the ears, and at once found its way to the hearts, of those admirable ladies in South Carolina, Sarah and Angelina Grimké, who erelong came to the North, and bore their emphatic, eloquent, thrilling testimony to the intrinsic, all-pervading sinfulness of that system of domestic servitude to which they had been accustomed from their birth. And, more than all, his word had reached that high-souled, brave, courteous civilian, philanthropist, and Christian in Alabama, Hon. James G. Birney, who, as I shall hereafter relate, having for several years devoted his time, his personal influence, and persuasive eloquence to the Colonization cause, when he came to see its essential injustice and proslavery tendency, earnestly renounced his error. He forthwith emancipated his slaves, paid them fairly for their services, did all he could for their improvement, and thenceforward consecrated himself, through much evil report and bitter persecution, to the dissemination of the sentiments and the accomplishment of the great object of the American Antislavery Society. Immediately after his conversion he wrote and published two letters addressed to the American Presbyterians, of whose body he had been a highly esteemed member. In those letters he set forth most clearly the sinfulness of slaveholding, and implored his brethren to turn from it, and rid themselves wholly of the awful guilt of holding, or allowing others to hold, human beings as their chattels personal, and treating them as domesticated brutes.

These and other instances might be adduced to show how far and widely the antislavery doctrines had been made known at the time of which I am writing. But, alas! there were a great many different and very disagreeable evidences that *the truth,* which alone could make our nation *free,* had been heard, or heard of, everywhere.

WALKER'S APPEAL.

It should be stated, however, that the excitement which had become so general and so furious against the Abolitionists throughout the slaveholding States was owing in no small measure to an individual with whom Mr. Garrison and his associates had had no connection. David Walker, a very intelligent colored man of Boston, having travelled pretty extensively over the United States, and informed himself thoroughly of the condition of the colored population, bond and free, had become so exasperated that he set himself to the work of rousing his fellow-sufferers to a due sense of "their degraded, wretched, abject condition," and preparing them for a general and organized insurrection. In the course of the year 1828 Mr. Walker gathered about him, in Boston and elsewhere, audiences of colored men, into whom he strove to infuse his spirit of determined, self-sacrificing rebellion against their too-long endured and unparalleled oppression. Little was known of these meetings, excepting by those who had been specially called to them. But in September, 1829, he published his "*Appeal to the colored citizens of the world, in particular and very expressly to those of the United States.*"

It was a pamphlet of more than eighty octavo pages, ably written, very impassioned and well adapted to its purpose. The second and third editions of it were published in less than twelve months. And Mr. Walker devoted himself until his death, which happened soon after, to the distribution of copies of this Appeal to colored men who were able to read it in every State of the Union.

Just as I had written the above sentence, Dr. W. H. Irwin, of Louisiana, came in with an introduction to me. He is one of many Union men who have been stripped of their property and driven out of the State by President Johnson's and Mayor Monroe's partisans. Learning that he had been a resident many years in the Southern States, I inquired if he saw or heard of Walker's Appeal in the time of it. He replied that he was living in Georgia in 1834, was acquainted with the Rev. Messrs. Worcester and Butler, missionaries to the Cherokees, and knew that they were maltreated and imprisoned in 1829 or 1830 for having one of Walker's pamphlets, as well as for admitting some colored children into their Indian school.

So soon as this attempt to excite the slaves to insurrection came to the knowledge of Mr. Garrison, he earnestly deprecated it in his lectures, especially those addressed to colored people. And in his first number of the *Liberator* he repudiated the resort to violence, as wrong in principle and disastrous in policy. His opinions on this point were generally embraced by his followers, and explicitly declared by the American Antislavery Society in 1833.

But as we wished that our fellow-citizens South as well as North should be assured of our pacific principles, and as we hoped to abolish the institution of slavery by convincing slaveholders and their abettors of the exceeding wickedness of the system, we did send our reports, tracts, and papers to all white persons in the Southern States with whom we were any of us acquainted, and to distinguished individuals whom we knew by common fame, to ministers of religion, legislators, civilians, and editors. *But in no case did we send our publications to slaves.* This we forbore to do, because we knew that few of them could read; because our arguments and appeals were not addressed to them; and especially because we thought it probable that, if our publications should be found in their possession, they would be subjected to some harsher treatment.

Notwithstanding our precaution, the Southern "gentlemen of property and standing" denounced us as incendiaries, enemies, accused us of intending to excite their bondmen to insurrection, and to dissolve the Union. They would not themselves give any heed to our *exposé* of the sin and danger of slavery, nor would they suffer others so to do who seemed inclined to hear and consider. They assaulted, lynched, imprisoned any one in whose possession they found antislavery publications. They waylaid the mails, or broke into post-offices, and tore to pieces or burnt up all papers and pamphlets from the North that contained aught against their "peculiar institution," and significantly admonished, if they did not summarily punish, those to whom such publications were addressed. Meetings were called in most, if not all, of the principal cities of the South, at which Abolitionists were denounced in unmeasured terms, and the friends of the Union, North and South, and East and West, were peremptorily summoned to suppress them. By the votes of such meetings, and still more by the acts of the Legislatures of several States, large rewards — $5,000, $10,000, $20,000 — were offered for the abduction or assassination of Arthur Tappan, William Lloyd Garrison, Amos A. Phelps, and other prominent antislavery men. Moreover, letters of the most abusive character were sent to us individually, threatening us with all sorts of violence, arson, and murder.

Sad to relate, the corrupting, demoralizing influence of slavery was not confined to those who were directly enforcing the great wrong upon their fellow-beings. Those who had consented to such desecration of humanity were found to be almost as much contaminated as the slaveholders themselves. "The whole head of the nation was sick, and the whole heart was faint." The "gentlemen of property and standing" at the North, yes, even in Massachusetts, espoused the cause of the slaveholders. The editors of most of the newspapers, religious as well as secular, and of some of the graver periodicals, nearly all of the popular orators, and very many of the ministers of religion, spoke and wrote against the doctrine of the Abolitionists. They extenuated the crime of denying to fellow-men the God-given, inalienable rights of humanity, apologized for those who had been born to an inheritance of slaves, and insisted that "slavery was an ordination of Providence, sanctioned by our sacred Scriptures, even the Christian Scriptures." This last was the chief weapon with which the religionists throughout the Northern as well as Southern States combated the Abolitionists. Not a few sermons were preached in various parts of New England, as well as New York and other Middle States, in justification of slaveholding. The professors of Princeton Theological School published a pamphlet in defence of slavery, and Professor Stuart, of Andover, the great leader of New England orthodoxy, gave the abomination his sanction. The record of our Cambridge Divinity School is much more honorable. Dr. Henry Ware, Jr., evinced a deep interest in our enterprise, and incurred some censure for manifesting his interest. Dr. Follen identified himself with us at an early day, and, as I shall tell hereafter, was one of the sufferers in the cause; and Dr. Palfrey, though at the time of which I am writing rather privately, expressed an appreciation of our principles, which a few years afterwards impelled him to pecuniary sacrifice and a course of conduct in Congress which deservedly placed him high on the list of the antislavery worthies.* All the large, influential ecclesiastical bodies in our country — the Presbyterian, the Episcopal, the Methodist, the Baptist — threw over the churches of their sects throughout the Southern States the shield of their consent to, if not their approval of, slaveholding; and, I grieve to add, the American Unitarian Association could not be induced to pronounce its condemnation of the tremendous sin, the sum of all iniquities.

Most religionists of every name, our own not excepted, insisted that slavery was a political institution, with which, as Christians, it would be inexpedient for us to meddle; and the politicians and merchants did all in their power to disseminate this view of the matter, and close the doors of the churches and the lips of the ministers against this "exciting subject." I need not add they were too successful.

Most of the prominent statesmen, and all the political demagogues of both parties, took the ground that the great question as to the enslavement of the colored population of the South was *settled* by the framers of the Constitution; that it was a matter to be left exclusively to the States in which slavery existed; that to meddle with it was to violate the provisions of the fundamental law of the land and loosen the bands of the Union. Therefore the Abolitionists were to be regarded as disturbers of the public peace, incendiaries, enemies of their country, traitors. And it was proclaimed by many in high authority, and shouted everywhere by the baser sort, "that the Abolitionists ought to be abolished," by any means that should be found necessary. Thus outlawed, given up to the fury of the populace, we were subjected to abuses and outrages, of which I can give only a brief account.

* See Appendix.

We were slow to believe that our fellow-citizens of the New England States could be so besotted by the influence of the institution of slavery, that they would *outrage our persons* in its defence. We had had proofs enough that "the gentlemen of property and standing," "the wise and prudent," with their dependants, had shut their ears against the truth, and turned away their eyes from the grievous wrongs we were imploring our country to redress. This treatment we had experienced, with increasing frequency, ever since the formation of the American Antislavery Society, in December, 1833. But we were unwilling to apprehend anything worse, certainly in Massachusetts. We trusted that our persons would be sacred, though we had learned that the liberty of speech and of the press was not.

Late in the fall of 1833 I delivered, in Boylston Hall, at the request of the New England Antislavery Society, a discourse "On the Principles and Purposes of the Abolitionists, and the Means by which they intended to subvert the Institution of Slavery." The audience was large, and among my hearers I was delighted to see my good friend (afterwards Dr.) F. W. P. Greenwood, then one of the editors of the *Christian Examiner*. He remained after the meeting was over, and to my great joy said to me, "I have liked your discourse much. I wish everybody who is opposed to the antislavery reform could hear or read it. If you will prepare it as an article for the *Examiner*, I will publish it there." Glad of this avenue to the minds and hearts of so many who I especially wished should understand and appreciate the work to which I had wholly committed myself, I set about converting my discourse into a review of our best antislavery publications, and making it, as a literary production, more worthy of a place in the chief periodical of our denomination. It was too late for the January number, 1834, so I aimed to have it in readiness for the March number. In due time I called at the office and inquired how soon my manuscript would be wanted. The publisher asked what was the subject of my article; and on learning that it was to be an explanation of the sentiments and purposes of the Abolitionists, he said, to my astonishment, with much emphasis, "We do not want it; it cannot be published." "Why," I said, "is not Mr. Greenwood one of the editors, and do not he and his colleague decide what shall be put into the *Examiner?*" "Generally they do," he replied; "indeed, I never interfered before. But in this case I must and shall. The *Examiner* is my property. It would be seriously damaged if an article favoring Abolition should appear in it. I should lose most of my subscribers in the slave, and many in the free States. And I cannot afford to make such a sacrifice." But I rejoined, "Mr. Greenwood has heard all the essential parts of the article. He approved of it, thought it would do good, and requested me to prepare it for publication." Mr. B. replied, with more earnestness than before, "Mr. May, it shall not be published. If I should find it all printed on the pages of the *Examiner*, just ready to be issued, I would suppress the number and publish another, with some other article in the place of yours."

I hastened to Mr. Greenwood for redress. With evident mortification and sorrow he confessed his inability to do me justice. Nevertheless, in the July number, 1834, there was allowed to be published, on the 397th page, a paragraph, written by one of the Boston ministers, "for the special instruction of such ardent, but mistaken philanthropists among us as think they are justified, from their abhorrence of slavery, and their zeal for universal emancipation, to interfere with the constitutions of civil governments, or the personal rights of individuals."

Having permitted such an assault to be made upon us in their pages, I could not doubt that the editors of the *Examiner* would suffer me to be heard in defence. I therefore prepared carefully a respectful "letter" to them, trusting it would appear in their next number. But, to my surprise and serious displeasure, it was excluded. The letter was accordingly published in the *Liberator*, which, here let me say to its distinctive honor, always allowed the foes as well as the friends of freedom and humanity a place in its columns. And the editors of the *Examiner*, unsolicited, did me the favor, in their November number, 1834, page 282, to refer to my letter, commending its "eloquence and its good spirit, although circumstances obliged them to decline publishing it, and advising their readers to procure it and read it, and the documents to which it refers." This evinced the willingness of those gentlemen to deal fairly, but showed that they were *in bondage.*

Immediately after the first New England Antislavery Convention, which closed on the 29th of May, 1834, I devoted four or five weeks to lecturing on the Abolition of Slavery in most of the principal towns between Boston and Portland. In several places there were strong expressions of hostility to our undertaking. But nothing like personal violence was offered me. I stopped over Sunday, 8th of June, at Portsmouth, to supply brother A. P. Peabody's pulpit, that he might preach in a neighboring town. I consented to do this, on the condition that I might deliver an antislavery lecture from his pulpit on Sunday evening. This he gladly agreed to, and took pains to publish my intention. But, greatly to my surprise, after the forenoon service, the Trustees of the church waited upon me, and informed me that, at the earnest demand of many prominent members, I should not be allowed to speak on slavery from their pulpit;

that the meeting-house would not be opened that evening. My remonstrance with them was of no avail. So at the close of my afternoon services I said to the congregation: "You are all doubtless aware that I had arranged with your excellent pastor to deliver a lecture on American slavery from this desk this evening. But during the intermission your Trustees called and peremptorily forbade my doing so. Has our consenting with the oppressors of the poor indeed brought us to this? That I, who am striving to be a minister of Him "who came to break every yoke" am forbidden to plead with you who are reputed to be an eminently Christian church the cause of millions of our countrymen who are suffering the most abject bondage ever enforced upon human beings? I know not, I do not wish to know, who those prominent members of your church are that have presumed to close this pulpit, and deny to others the right to manifest their sympathy for the down-trodden, and to hear what may and should be done for their relief. The time shall come when those prominent ones will be brought down, and their children and children's children will be ashamed to hear of their act."

With this exception, and an unsuccessful attempt to disturb a meeting that I was addressing in Worcester, I met with no serious molestation in any of the towns of Massachusetts, New Hampshire, or Maine, where I lectured during the summer and autumn of 1834. The faces of many of the rich and fashionable were averted from me; but "the common people" seemed to hear me gladly. Politicians and would-be statesmen often encountered me in the stage-coaches and at the hotels where I stopped. Many of our conflicts were amusing rather than terrible. They always based themselves upon "the provisions of the Constitution," about which it was soon made to appear, that they knew little or nothing. They took it for granted that the fathers of our Republic agreed that slavery should exist in any of the States where the white citizens chose to have it; and that the Constitution of our Union gave certain guarantees for the protection of their "peculiar institution" to the States in which it was maintained. Moreover, these political savans insisted that the Constitution provided that this matter should be left wholly to the slaveholders themselves; and that all condemnation of it as a wicked system, and the exposure of its evils and its horrors, was a violation of State comity, if not of the *rights* of our fellow-citizens of the South.

Perceiving how little most of such friends of the Union knew about the fundamental law of our Republic, and finding, on inquiry, that copies of the Constitution were in that day very scarce, I not unfrequently shut up my opponents almost as soon as they opened their mouths upon the subject. When they ventured to say, "The Constitution, sir, settled this question in the beginning," I would inquire, "My friend, have you ever read the Constitution?" "Everybody knows, sir, that slavery —" "Have you, yourself, read that document to which you appeal?" "Why, sir, do you presume to deny that guarantees —" "My friend, I ask again, have you yourself ever read the Constitution of the United States? I do not care to go into an argument with you until I know whether you are acquainted with our great national charter." In this way, time and again, I drew from my would-be opponents (sometimes justices of the peace), the acknowledgment that they had never themselves seen a copy of the Constitution, but supposed that what everybody, except the Abolitionists, said of its provisions must be true. Occurrences of this sort I reported to the managers of the Antislavery Society so frequently, that they caused a large edition of the

United States Constitution to be printed, so that copies of it might be distributed with our tracts, wherever the agents and lecturers saw fit. This was one of the *naughty* things we did, so inimical to the peace and well-being of our country.

The discussions which I had with sundry individuals who were acquainted with the subject led me to study the Constitution with greater care and deeper interest than ever before. It seemed to me that we owed it to the memory of those venerated men whose names are conspicuous in the early history of our Republic — those men who so solemnly pledged "their lives, their fortunes, and their sacred honor" to the cause of freedom and the inalienable rights of man — to exonerate them, if we fairly could, from the awful responsibility that was laid upon them by those who insisted that they *guaranteed* to the Southern States the unquestioned exercise of their assumed right to enforce the *enslavement* of one sixth part of the population of the land, many of whom had shared with them in all the hardships and perils of their struggles for independence. It seemed to me that every article of the Constitution usually quoted as intended to favor the assumptions of slaveholders admitted of an opposite interpretation, and that we were bound by every honorable and humane consideration to prefer that interpretation. The conclusions to which I was brought on this subject I gave some time afterwards in the *Antislavery Magazine* for 1836. But the publication of the "Madison Papers," in which was given the minutes, debates, etc., of the convention which framed the Constitution, I confess, disconcerted me somewhat. I could not so easily maintain my ground in the discussions which afterwards agitated so seriously the Abolitionists themselves, — some maintaining that the Constitution was, and was intended to be, proslavery; others maintaining that it was antislavery. It seemed to me that it might be whichever the people pleased to make it. I rejoice, therefore, with joy unspeakable that the question is at length practically settled, though by the issue of our late awful war.

THE CLERGY AND THE QUAKERS.

THE coming of George Thompson to our country in the fall of 1834, and his thrilling eloquence respecting our great national iniquity, awakened general attention to the subject, and caused more excitement about it than before. He came, as it were, a missionary from the philanthropists of Great Britain to show our people their transgression. The politicians tried to get up the public indignation against him as "a foreign emissary interfering with our political affairs." The religionists resented his coming as an impertinence, though *they* were much engaged in sending missionaries to the heathen to reclaim them from sins no more heinous than ours. Nevertheless, the people flocked to hear him, and many were converted. The demand for antislavery lectures came from all parts of New England, and from many parts of the Middle and Western States. A great work was to be done. The fields were whitening to the harvest, but the laborers were few. I therefore accepted the renewed invitation of the Massachusetts Antislavery Society to become its General Agent and Corresponding Secretary, and removed to Boston early in the spring of 1835. Many of my nearest relatives and dearest friends received me kindly, but with sadness. They feared I should lose my standing in the ministry and become an outcast from the churches. For a while it seemed as if their apprehensions were not groundless. None of the Boston ministers, excepting Dr. Channing, welcomed me. Dr. Follen, Dr. Ware, Jr., and Dr. Palfrey were then resident in Cambridge; Mr. Pierpont was in Europe. James Freeman Clarke had not left Louisville, and Theodore Parker was a student in the Divinity School. I was indeed soon made to feel that I was not in good repute. Dr. Ware, who had charge of the Hollis Street pulpit in the absence of the pastor, invited me to supply it, if I found I could do so consistently with my new duties. I engaged for two Sundays. But at the close of the first, one of the chief officers of the church waited upon me, by direction of the principal members, and requested me not to enter their pulpit again, assuring me, if I should do so, that a dozen or more of the prominent men with their families would leave the house. Of course I yielded that, and I was not invited into any other pulpit in the city, excepting Dr. Channing's, during the fifteen months that I resided there.

Soon after my removal to Boston I was informed that a young and very popular minister in a neighboring town had preached an antislavery sermon on the Fast Day then just past. I hurried to see him, and requested him to read to me the sermon. He did so. It was an admirable *exposé* of the wickedness of holding men in slavery, and of the duty incumbent upon all Christian and humane persons to do what they could to break such a yoke. It was the outpouring of an ingenuous, benevolent, generous heart, that deeply felt for the wrongs of the outraged millions in our country.

I begged a copy of the discourse for the press, assuring him it would be a most valuable contribution to the cause of the oppressed. He consented to let me have it, promising that, after retouching and fitting it for the press, he would send it to me. I returned to the Antislavery office and made arrangements to publish a large edition of that, which would then have been a remarkable sermon.

After waiting more than a week for the promised manuscript I called upon the author again. In answer to my inquiry why he had not fulfilled his promise he said: "I have concluded not to allow the discourse to be published. Some of the most prominent members of our church have earnestly advised me not to give it to the press." "Why," said I, "have they convinced you that slaveholding is not as sinful as you represented it to be, or that you have been misinformed as to the condition of our enslaved countrymen?" "O no," he replied, "but then this is a very complicated, difficult matter between our Northern and Southern States, and I have been admonished to let it alone." "Do you believe," I inquired, "that those who so admonished you were prompted to give you such advice by their sense of justice to the enslaved, their compassion for those millions to whom all rights are denied, and whose conjugal, parental, filial, and fraternal affections are trampled under foot? Or were they influenced by pecuniary, or by party political considerations?" "It is not for me, sir, to say what their motives were," he replied, in a tone that intimated displeasure. "They are among my best friends, and the most respectable members of my parish. I am bound to give heed to their counsel. I mean so to do. I shall not allow my sermon to be published. I shall not commit myself to the antislavery cause." "Let me only say," I added, "if you do not commit yourself to the cause of the *oppressed*, you will probably, erelong, be found on the side of the *oppressor*." So we parted. And my prediction was fulfilled.

Two or three years afterwards it was reported that the same gentleman, having visited the Southern States and enjoyed the hospitality of the slaveholders, returned and preached a discourse very like "The South Side View of Slavery," by Dr. Adams, of Essex Street.

On Fast Day, 1852, it so happened that I was visiting a parishioner of this brother minister. I accompanied him to church, and heard from that very able and eloquent preacher the most unjust and cruel sermon against the Abolitionists that I had ever listened to or read.

This incident and my reception in Boston prepared me in a measure for the warning given me by the New York merchant, as related on page 127. Still, I could not think so badly of my fellow-citizens, my fellow-Christians of the North, the New England States, as I was afterwards compelled to do.

That the cancer of slavery had eaten still deeper than I was willing to believe was soon after made too apparent to me.

THE QUAKERS.

We had always counted upon the aid and co-operation of the *Quakers*. We considered them "birthright" Abolitionists. And many of Mr. Garrison's earliest supporters, most untiring co-laborers, and generous contributors were members of "the Society of Friends," or had been. Besides John G. Whittier and James and Lucretia Mott, Evan Lewis, Thomas Shipley, and others, of whom I have already spoken, in my account of the Philadelphia Convention, there were the venerable Moses Brown, and the indefatigable Arnold Buffum, and that remarkable man, Isaac T. Hopper, and the large-hearted, open-handed Andrew Robeson and William Rotch, and Isaac and Nathan Winslow, and Nathaniel Barney, and Joseph and Anne Southwick,* and fifty more, whose praises I should delight to celebrate.

But we had received no expression of sympathy from any "Yearly" or "Monthly Meeting," and we felt moved to *seek a sign* from them. Accordingly, at the suggestion

* See Appendix.

of some of the Friends who were actively engaged with us, I went to Newport, R. I., in June, 1835, at the time of the great New England Yearly Meeting, to see if I could obtain from them any intimation of friendliness. My wife accompanied me. When we arrived at the principal hotel in the place, where I was told we should find "the weighty" as well as a large number of the lighter members of the Society, we were at a loss to account for the fluster of the landlord and his helpers, and the tardiness with which we were informed that we could be accommodated. After we had got established, I learned from one who had urged my coming, that there had been quite a commotion in consequence of the report that the General Agent of the Massachusetts Antislavery Society was about to visit the "Yearly Meeting." William ——, and William ——, and Oliver ——, and Isaac ——, and Thomas ——, wealthy cotton manufacturers and merchants, had bestirred themselves to prevent such "an intrusion," as they were pleased to term it. They had secured the public halls of Newport against me during the continuance of the "Yearly Meeting," and had been trying, on the morning of the day that I arrived, to induce the landlord to refuse me any accommodation in his house. And they would have succeeded, had not forty of his boarders informed him that if he did not receive me they would quit his premises. These forty, though of less account in the meeting, which, I learned, was governed by the aristocracy that occupied the high seats, were more weighty in the receipts of the hotel-keeper. He therefore compromised with the dignitaries by agreeing to serve their meals in a private parlor, so that their eyes might not be offended at the sight of the antislavery agent in the common dining-hall.

I sought, through several of their very respectable

members, permission to attend their "Meeting on Sufferings" and present to their consideration the principles and plans of the American Antislavery Society and its auxiliaries. This request was peremptorily denied. I then besought them to give their "testimony on slavery," as they had sometimes done in times past. This they also refused.

An arrangement was then made by the members who were Abolitionists, many of whom boarded with me at "Whitfield's," that I should address as many as saw fit to meet me in the large reception-room of the hotel, in the evening of the second day of my visit. So soon as this was known, it was asked of me if I would consent to let the meeting be conducted somewhat in the manner of "the Society of Friends" so that any who should be moved to speak might have the liberty. I acquiesced most cheerfully, not doubting that I should be moved, and should be expected to address the meeting first and give the direction to it.

Fifty or sixty persons assembled at the hour appointed. Deeming it respectful to my Quaker brethren to sit in silence a few minutes after the meeting came to order, I did so, and in so doing lost my chance to be heard. A wily brother took advantage of my sense of propriety, rose before me and delivered a long discourse upon slavery, made up of the commonplaces and platitudes of the subject, about which all were agreed. He was followed instantly by another in the same vein, and when the evening was far spent and the auditors were beginning to withdraw, I was permitted to speak a few minutes upon the vital points in the questions between the immediate Abolitionists and the slaveholders on the one hand, and the Colonizationists on the other hand.

However, the next morning, in the presence of twenty or more, I had unexpectedly a long and pretty thorough discussion with the distinguished John Griscom, so that my visit to Newport was not wholly lost.

I am sorry that truth compels me to add, that afterwards we had too many proofs that "the Society of Friends," with all their antislavery professions, were not, as a religious sect, much more friendly than others to the immediate emancipation of the enslaved without expatriation. They were disposed to be Colonizationists rather than Abolitionists.

THE REIGN OF TERROR.

Rejected as we Abolitionists were generally by the religionists of every denomination, denounced by many of the clergy as dangerous, yes, impious persons, refused a hearing in almost all the churches, it was not strange that the statesmen and politicians had no mercy upon us.

The first most serious opposition from any minister I myself directly encountered was in the pleasant town of Taunton. I went thither on the 15th of April, 1835, and had a very successful meeting in the Town Hall, which was filled full with respectable persons of both sexes. So much interest in the subject was awakened that a large number on the spot signified their readiness to co-operate with those who were laboring to procure the abolition of American slavery. To my surprise, the most prominent minister in the town, a learned and liberal theologian, and a gentleman of unexceptionable private character, took the utmost pains to prevent the formation of an auxiliary antislavery society there. He declared that "the slaves were the property of their masters," that "we of the North had no more right to disturb this *domestic arrangement* of our Southern brethren, and prevent the prosecution of their industrial operations, than the planters had to interfere with our manufactures and commerce." He dealt out to the Abolitionists no small number of opprobrious epithets; charged us with being the cause of the New York mobs of October, 1834, and insisted that, if we "were permitted to prosecute our measures, it would inevitably dissolve the Union and cause a civil war."

This was the substance of the *verbal* opposition that we met with everywhere throughout the Northern, Middle, and Western States; strengthened by the arguments of the civilians and statesmen, intended to show that the enslavement of the colored population of certain States was settled by the *founders* of our Republic, who made several compromises in relation to it, and gave sundry guarantees to the slaveholders which must be held sacred.

Many timid persons everywhere, by such assertions and appeals, were deterred from yielding to the convictions which the self-evident truths, urged by the Abolitionists, awakened. Still the cause of the oppressed made visible progress in all parts of the non-slaveholding States. Alarmed by this, the barons of the South, as Mr. Adams significantly styled them, stirred up their dependants and partisans to demand something more of their Northern brethren than denunciation and opprobrium against the Abolitionists. "They must be put down by law or *without law*, as the necessity of the case might require." And the determination to do *just this* was at length come to by "the gentlemen of property and standing" throughout the North, as the New York merchant, mentioned on the foregoing 127th page informed me.

In pursuance of this determination, the great meeting in Faneuil Hall, called, as I have said already, by fifteen hundred of the respectable gentlemen of Boston, was held on the 21st of August, 1835. The grave misrepresentations, the plausible arguments, the inflammatory appeals made by the very distinguished civilians who addressed that meeting, invoked those demon spirits throughout New England that did deeds, of which I hope the instigators themselves became heartily ashamed.

How devilish those spirits were I was made to know a few evenings after that never-to-be-forgotten meeting. I went to the quiet town of Haverhill, by special invitation from John G. Whittier and a number more of the genuine friends of humanity. I had lectured there twice before without opposition, and went again not apprehending any disturbance. The meeting was held in the Freewill Baptist Church, — a large hall over a row of stores. The audience was numerous, occupying all the seats and evidently eager to hear. I had spoke about fifteen minutes, when the most hideous outcries, yells, from a crowd of men who had surrounded the house startled us, and then came heavy missiles against the doors and blinds of the windows. I persisted in speaking for a few minutes, hoping the blinds and doors were strong enough to stand the siege. But presently a heavy stone broke through one of the blinds, shattered a pane of glass and fell upon the head of a lady sitting near the centre of the hall. She uttered a shriek and fell bleeding into the arms of her sister. The panic-stricken audience rose *en masse*, and began a rush for the doors. Seeing the danger, I shouted in a voice louder than I ever uttered before or since, "*Sit down, every one of you, sit down!* The doors are not wide; the platform outside is narrow; the stairs down to the street are steep. If you go in a rush, you will jam one another, or be thrown down and break your limbs, if not your necks. If there is any one here whom the mob wish to injure, it is myself. I will stand here and wait until you are safely out of the house. But you must go in some order as I bid you." To my great joy they obeyed. All sat down, and then rose, as I told them to, from the successive rows of pews, and went out without any accident.

When the house was nearly empty I took on my arm a brave young lady, who would not leave me to go through the mob alone, and went out. Fortunately none of the ill-disposed knew me. So we passed through the lane of madmen unharmed, hearing their imprecations and threats of violence to the —— Abolitionist when he should come out.

It was well we had delayed no longer to empty the hall, for at the corner of the street above we met a posse of men more savage than the rest, dragging a cannon, which they intended to explode against the building and at the same time tear away the stairs; so furious and bloodthirsty had "the baser sort" been made by the instigations of "the gentlemen of property and standing."

In October it was thought advisable for me to go and lecture in several of the principal towns of Vermont. I did so, and everywhere I met with contumely and insult. I was mobbed five times. In Rutland and Montpelier my meetings were dispersed with violence. Of the last only shall I give any account, because I had been specially invited to Montpelier to address the Vermont State Antislavery Society. The Legislature was in session there at that time, and many of the members of that body were Abolitionists. We were, therefore, without much opposition, granted the use of the Representatives' Hall for our first meeting, on the evening of October 20. A large number of persons — as many as the hall could conveniently hold — were present, including many members of the Legislature, and ladies not a few. There were some demonstrations of displeasure in the yard of the Capitol and a couple of eggs and a stone or two were thrown through the window before which I was standing. But their force was spent before they reached me, and therefore they were not suffered to interrupt my discourse. At the close, I was requested to tarry in Montpelier and address the public again the next evening from the pulpit of the First Presbyterian Church, the largest audience-room in the village. This I gladly consented to do. But the next morning placards were seen all about the village, admonishing "the people generally, and ladies in particular, not to attend the antislavery meeting proposed to be held that evening in the Presbyterian church, as the person who is advertised to speak will certainly be prevented, *by violence if necessary*." In the afternoon I received a letter signed by the President of the bank, the Postmaster, and five other "gentlemen of property and standing" in Montpelier, requesting me to leave town "without any further attempt to hold forth the absurd doctrine of antislavery, and save them the trouble of using any other measures to that effect." But as I had accepted the invitation to deliver a second lecture, I determined to make the attempt so to do, these threats notwithstanding. Accordingly, just before the hour appointed, with a venerable Quaker lady on my arm, I proceeded to the meeting-house and took a seat in the pulpit. After a prayer had been offered by Rev. Mr. Hurlbut, I rose to speak. But I had hardly uttered a sentence when the ringleader of the riot, Timothy Hubbard, Esq., rose with a gang about him and commanded me to desist. I replied, "Is this the respect paid to the *liberty of speech* by the free people of Vermont? Let any one of your number step forward and give reasons, if he can, why his fellow-citizens, who wish, should not be permitted to hear the lecture I have been invited here to deliver. If I cannot show those reasons to be fallacious, false, I will yield to your demand. But for the sake of one of our essential rights, the liberty of speech, I shall proceed if I can." While I was saying these words the rioters were still. But so soon as I commenced my lecture again, Mr. Hubbard and his fellows cried out, "Down with him!" "Throw him over!" "Choke him!" Hon. Chauncy L. Knapp, then, or afterwards, I believe, Secretary of State, remonstrated earnestly, implored his fellow-citizens not to continue disgracing themselves, the town, and the State. But his words were of no avail. The moment I attempted a third time to speak the rioters commenced a rush for the pulpit, loudly shouting their violent intentions. At this crisis Colonel Miller, well known as the companion of Dr. Howe in a generous endeavor to aid Greece in her struggle for independence in 1824, — Colonel Miller, renowned for his courage and prowess, sprang forward and planted himself in front of the leader, crying in a voice of thunder, "Mr. Hubbard, if you do not stop this outrage now, I will knock you down!" The rush for the pulpit was stayed; but such an alarm had spread through the house, that there was a hasty movement from all parts towards the doors, and my audience dispersed. Colonel Miller, Mr. Knapp, and several other gentlemen urged me to remain in town another day and attempt a meeting the next evening, assuring me that it should be protected against the ruffians. But it was Friday, and I had engaged to be in Burlington the next day, to preach for Brother Ingersoll the following Sunday, and deliver an antislavery lecture from his pulpit in the evening. So I was obliged to leave our good friends in the capital of Vermont mortified and vexed at what had occurred there.

But on my arrival at Burlington I received tidings from Boston of a far greater outrage that had been perpetrated at the same time, in the metropolis of New

England. On page 127 I made mention of the "well-dressed, gentlemanly" mob of October 21st, which broke up a regular meeting of the Female Antislavery Society. The fury of the populace had been incited to the utmost by articles in the *Commercial Gazette*, the *Courier*, the *Sentinel*, and other newspapers, of which the following is a specimen: "It is in vain that we hold meetings in Faneuil Hall, and call into action the eloquence and patriotism of our most talented citizens; it is in vain that speeches are made and resolutions adopted, assuring our brethren of the South that we cherish rational and correct notions on the subject of slavery, if Thompson and Garrison, and their vile associates in this city, are to be permitted to hold their meetings in the broad face of day, and to continue their denunciations against the planters of the South. They *must be put down* if we would preserve our consistency. The evil is one of the greatest magnitude; and *the opinion prevails very generally* that if there is no law that will reach it, it must be reached in some other way."

Though "the patriots" had been especially maddened by the report that "the infamous foreign scoundrel, Thompson," "the British emissary, the paid incendiary, Thompson," was to address the meeting, yet, when assured he was not and would not be there, they did not desist. "But Garrison is!" was the cry; "snake him out and finish him!" They tore down the sign of the Antislavery office and dashed it to pieces; compelled the excellent women to leave their hall, seized upon Mr. Garrison, tore off his clothes, dragged him through the streets, and would have hanged him, had it not been for the almost superhuman efforts of several gentlemen, assisted by some of the police and a vigorous hack-driver, who together succeeded in getting him to Leverett Street Jail, where he was committed for safe-keeping.

The disgraceful story was too well told at the time ever to be forgotten, especially by Mr. Garrison himself, and more especially by Mrs. Maria Weston Chapman, in a little volume entitled " Right and Wrong in Boston."

To show my readers still further how general the determination had become throughout the Northern States to put down the antislavery agitation by foul means, I will here only allude to the significant fact that on the same day, October 21, 1835, a mob, led on or countenanced by gentlemen of respectability, broke up an antislavery meeting in Utica, N. Y., and drove out of the city such men as Gerrit Smith, Alvan Stuart, and Beriah Green. Hereafter I will give a full account of the infamous proceeding, and of some of its consequences.

FRANCIS JACKSON.

There is a most interesting sequel to my brief narrative of the great outrage upon liberty in the metropolis of New England, which cannot be so pertinently told in any other connection.

After the first attempt of the Female Antislavery Society to hold their annual meeting on the 14th of October, in Congress Hall, was thwarted by the fears of the owner and lessee, Mr. Francis Jackson offered the use of his dwelling-house in Hollis Street for that purpose. But the ladies were unwilling to believe that they should be molested in their own small hall, No. 46 Washington Street, and thought it more becoming to meet there than to retreat to the protection of a private house. So the meeting was appointed to be held there on the 21st. The result, so disgraceful to the reputation of Boston, has just been given.

On the evening of that sad day, while the rioters were yet patrolling the city, exulting over their shameful deeds, and threatening the persons and property of the Abolitionists, Francis Jackson, called upon Miss Mary Parker, the truly devout and brave President of the Boston Female Antislavery Society, and renewed the offer of his dwelling in the following letter of invitation: —

"To the Ladies of the Boston Female Antislavery Society.

"Having with deep regret and mortification observed the manner in which your Society has been treated by a portion of the community, especially by some of our public journals, and approving as I do most cordially the objects of your association, I offer you the use of my dwelling-house in Hollis Street for the purpose of holding your annual meeting, or for any other meeting.

"Such accommodations as I have are at your service, and I assure you it would afford me great pleasure to extend this slight testimony of my regard for a Society whose objects are second to none other in the city.

"With great respect,

"Francis Jackson."

This heroic act thrilled with joy the hearts of the "faithful," and inspired them with new courage. For two or three years Mr. Jackson had evinced a deep interest in the antislavery cause, but we did not suspect that he had so much Roman virtue.

His invitation was gratefully accepted, and due notices were published in the usual form that the meeting would be held at his house on the 19th of November. Renewed efforts were made by our opposers to create another excitement. The air was filled with threats. But the editors of the newspapers did not come up to the work as before. Fewer prominent gentlemen encouraged "the baser sort," and therefore the mob did not come out in its strength. About a hundred and thirty ladies and four gentlemen gathered at the time appointed in Mr. Jackson's house, and were not molested on the way thither or while there, excepting by a few insulting epithets and an occasional ribald shout.

It was an intensely interesting meeting, conducted in the usual manner with the utmost propriety;* and an air of unfeigned solemnity was thrown over it by the consciousness of the dense cloud of malignant hatred that was hanging over us, and which might again burst upon us in some cruel outrage.

Among the ladies present were the celebrated Miss Harriet Martineau, of England, and her very intelligent travelling companion, Miss Jeffrey. At the right moment, when the regular business of the meeting had been transacted, Ellis Gray Loring, from the beginning a leading Abolitionist, — and one whose lead it was always well to follow, for he was a very wise, a single-hearted, and most conscientious man, — Mr. Loring handed me a slip of paper for Miss Martineau, on which was written an earnest request that she would then favor the meeting with some expression of her sympathy in the objects of the association. She immediately rose and said, with cordial earnestness: "I had supposed that my presence here would be understood as showing my sympathy with you. But as I am requested to speak, I will say what I have said through the whole South, in every family where I have been, that I consider slavery inconsistent with the law of God, and incompatible with the course of his providence. I should certainly say no less at the North than at the South concerning this utter abomination, and now I declare that in your principles I fully agree."

Hitherto Miss Martineau had received from the *élite* of Boston very marked attentions. She had been treated with great respect, as one so distinguished for her

* See "Right and Wrong in Boston," by Mrs. M. W. Chapman.

literary works and philanthropic labors deserved to be. But from the day of that meeting, and because of the words she uttered there, she was slighted, rejected, and in various ways made to understand that she had given great offence to "the best society in that metropolis."

Two days afterwards the Board of Managers of the Massachusetts Antislavery Society directed me, their Corresponding Secretary, by a unanimous vote, to express to Mr. Jackson the very high sense which they entertained of his generosity and noble independence in proffering, as he had done unsolicited, the use and protection of his dwelling-house to the Boston Female Antislavery Society, when they had just been expelled by lawless violence from a public hall.

My letter, written immediately in pursuance of this vote, drew from Mr. Jackson the following reply, which, considering the place where and the time when it was written, as well as its intrinsic excellence, deserves to be preserved among the most precious deposits in the Temple of Impartial Liberty, whenever such a structure shall be reared upon earth.

"BOSTON, November 25, 1835.

"DEAR SIR, — I have the honor to acknowledge the receipt of your highly esteemed letter of the 21st inst., written in behalf of the Managers of the Massachusetts Antislavery Society, and expressing in very flattering terms their approbation of my conduct in granting to the ladies of the Antislavery Society the use of my dwelling-house for their Annual Meeting.

"That meeting was a most interesting and impressive one. It will ever be treasured by me, among the most pleasing recollections of my life, that it was my good fortune to extend to those respectable ladies the protection of my roof after they had been reviled, insulted, and driven from their own hall by a mob.

"But in tendering them the use of my house, sir, I not only

had in view their accommodation, but also, according to my humble measure, to recover and perpetuate the right of free discussion, which has been shamefully trampled on. A great principle has been assailed, — one which lies at the very foundation of our republican institutions.

"If a large majority of this community choose to turn a deaf ear to the wrongs which are inflicted upon millions of their countrymen in other portions of the land, — if they are content to turn away from the sight of oppression, and 'to pass by on the other side,' so it must be.

"But when they undertake in any way to annul or impair my right to speak, write, and publish my thoughts upon any subject, more especially upon enormities which are the common concern of every lover of his country and his kind, so it must not be, — so it shall not be, if I can prevent it. Upon this great right let us hold on at all hazards. And should we, in its exercise, be driven from public halls to private dwellings, one house at least shall be consecrated to its preservation. And if in defence of this sacred privilege, which man did not give me, and shall not (if I can help it) take from me, this roof and these walls shall be levelled to the earth, let them fall! If it must be so, let them fall! They cannot crumble in a better cause. They will appear of very little value to me after their owner shall have been whipped into silence.

"Mobs and gag-laws, and the other contrivances by which fraud or force would stifle inquiry, will not long work well in this community. They betray the essential rottenness of the cause they are meant to strengthen. These outrages are doing their work with the reflecting.

"Happily, one point seems to be gaining universal assent, that slavery cannot long survive free discussion. Hence the efforts of the friends and apologists of slavery to break down this right. And hence the immense stake which the enemies of slavery hold, in behalf of freedom and mankind, in the preservation of this right. The contest is therefore substantially between liberty and slavery.

"As slavery cannot exist with free discussion, so neither can liberty breathe without it. Losing this, we shall not be freemen indeed, but little, if at all, superior to the millions we are now seeking to emancipate.

"With the highest respect,
"Your friend,
"FRANCIS JACKSON.

"REV. S. J. MAY, Cor. Sec. Mass. A. S. S."

Well said Mrs. Maria W. Chapman, who was usually the first to give the most pertinent expression to the best thought of every occasion, — well said Mrs. Chapman, "Ten such men would have saved our city and country from the indelible disgrace which has been inflicted upon them by the outrageous proceedings of the 21st and 24th of October. Mr. Jackson has by this act done all that *one* man can do to redeem the character of Boston." And were there not nine other men in the metropolis of New England, where dwelt descendants of Samuel Adams and Josiah Quincy, and relatives of Joseph Warren and James Otis and John Hancock, and other men of Revolutionary fame; were there not nine other men there to spring to the rescue of the ark of civil liberty? Alas! they did not appear. The abettors of slavery were in the ascendant. "The gentlemen of property and standing" thought it good policy, both politically and pecuniarily considered, to trample the Declaration of Independence under foot. And the people generally seemed willing to perpetrate wrongs far greater than Great Britain ever inflicted on their fathers.

RIOT AT UTICA, N. Y. — GERRIT SMITH.

The resort to mobocratic violence in so many parts of the Middle, Northern, and Eastern States showed how general had become the determination of the "gentlemen of property and standing" (as the leaders everywhere claimed or were reported to be) to put down the

Abolitionists by *foul means,* having found it impossible to do so by *fair* discussion. This had been peremptorily demanded of them by their Southern masters; and they had evidently come to the conclusion that no other means would be effectual to stay the progress of universal, impartial liberty. No one fact showed us how almost universally this plan of operations was adopted, so plainly as the fact that, at the very same time, October 21, 1835, antislavery meetings were broken up and violently dispersed in Boston, Mass., Utica, N. Y., and Montpelier, Vt.

Societies for the abolition of slavery had been formed in the city of New York, and in many towns and several counties of the State. And it had come to be obvious that their efficiency would be greatly increased if they should be united in a State organization. Accordingly, invitations were sent everywhere to all known associations, and to individuals where there were no associations, calling them to meet on the 21st of October in Utica, then the most central and convenient place, for the purpose of forming a New York State Antislavery Society.

So soon as it became public that such a Convention was to be held in their city, certain very "prominent and respectable gentlemen" set about to avert "the calamity and disgrace." It was denounced in the newspapers, and deprecated by loud talkers in the streets. Soon the excitement became general. When it was known that permission had been given for the Convention to occupy the Court-room, "the whole population was thrown into an uproar." A large meeting of the people was held on Saturday evening, October 17th, and adopted measures to preoccupy the room where the Convention were called to assemble; and in every way, by any means, prevent the proceedings of such a body of "fanatics," "incendiaries," "madmen." Hon. Samuel Beardsley, member of Congress from Oneida County, declared that "the disgrace of having an Abolition Convention held in the city is a deeper one than that of twenty mobs; and that it would be better to have Utica razed to its foundations, or to have it destroyed like Sodom and Gomorrah, than to have the Convention meet here." *

Nevertheless, delegates from all parts of the State and individuals interested in the great cause, at the appointed time, came into Utica in great numbers, — six or eight hundred strong. On arriving at the Court-house, they found the room pre-occupied by a crowd of their vociferous opponents, and therefore quietly repaired to the Second Presbyterian meeting-house.

As soon as practicable the Convention was organized by the choice of Hon. Judge Brewster, of Genesee County, Chairman, and Rev. Oliver Wetmore, of Utica, Secretary. The Hon. Alvan Stewart, a most excellent man and distinguished lawyer, as Chairman of the Committee of the Utica Antislavery Society, which had first proposed the calling of the Convention, rose, and after a few pertinent and impressive remarks, moved the formation of a New York State Antislavery Society, and read a draft of a Constitution. While he was reading a noisy crowd thundered at the doors for admission. One of the Aldermen of the city, in attempting to keep them back, had his coat torn to pieces. As soon as the reading of the draft was finished, it was unanimously adopted as the Constitution, and the *State Antislavery Society was formed.*

Mr. Lewis Tappan then proceeded to read a declaration of sentiments and purposes, that had been carefully prepared. But he had not half finished the document, when a large concourse of persons rushed into the house

* I have been told, and I record it here to his honor, that Hon. Joshua A. Spencer made an earnest, excellent speech, in behalf of free discussion.

and commanded him to stop. He, however, persisted in the discharge of his duty with increased earnestness to the end, when the declaration was adopted unanimously by a rising vote.

The Convention then gave audience to the leaders of the mob, who declared themselves to be a Committee of twenty-five, sent thither by a meeting of the citizens of Utica, held that morning in the Court-house. Hon. Chester Hayden, first Judge of the County, was Chairman of this Committee. He presented a series of condemnatory resolutions, which had just been adopted at the Court-house. They were respectfully listened to by the Convention, and then the mob gave loud utterance to their denunciations and threats. The Judge remonstrated with the rioters, saying: "We have been respectfully listened to by the Convention, I hope *my friends* will permit the answer of the Convention to be heard in peace." Mr. Tappan then moved that a committee of ten be appointed to report what answer should be made to the citizens.

Hon. Mr. Beardsley, mentioned above, one of the Committee of twenty-five, also said, "It is proper we should hear what the Convention have to say, either now or by their Committee. We are bound to hear them; we are bound to exercise all patience and long-suffering, *even towards such an assembly as this*. . . . For my part, I should like to hear what apology can be made for proceedings which we know, and they know, are intended to exasperate the members of our National Union against each other. They profess to come here on an errand of religion, while, under its guise, they are hypocritically plotting the dissolution of the American Union. They have been warned beforehand, have been treated with unexampled patience, and if they now refuse to yield to our demand, and any unpleasant circumstances should follow, we shall not be responsible." Such talk, and more of the same sort that he uttered, was adapted, if it was not intended, to inflame the mobocrats yet more. So when, in conclusion, he said, "But let us hear their justification for this outrage on our feelings, if they have any to offer," the cry rose, "No! we won't hear them; they sha'n't be heard. Let them go home. Let them ask our forgiveness, and we will let them go." Many of the rioters were too evidently inflamed with strong drink as well as passion; and this was easily accounted for, though it was in the forenoon of the day, by the fact afterwards stated in the New York *Commercial Advertiser*, that the grog-shops in the neighborhood were thrown open and liquor furnished *gratuitously* to the tools and minions of "the very respectable citizens, the best people of Utica," who were determined their city should not tolerate a Convention of Abolitionists. It was evident that these leaders held "the baser sort" under some restraint, for one of them cried out, "Let *them* say the word, and I am ready to tear the rascals in pieces." Loud threats of violence were reiterated, with imprecations and blasphemies. The leading members of the Committee of twenty-five besought the Convention to adjourn, and seeing that it was impossible to transact any more business, they did adjourn *sine die*.

Most of the members retired unmolested excepting by abusive, profane, and obscene epithets. A cry was raised by some of the Committee for "the minutes" of the Convention, and members pressed upon the venerable Secretary, demanding that he should give them up. But he resolutely refused, though they crowded him against the wall, seized him by the collar, and threatened to beat him. A member of the Committee of twenty-five, a man holding an important public office, raised his cane over that aged and faithful minister of the Gospel and cried out, "God damn you! give the papers up, or I will knock you on the head." At this, another of the Committee, a young man — his son — sprang forward and begged him, "Do, father, give them up and save your life. Give them to me, and I will pledge myself they shall be returned to you again." With this Rev. Mr. Wetmore complied, and was let off without any further harm.

Many of the newspapers, especially those of New York City, exulted over the results of the riots of the 21st of October in Boston and Utica. They boasted that, by thus dealing with the Abolitionists, the people of the Northern States proved themselves to be sound to the core on the subject of slavery. "Hereafter," said the New York *Sunday Morning News*, "hereafter the leaders of the Abolitionists will be treated with less forbearance than they have been heretofore. The people will consider them as out of the pale of the legal and conventional protection which society affords to its honest and well-meaning members. They will be treated as robbers and pirates, as the enemies of the human kind."

The most important incident of the Utica riot was the accession which it caused of *Gerrit Smith* to our ranks. The great and good man had, for many years, been an active opponent of slavery. He had always been in favor of immediate emancipation, and was unusually free from prejudice against colored people. But from almost the beginning of the Colonization Society he had been a member of it, deceived as we all were by the representations which its agents at the North made of its intentions and the tendency of its operations. He believed its scheme was intended to effect and would effect the abolition of slavery. He therefore joined it, and labored heartily in its behalf, and contributed most generously to its funds, — *ten thousand dollars*, if not more. Mr. Smith was repulsed from the American Antislavery Society, and kept away for nearly two years, because he thought Mr. Garrison and his associates were unjust in their denunciations of the Colonization Society, and too severe in their censures of the American churches and ministers, as virtually the accomplices of slaveholders.

But the outrages committed upon the Abolitionists in the fall of 1834, and throughout the year 1835, fixed his attention more fully upon them. He determined to know, to search, and prove those who had become the subjects of such general and unsparing persecution. When, therefore, the Convention for the formation of a State Antislavery Society was to be held in Utica (only twenty-five or thirty miles from his residence), he could not withhold himself from it. He went thither, not as a member of any Antislavery Society, not intending to become a member, but determined to hear for himself what should be said, see what should be done, learn what might be proposed, and decide as he should find reason to, between the Abolitionists and their adversaries. Alas, that the prominent, influential, professedly religious men in every part of our country did not do likewise! Then would the names of comparatively few of them have gone down, in the history of this generation, as the leaders and instigators of a most shameful persecution of the friends of freedom and humanity.

Mr. Smith was so disgusted, shocked, alarmed, at the proceedings of "the gentlemen of property and standing" in Utica, that he invited all the members of the antislavery convention to repair to Peterboro'. And a large proportion of the members accepted his invitation. Insults and threats of violence were showered upon them wherever they were met in the streets of Utica and at the hotels where they had quartered themselves. The same evil spirit of hatred pursued them on their way. Especially at Vernon, the hotel at which they had stopped for refreshment was beset by a mob, with an evident determination to rout them and drive them from the village. But the resolute action of Captain Hand, the landlord, dispersed the rioters.

Arrived at Peterboro', the Abolitionists were most cordially received, not only at the hospitable and spacious mansion of Gerrit Smith, but into the houses of most of his neighbors. And the next day was held in the Presbyterian Church the first meeting of the New York State Antislavery Society. At that meeting Mr. Smith brought forward the following resolution: —

"*Resolved*, That the right of FREE DISCUSSION given us by our God, and asserted and guarded by the laws of our country, is a right so vital to man's freedom and dignity and usefulness that we can never be guilty of its surrender, without consenting to exchange that liberty for slavery and that dignity and usefulness for debasement and worthlessness."

This resolution he supported and enforced by a speech of surpassing power, — a speech which deserves to be printed in letters of light large enough to be seen throughout our country.*

Ever since that eventful period of our history Gerrit Smith has been a most zealous fellow-laborer in the antislavery cause, and bountiful contributor of money in its behalf. He has made as many speeches in large meetings and small as any man who has not been a hired agent. He announced the doctrines of the immediate Abolitionists in the Congress of the United States and maintained them in several speeches of great ability. He has made frequent donations to some special, or to the general purposes of our Society of one, two, five, ten thousand

* See Appendix.

dollars at a time. He has in every way befriended the colored people of our country, and at one time gave forty acres of land, in the State of New York, to each one of three thousand poor, temperate men of that class. I shall have an occasion in another place to speak more particularly of the acts of this almost unequalled giver.

DR. CHANNING.

Another and a most auspicious event signalizes in my memory the year 1835. It was the publication of Dr. Channing's book on Slavery. He had for many years been the most distinguished minister of religion in New England, certainly in the estimation of the Unitarian denomination; and his fame as a Christian moralist, a philosopher, and finished writer had been spread far and wide throughout England, France, and Germany by a large volume of his Discourses, Essays, and Reviews published in 1830.

A few weeks after his graduation from Harvard College in 1798, when about nineteen years of age, determined to be no longer dependent upon his mother and friends for a living, he gladly accepted the situation of a tutor in the family of Mr. Randolph, of Richmond, Virginia. Here he often met many of the most distinguished gentlemen and ladies of the city and the State, and visited them freely at their city homes and on their plantations. He was delighted with their cordial and elegant courtesy. But he saw also their *slaves* and the sensuality which abounded amongst them. These made an impression upon his heart which was never effaced.

In the fall of 1830 he went to the West Indies for his health, and passed the winter in St. Croix. There he witnessed again the inherent wrongs of slavery and the vices which it engenders. On his return in May, 1831, he spoke freely and with the deepest feeling from his pulpit of the inhuman system, and its debasing effects upon the oppressors as well as the oppressed. At that time the public mind in New England had begun to be agitated upon the subject of slavery, as it never had been before by the scathing denunciations that were every week poured from *The Liberator* upon slaveholders and their abettors and apologists. Dr. Channing's sensitive nature shrank from the severity of Mr. Garrison's blows, and yet he acknowledged that the gigantic system of domestic servitude in our country ought to be exposed, condemned, and subverted. He found his highly esteemed friend, Dr. Follen, with his excellent wife and several others of the best women in Boston, and Ellis Gray Loring and Samuel E. Sewall and others, whom he highly esteemed, giving countenance and aid to the "young fanatic." This drew his attention still more to the subject of slavery. Soon after his return from the West Indies I visited Dr. Channing, and found his mind very much exercised. He sympathized with the Abolitionists in their abhorrence of the domestic servitude in our Southern States, and their apprehension of its corrupting influence upon the government of our Republic, and the political as well as moral ruin to which it tended. But he distrusted our measures, and was particularly annoyed, as I have already stated, by Mr. Garrison's "scorching and stinging invectives." Whenever I was in the city and called upon the Doctor, he would make particular inquiries respecting our doctrines, purposes, measures, and progress. Repeatedly he invited me to his house for the express purpose, as he said, of learning more about our antislavery enterprise. He always spoke as if he were deeply interested in it, but he was afraid of what he supposed to be some of our opinions and measures. I was surprised that he was so slow to accept our vital doctrine, "immediate emancipation." But owing, I suppose, to his great aversion to excited speeches and exaggerated statements, and his peculiar distrust of associations, he had never attended any of our antislavery meetings, where the doctrine of immediate emancipation was always explained. The Doctor, therefore, as well as the people generally, misunderstood it, and had been misinformed in several other respects as to the purposes, measures, and spirit of the Abolitionists. Still he persisted in abstaining from our meetings until after the alarming course taken by the Governor and Legislature of Massachusetts, in the spring of 1836, of which I shall give an account in the proper place.

Late in the year 1834, being on a visit in Boston, I spent several hours with Dr. Channing in earnest conversation upon Abolitionism and the Abolitionists. My habitual reverence for him was such that I had always been apt to defer perhaps too readily to his opinions, or not to make a very stout defence of my own when they differed from his. But at the time to which I refer I had become so thoroughly convinced of the truth of the essential doctrines of the American Antislavery Society, and so earnestly engaged in the dissemination of them, that our conversation assumed, more than it had ever done, the character of a debate. He acknowledged the inestimable importance of the object we had in view. The evils of Slavery he assented could not be overstated. He allowed that removal to Africa ought not to be made a condition of the liberation of the enslaved. But he hesitated still to accept the doctrine of immediate emancipation. His principal objections, however, were alleged against the severity of our denunciations, the harshness of our epithets, the vehemence, heat, and excitement caused by the harangues at our meetings, and still more by Mr. Garrison's *Liberator*. The Doctor dwelt upon these objections, which, if they were as well founded as he assumed them to be, lay against what was only incidental, not an essential part of our movement. He dwelt upon them until I became impatient, and, forgetting for the moment my wonted deference, I broke out with not a little warmth of expression and manner: —

"Dr. Channing," I said, "I am tired of these complaints. The cause of suffering humanity, the cause of our oppressed, crushed colored countrymen, has called as loudly upon others as upon us Abolitionists. It was just as incumbent upon others as upon us to espouse it. *We* are not to blame that wiser and better men did not espouse it long ago. The cry of millions, suffering the most cruel bondage in our land, had been heard for half a century and disregarded. 'The wise and prudent' saw the terrible wrong, but thought it not wise and prudent to lift a finger for its correction. The priests and Levites beheld their robbed and wounded countrymen, but passed by on the other side. The children of Abraham held their peace, and at last 'the very stones have cried out' in abhorrence of this tremendous iniquity; and you must expect them to cry out like 'the stones.' You must not wonder if many of those who have been left to take up this great cause, do not plead it in all that seemliness of phrase which the scholars and practised rhetoricians of our country might use. You must not expect them to manage with all the calmness and discretion that clergymen and statesmen might exhibit. But the scholars, the statesmen, the clergy had done nothing, — did not seem about to do anything, and for my part I thank God that at last any persons, be they who they may, have earnestly engaged in this cause; for no *movement* can be in vain. We Abolitionists are what we are, — babes, sucklings, obscure men, silly women, publicans, sinners, and we shall manage this matter just as might be expected of such persons as we are. It is unbecoming in abler men who stood by and would do nothing to complain of us because we do no better.

"Dr. Channing," I continued with increased earnestness, "it is not *our fault* that those who might have conducted this great reform more prudently have left it to us to manage as we may. It is not *our fault* that those who might have pleaded for the enslaved so much more wisely and eloquently, both with the pen and the living voice than we can, have been silent. We are not to blame, sir, that you, who, more perhaps than any other man, might have so raised the voice of remonstrance that it should have been heard throughout the length and breadth of the land, — we are not to blame, sir, that you have not so spoken. And now that inferior men have been impelled to speak and act against what you acknowledge to be an awful system of iniquity, it is not becoming in you to complain of us because we do it in an inferior style. Why, sir, have you not taken this matter in hand yourself? Why have you not spoken to the nation long ago, as you, better than any other one, could have spoken?"

At this point I bethought me to whom I was administering this rebuke, — the man who stood among the highest of the great and good in our land, — the man whose reputation for wisdom and sanctity had become world-wide, — the man, too, who had ever treated me with the kindness of a father, and whom, from my childhood, I had been accustomed to revere more than any one living. I was almost overwhelmed with a sense of my temerity. His countenance showed that he was much moved. I could not suppose he would receive all I had said very graciously. I awaited his reply in painful expectation. The minutes seemed very long that elapsed before the silence was broken. Then in a very subdued manner and in the kindliest tones of his voice he said, "Brother May, I acknowledge the justice of your reproof. I have been silent too long." Never shall I forget his words, look, whole appearance. I then and there saw the beauty, the magnanimity, the humility of a truly great Christian soul. He was exalted in my esteem more even than before.

The next spring, when I removed to Boston and became the General Agent of the Antislavery Society, Dr. Channing was the first of the ministers there to call upon me, and express any sympathy with me in the great work to which I had come to devote myself. And during the whole fourteen months that I continued in that office he treated me with uniform kindness, and often made anxious inquiries about the phases of our attempted reform of the nation.

Early in December, 1835, Dr. Channing's volume on Slavery issued from the press. A few days after its publication, he invited Samuel E. Sewall and myself to dine with him, that he might learn how we liked his book. Both of us had been delighted with some parts of it, but neither of us was satisfied with other parts; much dissatisfied with some. He requested and insisted on the utmost freedom in our comments. He listened to our objections very patiently, and seemed disposed to give them their due weight.

As was to be expected, the appearance of a work on Slavery, by Dr. Channing, caused a great sensation throughout the land. It was sought for with avidity. It found its way into many parlors from which a copy of *The Liberator* would have been spurned. Most of the statesmen of our country read it, and many slaveholders.

Not many days elapsed before the responses which it awakened began to be heard; and they were by no means altogether such as he had expected. Although he disclaimed the Abolitionists; stated that he had never attended one of our meetings, nor heard one of our lecturers; although he made several grave objections to our doctrines and measures, and unwittingly gave his sanction to several of the most serious misrepresentations of our sentiments, our objects, and means of prosecuting them; yet he so utterly repudiated the right of any man to *property* in the person of any other man, and gave such a fearful *exposé* of the sinfulness of holding slaves and the vices which infested the communities where human beings were held in such an unnatural condition, that the Southern aristocracy and their Northern partisans came soon to regard him as a more dangerous man than even Mr. Garrison. He was denounced as an enemy of his country, as encouraging the insurrection of the slaves, and as in effect laboring to do as much harm as the Abolitionists.

In due time an octavo pamphlet of forty-eight pages was published in Boston, entitled "Remarks on Dr. Channing's Slavery." It was evidently written by a very able hand, and was attributed to one of the most prominent lawyers in that city. The writer spoke respectfully of Dr. Channing, but condemned utterly his doctrines on the subject of slavery, and found in them all the viciousness of the extremest abolitionism. The author announced and labored to maintain the following false propositions: "First. Public sentiment in the free States in relation to slavery is perfectly sound and *ought not* to be altered. Second. Public sentiment in the slaveholding States, whether right or not, *cannot* be altered. Third. An attempt to produce any alteration in the public sentiment of the country will cause great additional evil, — moral, social, and political."

Such bald scepticism was not to be tolerated. "A Review of the Remarks" was soon sent forth. This called out a "Reply to the Review," and thus the subject of slavery was fully broached among a class of people who had given no heed to *The Liberator* and our antislavery tracts.

In future articles I shall have occasion gratefully to acknowledge the further services rendered by Dr. Channing to the antislavery cause, and to show how at last he came nearly to accord in sentiment with the ultra-Abolitionists.

SLAVERY,—BY WILLIAM E. CHANNING.

This was the title of Dr. Channing's book. It rendered the antislavery cause services so important that I am impelled to give a further account of it. It seemed to me at the time, it seems to me now, one of the most inconsistent books I have ever read. It showed how, all unconsciously to himself, the judgment of that wise man had been warped and his prejudices influenced by the deference, which had come to be paid pretty generally throughout our country, to the Southern slaveholding oligarchy; and by the denunciations which their admirers, sympathizers, abettors, and minions in the free States, poured without measure upon Mr. Garrison and his comparatively few fellow-laborers.

Dr. Channing's profound respect for human nature and the rights of man, and his heartfelt compassion for the oppressed, suffering, despised, were such that he could not but see clearly the essential, inevitable, terrible wrongs and evils of slavery to the master as well as to his subject. He portrayed these cruelties and vices so clearly and forcibly that the pages of his book contain as utter condemnations of the domestic servitude in our Southern States, and as awful exposures of the consequent corruption, pollution of families and the community in those States, — condemnations as utter and exposures as awful as could be found in *The Liberator*. To his chapters on "Property in Man," "Rights," and "Evils of Slavery," we could take no exceptions. But his chapter entitled "Explanations" seems to us, as Mr. Garrison called it, a chapter in *recantation*, — a disastrous attempt to make it appear as if there could be sin without a sinner. He says that the character of the master and the wrong done to the slave are distinct points, having little or no relation to each other. He therefore did not "intend to pass sentence on the character of the slaveholder." Jesus Christ taught that "by their fruits ye shall know men." But the Doctor said in this chapter, "Men are not always to be interpreted by their acts or their institutions." "Our ancestors," he continued, "committed a deed now branded as piracy," i. e. the slave-trade. "Were they, therefore, the offscouring of the earth?" No, — but they were *pirates*, their good qualities in other respects notwithstanding. They were guilty of kidnapping the Africans, and made themselves rich by selling their victims into slavery. Piracy was too mild a term for such atrocious acts. They were just as wicked before they were denounced by law as afterwards. And it was by bringing the people of England and of this country to see the enormity of the crimes inseparable from that trade in human beings, that they were persuaded to repent of it, to renounce and abhor it. Again Dr. Channing says under this head, "How many sects have persecuted and shed blood! Were their members, therefore, monsters of depravity?" I answer, their spirit was cruel and devilish, utterly unlike the spirit of Jesus. They were none of his, whatever may have been their professions. As well might we deny that David was a gross adulterer and mean murderer, because he wrote some very devotional psalms.

A more marvellous inconsistency in the book before us is this. The Doctor declares "that cruelty is not the habit of the slave States in this country." "He might have affirmed just as truly," said Mr. Garrison, "that idolatry is not the habit of pagan countries." What is cruelty? The extremest is the reducing of a human being to the condition of a domesticated brute, a piece of mere property. The Doctor himself has said as much in another part of this volume, see the 26th page in his excellent chapter on "Property." Having described what man is by nature, he adds, "The sacrifice of such a being to another's will, to another's present, outward, ill-comprehended good, *is the greatest violence which can be offered to any creature of God.* It is to cast him out from God's spiritual family into the brutal herd." "No robbery is *so great* as that to which the slave is *habitually* subjected." "The slave *must* meet cruel *treatment* either inwardly or outwardly. Either the soul or the body must receive the blow. Either the flesh must be tortured or the spirit be struck down." No Abolitionist, not even Mr. Garrison, has set forth more clearly the extreme cruelty, inseparable from holding a fellow-man in slavery one hour.

Still Dr. Channing objected to our primal doctrine,—"immediate emancipation." But could there have been a more obvious inference than this, which an upright mind would unavoidably draw from a consideration of the rights of man, the evils of slavery, and the unparalleled iniquity of subjecting a human being to such degradation. I ask, could there have been a more obvious inference than that any, every human being held in such a condition ought to be *immediately released* from it? It is plain to me that Dr. Channing himself drew the same inference that Elizabeth Heyrick,* of England,

* Of Leicester, England, who first demanded "immediate emancipation."

and Mr. Garrison had drawn, although he rejected the trenchant phrase in which they declared that inference. Having exhibited so faithfully and feelingly the wrongs and the evils of slavery, he says, on the 119th page of this book: "What, then, is to be done for the removal of slavery? *In the first place*, the slaveholder should solemnly disclaim the right of property in human beings. The great principle that man cannot belong to man should be distinctly recognized. The slave should be acknowledged as a partaker of a common nature, as having the essential rights of humanity. This great truth lies at the foundation of every wise plan for his relief." Would not any one suppose, if he had not been forbidden the supposition, that the writer of these lines intended to enjoin the *immediate* emancipation of the enslaved? Surely, he would have *the first thing* that is to be done for their relief done immediately. Surely, he would have the foot of the oppressor taken from their necks *at once*. He would have the heavy yoke that crushes them broken without delay. Surely, he would have the *foundation* of the plan for the removal of slavery laid *immediately*. He would not, could not counsel the slaveholder to postpone a day, nor an hour, the recognition of the right of his slave to be treated as a fellow-man. There is a remarkable resemblance between what Dr. Channing here says ought to be done *in the first place*, and what the Abolitionists had from the beginning insisted ought to be done *immediately*.

One of the Doctor's objections to our chosen phrase was that it was liable to be misunderstood. But, as we said at the time, "if *immediate emancipation* expresses our leading doctrine exactly, it ought to be used and explanations of it be patiently given until the true doctrine has come to be generally understood, received, and obeyed." Now, *immediate emancipation* was the comprehensive phrase that did best express the right of the slave and the duty of the master. In whatever sense we used the word *immediate,* whether in regard to time or order, the word expressed just what we Abolitionists meant. We insisted upon it in opposition to those who were teaching slaveholders to defer to another generation, or to some future time an act of common humanity that was due to their fellow-men *at once;* and would be due every minute until it should be done. We insisted upon it in opposition to the popular but deceptive, impracticable, and cruel scheme which proposed to liberate the slaves on condition of their removal to Africa.

Dr. Channing further objected that "the use of the phrase *immediate emancipation* had contributed much to spread far and wide the belief, that the Abolitionists wished immediately to free the slave from *all* his restraints." But ought we to have been held responsible for such a senseless, wanton misconstruction of words that had been explained a thousand times by our appointed lecturers, in our tracts, and in the "Declaration of the Sentiments, Purposes, and Plans of the American Antislavery Society," which was published three years before Dr. Channing's book appeared? Freemen, — Republican freemen were, are, and ever ought to be subject to the restraints of civil government, equal and righteous laws. From the commencement of our enterprise, our only demand for our enslaved countrymen has been that they should forthwith be admitted to all the rights and privileges of freemen upon the same conditions as others, after they shall have acquired (those of them who do not now possess) the qualifications demanded of others.

Still further the Doctor accused us Abolitionists of having "fallen into the common error of enthusiasts, — that of exaggerating their object, of feeling as if no evil existed but that which they opposed, and as if no guilt could be compared with that of countenancing or upholding it." We grieved especially that he suffered this censure to drop from his pen, as, coming from him, it would repress in many bosoms the concern which was beginning to be felt more than ever before for the slaves and the slaveholders. There was no danger that we should esteem or lead others to esteem the evils of their condition to be greater than they were. All about us there was still an alarming insensibility or indifference to the subject. This could not have been made to appear more glaring than by the Doctor himself, on the 137th page of his book. "Suppose," he there said, "suppose that millions of *white* men were enslaved, robbed of all their rights in a neighboring country, and enslaved by a black race who had torn their ancestors from the shores on which our fathers had lived. How deeply should we feel their wrongs!" Ay, how much more deeply would even the Abolitionists feel for them! Yet why should we not all feel as much, in the case that actually existed in our country as in the one supposed? We are unable to find a reason of which we ought not to be ashamed, because it must be one based upon a cruel prejudice, the offspring of the degradation into which we had forced the black men. I really wish if there are any who think with Dr. Channing that the Abolitionists did *exaggerate* the guilt of holding men in slavery, or consenting with slaveholders, — I really wish such persons would read Dr. Channing's chapter on the "Evils of Slavery," and then show us, if he can, wherein we exaggerated them.

Dr. Channing repelled with great emphasis the charge often brought against Abolitionists, that we were endeavoring to incite the slaves to violence, bloodshed, insurrection. He said, page 131: "It is a remarkable fact, that though the South and the North have been leagued to crush them, though they have been watched by a million of eyes, and though prejudice has been prepared to detect the slightest sign of corrupt communication with the slave, yet this crime has not been fastened on a single member of this body." No, not one of our number, that I was acquainted with, ever suggested the resort to insurrection and murder by the enslaved as the means of delivering them from bondage. And in our Declaration at Philadelphia we solemnly disclaimed any such intention.

We knew that slavery could be *peaceably* abolished only by the consent of the slaveholders and the legislators of their States. We knew that they could not fail to be affected, moved by the right action of our Federal Government, touching the enslavement of the colored population in the District of Columbia, and in the territories that were entirely under the jurisdiction of Congress. And we knew that the members of Congress could not be reached and impelled to act as we wished them to, but by the known sentiments and expressed wishes of their constituents, — the people of the nation North and South. It was needful, therefore, to press the subject upon the consideration of the people throughout the land. Accordingly, we did all in our power to awaken the public attention, to agitate the public mind, to touch the public heart. We sent able lecturers to speak wherever there were ears to hear them, and we sent newspapers and tracts wherever the mails would carry them.

Dr. Channing reproached us for this, especially for sending our publications to the slaveholders. But we know not how else we could have made them sensible of the horror with which their system of domestic servitude was viewed by thousands in the Northern States; and inform them correctly of our determination to effect the liberation of their bondmen; and the peaceful means and legal measures by which we intended, if possible, to accomplish our purpose. We wondered greatly at the Doctor's objection to our course in this direction. To whom should we have sent our publications, if not to those whose cherished institution we were aiming by them to undermine and overthrow? Would it have been open, manly, honorable not to have done so?

One more objection Dr. Channing made, which seemed to us as unreasonable as the last. It was to our *manner* of forming our Antislavery Associations. He said: "The Abolitionists might have formed an association, but it should have been an elective one. Men of strong principles, judiciousness, sobriety, should have been carefully sought as members. Much good might have been accomplished by the co-operation of such philanthropists." Alas! such philanthropists, the wise and prudent men, to whom he probably alluded, seemed to have made up their minds to acquiesce in the continuance of slavery, so long as our white brethren at the South saw fit to retain the institution; or to help them take it down very gradually, by removing the victims of it to the shores of Africa. Nearly fifty years had passed, and such philanthropists as he indicated had done little or nothing for the enslaved, and seemed to be growing more indifferent to their wrongs. If we had elected them, would they have associated with us? Are they the men to bear the brunt of a moral conflict? "Not many wise," — as this world counts wisdom, — "not many rich, not many mighty," were ever found among the leaders of reform. God has always chosen the foolish to confound the wise. It is left for imprudent men, enthusiasts, fanatics, to begin all difficult enterprises. They have usually been the pioneers of reform. Else why was not the abolition of slavery attempted and accomplished long before by that "better class"?

I have not dwelt so long upon this book, and criticised parts of it so seriously, in order to throw any shade upon the memory of that great man, whom I have so much reason to revere and love. But I have done this in order to reveal more fully to the present generation, and to those who may come after us, the sad state of the public mind and heart in New England thirty-five years ago. All the objections Dr. Channing alleged against us in this book were the common current objections of that day, hurled at us in less seemly phrases from the press, the platform, and the pulpit. They would not have been thought of, if we had been laboring for the emancipation of white men. It was sad that a man of such a mind and heart as Dr. Channing's could have thought them of sufficient importance to press them upon us as he did. Nevertheless, his book contained so many of the vital principles for which we were contesting, set forth so luminously and urged so fervently, that it proved to be, as I have already said, a far greater help to our cause than we at first expected. And we look back with no little admiration upon one who, enjoying as he did, in the utmost serenity, the highest reputation as a writer and a divine, put at hazard the repose of the rest of his life, and sacrificed hundreds of the admirers of his genius, eloquence, and piety, by espousing the cause of the oppressed, which most of the eminent men in the land would not touch with one of their fingers.

THE GAG-LAW.

In the winter of 1835 and 1836 the slaveholding oligarchy made a bolder assault than ever before upon the liberty of our nation, and the most alarming intimations were given of a willingness to yield to their imperious demands. The legislatures of Alabama, Georgia,

South Carolina, North Carolina, and Virginia passed resolutions of the same import, only those of Virginia and South Carolina were clothed, as might have been expected, in somewhat more imperative and threatening terms. These resolutions insisted that each State, in which slavery was established, had the exclusive right to manage the matter in the way that the inhabitants thereof saw fit; and that the citizens of other States who were interfering with slavery in any way, directly or indirectly, were guilty of violating their social and constitutional obligations, and ought to be punished. They therefore "claimed and earnestly requested that the non-slaveholding States of the Union should promptly and *effectually suppress* all abolition societies, and that they should make it *highly penal* to print, publish, and distribute newspapers, pamphlets, tracts, and pictorial representations calculated or having a tendency to excite the slaves of the Southern States to insurrection and revolt."

These resolutions further declared that "they should consider every interference with slavery by any other State, or by the General Government, as a direct and unlawful interference, to be resisted at once, and under every possible circumstance." Moreover, they insisted that they "should consider the abolition of slavery in the District of Columbia as a violation of the rights of the citizens of that District, and as a usurpation *to be at once resisted*, as nothing less than the commencement of a scheme of much more extensive and flagrant injustice."

Resolutions in these words, or to the same effect, passed by the legislatures of the above-mentioned States, were transmitted by the governors of those States severally to the governors of each of the non-slaveholding States, among them to the chief magistrate of Massachusetts, then the Hon. Edward Everett.

On the 15th of January, 1836, that gentleman delivered his address to both branches of the Legislature at the organization of the State Government. In the course of that address, as in duty bound to do under the circumstances, he alluded particularly to the subject of slavery, and to the excitement kindled throughout the country by the discussion of it in the free States.

But instead of showing that the subject of human rights was ever up, and must needs be ever up, for the consideration of the American people, in private circles and public assemblies; that it ought not and could not be prohibited, — instead of conceding the impossibility (in our country especially) of preventing the freest expression of the opinion, that such a glaring inconsistency, such a tremendous iniquity as the enslavement of millions ought not to be tolerated; that the genius of our Republic, the spirit of the age, the principles of Christianity, the impartial love of the Father of all mankind, each and all demanded the abolition of slavery, — instead of availing himself of the occasion so fully given him, from his high position, to reiterate the glorious doctrines of the Declaration of Independence, and to press upon the complaining States the obvious necessity of their yielding to the self-evident claims of humanity, — instead of this, His Excellency saw fit to commend the disastrous policy of the framers of our Republic; to pass a severe censure upon us Abolitionists, and to intimate his opinion that we were guilty of offences punishable at common law.

This part of his speech was referred to a joint committee of two from the Senate and three from the House of Representatives, Hon. George Lunt, Chairman. By order of the managers of the Massachusetts Antislavery Society, I addressed a letter to the above-named committee, asking permission to appear before them by representatives, and show reasons why there should be no legislative action condemnatory of the Abolitionists. The request was granted, and on the 4th of March the proposed interview took place in the chamber of the Representatives, in the presence of many citizens.

At first a member of the committee, Mr. Lucas, objected to our proceeding; said we were premature; that we should have waited until the committee had reported; that we had no reason to apprehend the Legislature would do anything prejudicial to us, or to the liberties of the people. I replied, "that formerly it would have been a gratuitous, an impertinent apprehension, but recent occurrences have admonished us, that we may not any longer safely rest in the assurance that our liberties are secure. Alarming encroachments have been made upon them, even in the metropolis of New England. We do not fear," I continued, "that your committee will recommend, or that our Legislature will enact, a penal law against Abolitionists. But we do apprehend that condemnatory resolutions may be reported and passed; and these we deprecate more than a penal law for reasons that we wish to press upon your consideration."

After some discussion between the members of the committee Mr. Lucas withdrew his objection, and we were allowed to proceed. I commenced, being the General Agent of the Society, and gave a sketch of the origin, the organization, and progress of the abolition enterprise, — stating distinctly our purpose and the instrumentalities by which we intended to accomplish it. I laid before the committee copies of our newspapers, reports, and tracts, — especially the constitutions of several State and County Antislavery Societies, and more especially the report of the convention that met in Philadelphia, in December 1833, and organized the American Antislavery Society, and issued a declaration of sentiments and purposes. All these documents, I insisted, would make it plain to the committee that we were endeavoring to effect the abolition of slavery by moral means, — not by rousing the enslaved to insurrection, but by working such changes in the public sentiment of the nation respecting the cruelty and wickedness of our slave system, that strong, earnest remonstrances would be sent from the Legislature, and still more from the ecclesiastical bodies in all the free States to corresponding bodies in the slave States, imploring them to consider the awful iniquity of making merchandise of fellow-men, and treating them like domesticated brutes; at the same time offering to co-operate with them and share generously in the expense of abolishing slavery, and raising their bondmen to the condition and privileges of the free.

Some discussion here ensued as to the character of some of our publications, and the propriety of certain expressions used by some of our speakers and writers. And then Ellis Gray Loring was heard in our behalf. This gentleman had been prominent among the New England Abolitionists from the very beginning of Mr. Garrison's undertaking. There were combined in him the strength and resolution of a man with the intuitive wisdom and delicacy of a woman. He addressed the committee more than half an hour in a most pertinent manner, replying aptly to their questions and objections. "The general duty," said Mr. Loring, "of sympathizing with and succoring the oppressed will probably be conceded. It is enjoined by Christianity. We are impelled to it by the very nature which our Creator has conferred upon us. What, then, is to limit our exercise, as Abolitionists, of this duty and this right? The relations we bear to the oppressor control, it is said, our duty to the oppressed. If we are bound to abstain from the discussion of slavery, it must be either because we are restrained by the principles of international law, or by some provisions of the Constitution of the United States. But, gentlemen, if the slaveholding States were foreign nations, it could not be shown that we have done anything which the law of nations forbids. We have done nothing for the overthrow of slavery in our Southern States which that law forbids, more than our foreign missionary societies have for many years been doing for the subversion of idolatry in pagan lands, — nothing more than was done in this city and all over our country to aid the Poles and the Greeks in their struggle for freedom, of which our ancient allies, the Russians and the Turks, were determined to deprive them. If, then, the Law of nations does not restrain us, is it in the Constitution of the United States that such restraint is imposed? Far from it. I find in that, our Magna Charta, an abundant guaranty for the liberty of speech; but I look in vain in the letter of the Constitution for any prohibition of the use of moral means for the extirpation of slavery or any other evil."

Mr. Loring here took up the three clauses of the Constitution in which alone any allusion is made to the subject of slavery, and showed clearly that there was nothing in them which forbade the fullest and freest discussion of the political expediency or moral character of that system of oppression. And he confirmed his position by referring to the fact, that the framers of that great document did not understand it as the proslavery statesmen and politicians of our day would have it understood. Washington declared himself warmly in favor of emancipation. Jefferson's writings contain more appalling descriptions and more bitter denunciations of slavery than are to be found in the publications of modern Abolitionists; and Franklin, Rush, and John Jay were members of an antislavery society formed a few years after they had signed the Constitution, and they joined in a petition to Congress praying for the abolition of that system of domestic servitude, so inconsistent with our political principles and disastrous to our national honor and prosperity."

I have not given, nor have I room to give, anything like a full report of Mr. Loring's speech. He closed with these words: "A great *principle*, gentlemen, is involved in the decision of this Legislature. I esteem as nothing in comparison our feelings or wishes as individuals. Personal interests sink into insignificance here. Sacrifice us if you will, but do not wound liberty through us. Care nothing for men, but let the oppressor and his apologist, whether at the North or the South, beware of the certain defeat which awaits him who is found fighting against God."

The next one who addressed the committee was the Rev. William Goodell, one of the sturdiest, most sagacious and logical of our fellow-laborers. We are indebted to him for "a full statement of the reasons which were in part offered to the committee," &c., &c., given to the public in a pamphlet which was issued from the press a few days after our interviews with said committee.

I shall here quote only the most important passage in his speech: "We would deprecate the passage of any condemnatory resolutions by the Legislature, even more than the enactment of a penal law, for in the latter case we should have some redress. We could plead the unconstitutionality of such a law, at any rate, it could not take effect until we had had a fair trial. Not so, gentlemen of this committee, in the case of resolutions. We should have no redress for the injurious operation of such an extra-judicial sentence. The passage of such resolutions by this and other legislatures would help to fix in the public mind the belief that Abolitionists are a specially dangerous body of men, and so prepare the public to receive such a law as the slave-holding States might dictate. We solemnly protest against a legislative censure, because it would be a usurpation of an authority never intrusted to the Legislature. They are not a judicial body, and have no right to pronounce the condemnation of any one."

"Hold," said Mr. Lunt, the Chairman of the committee, "you must not indulge in such remarks, sir. We cannot sit here and permit you to instruct us as to the duties of the Legislature."

Mr. Goodell resumed, justified the remark for which he had been called to order, and completed his very able argument against any concurrence on the part of the General Court of Massachusetts with the demands of the Southern States.

Mr. Garrison next addressed the committee in a very comprehensive and forcible speech. But he neglected to give any report of it in his *Liberator*. I can therefore lay before your readers only this brief passage: "It is said, Mr. Chairman, that the Abolitionists wish to destroy the Union. It is not true. We would save the Union, if it be not too late. To us it would seem that the Union is already destroyed. To us there is no Union. We, sir, cannot go through these so-called United States enjoying the privileges which the Constitution of the Union professed to secure to all the citizens of this Republic. And why? Because, and only because, we are laboring to accomplish the very purposes for which it is declared in the preamble to the Constitution that the Union was formed! Because we are laboring 'to establish justice, insure domestic tranquillity, and promote the general welfare.'"

Dr. Follen then arose. He was extensively known

and very much respected and beloved by all who had known him, as a Professor in Harvard College, or as a preacher of true Christianity in several parishes in the vicinity of Boston. He had done and suffered much for the sake of civil and religious liberty in his own country, — Germany, — and had come to our country in the high hope of enjoying the blessings and privileges of true freedom. He early espoused the antislavery cause, and rendered us essential services by his wise counsels and his labors with several prominent persons whom we had failed to reach. He was selected as one of the nine to maintain our rights before the legislative committee, and avert the wrong that seemed impending over us from the unhappy suggestions in the speech of Governor Everett.

The Doctor evidently felt very deeply the grave importance of the occasion. He commenced his speech with some profound remarks upon the rights of man and the spirit and purpose of our republican institutions, and then proceeded to point out the fearful encroachments, that had been made on the fundamental principles of our Republic by slaveholders and their Northern partisans. "And now," said he, "they are calling upon the Northern legislatures to abolish the Abolitionists by law. We do not apprehend, gentlemen, that you will recommend, or that our General Court will enact, such a law. But we do apprehend that you may advise, and the Legislature may pass, resolutions severely censuring the Abolitionists. Against this measure we most earnestly protest. We think its effects would be worse than those of the penal law. The outrages committed in this city upon the liberty of speech, the mobs in Boston last October, were doubtless countenanced and incited by the great meeting of August, in Faneuil Hall. Now, gentlemen, would not similar consequences follow the expression by the Legislature of a similar condemnation? Would not the mobocrats again undertake to execute the informal sentence of the General Court? Would they not let loose again their bloodhounds upon us?"

"Stop, sir!" cried Mr. Lunt. "You may not pursue this course of remark. It is insulting to the committee and to the Legislature which they represent."

Dr. Follen sat down, and an emotion of deep displeasure evidently passed through the crowd of witnesses.

I sprang to my feet and remonstrated with Mr. Lunt. Mr. Loring and Mr. Goodell also expressed their surprise and indignation at his course. But it was of no avail. He would not consent that Dr. Follen should proceed to point out what we considered the chief danger to be guarded against. We therefore declined to continue our interview with the committee; and gave them notice that we should appeal to the Legislature for permission to present and argue our case in our own way before them, or before another committee.

THE GAG-LAW.—SECOND INTERVIEW.

We left the committee very much dissatisfied with the treatment we had received from Mr. Lunt and the majority of his associates. Hon. Ebenezer Moseley was an honorable exception. From the first he had treated us in the most fair and gentlemanly manner. And at the last he protested against the procedure of the Chairman.

We forthwith drew up, and the next morning presented, a memorial to the Legislature, intimating that we had not been properly treated by the committee, and asking that our *right* to be heard might be recognized; and that we might be permitted to appear and show our reasons in full, why the Legislature of Massachusetts should not enact any penal law, nor pass any resolutions condemning Abolitionists and antislavery societies. The remonstrance was read in both branches of the Legislature and referred to the same committee, with instructions to hear us according to our request.

On the afternoon of the 8th, therefore, we met the committee again in the Hall of the Representatives. The reports which had gone forth of our first interview had so interested the public, that the house was now quite filled with gentlemen and ladies, many of whom had never before shown any sympathy with the antislavery reform.

It was intended that Dr. Follen should address the committee first, beginning just where he had been, on the 4th, so rudely commanded by Mr. Lunt to leave off, and that he should press home that part of his argument which we all deemed so important. But he was detained from the meeting until a later hour. It devolved upon me, therefore, to commence. I confined my remarks to two points. First, I contended that our publications were not incendiary, not intended nor adapted to excite the oppressed to insurrection. Secondly, I assured the committee that, whatever they might think of the character of our publications, we had never sent them to the slaves nor to the colored people of the South, and gave them our reasons for having refrained so to do.

Samuel E. Sewall, Esq., then made a somewhat extended, but very close legal and logical argument against the demands of the slaveholding States, — "arrogant, insolent demands," as he called them. "To yield to them would be to subvert the foundations of our civil liberties, and make it criminal to obey the laws of God, and follow the example of Jesus Christ." His excellent speech evidently made an impression upon the committee as well as his larger audience. But I have not room here for such an abstract of it as I should like to give.

While Mr. Sewall was speaking Dr. Follen came in, and when he had ended the Doctor arose and commenced by showing very clearly that we Abolitionists were accused of *crime* by the legislatures of several of our Southern States, and that the Governor of Massachusetts had indorsed the accusation, because we had exercised in the cause of humanity that liberty of speech and of the press which was guaranteed to us in the Constitution of our Republic, not less explicitly than in the fundamental law of this State. "We have endeavored by persuasion, by argument, by moral and religious appeals to urge upon the nation, and especially upon our Southern brethren, the necessity of freeing themselves from the sin, the evils, and the shame of slavery. You cannot punish or censure freedom of speech in Abolitionists, without preparing the way to censure it in any other class of citizens who may for the moment be obnoxious to the majority. A penal enactment against us is less to be dreaded than condemnatory resolutions; for these are left to be enforced by Judge Lynch and his minions, and I must say, as I said the other day — "

"I call you to order, sir," said Mr. Lunt, with great emphasis. "This is not respectful to the committee."

Dr. Follen replied, "I am not conscious of having said anything disrespectful to the committee. I beg to be informed in what I am out of order."

Mr. Lunt replied, "Your allusion to mobs, for which you were called to order at our first interview, is not proper."

"Am I then to understand," said Dr. Follen, "that deprecating mobs is disrespectful to this committee?"

Mr. Moseley, one of the committee, here spoke with much feeling; said he dissented wholly from the action of the Chairman. "I see nothing in the allusion to mobs disrespectful to the committee or the Legislature; and I consider Dr. Follen entirely in order."

Some discussion ensued. Two others of the committee, making a majority, silently assented to the opinion of Mr. Lunt. So it was decided that the Doctor was out of order, and must not allude to mobs.

Here I called the attention of Mr. Lunt to the memorial, in answer to which we were permitted by the Legislature to appear before the committee, and they were instructed to hear us. "It seemed, on the fourth instant, that the Chairman considered that we came here by his grace to exculpate ourselves from the charges alleged against us by the Legislatures of several of the Southern States; and that we were not to be permitted to express our anxious apprehensions of the effects of any acts by our Legislature intended to gratify the wishes of those States. In order, therefore, that we might appear before you in the *exercise of our right as free citizens*, we have appealed to the Senate and House of Representatives, and have received their permission so to do. Dr. Follen was setting before you what we deem the most probable and most serious evil to be apprehended from any condemnatory resolutions which the Legislature might be induced to pass; and if he is not permitted to press this upon your consideration our interview with the committee must end here." Mr. Lunt then consulted with his associates and intimated that Dr. Follen might proceed. He did so, and having referred to the disastrous influence of the great meeting in Faneuil Hall, August, 1835, and of the condemnatory resolutions there passed, he showed clearly that far greater outrages upon the property and persons of Abolitionists would be likely to follow the passage of similar resolutions by the Legislature of the Commonwealth.

Rev. William Goodell then arose and made a most

able and eloquent speech. He ignored for the time being all the personal dangers and private wrongs of the Abolitionists; he set aside for the moment the consideration of everything else but the imminent peril that seemed to be impending over the very life of liberty in our country. "For what, Mr. Chairman," said he, "are Abolitionists accused by the Southern States, and our own Legislature called upon to condemn them? For nothing else but exercising and defending the inalienable rights of the people. What have we said that is not said in your Declaration of Independence? and why are we censured for carrying into practice what others have been immortalized as patriots for writing and adopting? In censuring us you censure the Father of our Country. I turn to the portrait of Washington as it looks upon us in this hall, and remind you how he declared that he earnestly desired to see the time when slavery should be abolished. For saying this, and urging it upon our countrymen, the mandate has come from the South to stop our mouths, and we are here to avert the sentence our own Legislature is called upon to pronounce upon us." Mr. Goodell then went on to quote the strongest antislavery sentiments uttered by President Jefferson, Chief Justice John Jay, and Hon. William Pinckney, a distinguished member of the Legislature of Maryland, the last in stronger language of condemnation than ever issued from an antislavery press. "Shall the men of the South speak thus, and we be compelled to hold our peace? Mr. Chairman, in this hour of my country's danger, I should disdain to stand here pleading for my personal security. In behalf of my fellow-citizens throughout the land, I implore the Legislature of this Commonwealth to pause before they act on those documents of the South. What are they? A demand for the unconditional surrender to the South of the first principles of your Constitution, the surrender of your liberties. It is a blow particularly aimed at the independence of your laboring classes." Mr. Goodell here quoted the declaration of Governor McDuffie and other distinguished Southern gentlemen, distinctly asserting the doctrine that "the laboring population of no nation on earth are entitled to liberty or capable of enjoying it." "Mr. Chairman, we are charged with aiming at disunion, because we seek what only can save the Union. I charge upon those who promulgate the doctrines on your table, a deep and foul conspiracy against the liberties of the laboring people of the North." Mr. Lunt here interrupted him.

"Mr. Goodell, I must interfere," he said. "You must not charge other States with a foul conspiracy, nor treat their public documents with disrespect." Mr. Goodell replied: "Something may be pardoned to a man when he speaks for the liberties of a nation." Mr. Lunt continued: "The documents emanating from other States are required by our Federal Constitution to be received with full faith and credit here." "Certainly, sir," responded Mr. Goodell. "I wish them to be regarded as official, accredited documents, and I have referred to an accredited document from the Governor of South Carolina, in which he says, *that the laborers of the North are incapable of understanding or enjoying freedom, that liberty in a free State best subsists with slavery, and that the laborers must be reduced to slavery, or the laws cannot be maintained.* This, sir, is also a document entitled to full faith and credit, — holding up a report of the doings of the Legislature of South Carolina, in which they declared an entire accordance with Governor McDuffie in the sentiments expressed in his message." Mr. Lunt here interposed with great warmth. "Stop, sir!" Mr. Goodell stopped, but remained standing. "Sit down, sir," said Mr. Lunt; "the committee will hear no more of this." Mr. Goodell said: "My duty is discharged, Mr. Chairman, if I cannot proceed in the way that seems to me necessary to bring our case properly before the committee and the Legislature. We came here as free men, and we will go away as freemen should." Some one in the vast audience that had been watching our proceedings with intensest interest cried out, "Let us go quickly lest we be made slaves." I here made one more appeal to Mr. Lunt. "Are we, sir, to be again denied our right of being heard in pursuance of our memorial to the Legislature?" The Chairman intimated that they had heard enough.

The audience here began to leave the hall, but were arrested by a voice in their midst. It was that of Dr. Gamaliel Bradford, not a member of the Antislavery Society, who had come there only as a spectator, but had been so moved by what he had witnessed that he pronounced an eloquent, thrilling, impassioned, but respectful appeal in favor of free discussion. I wish that I could spread the whole of it before my readers. So soon as he sat down Mr. George Bond, one of the most prominent merchants and estimable gentlemen of Boston, expressed a desire to say a few words to the committee. "I am not a petitioner nor an Abolitionist," said he; "but, though opposed to some of the measures of these antislavery gentlemen, I hold to some opinions in common with them. If under these circumstances the committee will permit, I beg leave to offer a few remarks." The Chairman preserved silence; but another member of the committee intimated to Mr. Bond that he might proceed. "It strikes me," said Mr. Bond, "that this is a subject of deep and vital importance; and I fear as a citizen that the manner in which it has been treated by the committee will produce an excitement throughout the Commonwealth. With due respect to the committee, I beg leave to say that, from the little experience I have had in legislative proceedings, it is not the practice to require of persons, appearing before a committee, a strict conformity to rules. They are usually indulged in telling their own story in their own way, provided it be not disrespectful. I have certainly heard nothing from the gentlemen of the Antislavery Society that called for the course that has been adopted. It does seem to me that some of the committee have been too fastidious, too hypercritical."

Mr. Lunt here broke out again. "Be careful, sir, what you say. The committee will not submit to it." Mr. Bond replied: "I certainly have no wish to say anything unpleasant to the committee, but I cannot help regretting the course that has been taken to withhold a full hearing from the parties interested. They came here through their memorial, which had been received by the Legislature and referred to this committee, and I expected that the committee would have allowed them to say what they pleased, using proper language. If they state their case improperly, it will injure them and not the committee. I may be wrong, but I regret to see the grounds given for the gentlemen and their friends to say they have been denied a hearing. The action on this question here is of immense importance in the influence it may have, not only upon those who have appeared before the committee, but upon the Legislature, the community, the Commonwealth, and the whole country." When Mr. Bond had closed, instead of proffering to us a further hearing, the committee broke up without a formal adjournment, the Chairman immediately retiring, conscious, as it seems to me he must have been, of the very general indignation which his conduct had excited. Just as he was leaving, Mr. Moseley, one of the committee, said to him, "I am not satisfied with your course. You have been wrong from the beginning. I will not sit again on such a committee."

The large audience retired from the hall murmuring their astonishment, shame, indignation at the conduct of the Chairman. Many gentlemen and ladies, who had never shown us favor before, came to assure us that they had been led, by what they had heard and seen that afternoon, to take a new view of the importance of the great reform we were laboring to effect.

Nothing, however, gratified us so much as seeing Dr. Channing approach Mr. Garrison, whom until then he had appeared to avoid, shake him cordially by the hand, and utter some words of sympathy. From that time until his death the larger portion of his publications were upon the subject of slavery, increasing in earnestness and power to the last.

The conduct of the committee, especially the Chairman, was severely censured next day in the Senate by Hon. Mr. Whitmarsh, and other members of that body. Reports of our interviews were published and republished throughout the Commonwealth, and called out from almost every part of it condemnatory comments. Many were brought over to the antislavery faith, and our party became not a little significant in the estimation of the politicians. Governor Everett's too evident inclination to yield to the insolent demands of the slaveholding oligarchy damaged him seriously in the confidence of his fellow-citizens, and, if I remember correctly, at the very next election he was beaten by the opposing candidate, whose sentiments on slavery were thought to be more correct than his.

HON. JAMES G. BIRNEY.

Let me again beg my readers to bear in mind, that I am not attempting to write a complete history of the antislavery conflict. Many individuals rendered essential services to the cause in different parts of our country whose names even may not be mentioned on any of my pages, for the reason that I had little or no personal acquaintance with them. My purpose is merely to give my recollections of the most important incidents in the progress of the great reform, and of the individuals whom I personally knew in connection with those incidents.

Although I did not enjoy a very intimate acquaintance with the distinguished gentleman whose name stands at the head of this article, my connection with him was such that it will be very proper, as well as very grateful to me, to give some account of him and of his inestimable services.

At the annual meetings of the American Antislavery Society in New York, and of the Massachusetts Society in Boston in May, 1835, our hearts were greatly encouraged and our hands strengthened by the presence and eloquence of the Hon. James G. Birney, then of Kentucky, lately of Alabama. We had repeatedly heard of him during the preceding twelve months, and of his labors and sacrifices in the cause of our enslaved countrymen. As I said in my report at the time, all were charmed with him. He was mild yet firm, cautious yet not afraid to speak the whole truth, candid but not compromising, careful not to exaggerate in aught, and equally careful not to conceal or extenuate. He imparted much valuable information and animated us to persevere in our work.

Mr. Birney was a native of Kentucky, the only son of a wealthy planter, who gave him some of the best opportunities that our country then afforded for acquiring a thorough classical, scientific, and professional education, to which were added the advantages of extensive foreign travel. When he had completed his preparations for the practice of the law he opened an office in Danville, his native place, and married a Miss McDowell, of Virginia. Thus he was allied by marriage as well as birth to a large circle of prominent slaveholders in two States. Soon after he removed to Huntsville, Alabama, where he rapidly rose to great distinction in his profession and in the estimation of his fellow-citizens. He was elected Solicitor-General of the State, and in 1828, when John Q. Adams was nominated for the Presidency, Mr. Birney was chosen by the Whig party one of the Alabama Electors. Moreover, he was an honored member of the Presbyterian church, and was zealous and active as an elder in that denomination. I make these statements to show that Mr. Birney occupied a very high position, both civil and ecclesiastical.

He had been accustomed to slavery from his birth. So he purchased a cotton plantation near Huntsville and directed the management of it. But his kind heart was ill at ease in view of the condition of the slaves. He could not regard them as brute animals, and felt that there must be a terrible wrong in treating them as if they were. He gladly entered into the project of the Colonization Society, hoping it would lead ultimately to the deliverance of the bondsmen. He became so interested in it that he turned from his legal practice, which had become very lucrative, that he might discharge the duties of General Superintendent of the Colonization Society in the States of Alabama, Mississippi, Louisiana, Tennessee, and Arkansas. He travelled extensively throughout those States, was everywhere treated with respect, and had abundant opportunities for forming an opinion of the real effect of the Colonization scheme upon the institution of slavery. He saw that it was tending to perpetuate rather than to put an end to the great iniquity.

Towards the close of 1833 Mr. Birney removed back to his native place, that he might be near and minister to the comfort of his aged father. He returned carrying with him his new-formed opinions of Colonization. He found a few who had come to feel, with him, that something else and more should be done for the relief of the oppressed. In December of that year he joined them and formed the "Kentucky Gradual Emancipation Society." But the principles of it did not long satisfy him.

Mr. Garrison's "Thoughts on Colonization," published more than a year before in Boston, had reached that neighborhood, and probably had come under the consideration of Mr. Birney. It contained a faithful searching review of the purposes, the spirit and tendency of Colonization. Soon after, the famous discussion arose in Lane Seminary, of which I have given some account on a previous page, and which resulted in an eruption that threw eighty "live coals" in as many directions over the country, — fervent young men, who went diligently about, kindling up the minds of the people on the question of *immediate* emancipation.

That remarkable young man, Theodore D. Weld, leader of the antislavery party in Lane Seminary, visited Mr. Birney, and found him ready for conversion, if not already a convert to the highest antislavery truth. Their interviews resulted in Mr. Birney's entire conviction that the Colonization plan tended to uphold rather than to subvert slavery; and that immediate emancipation, without removal from their homes, was the right of every slave, and the duty of every slaveholder.

Without delay, he acted in accordance with this conviction. He addressed an admirable letter to Rev. Mr. Mills, Corresponding Secretary of the Kentucky Colonization Society, announcing that he must no longer be considered a member of that association, and stating, in a very lucid and impressive manner, his weighty reasons for disapproving of, and feeling impelled to oppose, an enterprise in which he had taken so much interest, and to which he had devoted so much time and labor. Better than this, he summoned all his slaves into his presence, acknowledged that he had been guilty of great wrong in holding them as his property, informed them that he had executed deeds of manumission for each and all of them, and that henceforth they were free men, free women, free children. He offered to retain in his service all who preferred to remain with him, and to pay them fair wages for their labor. None left him, and, as he himself told me, they afterwards toiled not only more cheerfully than before, but more effectively, and for a greater number of hours. In several instances he had been impelled to go to them in person, and insist upon their "hanging up the shovel and the hoe." In the fall of 1834 he addressed a letter to the members of the Presbyterian Synod, in the vicinity of Danville, in which he pressed upon them the sinfulness of holding their fellow-beings as property, and showed them the true Scripture doctrine respecting slavery. He also visited the seat of government during the session of the Kentucky Legislature, and conversed with many members. He found that most of them regarded slavery as an evil which could not be perpetual, but most of them recoiled from the plan of immediate emancipation.

Convinced that this was the vital doctrine, he determined to do all in his power to disseminate it among the people. For this purpose he purchased a printing-press and types, and engaged a man to print for him at Danville a paper to be called *The Philanthropist.* So soon as his intention became known, his neighbors roused themselves to prevent the execution of it. While he continued a slaveholder and in favor of Colonization, it was proper and safe enough for him to express freely his opinions. But when he became an immediate emancipationist, and liberated his slaves, he was regarded as a dangerous man. And now that he was preparing to disseminate his doctrines through the press, he was to be denounced and silenced.

On the 12th of July, 1835, the slaveholders of his neighborhood assembled in mass meeting, in the town of Danville, and after rousing themselves and each other to the right pitch of madness, they addressed a letter to Mr. Birney, vehemently remonstrating with him, and pledging themselves to prevent the publication of his paper, by the most violent means, if necessary. Mr. Birney respectfully but firmly refused to yield to their demand, assured them that he understood the rights of an American citizen, and that he should exercise and defend them. However, their threats, which did not intimidate him, so far excited the apprehensions of his printer that he utterly refused to undertake the publication.

When the report reached Alabama that Mr. Birney had become an immediate Abolitionist, had renounced the Colonization Society, and had liberated his slaves, most of those who had formerly known and honored him there united in expressing very emphatically their displeasure, and declaring their contempt for his new fanatical opinions. The Supreme Court of that State expunged his name from the roll of attorneys practising at its bar. And in the University of Alabama, of which he had been a most useful trustee, several literary societies, of which he had been an honorary member, hastened to pass resolutions expelling him from their bodies. These acts convinced him of their hatred, but not of his error.

Finding that he could not get his paper printed in Danville, he removed his press and types to Cincinnati, in order that he might publish his *Philanthropist* as near to his father's home and his native State as possible, and under the ægis of Ohio, whose constitution explicitly guarantees to her citizens freedom of speech and of the press.

But he had not got himself and family settled in Cincinnati, before he found that the inhabitants of that city were so swayed by Southern influence that it would be useless to attempt to issue a paper there, opposed to slavery and to the expatriation of the free colored people. He therefore removed twenty miles up the river to the town of New Richmond, where the dominant influence was in the hands of Quakers. *The Philanthropist* was much better received by the public than he expected, and was so generally commended for the excellent spirit with which the subject of slavery was discussed, that he thought it best to remove his press back to Cincinnati. But he had hardly got it established there before "the gentlemen of property and standing" bestirred themselves and their minions to the determination that the incendiary paper "must be suppressed by all means, right or wrong, peaceably or forcibly." Mr. Birney contended manfully, nobly, for the liberty of speech and of the press. He met his opponents in public and in private, refuted their arguments and exposed the fearful consequences of their conduct, if persisted in. But his facts, his logic, and his eloquence were of no avail. What had not been reasoned into them could not be reasoned out of them. His opponents were fixed in a foregone conclusion that slavery was a matter with which the citizens of the free States were bound not to meddle, and were made more impetuous by that dislike of the colored people, which was intensified by the consciousness that they were living witnesses to the inconsistency, cruelty, and meanness of our nation. I wish I had room for a full account of Mr. Birney's courageous and persistent defence of his antislavery opinions, and of his right to publish and disseminate them.

Suffice it to add that, on the evening of the 1st of August, 1836, Mr. Birney having gone to a distant town to deliver a lecture, large numbers of persons, among them some of the *most respectable* citizens of Cincinnati, went to the office of *The Philanthropist*, demolished or threw into the streets everything they found there excepting the printing-press. That they dragged to the bank of the Ohio, half a mile distant, conveyed it in a boat to the middle of the river and threw it in.

In the fall of 1837 Mr. Birney removed to New York, and for two years or more rendered inestimable services as one of the Corresponding Secretaries of the American Antislavery Society.

While there, some time in 1839, his father died, leaving a large amount of property in lands, money, and slaves to him and his only sister, Mrs. Marshall. Mr. Birney requested that all the slaves, twenty-one in number, might be set off to him at their market value, as a part of his patrimony. This was done. He immediately wrote and executed a deed manumitting them all. Thus he sacrificed to his sense of right, his respect for humanity, that which he might legally have retained or disposed of as property, amounting to eighteen or twenty thousand dollars.*

This act, added to all else that he had done and said

* See Appendix.

in the cause of liberty, and the invaluable contributions from his pen, and the noble traits of character that were ever manifest in all his deeds and words, raised Mr. Birney to the highest point in the estimation of all Abolitionists. When, therefore, they had become weary of striving to induce one or the other of the political parties to recognize the rights of the colored population of the country; when they had found that neither the Whigs nor the Democrats would attempt anything for the relief of the millions of the oppressed, but what their *oppressors* approved or consented to; when thus forced to the conclusion that a Third Party must needs be formed in order to compel politicians and statesmen to heed their demands for the relief of suffering outraged millions in our land, James G. Birney was unanimously selected to be their candidate for the presidency. He unquestionably possessed higher qualifications for that office than either of the candidates of the other parties. But, with shame be it said, he had too much faith in the glorious doctrine of the Declaration of Independence, and in the declared purpose of the Constitution of the United States to suit the depraved policy of the nation in 1840. In that year the Liberty party gave a very significant number of votes for Mr. Birney. And again in 1844 their votes for him amounted to 62,300. These votes, if given for Mr. Clay, as they would have been had he been true to "the inalienable rights of man," would have secured his election by a majority of 23,119. This number was too large to be ignored. It showed that the Abolitionists held the balance of power between the Whigs and the Democrats. Their opinions and wishes thenceforward were more respected by politicians and their partisans. Various attempts were made to conciliate them, which, after several political abortions, gave birth to the *Republican party.* This party, we hope and trust, will be guided or forced to pursue such measures as will not only abolish slavery, but raise the colored population of our country to the enjoyment of all the privileges and the exercise of all the prerogatives of American citizens.

JOHN QUINCY ADAMS.

Although this gentleman — so prominent for more than half a century among our American statesmen and scholars—was not a member of our Antislavery Society, he rendered us and our cause, in one respect, a most important service. And as I have some interesting recollections of him, a few pages devoted to them will be german to my plan.

In January, 1835, a petition was committed to Mr. Adams, signed by more than a hundred women of his congressional district, praying for the abolition of slavery in the District of Columbia. He presented it and moved its reference to a select committee. Instantly several Southern representatives sprang to their feet and vehemently opposed even the reception of it. They insisted that Congress ought not to receive such petitions, adapted as they were, if not intended, to create an excitement, and wound the feelings of members from the slaveholding States. Mr. Adams urged the reception of the petition with earnestness and eloquence, reminding his opponents that the feelings of his constituents, and of many of the people of the non-slaveholding States, were deeply wounded by being held in any way responsible for the continuance of such a system of oppression as they considered slavery. No right of the people, he said, could be more vital, or should be held as more sacred, than the *right of petition*, — the right to implore their rulers to relieve them of any unnecessary burden, or to correct what seemed to them a grievous wrong. He besought the representatives of the American people to show their respect for the right of petition by receiving the paper he now presented. If there were any expressions in the language of this petition disrespectful or improper, let the signers of it be reproved. It might be easy, he added, to show that this prayer of his constituents ought not to be granted, but that was no reason for refusing to hear their request. To petition is a right guaranteed to every one by the Constitution, of our Republic, — yes, a right inherent in the constitution of man, and Congress is not authorized to deny it or to abridge it. Such was the effect of his speech that the petition was received. But it was immediately laid on the table.

Again in January, 1837, Mr. Adams offered a petition of the same tenor, signed by a hundred and fifty women. Forthwith several Southern members passionately objected to the reception of it. Mr. Adams planted himself as firmly as before in defence of the *right of petition*. He charged upon the opposers that they were violating most fearfully the federal Constitution, which they had sworn to support. He besought the House not to give its countenance, its sanction, to the violent assaults which had been made in our country within the last eighteen months upon the freedom of the press and the liberty of speech, by denying the still more fundamental right, — the *right of petition;* and this "to a class of citizens as virtuous and pure as the inhabitants of any section of the United States."

A violent debate ensued, in which Mr. Adams maintained his part with so much fortitude, dignity, and force of argument that the petition was received by a large majority. I am sorry to add that it was soon after laid on the table by a majority almost as large. And a few days afterwards, on the 18th of January, 1837, the House of Representatives passed this infamous resolution:

"That all petitions relating to slavery, *without being printed or referred*, shall be laid on the table, and no action shall be had thereon." This resolution, intended to shut the door of legislative justice and mercy against millions of the most cruelly oppressed people on earth, was passed in the Congress of these United States by a vote of 139 ayes to 96 nays.

Petitions for the abolition of slavery in the District of Columbia had been sent to Mr. Adams and to other members of Congress, from various parts of the country. For it was the feeling of Abolitionists everywhere that we were all, in some measure, directly responsible for the continuance of slavery in that District, over which Congress had then, and has now, exclusive jurisdiction. Seeing how such petitions were to be spurned, by the advice of the managers of the Antislavery Society, I addressed a letter to Mr. Adams, proposing that thereafter our petitions should be "for the removal of the national capital to some place north of Mason and Dixon's line." He replied that nothing would be gained by such a change. Petitions so worded, coming from Abolitionists, would be treated with the same contempt. And he thought it better to persist in demanding the abolition of slavery in the District, and contend for the right of petition on that issue.

Nothing daunted by the high-handed measure of January 18th, Mr. Adams, on the 6th of the following month, announced to the Speaker that he held in his hand a petition which purported to come from a number of slaves, without, however, stating what it prayed for. Before presenting it, he wished to be informed by the Speaker whether such a paper would come under the order of the 18th ult. Without waiting for the decision, several slaveholders rose in quick succession and poured out their astonishment, their indignation, their wrath at the effrontery of the man who could propose to offer such a petition, — a petition from slaves! One said it was so gross an insult to the House that the paper ought to be taken and burnt. Another insisted that the representative from Massachusetts deserved the severest censure, yes, that he ought to be immediately brought to the bar of the House and reproved by the Speaker. Others demanded that Mr. Adams should be forthwith expelled from his seat with those he had so grossly insulted.

Amidst this storm Mr. Adams remained as little moved as "the house that was founded upon a rock." When it had spent its rage enough for a human voice to be heard, the brave "old man eloquent" rose and said: "Mr. Speaker, to prevent further consumption of the time of the House, I deem it my duty to request the members to modify their several resolutions so that they may be in accordance with the facts. I did not present the petition. I only informed the Speaker that I held in my hand a paper purporting to be a petition from slaves, and asked if such a petition would come under the general order of January 18th. I stated distinctly that I should not send the paper to the table until that question was decided. This is one *fact*, and one of the resolutions offered to the House should be amended to accord with it.

"Another gentleman alleged in his resolution that the paper I hold is a petition from slaves, praying for the abolition of slavery. Now, Mr. Speaker, that is not the fact. If the House should choose to hear this paper read they would learn that it is a petition the reverse of what the resolution states it to be. If, therefore, the gentleman from Alabama still shall choose to call me to the bar of the House, he will have to amend his resolution by stating in it that my crime has been attempting to introduce a petition from slaves, praying that slavery may *not* be abolished, — precisely that which the gentleman desires."

A variety of absurd and incoherent resolutions were proposed, and as many abusive speeches were made, after which the following were adopted: "*Resolved,* That this House cannot receive the said petition without disregarding its own dignity, the rights of a large class of citizens of the South and West, and the Constitution of the United States." Yeas, 160. Nays, 35. "*Resolved,* That slaves do not possess the right of petition secured to the people of the United States by the Constitution." Yeas, 162. Nays, 18.

None of the Northern representatives interposed to aid Mr. Adams in the conflict, excepting only Messrs. Lincoln and Cushing, of Massachusetts, and Mr. Evans, of Maine. These gentlemen defended his positions with distinguished ability. But the "old man eloquent" was a host in himself, — a match for all who rose up against him. Through the whole of the unparalleled excitement he behaved with exemplary equanimity and admirable self-possession. "His speech, in vindication of his cause," said Mr. Garrison, "was the hewing of Agag in pieces by the hand of Samuel." His exposure of the vice and licentiousness of slaveholding communities was unsparing. His sarcasms were as cutting as the surgeon's knife. His rebukes were terrible. He contended that there was not a word, not an intimation in the Constitution, excluding petitions from slaves. "The right of petition," said he, "God gave to the whole human race when he made them *men,* — the right of prayer, — the right of those who need to ask a favor of those who can bestow it. It belongs to humanity; it does not depend upon the condition of the petitioners. It belongs to the wronged, the destitute, the wretched. Those who most need relief of any kind have the best right to petition for it, *enslaved men more than all others.* Did the gentleman from South Carolina think he could frighten me by his threat of a grand jury? Let me tell him *he mistook his man;* I am not to be frightened from the discharge of a duty by his indignation, nor by all the grand juries in the universe. Mr. Speaker, I never was more serious in any moment of my life. I never acted under a more solemn sense of duty. What I have done I should do again under the same circumstances if it were to be done to-morrow."

For this dignified, persistent, heroic defence of the right of petition Mr. Adams deserved the gratitude of all the suffering, and those who desired their relief, — of the enslaved and those who were laboring for their redemption. But in the course of the debate he said, "It is well known to all the members of this house that, from the day I entered this hall to the present moment, I have invariably, here and elsewhere, declared my opinion to be adverse to the prayer of petitions which call for the abolition of slavery in the District of Columbia. I have, however, uniformly insisted, and do insist, that such petitions ought to be respectfully received, duly considered, and our reasons given for refusing to grant them."

Such a declaration from the champion of our petitions, it will readily be believed, disconcerted us Abolitionists not a little. Some denounced him. Many thought he certainly ought not to be returned to Congress again.

I was then one of his constituents, living about thirteen miles from his residence. I was as much disconcerted as any were by Mr. Adams's opposition to the prayer of our petition, and could not rest without hearing from himself his reasons for that opposition. Accordingly, soon after his return to Quincy, in the summer of 1837, I called at his house. He received me graciously, and, on being told what was the object of my visit, he thanked me for coming to himself to learn what were the principles by which he endeavored to govern his conduct as a member of the National Legislature, and what the reasons for the opinion he held respecting the abolition of slavery in the District of Columbia by an act of Congress. "You cannot doubt," said he, "that I desire the abolition of slavery there, and everywhere, as much as you or any Abolitionist desires it. I am ready to do all that I think can be done legally to exterminate that great wrong, that alarming evil, that dark shame from our country. I shall ever withstand any plan for the extension of slavery in any direction an inch beyond the limits within which unhappily it existed at the formation of our Union. I have repeatedly declared myself at any time ready to go for the most stringent prohibition of our interstate slave-trade, putting it under the same ban with the foreign slave-trade.* But, sir, the citizens of the District of Columbia are in an anomalous condition, — a condition not to be reconciled with one of the fundamental principles of our democratic institutions. They are governed by laws enacted by a Legislature in which they have no representative, and to the enactment of which they have given no consent. Whenever, therefore, I am called upon to act as a legislator for the District of Columbia, I feel myself to be all the more bound in honor to act as if I were a representative chosen by the people of that District, that is, to act in accordance with what I know to

* On that occasion, or another, I am not sure which, Mr. Adams announced another very pregnant opinion which he was ready to maintain; namely, that slaveholders had no right to bring or send their slaves into a free State, and keep them in slavery there; but that whenever slaves were brought into any State where all the people were free, they became partakers of that freedom, were slaves no longer.

be the will of my quasi constituents. Therefore, until I know that the people of that District generally desire the abolition of slavery, I cannot vote for it consistently with my idea of the duty of a representative."

Of course I demurred at the sufficiency of this reason, and urged several objections to it. But I need not add a stern old statesman was not to be moved from his allegiance to a principle which he said had governed him through his long political life.

I left him dissatisfied and doubting whether I could help by my vote to re-elect him to Congress. I conferred much with some of the leading Abolitionists in his district. They were troubled in like manner. But we could think of no man who could be elected in his place that would go further in opposition to slavery than Mr. Adams had gone, or could utter such scathing condemnation of our American despotism. When, too, we reviewed the course he had pursued in Congress in defence of the right of petition, and considered his venerable age, his high official and personal character, his intimate acquaintance with every part of the history of our country, his unequalled adroitness in the conduct of a legislative debate, the insults and abuse he had endured in Congress, because of his words and acts bearing upon the subject of slavery, and his perfect fearlessness in the midst of the angry, violent, bullying slaveholders, we came to the conclusion that it would be most unjust, ungrateful, and unwise in Abolitionists to withhold their support from Mr. Adams. We determined rather to rally about him.

And first we thought it would be becoming in his constituents to give some public and emphatic expression of their high and grateful appreciation of his faithfulness and heroic courage, in advocating and maintaining the sacred right of petition. Accordingly, we conferred with the prominent members of the Whig party in his district, who, after some hesitation, agreed to unite with us in calling a delegated convention to consider the alarming assaults that had been made in the Congress of the nation upon the right of petition, and the noble defence of that right by the venerable and illustrious representative of the twelfth Congressional District.

Such a convention was held in Quincy, on the 23d of August, 1837. Seventeen towns were represented by delegates, and a large number of other citizens were present.

Hon. Thomas Greenleaf, of Quincy, was chosen President. Hon. Cushing Otis, of South Scituate, and Hon. John B. Turner, of Scituate, Vice-Presidents. Hon. Gershom B. Weston, of Duxbury, and Orrin P. Bacon, Esq., of Dorchester, Secretaries. The forenoon was spent in listening to speeches upon the sacredness of the right of petition, the assaults made upon that right in the Congress of our nation, and the persistent, dauntless, noble defence of it by our representative. A series of appropriate resolutions was passed and a committee appointed to present a copy of them to Mr. Adams, and request him to favor the convention with his presence in the afternoon.

We reassembled soon after 2 P. M., and were informed by the committee that Mr. Adams would be with us at three o'clock. There was no other business before the convention. Several topics were proposed by resolutions or motions that were ruled out of order, as not german to the purpose of the meeting. Members were getting impatient. I had begun to fear that some of our ardent ones would break over the agreement under which the convention had been called. Just at this crisis our excellent friend, Francis Jackson, of Boston, came into the hall. His face was radiant with his message of glad tidings. He came straight towards me, and placed in my hand a paper covered with lines, in the clear, beautiful handwriting of that true philanthropist, John Pierpont, with which I was familiar. "A Word from a Petitioner." Nothing could have been more timely, nothing more appropriate. I seized it, and commenced reading at once: —

"What! our petitions spurned! The prayer
Of thousands, tens of thousands, cast
Unheard beneath your Speaker's chair!
But you *will* hear us first or last.
The thousands that last year ye scorned
Are millions now. Be warned! Be warned!"

The reading of this first stanza brought down the house in rapturous applause. It struck the key-note to which the feelings of all were attuned. Every stanza was received with some response of approval or delight. When the last line was read and I began to fold the paper, "Encore! Encore!!" resounded from every part of the hall. So I read the admirable poem again and better than the first time. And just as I was reading the last stanza, Mr. Adams entered the convention escorted by the committee. Now the applauses rose in deafening cheers. "Hurrah! Hurrah!! Hurrah!!! the hero comes!!!!" Three times three and then again. Mr. Adams tottered to his seat next the President, wellnigh overcome with emotion. And when the uproar ceased and he rose to speak he seemed for the moment no more "the old man eloquent." He could not utter a word. He stood trembling before us. But the moment passed, and the orator was himself again. His first words were: "My friends, my neighbors, my constituents, though I tremble before *you*, I hope, I trust you know that I have never trembled before the enemies of your liberties, your sacred rights." Again was the assembly thrown into an uproar of applause, which did not die away until his self-possession had entirely revived. And then he addressed us for nearly an hour, giving a very graphic account of his conflict with the slaveholders in Congress, and making it evident, perhaps more evident to us than to himself, that some of them were determined to rule or else to ruin our Republic.

By order of the convention a memorial was sent to our fellow-citizens of each congressional district in the Commonwealth, commending to their just appreciation the conduct of Mr. Adams in defence of the right of petition, and praying them to send representatives who would be equally true, faithful, fearless in withstanding the enemies of freedom.

THE ALTON TRAGEDY.

Rev. Elijah P. Lovejoy was a young Presbyterian minister, a native of Maine, who soon after his graduation from college settled in the city of St. Louis, first as a school-teacher, then as a preacher, and lastly as the editor of a religious paper. In all these offices he had commended himself to the respect and affectionate regards of a large circle of friends. He conducted his paper to very general acceptance, until he became an Abolitionist. An awful, a diabolical deed perpetrated in or near St. Louis, compelled him to look after the evil influences which could have prepared any individuals to be guilty of such an atrocity, and the community in which it was done to tolerate it.

Some time in the latter part of 1836, or the beginning of 1837, a slave was accused of a heinous crime (not worse, however, than many white men had been guilty of). He was tried by a Lynch Court, over which a man most appropriately named Judge Lawless presided. He was found guilty, sentenced *to be burned alive*, and actually suffered that horrid death at the hands of American citizens, some of whom were called "most respectable." Mr. Lovejoy faithfully denounced the horrible outrage as belonging to the Dark Ages and a community of savages, and thenceforward devoted a portion of his paper to the exposure of the sinfulness and demoralizing influence of slaveholding. This was not long endured. His printing-office was broken up, his press destroyed, and he was driven out of the State of Missouri. He removed about twenty miles up the Mississippi River to Alton, Illinois, and there commenced the publication of a similar paper, called the *Alton Observer*. But though in a nominally free State, he was not beyond the power of the slaveholders. The people of that town, obsequious to the will and tainted with the spirit of their Southern and Southwestern neighbors, soon followed the example of the Missourians, demolished his printing-office and threw his press into the river.

Mr. Lovejoy was a man whose determination to withstand oppression was a high moral principle rather than a resentful passion. He therefore set about, with calm resolution, to re-establish his office and his paper. In this he was encouraged and assisted by the sympathy and the contributions of some of the best people in Alton, St. Louis, and that region of country. But he had issued only one or two numbers of his *Observer*, before the ruffians again fell upon his establishment and destroyed it.

This second violation of his rights, in a State professedly free, brought him and his patrons to feel that they were indeed "set for the defence" of the liberty of the press. They appealed in deeper tones of earnest remonstrance and solemn warning to their fellow-citizens, to their countrymen, to all who appreciated the value of our political institutions, to help them re-establish and maintain their desecrated press. They called a convention of the people to consider the disgrace that had been brought upon their town and State, and to awaken a public sentiment that would overbear the minions of the slaveholding oligarchy, which was assuming to rule our nation. Dr. Edward Beecher, of Jacksonville, came to Alton and spoke with wisdom and power in defence of the *Alton Observer*, and its devoted editor.

Mr. Lovejoy gave notice that he felt it to be a momentous duty incumbent on him, there to vindicate the precious right which had been so ruthlessly outraged in his person and property. He gave notice that he had taken measures to procure another printing-press and materials for the publication of his paper. He hoped the violent men, who had twice broken up his office, would see their fearful mistake and molest him no more. He trusted the good people of Alton and the officials of their city would see to it that he should be protected, if the spirit of outrage should again appear in their midst.

Many of the good people of the place gathered about him with assurances of help, if needed. A Mr. Gilman, by all acknowledged to be one of the very best men in the community, readily consented to receive the press into his store for safe-keeping, and many other gentlemen agreed to come there to defend it, if any attempt to take it away should be made.

As the day drew near on which the press was to arrive, alarming threats were heard about the city, and evidences of preparation for another deed of violence were too plain to be mistaken. Mr. Gilman called upon the Mayor for protection, — to appoint a special police for the occasion, or to have an armed force in readiness, if the emergency should require their interposition. That official informed him that he had no military at his service, and did not feel authorized to appoint a special police. Then Mr. Gilman craved to know if the Mayor would authorize him to collect an armed force to protect his property if it should be assaulted. The Mayor gave him to understand that he would be justified in so doing.

The boat arrived in the night of the 6th of November, and the press was safely deposited in Messrs. Godfrey & Gilman's store. The next evening a mob assembled with the declared purpose of destroying the press or the building that contained it, in which were goods valued at more than $100,000. Mr. Gilman went out and calmly remonstrated with the mob. He assured them that it was his determination, as it was his right, to defend his own property and that of another, which had been committed to him for safe-keeping, and that he was prepared so to do; that there were a considerable number of loaded muskets in his store and resolute men there to use them. He had no wish to harm any one, and besought them to refrain from their threatened assault, which would certainly be repulsed. They heeded him not, but reiterated their cries for the onset. It was agreed between himself, Mr. Lovejoy, and their helpers that they would forbear until there could be no longer any doubt of the fell purpose of the assailants. The suspense was brief. Stones and other heavy missiles were thrown against the building and through the windows. These were quickly followed by bullets. At this several of the besieged party fired upon the mob, killing one man and wounding another. After a temporary retreat, the madmen returned bringing materials with which to fire the store. A ladder was raised and a torch applied to the roof. Mr. Lovejoy came out and aimed his musket at the incendiary. So soon as he was recognized he was fired upon and fell, his bosom pierced by five bullets.

Mr. Garrison and most of the oldest Abolitionists regretted that Mr. Lovejoy and his friends had resorted to deadly weapons. If he was to fall in our righteous cause we wished that he had chosen to fall an unresisting martyr. From the beginning we had determined not to harm our foes. And though we had been insulted, buffeted, starved, imprisoned, our houses sacked, our property destroyed, our buildings burnt, not the life of one of our number had hitherto been lost. But we doubted not that our devoted brother had been governed by his highest sense of right. He had acted in accordance with the accepted morality of the Christian world, and in the spirit of our Revolutionary fathers. A sensation of horror at the murder of that amiable and excellent young man thrilled the hearts of all the people that were not steeped in the insensibility to the rights of humanity which slaveholding produces. The 7th of November, 1837, was fixed in the calendar as one of the days never to be forgotten in our country, nor remembered but with shame.

The American Antislavery Society, the Massachusetts, and other kindred societies took especial and very appropriate notice of the dreadful outrage, and renewed their solemn pledges to labor all the more assiduously, for the utter extermination of that system of iniquity in the land, which could be upheld only at the expense of our freedom of speech and the liberty of the press.

Rev. Dr. Channing and many more of the prominent citizens of Boston were moved to call a public meeting in their "Old Cradle of Liberty," without distinction of sect or party, there to express the alarm and horror which were felt at the outrage on civil liberty, and the murder of a Christian minister, for attempting to maintain his constitutional and inalienable rights. Accordingly, the Doctor and a hundred other gentlemen made an application to the Mayor and Aldermen of the city for permission to occupy Faneuil Hall for that purpose. Their application was rejected as follows:—

"City of Boston. In Board of Aldermen, November 29, 1837: On the petition of William E. Channing and others, for the use of Faneuil Hall on the evening of Monday, the 4th of December,

"*Resolved*, That in the opinion of this Board, it is inexpedient to grant the prayer of said petition, for the reason that resolutions and votes passed by a public meeting in Faneuil Hall are often considered, in other places, as the expression of public opinion in this city; but it is believed by the Board that the resolutions which would be likely to be sanctioned by the signers of this petition on this occasion ought not to be regarded as the public voice of this city."

This extraordinary conduct of the city authorities kindled a fire of indignation throughout the city and the Commonwealth, that sent forth burning words of surprise and censure. Dr. Channing addressed an eloquent and impressive "letter to the citizens of Boston," that produced the intended effect. It was widely circulated, and everywhere read with deep emotion. A public meeting was called by gentlemen who were not Abolitionists, to be held in the old Supreme Court Room, "to take into consideration the reasons assigned by the Mayor and Aldermen for withholding the use of Faneuil Hall, and to act in the premises as may be deemed expedient." A large concourse of citizens assembled. George Bond, Esq., was chosen chairman, and B. F. Hallett, Secretary. Dr. Channing's letter was read, and then a series of resolutions, "drawn up with consummate ability and strikingly adapted to the occasion," were offered by Mr. Hallett, and after an animated discussion were unanimously adopted. A committee of two from each ward was appointed to renew the application (precisely in the words of the former one) for the use of Faneuil Hall, and to obtain signatures to the same. This request was not to be denied. The Mayor and Aldermen yielded to the pressure.

On the 8th of December the doors of Faneuil Hall were thrown open, and as many people as could find a place pressed in. Hon. Jonathan Phillips was called to the chair, and made some excellent introductory remarks. Dr. Channing then made an eloquent and impressive address, after which B. F. Hallett, Esq., read the resolutions which Dr. Channing had drawn up. These were seconded by George S. Hillard, Esq., in a very able speech. Then arose James T. Austin, the Attorney-General, and made a speech in the highest degree inflammatory and mobocratic. He declared that "Lovejoy died as the fool dieth." He justified the riotous procedure of the Altonians, and compared them to "the patriotic Tea-Party of the Revolution." What he said of the slaves was really atrocious. Hear him!

"We have a menagerie in our city with lions, tigers, hyenas, an elephant, a jackass or two, and monkeys in plenty. Suppose, now, some new cosmopolite, some man of philanthropic feelings, not only towards men but animals, who believes that all are entitled to freedom as an inalienable right, should engage in the humane task of giving liberty to these wild beasts of the forest, some of whom are nobler than their keepers, or, having discovered some new mode to reach their understandings, should try to induce them *to break their cages and be free?* The people of Missouri had as much reason to be afraid of their *slaves* as we should have to be afraid of the wild beasts of the menagerie. They had the same dread of Lovejoy that we should have of this supposed instigator, if we really believed the bars would be broken and the caravan let loose to prowl about our streets."

Though this was the most disgusting passage in Mr.

Austin's speech, nearly all of it was offensive to every true American heart, and some parts were really impious. He likened the Alton and St. Louis rioters to the men who inspired and led our Revolution. He infused so much of his riotous spirit into a portion of his audience that at the close of his speech they attempted to break up the meeting in an uproar. Happily for the reputation of Boston, there were present a preponderance of the moral *élite* of the city. So soon as the disorder had subsided, a young man, then unknown to most of his fellow-citizens, took the platform, and soon arrested and then riveted the attention of the vast assembly to a reply to the Attorney-General that was "sublime, irresistible, annihilating." I wish there were room in these columns for the whole of it. I can give you but a brief passage.

"Mr. Chairman, when I heard the gentleman lay down principles which placed the rioters, incendiaries, and murderers of Alton side by side with Otis and Hancock, with Quincy and Adams, I thought those pictured lips [pointing to the portraits in the hall] would have broken into voice to rebuke the recreant American, the slanderer of the dead. [Great applause and counter-applause.] Sir, the gentleman said that he should sink into insignificance if he dared not to gainsay the principles of the resolutions before this meeting. Sir, for the sentiments he has uttered on soil consecrated by the prayers of Puritans and the blood of patriots, the earth should have yawned and swallowed him up!"

I need only tell my readers that this was the *début* of our Wendell Phillips, who has since become the leading orator of our nation, and the dauntless champion of our enslaved, down-trodden countrymen. He was then just established in the practice of law in Boston, with the most brilliant prospect of success in his profession. No young man would have risen so soon as he, or to so great a height as an advocate at the bar and a speaker in the forum, if he had pursued his course as a lawyer and a politician. But, blessed be the God of the oppressed, the cry of the millions, to whom in our Republic every right of humanity was denied, entered into his bosom. He espoused their cause with no hope of fee or reward, but that best of all compensations, the consciousness of having relieved suffering, and maintained great moral and political principles, and throughout the thirty-two years that have since passed away, he has consecrated his brilliant powers to the service of the enslaved with an assiduity and effect of which our whole nation has been the admiring witness.

Another young man, to whom we owe scarcely less than to Mr. Phillips, was brought into our ranks and impelled to take upon himself the odium of an Abolitionist by the awful catastrophe at Alton, — a young man bearing a name illustrious in the history of our country, and still highly honored in our State and nation. I allude to Edmund Quincy, a son of Hon. Josiah Quincy, who, having filled almost every other office in the gift of the people, was then President of Harvard College, and grandson of Josiah Quincy, Jr., one of the leading spirits of the American Revolution.

From the beginning of our antislavery efforts Mr. Edmund Quincy had been deeply interested in our undertaking. But, like very many others, he distrusted the wisdom of some of our measures, and especially the terrible severity of Mr. Garrison's condemnation of slaveholders.

The outrages perpetrated upon Mr. Lovejoy and the liberty of the press at St. Louis and Alton dispelled all doubt of the unparalleled iniquity of holding human beings in the condition of domesticated brutes, and of the sinfulness of all who consent thereto. He has since been one of the towers of our strength; has presided, often with signal ability, at our meetings in the most troublous times, and occasionally spoken with force and marked effect. But he has rendered us especial services by his able pen. His contributions to *The Anti-slavery Standard* and *The Liberator* have been numerous and invaluable. His style has been as vigorous and penetrating as that of Junius, and his satire sometimes as keen. Thus have the attempts of slaveholders and their minions to crush the spirit of liberty served rather to bring to her standard the ablest defenders.

WOMAN QUESTION. — MISSES GRIMKÉ.

The title of this article announces a great event in the progress of our antislavery conflict, and opens a subject the adequate treatment of which would fill a volume much larger than I intend to impose upon the public.

From the beginning of Mr. Garrison's enterprise excellent women were among his most earnest, devoted, unshrinking fellow-laborers. Their moral instincts made them quicker to discern the right than most men were, and their lack of political discipline left them to the guidance of their convictions and humane feelings. Would that I could name all the women who rendered us valuable services when we most needed help. In our early meetings, at our lectures, public discussions, &c., a large portion of our auditors were females, whose sympathy cheered and animated us. Among our first and fastest friends in Boston were Mrs. L. M. Child, Mrs. M. W. Chapman, and her sisters, the Misses Weston, and her husband's sisters, Miss Mary and Miss Ann G. Chapman, and their cousin, Miss Anna Green, now Mrs. Wendell Phillips,—then, as now, in feeble health, but strong in faith and unfaltering in purpose. There, too, were Mrs. E. L. Follen and her sister, Miss Susan Cabot, Miss Mary S. Parker, Mrs. Anna Southwick, Mrs. Mary May, Mrs. Philbrick, Miss Henrietta Sargent, and others. In Philadelphia we found wholly with us, Lucretia Mott, Esther Moore, Lydia White, Sarah Pugh, Mrs. Purvis, the Misses Forten, and Mary Grew. In New York, too, there were many with whom I did not become personally acquainted. And indeed wherever in our country the doctrine of "immediate, unconditional emancipation" (first taught by a woman *) was proclaimed there were found good women ready to embrace and help to propagate it. Often were they our self-appointed committees of ways and means, and by fairs and other pleasant devices raised much money to sustain our lecturers and periodicals. The contributions from their pens were frequent and invaluable. I have already spoken of Mrs. Child's "Appeal," and of her many other excellent antislavery writings. I ought also to acknowledge our indebtedness to her as the editor, for several years, of *The Antislavery Standard*, which, without compromising its fidelity or efficiency, she made very attractive by its literary qualities and its entertaining and instructive miscellany.

Mrs. Maria W. Chapman, who wielded gracefully a trenchant pen, plied it busily in our cause with great effect. Her successive numbers of "Right and Wrong in Boston" were too incisive not to touch the feelings of the good people of that metropolis, which claimed to be the birthplace of American independence, but had ceased to be jealous for "the inalienable rights of man." Year after year her "Liberty Bell" rung out the clearest notes of personal, civil, and spiritual liberty, and she

* Elizabeth Heyrick, of Leicester, England.

compiled our Antislavery Hymn Book, — "The Songs of the Free," — effusions of her own and her sisters' warm hearts, and of their kindred spirits in this country and England.

But though the excellent women whom I have named, and many more like them, constantly attended our meetings, and often *suggested* the best things that were said and done at them, they could not be persuaded to utter their thoughts aloud. They were bound to silence by the almost universal sentiment and custom which forbade "women to speak in meeting."

In 1836 two ladies of a distinguished family in South Carolina — Sarah and Angelina E. Grimké — came to New York, under a deep sense of obligation to do what they could in the service of that class of persons with whose utter enslavement they had been familiar from childhood. They were members of the "Society of Friends," and were moved by the Holy Spirit, as the event proved, to come on this mission of love. They made themselves acquainted with the Abolitionists, our principles, measures, and spirit. These commended themselves so entirely to their consciences and benevolent feelings that they advocated them with great earnestness, and enforced their truth by numerous facts drawn from their own past experience and observation.

In the fall of 1836 Miss A. E. Grimké published an "Appeal to the Women of the South," on the subject of slavery. This evinced such a thorough acquaintance with the American system of oppression, and so deep a conviction of its fearful sinfulness, that Professor Elizur Wright, then Corresponding Secretary of the American Antislavery Society, urged her and her sister Sarah to come to the city of New York and address ladies in their sewing-circles, and in parlors, to which they might be invited to meet antislavery ladies and their friends.

No man was better able than Professor Wright to appreciate the value of the contributions which these South Carolina ladies were prepared to make to the cause of impartial liberty and outraged humanity. As early as 1833, while Professor of Mathematics and Natural Philosophy in Western Reserve College, he published an elaborate and powerful pamphlet on "The Sin of Slaveholding," which we accounted one of our most important tracts. Commended by him and by others who had read her "Appeal," Miss Grimké and her sister attracted the antislavery women of New York in such numbers that soon no parlor or drawing-room was large enough to accommodate those who were eager to hear them. The Rev. Dr. Dunbar, therefore, offered them the use of the vestry or lecture-room of his church for their meetings, and they were held there several times. Such, however, was the interest created by their addresses, that the vestry was too small for their audiences. Accordingly, the Rev. Henry G. Ludlow opened his church to them and their hearers, of whom a continually increasing number were gentlemen.

Early in 1837 the Massachusetts Antislavery Society invited these ladies to come to Boston to address meetings of those of their own sex. But it was impossible to keep them thus exclusive, and soon, wherever they were advertised to speak, there a large concourse of men as well as women was sure to be assembled. This was an added offence, which our opposers were not slow to mark, nor to condemn in any small measure. It showed plainly enough that "the Abolitionists were ready to set at naught the order and decorum of the Christian church."

My readers may smile when I confess to them that at first I was myself not a little disturbed in my sense of propriety. But I took the matter into serious consideration. I looked the facts fully in the face. Here were millions of our countrymen held in the most abject, cruel bondage. More than half of them were females, whose condition in some respects was more horrible than that of the males. The people of the North had consented to this gigantic wrong with those of the South, and those who had risen up to oppose it were denounced as enemies of their country, were persecuted, their property and their persons violated. The pulpit for the most part was dumb, the press was everywhere, with small exceptions, wielded in the service of the oppressors, the political parties were vying with each other in obsequiousness to the slaveholding oligarchy, and the petitions of the slaves and their advocates were contemptuously and angrily spurned from the legislature of the Republic. Surely, the condition of our country was wretched and most perilous. I remembered that in the greatest emergencies of nations women had again and again come forth from the retirement to which they were consigned, or in which they preferred to dwell, and had spoken the word or done the deed which the crises demanded. Surely, the friends of humanity, of the right and the true, never needed help more than we needed it. And here had come two well-informed persons of exalted character from the midst of slavedom to testify to the correctness of our allegations against slavery, and tell of more of its horrors than we knew. And shall they not be heard because they are women? I saw, I felt it was a miserable prejudice that would forbid woman to speak or to act in behalf of the suffering, the outraged, just as her heart may prompt and as God has given her power. So I sat me down and penned as earnest a letter as I could write to the Misses Grimké, inviting them to come to my house, then in South Scituate, to stay with us as long as their engagements would permit, to speak to the people from my pulpit, from the pulpit of my excellent cousin, Rev. E. Q. Sewall, Scituate, and from as many other pulpits in the county of Plymouth as might be opened to them.

They came to us the last week of October, 1837, and tarried eight days. It was a week of highest, purest enjoyment to me and my precious wife, and most profitable to the community.

On Sunday evening Angelina addressed a full house from my pulpit for two hours in strains of wise remark and eloquent appeal, which settled the question of the propriety of her "speaking in meeting."

The next afternoon she spoke to a large audience in Mr. Sewall's meeting-house in Scituate, for an hour and a half, evidently to their great acceptance. The following Wednesday I took the sisters to Duxbury, where, in the Methodist Church that evening, Angelina held six hundred hearers in fixed attention for two hours, and received from them frequent audible (as well as visible) expressions of assent and sympathy.

On Friday afternoon I went with them to the Baptist meeting-house in Hanover, where a crowd was already assembled to hear them. Sarah Grimké, the state of whose voice had prevented her speaking on either of the former occasions, gave a most impressive discourse of more than an hour's length on the dangers of slavery, revealing to us some things which only those who had lived in the prison-house could have learnt. Angelina followed in a speech of nearly an hour, in which she made the duty and safety of immediate emancipation appear so plainly that the wayfaring man though a fool must have seen the truth. If there was a person there who went away unaffected, he would not have been moved though an angel instead of Angelina had spoken to him. I said then, I have often said since, that I never have heard from any other lips, male or female, such eloquence as that of her closing appeal. Several gentlemen who had come from Hingham, not disposed nor expecting to be pleased, rushed up to me when the audience began to depart, and after berating me roundly for "going about the neighborhood with these women setting public sentiment at naught and violating the decorum of the church," said "there can be no doubt that they have a right to speak in public, and they ought to be heard; do bring them to Hingham as soon as may be. Our meeting-house shall be at their service." Accordingly, the next day I took them thither, and they spoke there with great effect on Sunday evening, November 5th, from the pulpit of the Unitarian Church, then occupied by Rev. Charles Brooks.

The experience of that week dispelled my Pauline prejudice. I needed no other warrant for the course the Misses Grimké were pursuing than the evidence they gave of their power to speak so as to instruct and deeply impress those who listened to them. I could not believe that God gave them such talents as they evinced to be buried in a napkin. I could not think they would be justified in withholding what was so obviously given them to say on the great iniquity of our country, because they were women. And ever since that day I have been steadfast in the opinion that the daughters of men ought to be just as thoroughly and highly educated as the sons, that their physical, mental, and moral powers should be as fully developed, and that they should be allowed and encouraged to engage in any employment, enter into any profession, for which they have properly qualified themselves, and that women ought to be paid the same compensation as men for services of any kind equally well performed. This radical opinion is spreading rapidly in this country and in England, and it will ultimately prevail, just as surely as that God is impartial and that "in Christ Jesus there is neither bond nor free, neither male nor female." And yet it has been, and is, as strenuously opposed and as harshly denounced as was our demand of the immediate emancipation of the enslaved. Men and women, press and pulpit, statesmen and clergymen, legislative and ecclesiastical bodies have raised the cry of alarm, and pronounced the advocates of the equal rights of women dangerous persons, disorganizers, infidels.

The first combined assault was made upon "The Rights of Women" by the "Pastoral Association of Massachusetts in the fall of 1837 or the spring of 1838, in their spiritual bull against the antislavery labors of the Misses Grimké, which it utterly condemned as unchristian and demoralizing. This, of course, made it the duty, as it was pleasure, of the New England Abolitionists to stand by those excellent women, who had rendered such inestimable services to the cause of the enslaved, the downtrodden, the despised millions of our countrymen. Therefore, at the next New England Antislavery Convention, held in Boston, May, 1838, attended by delegates from eleven States, it was "*Voted*, That all persons present, or who may be present, at subsequent meetings, whether men or women, who agree with us in sentiment on the subject of slavery, be invited to become members and participate in the proceedings of the Convention."

This gave rise to a long and very animated discussion, but was passed by a very large majority. Immediately eight Orthodox clergymen requested to have their names erased from the roll of that Convention, and seven others, including some of our faithful fellow-laborers, presented a protest against the vote, which, by their request, was entered upon the records, and published with the doings of the Convention.

At that same great gathering a committee of three persons was appointed to prepare and transmit a memorial to each and all of the ecclesiastical associations in New England, of every sect, beseeching them to testify against the further continuance in our country of slavery, and take such measures as they might deem best to induce the members of their several denominations who were guilty of the dreadful iniquity to consider and turn away from it. One of that committee was a much respected woman, as well qualified as either of her associates to discharge the duties assigned them. An excellent memorial was prepared and presented in accordance with the vote. But it was very coldly received by some, and rudely treated by others of the ecclesiastical bodies to which it was sent. On the presentation of it to the Rhode Island Congregational Consociation, a scene of great excitement ensued. The memorial was treated with all possible indignity. Most of the brethren who had been earnest for the reception of it, and for such action as it requested, when they were informed that one of the committee by whom the memorial was prepared was a woman, united in a vote "*to turn the illegitimate product from the house, and obliterate from the records all traces of its entrance.*" No deliberative assembly ever behaved in a more indecorous manner. And those who were most active in trampling upon that respectful petition in behalf of bleeding humanity were the professed ministers of Him who came to preach deliverance to the captive. "*O tempora! O mores!!*"

"THE PASTORAL LETTER" AND "THE CLERICAL APPEAL."

Abolitionists from the first were persons of both sexes and all complexions, of every class in society, of every religious denomination, of each of the three learned professions, of both political parties, and of all the various trades and occupations in which men and women engage. Although it is too true that most ministers, especially in the cities, were slow to espouse the cause of the oppressed, yet it is due to them to say that, taking the country through, there were, in proportion to their numbers, more of that profession than of either of the others who embraced the doctrine of "immediate emancipation," advocated it publicly, wrote columns, pamphlets, and volumes in its defence, and suffered no little obloquy and persecution for so doing. And they were, as I have said, of every Protestant sect. Whenever a complete history of our antislavery conflict shall be written, grateful and admiring mention will be made of the valuable services and generous sacrifices of many ministers whose names may not appear in my slight sketches.

These various individuals were evidently moved by one spirit, drawn together by the conviction that there was a great, a fearful iniquity involved in the enslavement of millions of the inhabitants of our land, that if the God-given rights of humanity were (as the founders of our Republic declared them to be) inalienable, then those men, who were holding human beings as their chattels, were setting the will and authority of the Almighty at defiance, and would bring themselves to ruin. Moreover, there was a deep conviction awakened in the hearts of those who openly espoused the cause of the bondmen, that the people of the North were verily guilty in consenting to their enslavement; and, as the States and the churches refused to interfere for their deliverance, it was left for individuals and voluntary associations to do what might be done, so to correct public opinion and awaken the public conscience that slavery could not be tolerated in the land.

Further than this there was little agreement among the early Abolitionists. But this proved to be a mighty solvent. And for years the wonderful, the beautiful, the Christian sight was seen, — Trinitarians and Unitarians, Methodists and Universalists, Baptists and Quakers, laboring together in the cause of suffering fellow-beings, with so much earnestness that they had set aside, for the while, their theological and ritualistic peculiarities, and seemed to rejoice in their release from those narrow enclosures. Coming out of our hall on the second evening of our Convention in Philadelphia, in December, 1833, a young Orthodox minister took my arm with an affectionate pressure, and said, "Brother May, I never thought that I could feel towards a Unitarian as I feel towards you." My reply was: "Dear M., if professing Christians were only real Christians, engaged in the work of the Lord, they could not find the time nor the heart to quarrel about creeds and rites." Wherever I went, preaching the gospel of impartial liberty, I was as cordially received by Orthodox as by Unitarian Abolitionists, until I came to have a much more brotherly feeling towards an antislavery Presbyterian or Baptist or Methodist than I did towards a Unitarian who was proslavery, or indifferent to the wrongs of the bondmen. And this feeling was obviously reciprocated. I was repeatedly invited to preach in the pulpits of Orthodox ministers, and to commune with Orthodox churches. Once I attended a church in company with Miss Ann G. Chapman, one of the most single-minded and true-hearted of women. The invitation to the Lord's table was given in such words as virtually excluded us. Of course we arose and departed. But so soon as the service was over both the minister and deacon (beloved antislavery brethren) came to my lodgings to assure me that the exclusion was not intended, and that whenever Miss Chapman and myself might again be at their church on a similar occasion, they hoped that we would commune there.

I give these facts, and could give many more like them, to show the anti-sectarian tendency of the antislavery reform. This was perceived by many of "the wise and prudent" leaders of the sects, and was evidently watched by them with a jealous eye. As the number of Abolitionists increased, and our influence in the churches came to be felt more and more, many of those leaders joined antislavery societies, partly, no doubt, because they had been brought to see the truth of our doctrines and the importance of the work we were laboring to accomplish, but also in part, if not chiefly (as I was afterwards forced to suspect), because they wished to maintain the ascendency over their sects, and to prevent the obliteration of the lines which separated them from such as they were pleased to consider unsound in faith.

We were greatly encouraged and gladdened by the accessions we received in 1835 and 1836. Many ministers of the evangelical sects joined us, not a few of them Doctors of Divinity. And the obligations of Christians to the bondmen in our land, and the discipline that should be brought to bear on those professing Christians who were holding them in slavery, became the subjects of earnest debate in several of the large ecclesiastical bodies. But we found these new-comers were much disposed to object to the liberty that was allowed on our platform. Generally the president or chairman of our meetings would call upon some one to invoke the divine blessing upon our undertaking. Sometimes, in deference to our Quaker brethren, we would sit in silence until the Spirit moved some one to offer prayer. Then again, persons who were not members of any religious denomination, nay, even some who were suspected of being, if not known to be, unbelievers, infidels, were permitted to co-operate with us, to contribute to our funds, to take part in our deliberations, and to be put upon our committees. This was a scandal in the estimation of those of the "straitest sect." Our only reply was, that as so many, who made the highest professions of Christian faith, turned a deaf ear to the cries of the millions who were suffering the greatest wrongs, we were grateful for the assistance of such as made no professions. Not those who cried Lord, Lord, but those who were eager to do the will of the impartial Father, were the persons we valued most.

But nothing gave so much offence as the admission of women to speak in our meetings, to act on our committees, and to co-operate with us in any way they saw fit. In my last I gave some account of the rupture it caused in our New England Antislavery Convention in 1838. This was foreshadowed the year previous. Some time in the summer of 1837 the General Association of Massachusetts issued a "Pastoral Letter to the churches under their care," intended to avert the alarming evils which were coming upon them from the over-heated zeal of the Abolitionists. First, the extraordinary document mourns over the loss of deference to the pastoral office, which is enjoined in Scripture, and which is essential to the best influence of the ministry. At this day, when all but Roman Catholics and High Church Episcopalians are wondering at, if not amused by, the dealing of Bishop Potter with Mr. Tyng, it may surprise my readers to be told that thirty years ago the Orthodox Congregational ministers of Massachusetts set up the same claim of authority in their several parishes, that the diocesan of New York and New Jersey demands for his clergymen. "One way," they said in their Pastoral Letter, "one way in which the respect due to the pastoral office has been in some cases violated, is in encouraging lecturers or preachers on certain topics of reform to present their subjects within the parochial limits of settled pastors, *without their consent.*" "Your minister is ordained of God to be your teacher, and is commanded to feed that flock over which the Holy Ghost hath made him overseer. If there are certain topics upon which he does not preach with the frequency, or in the manner that would please *you*, it is a violation of *sacred and important* RIGHTS to encourage a stranger to present them." "Deference and *subordination* are essential to the happiness of society, and *peculiarly so* in the relation of a people to their pastor." Happily for those who may come after us, we Abolitionists have done much to emancipate the people from such spiritual bondage, and secure to them the privilege of seeking after knowledge wherever it may be found, and yielding themselves to good influences, let them come through whatever channel they may.

But the "Pastoral Letter" dwelt at greater length upon the dangers which threatened the female character with wide-spread and permanent injury. Forgetting that women were the *bravest*, as well as the most devoted and affectionate of the first disciples of Jesus, that in all ages since they have been prominent among the confessors of Christianity, and that in our day they do more than men to uphold the churches, — forgetting these facts, the frightened authors and signers of that letter uttered themselves thus: "The power of woman is in her *dependence*, flowing from the consciousness of that weakness which God has given her *for* her protection, and which keeps her in those departments of life that form the characters of individuals and of the nation. . . . . But, when she assumes the place and tone of man as a public reformer, *our care and protection of her seem unnecessary*; we put ourselves in self-defence against her; she yields the power which God has given her for protection, and her character becomes unnatural. If the vine, whose strength and beauty is to lean upon the trellis-work and half conceal its clusters, thinks to assume the independence and the overshading nature of the elm, it will not only cease to bear fruit, but will fall in shame and dishonor into the dust." Did not those ministers know — were there not in their day wives who sustained their husbands instead of leaning upon them? women who were the stay and staff of the men of their families — their mental and moral stamina? There have been such women in all other times; we have known and do know such women now. If our antislavery conflict has done nothing else, it has shown that there is neither orthodox nor heterodox, neither white nor black, neither male nor female, but all *are one in the work of the Lord.*

Undismayed by the censure and warning of so exalted a body as the General Association, we Abolitionists continued to labor as we had done, pursuing the same measures, using the same instrumentalities, employing as our agents and lecturers women no less than men, whom we found able as well as willing to do good service. And to several, besides those I have already named, the bondmen and their advocates were immeasurably indebted. Abby Kelly (now Mrs. Foster) performed for years an incredible amount of labor. Her manner of speaking in her best days was singularly effective. Her knowledge of the subject was complete, her facts were pertinent, her arguments forcible, her criticisms were keen, her condemnation was terrible. Few of our agents of either sex did more work while her strength lasted, or did it better.

Susan B. Anthony was one of the living spirits of our financial department, indomitable in her purposes, ingenious in her plans, untiring in her exertions, she not only kept herself continually at work, but spurred all about her to new effort. She has often herself spoken to excellent effect, and more frequently stimulated others to their best efforts.

Miss Sallie Holley has seldom consented to speak in our largest assemblies, or in our cities. But we have very frequently heard of her diligent labors in the rural districts, and of the good fruits she has gathered there. Her eloquence is particularly dignified and impressive.

I should love to tell of Lucy Stone, and Antoinette L. Brown, and Mrs. E. C. Stanton, and Ernestine L. Rose, all wise women and attractive speakers, but their word and work has been given more to the advocacy of "Woman's Rights." The reformation for which they have toiled so long and so well, though the offspring of Abolitionism, is still *more radical;* and to the history of it volumes will hereafter be devoted.

I can here only name Miss Anna E. Dickinson, now one of the most attractive of the popular lecturers. Although another of the women who have been brought out of their retirement by the exigency of the times, yet she came upon the platform about the period at which I intend these recollections shall cease.

As surely as the conflict with slavery has been found to be irrepressible, so surely will it be found to be impossible to suppress the conflict for the rights of women until they shall be securely placed where the Creator intended them to stand, on an entire equality with men in their domestic, social, legal, and political relations.

Not long after the "Pastoral Letter," there came forth from some of the members of the Massachusetts General Association a still more pointed attack upon *The Liberator*, Mr. Garrison and his associates, one which would have been very damaging if it had not been so easily repelled. It was entitled the "Appeal of Clerical

Abolitionists on Antislavery Measures," signed by two Orthodox ministers of Boston, and three in the vicinity of that city. As these gentlemen had belonged to the Antislavery Society, and two of them had been vehement if not fierce in their advocacy of our doctrines, it would seem that they must have known whereof they affirmed. They prefaced their Appeal with a declaration of their lively interest in the cause of the oppressed, their clear perception of the sinfulness and their detestation of slavery. Then they went on to accuse the leading Abolitionists, 1st, of hasty, unsparing, and almost ferocious denunciation "of a certain reverend gentleman because he had resided in the South," without having taken pains to ascertain whether he had been a slaveholder or not; 2d, They accused us of "hasty insinuations" against an Orthodox minister of high standing in Boston, that he was a slaveholder, without having had any proof of the *truth* of the reports we may have heard so damaging to the reverend gentleman's reputation. Their third, fourth, and fifth accusations were, that we had demanded of ministers what we had no right to require of them; had abused them for not doing as we called upon them to do, and, through our zeal in the cause of the enslaved, we had become indifferent to other Christian enterprises, and would withdraw from them the regards of those who co-operated with us, and that we had censured and denounced excellent Christian ministers and church-members because they were not prepared to enter fully into the work of antislavery societies.

This document, coming from such persons, of course was the occasion of no little excitement. Our enemies exulted over it as testimony against us, given by those who had been in our councils and well knew what spirit animated us. Others who had been timid friends, or half inclined to join our ranks, were at first repulsed from us by the apprehension that there was too much truth in these charges.

But as soon as possible elaborate and thorough replies were published to this Appeal, denying the truth of each of the above-named accusations, and showing them to be false. One of the replies was written by Mr. Garrison, in his clear and trenchant style, and showed up the inconsistency as well as the falseness of the accusations by ample quotations from the writings and speeches of Mr. Fitch, the author of the Appeal. The other reply was from the pen of Rev. A. A. Phelps.

This good orthodox brother was then the General Agent of the Antislavery Society, and therefore felt it to be incumbent upon him to repel charges so unjust and so injurious. No one but Mr. Garrison was so competent as he to do this. From an early period Mr. Phelps had been engaged in this great reform. In 1833 or 1834 he published a volume on the subject, which showed how thoroughly he understood the principles, how deeply he was imbued with the spirit, of the undertaking. He gave years of undivided attention to the cause, and by the labors of his pen and his voice rendered essential services. His reply to the Appeal was complete, exhaustive, unanswerable. And thus what was intended to do us harm was overruled for our good. It gave a fair and proper occasion for the fullest exposition to the public of our doctrines, our measures, and of the spirit in which we intended to prosecute them.

I am most happy to conclude this narrative by stating, because it is so highly honorable to Rev. Charles Fitch, the author of the Appeal, that some time afterwards he saw and frankly confessed his fault. On the 9th of January, 1840, in a letter addressed to Mr. Garrison, after a very proper introduction to such a confession, Mr. Fitch said : —

"I feel bound in duty to say to you, sir, that to gain the good-will of man was the only object I had in view in everything which I did relative to the 'Clerical Appeal.' As I now look back upon it, in the light in which it has of late been spread before my own mind (as I doubt not by the Spirit of God), I can clearly see that in all that matter I had no regard for the glory of God or the good of man. If you can make any use of this communication that you think will be an honor to Him, or a service to the cause of truth, dispose of it at your pleasure."

It surely will do good to republish this magnanimous, noble, Christian confession of the wrong that was attempted to be done by that "Clerical Appeal."

DR. CHARLES FOLLEN.

The name of Dr. Follen will send a grateful thrill through the memory of every one who really knew him. He was a dear son of God, and attracted all but such as were repulsed by the spirit of righteousness and freedom. He was a native of that country which gave birth to Luther. The light of civil and religious liberty kindled in Wittenberg shone upon his cradle. He was the son of Protestant parents, and received a religious education with little reference to the dogmas of any sect. He was born in the early years of the French Revolution, — that event which at first revived the hopes of the oppressed subjects of European despots. The Germans, especially those of the smaller members of the Confederacy, hailed the prospect of more liberal institutions in France as the harbinger of a better day for themselves. Charles Follen was just then at the age to receive into the depths of his soul the generous sentiments that were uttered by the purest, best men of Germany. His father, an enlightened civilian and liberal Christian, encouraged the growing ardor of his son in the cause of freedom and humanity.

When, therefore, the German States, finding themselves deceived by Bonaparte, united with one accord to oppose him, Charles Follen, then a student at the University of Giesen, and only nineteen years of age, came forward to act his first public part in the great struggle for civil liberty. He entered the allied army in a volunteer corps of young men, and endured the fatigues and incurred the dangers of those battle-fields, on which were witnessed the death-throes of the first Napoleon's ambition. I have heard him describe his feelings, and what he believed to be the feelings of his youthful comrades, in that so-called "holy war of the people." They refused to wear the trappings of soldiers. They needed not "the pomp and circumstance of war" to rouse or sustain the purpose of their souls. They came into the field of mortal strife as men, not soldiers, to contend for liberty, not laurels. Whenever he spoke of that momentous period of his life, a solemnity came over the calm, sweet face of Dr. Follen, his utterance was subdued, his whole frame pervaded by a deep emotion, so that, much as I differed from him in my opinion of that resort to carnal weapons, I could not doubt that he had thrown himself into the dread conflict with a self-sacrificing, I had almost said, a holy spirit. Körner, "the patriot poet of Germany," was his personal friend, and it is a touching incident that some of his last mental efforts were most successful translations into our language of the breathing thoughts and burning words of that enthusiast of liberty.

Although the issue of the French Revolution cast down the hope of the friends of freedom, that hope was not destroyed. True they had been deceived. But they could not doubt that freedom was a reality, the birthright of man. When, therefore, the real design of the self-styled "Holy Alliance" between Russia, Austria, and Prussia became manifest, many of the choicest spirits who had united under their banner to overthrow the tyrant of France uprose to withstand them. None were more resolute, few became more conspicuous, than the still youthful Follen, who had scarcely entered upon his professional career. He boldly claimed for his fellow-subjects of Hesse Darmstadt a mitigation of the feudal tenures under which they were oppressed. Thus he incurred the displeasure of the Grand Duke. But the farmers of that country gratefully acknowledged the importance of his service in letters that are still extant.

In 1817, when twenty-two years of age, he took his degree of Doctor of Laws, and became a teacher in the University of Jena. Here he found an atmosphere congenial to his free spirit. The most distinguished professors there were friends of liberal institutions. And the Duke of Saxe-Weimar was for a while indulgent towards them. At Jena appeared the first periodical publications that disturbed the diplomatists of Frankfort and Vienna. To these publications Dr. Follen contributed, and, even among such men as Dr. Oken and Professors Fries and Luden, he distinguished himself as an advocate of the rights of man.

The sovereigns of Austria and Prussia were alarmed. The professors of the University at Jena were proscribed, and the young men of Austria and Prussia who were students there were required to leave the infected spot. The persecution of Dr. Follen was carried further. An attempt was made to involve him in the guilt of the deluded murderer of Kotzebue, "that unblushing hireling of the Russian Autocrat," and he was arrested on the charge. He was fully exonerated, but the spirit which dictated his arrest made it uncomfortable for him to remain in Germany.

He went to Switzerland, the resort of the free spirits of that day, and was appointed Professor of Civil Law at the University of Basle. Here he continued, both in his lectures and through the press, to give utterance to his liberal opinions. Consequently, in August, 1824, the governments of Prussia, Austria, and Russia demanded of the government of Basle to deliver him up, with the other Professors of Law in their university. At first this demand was refused. But, being afterwards enforced by a threat of the serious displeasure of the allied powers, it was yielded to, and Dr. Follen was compelled to depart, with no reproach upon his character but that which was cast upon it by the enemies of freedom. Exiled from Germany as the dreaded foe of the oppressors of his country, hunted by the allied sovereigns out of Europe, as if their thrones were insecure while he dwelt on the same continent with themselves — surely the man who made himself such a terror to despots was entitled to a *carte-blanche* on the confidence of freemen!

Thus recommended, he came to our country in December, 1824, a few months after the arrival of Lafayette. The illustrious Frenchman came to feast his eyes and rejoice his heart with the sight of the astonishing growth and unexampled prosperity of the nation for whose deliverance from a foreign yoke he had in his early manhood lavished his fortune and exposed his life. The illustrious German came, as it proved, to assist in a great moral enterprise, the success of which was indispensably necessary to complete the American Revolution, and verify the truths which it declared to the world.

Nearly a year after his arrival he spent in Philadelphia

perfecting himself in the language of our country. But by the advice of Lafayette, who highly esteemed him, he came to Boston, and in December, 1825, was appointed teacher of the German language in Harvard College, where, in 1830, he was raised to a professorship of German literature.

He had not been long in the United States before he was struck by the contrast between our institutions and our habits of thought and conversation. He was surprised that he so seldom met with a free mind, or saw an individual who acted independently. Most persons seemed to be in bonds to a political party or a religious sect, or both. "I perceive," said he to an intimate friend, "that liberty in this country is a fact rather than a principle."

Such a soul as Dr. Follen could not be indifferent to any movement tending to liberate more than three millions of people in the country, of which he had become a citizen, from the most abject cruel slavery, and his fellow-citizens from the awful iniquity of keeping them in such bondage. The bugle-blast of *The Liberator* in 1831 summoned him to the conflict. Worldly wisdom, prudential considerations, would have withheld him if he had been like too many other men. He had then been in a professor's chair at Cambridge about a year. He had married a lady worthy of his love. He had become a father. He had made many friends. He was admired for his rich and varied endowments, his extensive and accurate knowledge, and sound understanding. He was honored for his exertions and sacrifices in the cause of liberty in Europe. He was cherished as an invaluable acquisition to the literature of our country, and as a most successful teacher of youth. How obvious, then, that he had as many reasons as any, and more reasons than most, for remaining quiet, contenting himself with an occasional sigh over the wrongs of the slaves, or an eloquent condemnation of slavery in the abstract, or the utterance of the form of prayer, — that the Sovereign Disposer of all events would, in his own good time, cause every yoke to be broken and oppression to cease. He was occupying a sphere of great responsibility, where, as was intimated to him, he might find enough to fill even the large measure of his ability for labor. Then he was wholly dependent upon his own exertions for the support of his family. Moreover, being a foreigner by birth, he was reminded that it was less decorous in him, than it might be in others, to meddle with the "delicate question" which touched so vitally the institutions of a very sensitive portion of the country.

But Charles Follen was a genuine man. In godly sincerity he felt as well as said, "that whatever affected the welfare of mankind was a matter of concern to himself." He was astonished at the apathy of so large a portion of the respectable and professedly religious of our country to the wretched condition of more than a sixth part of the population, to the disastrous influence of their enslavement upon the characters of their immediate oppressors, upon the well-being of the whole Republic, and the cause of liberty throughout the world. When, therefore, the words of Garrison came to his ears, "he rejoiced in spirit and said, I thank thee, O Father, that thou hast hid these things from the wise and prudent, and hast revealed them unto the babes; even so, Father, for so it seemed good in thy sight." He sought out the editor of *The Liberator*. He clambered up into his little chamber in Merchants' Hall, where were his writing-desk, his types, his printing-press; and where, with the faithful partner of his early toils, Isaac Knapp, he was living like the four children of Israel in the midst of the corruptions of Babylon, living on pulse and water. This was a sight to fill with hope Follen's sagacious soul. While, therefore, many who counted themselves servants of God and friends of humanity thought, or affected to think, that no good could come out of such a Nazareth, he often went to *The Liberator* office to converse with and encourage the young man who had dared to brave the contumely and detestation of the world in "preaching deliverance to the captives and liberty to them that are bruised."

He stopped not to inquire how it might affect his temporal interests, or even his good name, to espouse so unpopular a cause. "Some men," said he, "are so afraid of doing wrong that they never do right." The shameful fact, that the *cause* of millions of enslaved human beings in a country that made such high pretensions to liberty as ours was *unpopular*, so astonished and alarmed him that he felt all the more called to rise above personal considerations. Therefore, soon after the New England Antislavery Society was instituted, he made known his intention to join it. Some friends remonstrated. They admonished him that so doing would be very detrimental to his professional success. He hesitated a little while on account of his wife. But that gifted, high-minded, whole-hearted lady reproved the hesitation, and bade him act in accordance with his sense of duty, and in keeping with his long devotion to the cause of liberty and humanity. He joined the society, became one of its vice-presidents, was an efficient officer, and rendered us invaluable services. At that time I became intimately acquainted with him, and soon learned to love him tenderly and respect him profoundly.

The apprehensions of his friends proved to be too well founded. The funds for the support of his professorship at Cambridge were withheld; and he was obliged to retire from a position which had been most agreeable to himself, for which he was admirably qualified, and in which he had been exceedingly useful. It was a severe trial to his feelings, and the loss of his salary subjected him to no little inconvenience. But liberty, the rights of man, and his sense of duty were more precious to him than physical comforts or even life.

In May, 1834, was held in Boston the first New England Antislavery Convention. It was a large gathering. Dr. Follen was one of the committee of arrangements, and evinced great interest in making the meeting effective.* He was also appointed Chairman of the "address" that was ordered "to the people of the United States," and was the writer of it. His spirit breathes throughout it. It showed how wholly committed he was to the enterprise of the Abolitionists, how thoroughly he understood the principles on which we had from the first relied, and how unfeignedly he desired to make them acceptable to his fellow-citizens by the most lucid exposition of them, and the most earnest presentation of their importance.

In 1835 and 1836 I was the General Agent of the Society. This brought me into a much closer connection with him. It was during the most stormy period, — the time that tried men's souls. I have given some account of it in previous articles, and have made some allusions to Dr. Follen's fidelity and fearlessness. He never quailed. His countenance always wore its accustomed expression of calm determination. He aided us by his counsels, animated us by his resolute spirit, and strengthened us by the heart-refreshing tones of his voice. In this crisis it was, at our annual meeting in January, 1836, that he made his bravest speech. There was not a word, not a tone, not a look of compromise in it. He met our opponents at the very points where some of our

* I am most happy to preserve and make known the fact that Dr. Henry Ware, Jr., then at the head of the Divinity School, and Professor Sidney Willard, of the college in Cambridge, were also members of that Convention.

friends thought us deserving of blame, and he manfully maintained every inch of our ground. That speech may be found in the Appendix to the Memoir of his life. It is not easy even for us to recall, and it is impossible to give to those who were not Abolitionists then, a clear idea of the state of the community at the time the above-named speech was made. The culmination of our trials was the sanction which the Governor of Massachusetts gave to the opinion of one of the judges, that we had committed acts that were punishable at common law. I have given some description of the scenes that were witnessed in the Hall of Representatives. Dr. Follen distinguished himself there. We can never cease to be grateful to him for his pertinacity in withstanding the aggressive overbearance of the Chairman of the joint-committee of the Senate and House appointed to consider our remonstrance against Governor Everett's condemnation of us. I have sometimes thought it was the turning-point of our affairs in the old Commonwealth.

Soon afterwards Dr. Follen removed to New York and became pastor of the first Unitarian church. It was a situation so eligible, and in every respect so desirable to him, that many supposed he would suffer his Abolitionism to become latent, or at least would refrain from giving full and free expression to it in the pulpit. They knew not the man. He did there as he had done elsewhere. Modestly, mildly, yet distinctly, he avowed his antislavery sentiments, and endeavored to make his hearers perceive how imperative was the obligation pressing upon them as patriots, scarcely less than as Christians, to do all in their power to exterminate slavery from our country. He was chosen a member of the Executive Committee of the American Antislavery Society, and promptly accepted the appointment. The members of that Board testified that "his sound judgment, his discriminating intellect, his amenity of manners, and his uncommonly single-hearted integrity greatly endeared him to his associates." Yet was the offence he gave by his antislavery preaching such that, after about two years, his services were dispensed with by the Unitarian church.

He returned to Massachusetts, and soon interested so highly the liberal Christians at East Lexington that he was invited to become their pastor. They set about in 1839 the building of a meeting-house, in accordance with his taste, and after a plan which I believe he furnished. The 15th day of January, 1840, was fixed upon as the day for the dedication, and Dr. Channing was engaged to preach on the occasion.

In December Dr. Follen went to New York and delivered a course of lectures. On the evening of the 13th of January he embarked on board the ill-omened steamer Lexington to return. She took fire in the night, and all the passengers and crew excepting three perished in the flames, or in their attempts to escape from them. Dr. Follen, alas! was not one of the three.

The grief and consternation caused by that awful catastrophe need not be described. Few if any persons in the community had so great cause for sorrow as the Abolitionists. One of the towers of our strength had fallen. The greatness of our loss was dwelt upon at the annual meeting of the Massachusetts Society a few days afterward, and it was unanimously voted: "That an address on the life and character of Charles Follen, and in particular upon his early and eminent services to the cause of abolition, be delivered by such person and at such time and place as the Board of Managers shall appoint." Their appointment fell upon me, and I was requested to give notice so soon as my eulogy should be written. I gave such a notice early in February, when I was informed by the managers that they had not yet been able to procure a suitable place, for such a service as they wished to have in connection with my discourse. They had applied for the use of every one of the Unitarian and for several of the Orthodox churches in Boston, and all had been refused them. It was said that Dr. Channing did obtain from the trustees of Federal Street Church consent that the eulogy on Dr. Follen, whom he esteemed so highly, might be pronounced from his pulpit. But another meeting of the trustees, or of the proprietors, was called, and that permission was revoked. More sad still the meeting-house at East Lexington, which had been built under his direction, which he was coming from New York to dedicate, and in which he was to have preached as the pastor of the church if his life had been spared, — even that meeting-house was refused for a eulogy and other appropriate exercises in commemoration of the early and eminent services of Dr. Follen to the cause of freedom and humanity in Europe, and more especially in our country. Such was the temper of that time, such the opposition of the people in and about the metropolis of New England to Mr. Garrison and his associates.

In consequence of this treatment by the churches, and as a protest against it, the Board of Managers determined to defer the delivery of the eulogy, until the meeting-house of some religious body in Boston should be granted for that purpose. No door was unbarred to us for more than two months. In April one of our fellow-laborers, Hon. Amasa Walker, having become one of the proprietors of Marlborough Chapel, succeeded in getting permission for the Massachusetts Antislavery Society, and other friends of Dr. Follen, to meet in that central and very ample room on the evening of the 17th of April, there to express in prayer, in eulogy, and hymns our gratitude to the Father of spirits for the gift of such a brother, so able, so devoted, so self-sacrificing; to attempt some delineation of his admirable character, some acknowledgment of his inestimable services, and thus make manifest our deep sense of bereavement and loss occasioned by his sudden and as we supposed dreadful death.

It so happened that the 17th of April, 1840, was Good Friday, — a most appropriate day on which to mourn the death and commemorate the glorious life of one who had been so true a disciple of Him, who was crucified on Calvary for his fidelity to God and to the redemption of man.

The assemblage was large, estimated by some at two thousand. A prayer was offered by Rev. Henry Ware, Jr., — such a prayer as we expected would rise from the large, liberal, loving, devout heart of that excellent man. A most appropriate hymn, written by himself, was then read by Rev. John Pierpont. After my discourse was delivered another touching hymn from the pen, or rather the heart, of Mrs. Maria W. Chapman was read by Rev. Dr. Channing, and sung very impressively by the congregation, after which the services were closed by a benediction from Rev. J. V. Himes, a zealous antislavery brother of the Christian denomination.

JOHN G. WHITTIER AND THE ANTISLAVERY POETS.

All great reformations have had their bards. The Hebrew prophets were poets. They clothed their terrible denunciations of national iniquities and their confident predictions of the ultimate triumph of truth and righteousness in imagery so vivid that it will never fade. Mr. Garrison was bathed in their spirit when a child by his pious mother. He is a poet and an ardent lover of poetry. The columns of *The Liberator*, from the beginning, were every week enriched by gems in verse, not unfrequently the product of his own rapt soul. No sentiment inspires men to such exalted strains as the love of liberty. Many of the early Abolitionists uttered themselves in fervid lines of poetry, — Mrs. M. W. Chapman, Mrs. E. L. Follen, Miss E. M. Chandler, Miss A. G. Chapman, Misses C. and A. E. Weston, Mrs. L. M. Child, Mrs. Maria Lowell, Miss Mary Ann Collier, and others, male and female. In 1836 — the time that tried men's souls — Mrs. Chapman gathered into a volume the effusions of the above-named, together with those of kindred spirits in other lands and other times. The volume was entitled, "Songs of the Free and Hymns of Christian Freedom." Many of these songs and hymns will live so long as oppression of every kind is abhorred, and men aspire after true liberty. This book was a powerful weapon in our moral welfare. My memory glows with the recollections of the fervor, and often obvious effect, with which we used to sing in true accord the 13th hymn, by *Miss E. M. Chandler :* —

> "Think of our country's glory
> All dimmed with Afric's tears!
> Her broad flag stained and gory
> With the hoarded guilt of years!"

Or the 15th, by *Mr. Garrison :* —

> "The hour of freedom! come it must.
> O, hasten it in mercy, Heaven!
> When all who grovel in the dust
> Shall stand erect, their fetters riven."

Or the 7th, by *Mrs. Follen :* —

> "'What mean ye, that ye bruise and bind
> My people,' saith the Lord;
> 'And starve your craving brother's mind,
> That asks to hear my word?'"

Or the 102d, by *Mrs. Chapman :*—

"Hark! hark! to the trumpet call,—
'Arise in the name of God most high!'
On ready hearts the deep notes fall,
And firm and full is the strong reply:
'The hour is at hand to do and dare!
Bound with the bondmen now are we!
We may not utter the patriot's prayer,
Or bend in the house of God the knee!'"

Or that stirring song, by *Mr. Garrison :*—

"I am an Abolitionist;
I glory in the name."

The singing of such hymns and songs as these was like the bugle's blast to an army ready for battle. No one seemed unmoved. If there were any faint hearts amongst us, they were hidden by the flush of excitement and sympathy.

In 1838 or 1839 Mrs. Chapman, assisted by her sisters, the Misses Weston, and Mrs. Child, commenced the publication of *The Liberty Bell.* A volume with this title was issued annually by them for ten or twelve years, especially for sale at the yearly antislavery fair. These volumes were full of poetry in prose and verse. The editors levied contributions upon the true-hearted of other countries besides our own, and enriched their pages with articles from the pens of all the above-named, and from Whittier, Pierpont, Lowell, Longfellow, Phillips, Quincy, Clarke, Sewall, Adams, Channing, Bradburn, Pillsbury, Rogers, Wright, Parker, Stowe, Emerson, Furness, Higginson, Sargent, Jackson, Stone, Whipple, our own countrymen and women; and Bowring, Martineau, Thompson, Browning, Combe, Sturge, Webb, Lady Byron, and others, of England; and Arago, Michelet, Monod, Beaumont, Souvestre, Paschoud, and others, of France. It would not be easy to find elsewhere so full a treasury of mental and moral jewels.

The names of most of our illustrious American poets

appear in *The Liberty Bell* more or less frequently. To all of them we were and are much indebted. James Russell Lowell was never, I believe, a member of the Antislavery Society. He was seldom seen at our meetings. But his muse rendered us essential services. His poems — "The Present Crisis," "On the Capture of Fugitive Slaves near Washington," "On the Death of Charles T. Torrey," "To John G. Palfrey," and especially his "Lines to William L. Garrison," and his "Stanzas sung at the Antislavery Picnic in Dedham, August 1, 1843" — committed him fully to the cause of freedom, — the cause of our enslaved countrymen.

Rev. John Pierpont gave us his hand at an earlier day. He took upon himself "our reproach" in 1836, when we most needed help. I have already made grateful mention of his "Word from a Petitioner," sent to me by the hand of the heroic Francis Jackson in the midst of the convention of the constituents of Hon. J. Q. Adams, called at Quincy to assure their brave, invincible representative of their deep, admiring sense of obligation to him for his persistent and almost single-handed defence of the sacred right of petition on the floor of Congress.

Mr. Pierpont's next was a *tocsin* in deed as well as in name. He was impelled to strike his lyre by the alarm he justly felt at the tidings from Alton of the destruction of Mr. Lovejoy's antislavery printing-office, and the murder of the devoted proprietor. His indignation was roused yet more by the burning of "Pennsylvania Hall" in Philadelphia, and the shameful fact that at the same time, 1838, no church or decent hall could be obtained in Boston for "love or money," in which to hold an antislavery meeting; but we were compelled to resort to an inconvenient and insufficient room over the stable of Marlborough Hotel.

His next powerful effusion was *The Gag*, a caustic and

scathing satire upon the Hon. C. G. Atherton, of New Hampshire, for his base attempt in the House of Representatives at Washington to put an entire stop to any discussion of the subject of slavery.

His next piece was *The Chain*, a most touching comparison of the wrongs and sufferings of the slaves with other evils that injured men have been made to endure.

Then followed *The Fugitive Slave's Apostrophe to the North Star*, which showed how deeply he sympathized with the many hundreds of our countrymen who, to escape from slavery, had toiled through dismal swamps, thickset canebrakes, deep rivers, tangled forests, alone, by night, hungry, almost naked and penniless, guided only by the steady light of the polar star, which some kind friend had taught them to distinguish, and had assured them would be an unerring leader to a land of liberty. They who have heard the narratives of such as have so escaped need not be told that Mr. Pierpont must have had the tale poured through his ear into his generous heart.*

But of all our American poets, John G. Whittier has from first to last done most for the abolition of slavery. All my antislavery brethren, I doubt not, will unite with me to crown him our laureate. From 1832 to the close of our dreadful war in 1865 his harp of liberty was never hung up. Not an important occasion escaped him. Every significant incident drew from his heart some per-

* Would that justice would allow shame to wipe forever from the memory of man the disgraceful fact that, on the 27th of July, 1840, the Rev. John Pierpont was arraigned before an Ecclesiastical Council in Boston, by a committee of the parish of Hollis Street, as guilty of offences for which his connection with that parish ought to be dissolved, — and was dissolved. His offences were "his too busy interference with questions of legislation on the subject of prohibiting the sale of ardent spirits, his too busy interference with questions of legislation on the subject of imprisonment for debt, *and his too busy interference with the popular controversy on the subject of the abolition of slavery.*"

tinent and often very impressive or rousing verses. His name appears in the first volume of *The Liberator*, with high commendations of his poetry and his character. As early as 1831 he was attracted to Mr. Garrison by sympathy with his avowed purpose to abolish slavery. Their acquaintance soon ripened into a heartfelt friendship, as he declared in the following lines, written in 1833: —

"Champion of those who groan beneath
Oppression's iron hand:
In view of penury, hate, and death,
I see thee fearless stand.
Still bearing up thy lofty brow,
In the steadfast strength of truth,
In manhood sealing well the vow
And promise of thy youth.

. . . . .

"I love thee with a brother's love;
I feel my pulses thrill,
To mark thy spirit soar above
The cloud of human ill.
My heart hath leaped to answer thine,
And echo back thy words,
As leaps the warrior's at the shine
And flash of kindred swords!

. . . . .

"Go on — the dagger's point may glare
Amid thy pathway's gloom, —
The fate which sternly threatens there
Is glorious martyrdom!
Then onward with a martyr's zeal;
And wait thy sure reward,
When man to man no more shall kneel,
And God alone be Lord!"

Mr. Whittier proved the sincerity of these professions. He joined the first antislavery society and became an active official. Notwithstanding his dislike of public speaking, he sometimes lectured at that early day, when so few were found willing to avow and advocate the right of the enslaved to immediate liberation from bondage without the condition of removal to Liberia. Mr. Whittier attended the convention at Philadelphia in December,

1833, that formed the American Antislavery Society. He was one of the secretaries of that body, and a member, with Mr. Garrison, of the committee appointed to prepare the "Declaration of our Sentiments and Purposes." Although, as I have elsewhere stated, Mr. Garrison wrote almost every sentence of that admirable document just as it now stands, yet I well remember the intense interest with which Mr. Whittier scrutinized it, and how heartily he indorsed it.

In 1834, by his invitation I visited Haverhill, where he then resided. I was his guest, and lectured under his auspices in explanation and defence of our abolition doctrines and plans. Again the next year, after the mob spirit had broken out, I went to Haverhill by his invitation, and he shared with me in the perils which I have described on a former page.

In January, 1836, Mr. Whittier attended the annual meeting of the Massachusetts Antislavery Society, and boarded the while in the house where I was living. He heard Dr. Follen's great speech on that occasion, and came home so much affected by it that, either that night or the next morning, he wrote those "Stanzas for the Times," which are among the best of his productions:—

"Is this the land our fathers loved,
    The freedom which they toiled to win?
Is this the soil whereon they moved?
    Are these the graves they slumber in?
Are *we* the sons by whom are borne
The mantles which the dead have worn?

"And shall we crouch above these graves
    With craven soul and fettered lip?
Yoke in with marked and branded slaves,
    And tremble at the driver's whip?
Bend to the earth our pliant knees,
And speak but as our masters please?

. . . . .

"Shall tongues be mute when deeds are wrought
Which well might shame extremest hell?
Shall freemen lock the indignant thought?
Shall Pity's bosom cease to swell?
Shall Honor bleed? Shall Truth succumb?
Shall pen and press and soul be dumb?

"No; — by each spot of haunted ground,
Where Freedom weeps her children's fall, —
By Plymouth's rock and Bunker's mound, —
By Griswold's stained and shattered wall, —
By Warren's ghost, — by Langdon's shade, —
By all the memories of our dead!

. . . . . .

"By all above, around, below,
Be our indignant answer, — NO!"

I can hardly refrain from giving my readers the whole of these stanzas. But I hope they all are, or will at once make themselves, familiar with them. As I read them now, they revive in my bosom not the memory only, but the glow they kindled there when I first pored over them. Then his lines entitled "Massachusetts to Virginia," and those he wrote on the adoption of Pinckney's Resolution, and the passage of Calhoun's Bill, excluding antislavery newspapers and pamphlets and letters from the United States Mail, — indeed, all his antislavery poetry helped mightily to keep us alive to our high duties, and fired us with holy resolution. Let our laureate's verses still be said and sung throughout the land, for if the portents of the day be true, our conflict with the enemies of liberty, the oppressors of humanity, is not yet ended.

PREJUDICE AGAINST COLOR.

If the enslaved millions of our countrymen had been white, the task of emancipating them would have been a light one. But as only colored persons were to be seen in that condition, and they were ignorant and degraded, and as all of that complexion, with rare exceptions, even in the free States, were poor, uneducated, and held in servile relations, or engaged in only menial employments, it had come to be taken for granted that they were fitted only for such things. It was confidently assumed that they belonged to an *inferior race* of beings, somewhere between monkey and man; that they were made by the Creator for our service, to be hewers of wood and drawers of water; and pious ministers, and some who were reputed to be wise in the sacred Scriptures, gave their sanction to the arrogant assumption by proving (to those who were anxious to believe) that negroes were descendants from the impious son of Noah, whom that patriarch cursed, and in his wrath decreed that his posterity should be the lowest of servants.

Our opponents gave no heed to the glaring facts, that the colored people were not permitted to rise from their low estate, were *held down* by our laws, customs, and contemptuous treatment. Not only were they prevented from engaging in any of the lucrative occupations, but they were denied the privileges of education, and hardly admitted to the houses dedicated to the worship of the impartial Father of all men.

I have given in early numbers of this series a full account of the fight we had in defence of the Canterbury School in Connecticut. More than a year before that, a number of well-qualified young men having been refused admission into Yale College and the Wesleyan Seminary at Middletown, *because of their complexion*, the Rev. Simeon S. Jocelyn, one of the best of men, generously assisted by Arthur Tappan and his brother Lewis Tappan, and others, endeavored to establish in New Haven an institution for the collegiate education of colored young men. The benevolent project was so violently opposed by "the most respectable citizens" of the place,

Hon. Judge Daggett among them, that it was abandoned. A year or two afterwards the trustees of "Noyes Academy," in Plymouth, New Hampshire, after due consideration, consented to allow colored pupils to be admitted into the academy. The respectable people of the town were so incensed, enraged by this encroachment upon the prerogative of white children, that, readily helped by the rougher but not baser sort of folks, they razed the building in which the school was kept from its foundation and carted it off into a meadow or swamp. In none of our cities, that I was acquainted with before the antislavery reform commenced, were colored children admitted into the "common schools" with white children. Hon. Horace Mann and his fellow-laborers in the cause of humanity, as well as education, put this injustice to shame in Massachusetts, if not elsewhere, and the doors of all public schools were opened to the young, without regard to complexion.

But this was not the utmost of the contempt with which colored people were treated. They were not permitted to ride in any public conveyances, stage-coaches, omnibuses, or railroad-cars; nor to take passage on any steamboats or sail-packets, excepting in the steerage or on deck. Many instances of extreme suffering, as well as great inconvenience and expense, to which worthy, excellent colored persons were subjected came to the knowledge of Abolitionists, and were pressed upon the public consideration, until the crying iniquity was abated.

And still there was a deeper depth to the wrong we did to these innocent victims of prejudice. In all our churches they were set apart from the white brethren, often in pews or pens, built high up against the ceiling in the corners back of the congregation, so that the favored ones who came to worship the "*impartial* Father" of all men might not be offended at the sight of those to whom in his *inscrutable* wisdom he had given a dark complexion.

There was quite an excitement caused in the Federal Street Church in 1822 or 1823, because one of the very wealthy merchants of Boston introduced into his pew in the broad aisle, one Sunday, a black gentleman. To be sure he was richly dressed, and had a handsome person, but he was black, — very black.

> "That Sunday's sermon all was lost,
> The very text forgot by most."

The refined and sensitive were much disturbed, offended, felt that their sacred rights had been invaded. They upbraided their neighbor for having so egregiously violated the propriety of the sacred place, and given their feelings such a shock. "Why," said the merchant, "what else could I do? That man, though black, is, as you must have seen, a gentleman. He is well educated, of polished manners. He comes from a foreign country a visitor to our city. He has long been a business correspondent of mine." "Then he is very rich." "Why, bless you, he is worth a million. How could I send such a gentleman up into the negro pew?"

In 1835, if I remember correctly, a wealthy and pious colored man bought a pew on the floor of Park Street Church. It caused great disturbance. Some of his neighbors nailed up the door of his pew; and so many of "the aggrieved brethren" threatened to leave the society, if they could not be relieved of such an offence, that the trustees were obliged to eject the colored purchaser. Another of the churches* of Boston, admonished by the above-mentioned occurrence, inserted in their *pew-deeds* a clause, providing that they should "*be held by none but respectable white persons.*"

* The one of which Rev. Baron Stow, D. D., was pastor.

Belonging to the society to which I ministered in Connecticut was a very worthy colored family. They were condemned to sit only in the negro pew, which was as far back from the rest of the congregation as it could be placed. Being blessed with a numerous family, as the children grew up they were uncomfortably crowded in that pew. Our church occupied the old meeting-house, which was somewhat larger than we needed, so that the congregation were easily accommodated on the lower floor. Only the choir sat in the gallery, except on extraordinary occasions. I therefore invited my colored parishioners to occupy one of the large, front pews in the side-gallery. They hesitated some time, lest their doing so should give offence. But I insisted that none would have any right to be offended, and at length persuaded them to do as I requested. But one man, a political partisan of the leader of Miss Crandall's persecutors, was or pretended to be much offended. He said with great warmth, "How came that nigger family to come down into that front pew?" "Because," I replied, "it was unoccupied; they were uncomfortably crowded in the pew assigned them, and I requested them to remove." "Well," said he, "there are many in the society besides myself who will not consent to their sitting there." "Why?" I asked. "They are always well dressed, well behaved, and good-looking withal." "But," said he, "they are niggers, and niggers should be kept to their place." I argued the matter with him till I saw he could not be moved, and he repeated the declaration that they should be driven back. I then said, with great earnestness: "Mr. A. B., if you do anything or say anything to hurt the feelings of that worthy family, and induce them to return to the pew which you know is not large enough for them, so sure as your name is A. B. and my name is S. J. M., the first time you afterwards appear in the congregation, I will state the facts of the case exactly as they are, and administer to you as severe a reproof as I may be able to frame in words." This had the desired effect. My colored friends retained their new seat.

To counteract as much as possible the effect of this cruel prejudice, of which I have given a few specimens, we Abolitionists gathered up and gave to the public the numerous evidences that were easily obtained of the intellectual and moral equality of the colored with the white races of mankind. Mrs. Child, in her admirable "Appeal," devoted two excellent chapters to this purpose. The Hon. Alexander H. Everett also, in 1835, delivered in Boston a lecture on "African Mind," in which he showed, on the authority of the fathers of history, that the colored races of men were the leaders in civilization. He said: "While Greece and Rome were yet barbarous, we find the '*light of learning and improvement* emanating from them,' the inhabitants of the degraded and accursed continent of Africa,—out of the very midst of this woolly-haired, flat-nosed, thick-lipped, coal-black race which some persons are tempted to station at a pretty low intermediate point between men and monkeys." Again he said: "The high estimation in which the Africans were held for wisdom and virtue is strikingly shown by the mythological fable, current among the ancient Greeks, and repeatedly alluded to by Homer, which represented the Gods as going annually in a body to make a long visit to the Ethiopians." Referring my readers to Mrs. Child's chapters, and Mr. Everett's oration on this subject, I will give a few of my own recollections of facts going to establish the natural equality of our colored brethren.

Since the admission of their children to the public schools, a fair proportion of them have shown themselves to be fully equal to white children in their aptness to learn. And surely no one who is acquainted with them will presume to speak of the inferiority of such men as Frederick Douglass, Henry H. Garnett, Samuel R. Ward, Charles L. Remond, William Wells Brown, J. W. Loguen, and many more men and women who have been our faithful and able fellow-laborers in the antislavery cause.*

But I have, recorded in my memory, many touching evidences of the *moral* equality, if not superiority, of the colored race. Let me premise these recollections by stating the general fact that, notwithstanding the serious disadvantages to which our prejudices have subjected them, the colored population of our country have nowhere imposed upon the public their proportion of paupers or of criminals. In this respect they are excelled only by the Quakers and the Jews.

I shall always remember with great pleasure once meeting the Rev. Dr. Tuckerman in Tremont Street, in 1835. He hurried towards me, his countenance beaming with a delight which only such a benevolent heart as his could give to the human countenance, saying: "O Brother May, I have a precious fact for you Abolitionists. Never in all my intercourse with the poor, or indeed with any class of my fellow-beings, have I met with a brighter instance of true, self-sacrificing Christian benevolence than lately in the case of a poor *colored* woman. Two colored women, not related, have been living for several years on the same floor in a tenement-house, each having only a common room and a small bedroom. Each of them was getting a living for herself and a young child by washing and day-labor. They had managed to subsist, earning about enough to meet current expenses. Several months ago one of them was taken very sick with inflammatory rheumatism. All was done for her relief that medical skill could do, but without avail. She grew worse rather than better, until she became utterly helpless. The

* See Appendix.

overseers of the poor made the customary provision for her, and benevolent individuals helped her privately. But it came to be a case for an infirmary. The overseers and others thought best to remove her to the almshouse. When this decision was made known to her she became much distressed. The thought of going to the poorhouse — of becoming a public pauper — was dreadful to her. We tried to reconcile her to what seemed to us the best provision that could be made for her, not only by assuring her that she would be kindly cared for, but by reminding her that she had been brought to her condition, as we believed, by no fault of her own, and by such considerations as our blessed religion suggests. But she could not be comforted. We left her, trusting that private reflection would in a few days bring her to acquiesce in what seemed to be inevitable. In due time I called again to learn if she was prepared for her removal to the almshouse. I found her not in her own but in her generous-hearted neighbor's room. Thither had been removed all her little furniture. So deep was that neighbor's sympathy with her feeling of shame and humiliation at becoming a public pauper, — an inmate of the almshouse, — that she had determined to take upon herself the care and support of this sick, infirm, helpless woman, and had subjected herself to all the inconvenience of an over-crowded room, as well as the great additional labor and care which she had thus assumed."

Whatever Dr. Tuckerman thought, or we may think, of the unreasonableness of the poor helpless invalid's dread of the almshouse, or of the *imprudence* of her poor friend in undertaking to support and nurse her, we cannot help admiring, as he did, that ardor of benevolence which impelled to such a labor of loving-kindness, and pronounce it a very rare instance of self-sacrificing charity. Let it redound as it should to the credit of that portion of the human race which our nation has so wickedly dared to despise and oppress.

I have several more precious recollections of elevated moral sentiment and principle evinced by black men and women whom I have known. Two of these I will give.

It was my privilege to see much of Edward S. Abdy, Esq., of England, during his visit to our country in 1833 and 1834. The first time I met him was at the house of Mr. James Forten, of Philadelphia, in company with two other English gentlemen, who had come to the United States commissioned by the British Parliament to examine our systems of prison and penitentiary discipline. Mr. Abdy was interested in whatsoever affected the welfare of man, but he was more particularly devoted to the investigation of slavery. He travelled extensively in our Southern States and contemplated with his own eyes the manifold abominations of our American despotism. He was too much exasperated by our tyranny to be enamored of our democratic institutions; and on his return to England he published two very sensible volumes, that were so little complimentary to our nation that our booksellers thought it not worth their while to republish them.

This warm-hearted philanthropist visited me several times at my home in Connecticut. The last afternoon that he was there we were sitting together at my study window, when our attention was arrested by a very handsome carriage driving up to the hotel opposite my house. A gentleman and lady occupied the back seat, and on the front were two children tended by a black woman, who wore the turban that was then usually worn by slave-women. We hastened over to the hotel, and soon entered into conversation with the slaveholder. He was polite, but somewhat nonchalant and defiant of our sympathy with his victim. He readily acknowledged, as slaveholders of that day generally did, that, abstractly considered, the enslavement of fellow-men was a great wrong. But then he contended that it had become a necessary evil, — necessary to the enslaved no less than to the enslavers, the former being unable to do without masters as much as the latter were unable to do without servants, and he added, in a very confident tone, "You are at liberty to persuade our servant-woman to remain here if you can."

Thus challenged, we of course sought an interview with the slave, and informed her that, having been brought by her master into the free States, she was, by the laws of the land, set at liberty. "No, I am not, gentlemen," was her prompt reply. We adduced cases and quoted authorities to establish our assertion that she was free. But she significantly shook her head, and still insisted that the examples and the legal decisions did not reach her case. "For," said she, "I promised mistress that I would go back with her and the children." Mr. Abdy undertook to argue with her that such a promise was not binding. He had been drilled in the moral philosophy of Dr. Paley, and in that debate seemed to be possessed of its spirit. But he failed to make any visible impression upon the woman. She had *bound* herself by a promise to her mistress that she would not leave her, and that promise had fastened upon her conscience an obligation from which she could not be persuaded that even her natural right to liberty could exonerate her. Mr. Abdy at last was impatient with her, and said in his haste: "Is it possible that you do not wish to be free?" She replied with solemn earnestness: "Was there ever a slave that did not wish to be free? I long for liberty. I will get out of slavery if I can the day after I have returned, but go back I must because I *promised* that I would." At this we desisted from our endeavor to induce her to take the boon that was apparently within her reach. We could not but feel a profound respect for that moral sensibility, which would not allow her to embrace even her freedom at the expense of violating a promise.

The next morning at an early hour the slaveholder, with his wife and children, drove off, leaving the slave-woman and their heaviest trunk to be brought on after them in the stage-coach. We could not refrain from again trying to persuade her to remain and be free. We told her that her master had given us leave to persuade her, if we could. She pointed to the trunk and to a very valuable gold watch and chain, which her mistress had committed to her care, and insisted that fidelity to a trust was of more consequence to her soul even than the attainment of liberty. Mr. Abdy offered to take the trunk and watch into his charge, follow her master, and deliver them into his hands. But she could not be made to see that in this there would be no violation of her duty; and then her own person, that too she had promised should be returned to the home of her master. And much as she longed for liberty, she longed for a clear conscience more.

Mr. Abdy was astonished, delighted, at this instance of heroic virtue in a poor, ignorant slave. He packed his trunk, gave me a hearty adieu, and when the coach drove up he took his seat on the outside with the trunk and the slave-chattel of a Mississippi slaveholder, that he might study for a few hours more the morality of that strong-hearted woman who could not be bribed to violate her promise, even by the gift of liberty. It was the last time I saw Mr. Abdy, and it was a sight to be remembered, — he, an accomplished English gentleman, a Fellow of Oxford or Cambridge University, riding on the driver's box of a stage-coach side by side with an

American slave-woman, that he might learn more of her history and character.

> "Full many a gem, of purest ray serene,
> The dark, unfathomed caves of ocean bear;
> Full many a flower is born to blush unseen,
> And waste its sweetness on the desert air."

In this connection I must be allowed to narrate an incident (though not an antislavery one), because it may interest my readers generally, and, should it come to the notice of any of my English friends, may lead to the return of a valuable manuscript which I wish very much to recover.

I had been for several years in possession of a letter of seven pages in the handwriting of General Washington, given me by a lady who obtained it in Richmond, Va. It was a letter addressed to Mr. Custis in 1794, while Washington was detained in Philadelphia in attendance upon his duties as President. He had left Mr. Custis in charge of his estates at Mount Vernon. The letter was one of particular instructions as to the management of "the people" and the disposition of the crops. It showed how exact were the business habits of that great man, and his anxiety that his slaves should be properly cared for.

Mr. Abdy read it and reread it with the deepest interest, and seemed to me to covet the possession of it. Just as he was about to take his departure I longed to give him something that he would value as a memento of his visit to me. There was nothing I could think of at the moment but the letter, so I put it into his hand, saying, "Keep it as my parting token of regard for you." "What!" said he, seizing it with surprise as well as delight, "will you give me this invaluable relic?" "Yes," I replied; "there are a great many of General Washington's letters in our country, but not many in England. Take it, and show your countrymen that he was a man of method as well as of might."

Some time after he had gone, and the fervor of feeling which impelled me to the gift had subsided, I began to regret that I had parted with the letter. There were in it, incidentally given, some traits of the character of Washington that might not be found elsewhere. It came to me that such a letter should not have been held or disposed of as my private property. It belonged rather to the nation.

A few years afterwards Mr. Abdy died. I learned from an English paper the fact of his demise and the name of the executor of his estate. To that gentleman I wrote, described the letter of Washington, the circumstances under which I had given it to Mr. Abdy, and requested that, as he had departed this life, the letter might be returned to me, with my reasons for wishing to possess it again. In due time I received a very courteous reply from that gentleman, assuring me that he sympathized with my feelings, and appreciated the propriety of my reclaiming the letter. But he added that he had searched for it in vain among Mr. Abdy's papers, and presumed he had deposited it in the library of some literary or historical institution, but had left no intimation as to the disposal of it.

When in England, in 1859, I inquired for it of the librarian of the British Museum, and of Dr. William's Library in Red-cross Street, but without success. If these lines should meet the eye of any friend in England who may know, or be able to find, where the valuable autograph is, I shall be very grateful for the information.*

A NEGRO'S LOVE OF LIBERTY.

A year or two after my removal to Syracuse a colored man accosted me in the street, and asked for a private

* I advertised my request in "Notes and Queries" for August, 1859.

interview with me on a matter of great importance. I had repeatedly met him about the city, and supposed from his appearance that he was a smart, enterprising, free negro.

At the time appointed he came to my house, and after looking carefully about to be sure we were alone, he informed me that he was a fugitive from slavery; that he had resided in our city several years, but nobody here except his wife knew whence he came, and he was very desirous that his secret should be kept.

"I have come," he continued, "to ask your assistance to enable me to get my mother out of slavery. I have been industrious, have lived economically, and have saved three hundred dollars. With this I hope to purchase my mother, and bring her here to finish her days with me." "You say," I replied, "that you are a fugitive slave; from what place in the South did you escape?" "From W——, in Virginia," he answered. I opened my atlas, and found a town so named in that State. "What towns are there adjoining or near W——?" I asked. He named several, enough to satisfy me that he was acquainted with that part of Virginia. "Well," said I, "how did you get here?" "By the light of the north-star," was his prompt reply. "How did you know anything about the north-star, and that it would guide you to freedom?" I doubtingly inquired. "I have *heard* of a great many Southern slaves who have made their way into the free States and to Canada by the light of that star, but I have never before seen one who had done so. I am very desirous to hear particularly about your escape." "Well, sir," said he, "a good man in W——, a member of the Society of Friends, knowing how much I longed to be free, pointed out to me the north-star, and showed me how I might always find it. And he assured me, if I would travel towards it, that I should at length reach a part of the country where slavery was not allowed. I need not tell you, sir, how impatient I became to set off. After a while my master left home to be absent several days, and the next Saturday night I started with a bundle on my back, containing a part of the very few clothes I had, and all the food I could get with my mother's help, and a little money in my pocket — not three dollars — that I had been gathering for a long time. The first and the second nights were pleasant, the stars shone bright, and there was no moon, so I travelled from the moment it was dark enough to venture out until the light of day began to appear. Then I found some place to hide, and there I lay all day until darkness came again. Thus I travelled night after night, always looking towards the north-star. Sometimes I lost sight of it in the woods through which I was obliged to pass, and oh! how glad I was to see it again. Sometimes I had to go a great ways round to avoid houses and grounds that were guarded by dogs, or that I feared it would not be safe for me to cross, but still I kept looking for the star, and turned and travelled towards it when I could. At other times (thank God, not often) the nights were so cloudy I could not see, and so was obliged to stay where I had been through the previous days. O sir, how long those nights did seem!

"When the food I had brought away in my bundle was all eaten up, I was forced to call at some houses and beg for something to relieve my hunger. I was generally treated kindly, for, as I learnt, I had gotten out of Virginia and Maryland. Still, I did not dare to stop so soon, but kept on until I reached this place, where I saw many colored people, evidently as free as the white folks. So I thought it would be safe to look about for employment here and a home. Here I have been living seven or eight years; have married a wife, and we have two children. As I told you at first, I have saved money enough, I believe, to buy my mother, and I want you, sir, to help me get her here."

It cannot be necessary for me to assure my readers that I was deeply interested in this narrative, which I have repeated so often that I have kept its essential parts fresh in my memory. But, wishing to test its truth still further, I asked him what towns he had passed through in coming from W—— to Syracuse. "O," said he, "as I travelled at night and avoided people all I could, and asked few questions of those I did meet, I learned the names of only a few places through which I came. I remember M—— and D—— and B——," and so on, giving the names of six or eight towns in all. "Ah," said I, "how did you get to B——, if you travelled only towards the north-star?"

"O," he replied, "I got scared there. I thought the slave-catchers were after me. I ran for luck. I travelled two nights in the road that was easiest for me, without caring for anything but to escape. Then, supposing I had got away from those who were after me, I took to the north-star again, and that brought me here."

The few towns which he named as having passed through after his last starting-point, I found on the map lying almost directly in the line running thence due north to this city.

Being thus assured of the correctness of his story, I began to question the expediency of his attempting to bring his mother away from her old home, even if I should be able to get possession of her for him. "She must be an aged woman by this time," said I. "You look as if you were forty years old; she probably is sixty, perhaps nearly or quite seventy."

"It may be so," he replied; "but she used to be mighty smart and healthy, and may live a good many years yet, and I want to do what I can for my mother. I am her only child I believe, and I know she would be mighty glad to see me again before she dies."

"Very true," I rejoined; "but you have been so long separated she must have got used to living without you. Like other old slave-women in our Southern States (*mammies* or *aunties*, as they are called), I presume she is pretty kindly treated, and such a change as you propose at her time of life might make her much less comfortable than she would be to continue to the last in her accustomed place and condition."

"O sir!" he said, with great earnestness, "she is a slave. Every one in slavery longs to be free. I am sure she would rather suffer a great deal as a free woman than to live any longer, however comfortably, as a slave."

"Yes," I replied, with all apparent want of sympathy, "but it will cost you all the money you have saved, and I fear much more, to buy her and get her brought on to you here, so that you may then be too poor to make her comfortable. But your three hundred dollars will enable you to increase in many ways the comfort of your wife and children. That sum will go far towards the purchase of a nice little home for them. Now, do you not owe them quite as much as you do your mother?" "My wife," he exclaimed, "is just as anxious as I am to get mother out of slavery. She is willing to work as hard as I will to make mother comfortable after we get her here. I am sure we shall not let mother suffer for anything she may need in her old age. Do, sir, help us get her here, and you shall see what we will do for her." Repressing my feelings as much as possible, I said once more: "But, my good fellow, your mother is so old she can live but a little while after you have spent your all and more to get her here. Very likely the excitement and the fatigue of the journey and the change of the climate will kill her very soon." With the deepest emotion and in a most subdued manner, he replied, "No matter if it does, — buy her, bring her here, and *let her die free.*" This was irresistible. I seized his hand. "Sanford, you must not think me as unsympathizing and cold as I have appeared. I have been trying you, proving you. I am satisfied that you know the value of liberty, that you hold it above all price. Be assured I will do all in my power to help you to accomplish your generous, your pious purpose. Nothing will give me more heartfelt satisfaction than to be instrumental in procuring the release of your mother and presenting her to you a free woman."

The sequel to my story is sad, but most instructive. It will show how demoralizing, dehumanizing it has been and must be to hold human beings, fellow-men, as property, chattels; that, as Cowper wrote long ago, "it were better to be a slave and wear the chains, than to fasten them on another."

How to compass the purpose which had thus been so forcibly fixed in my heart required some device. It would not have done for Sanford himself to have gone for his mother. That would have been like going into the den of an angry tiger. No sin that a slave could commit was so unpardonable then, in the estimation of a slaveholder, as running away.

I did not, until five years afterwards, become acquainted with that remarkable woman, *Harriet Tubman*, or I might have engaged her services in the assurance that she would have brought off the old woman without *paying* for what belonged to her by an inalienable right, — *her liberty.*

I therefore soon determined to intrust the undertaking to John Needles, of Baltimore, a most excellent man and member of the Society of Friends. Accordingly.

I wrote to him, giving all the particulars of the case, — the name of the town in Virginia where the slave-woman was supposed to be still living, usually called Aunt Bess or Old Bess, and the name of the planter who held her as his chattel. I promised to send him the three hundred dollars which Sanford had put at my disposal, and more, if more would be needed, so soon as he should inform me that he had gotten or could get possession of the woman.

After six or eight weeks I received a letter, informing me that he had secured the ready assistance of a very suitable man, — a Quaker, residing in the town of W——, not far from the plantation on which was still living the mother of Sanford, an old woman in pretty good health. But alas! his endeavor to purchase her had been utterly unavailing. He had approached the business as warily as he knew how to. Yet almost instantly the truth had been seen by the jealous eyes of the planter, through the disguise the Quaker had attempted to throw around it. "You don't want that old black wench for yourself," said the master. "She would be of no use to you. You want to get her for Sanford. And, damn him, he can't have her, unless he comes for her himself. And then, I reckon, I shall let Old Bess have him, and not let him have her. He may stay here where he belongs, the damned runaway!" No entreaty or argument the Quaker used seemed to move the master. Even the offer of two hundred dollars and two hundred and fifty dollars — much more than the market value of the old woman — was spurned. It was better to him than money to punish the runaway slave through his disappointed affections, now that he could not do it by lacerating his back or putting him in irons.

I need not attempt to describe the sorrow and vexation of the son thus wantonly denied the satisfaction of contributing to the comfort of his mother through the few last days of her life, in which her services could have been of little or no worth to the tyrant. Nor need I measure for my readers the vast *moral superiority* of the poor black man, who had been the slave, to the rich white man, who had been the master.

DISTINGUISHED COLORED MEN.

I have given above some instances of exalted *moral* excellence which greatly increased my regard for colored men, — instances of self-sacrificing benevolence, of rigid adherence to a promise under the strongest temptation to break it, and of their inestimable value of liberty. I wish now to tell of several colored men who have given us abundant evidences of their mental power and executive ability.

DAVID RUGGLES, LEWIS HAYDEN, AND WILLIAM C. NELL.

David Ruggles first became known to me as a most active, adventurous, and daring conductor on the underground railroad. He helped six hundred slaves to escape from one and another of the Southern States into Canada, or to places of security this side of the St. Lawrence. So great were the dangers to which he was often exposed, so severe the labors and hardships he often incurred, and so intense the excitement into which he was sometimes thrown, that his eyes became seriously diseased, and he lost entirely the sight of them. For a while he was obliged to depend for his livelihood upon the contributions of his antislavery friends, which they gave much more cheerfully than he received them. Dependence was irksome to his enterprising spirit. So soon, therefore, as his health, in other respects, was sufficiently restored, he eagerly inquired for some employment by which, notwithstanding his blindness, he could be useful to others and gain a support for himself and family. Having a strong inclination to, and not a little tact and experience in the curative art, he determined to attempt the management of a Water-cure Hospital. He was assisted to obtain the lease of suitable accommodations in or near Northampton, and conducted his establishment with great skill and good success, I believe, until his death.

Lewis Hayden and William C. Nell were active, devoted young colored men, who, in the early days of our antislavery enterprise, rendered us valuable services in various ways. The latter — Mr. Nell — especially assisted in making arrangements for our meetings, gathering important and pertinent information, and sometimes addressing our meetings very acceptably. He was always careful in preserving valuable facts and documents, and grew to be esteemed so highly for his fidelity and carefulness, that, when the Hon. J. G. Palfrey came to be the Postmaster of Boston, he appointed W. C. Nell one of his clerks; and, if I mistake not, he retains that situation to this day.

JAMES FORTEN.

While at the Convention in Philadelphia, in 1833, I became acquainted with two colored gentlemen who interested me deeply, — Mr. James Forten and Mr. Robert Purvis. The former, then nearly sixty years of age, was evidently a man of commanding mind, and well informed. He had for many years carried on the largest private sail-making establishment in that city, having at times forty men in his employ, most, if not all of them, white men. He was much respected by them, and by all with whom he had any business transactions, among whom were many of the prominent merchants of Philadelphia. He had acquired wealth, and he lived in as handsome a style as any one should wish to live. I dined at his table with several members of the Convention, and two English gentlemen who had recently come to our country on some philanthropic mission. We were entertained with as much ease and elegance as I could desire to see. Of course, the conversation was, for the most part, on topics relating to our antislavery conflict. The Colonization scheme came up for consideration, and I shall never forget Mr. Forten's scathing satire. Among other things he said: "My great-grandfather was brought to this country a slave from Africa. My grandfather obtained his own freedom. My father never wore the yoke. He rendered valuable services to his country in the war of our Revolution; and I, though then a boy, was a drummer in that war. I was taken prisoner, and was made to suffer not a little on board the Jersey prison-ship. I have since lived and labored in a useful employment, have acquired property, and have paid taxes in this city. Here I have dwelt until I am nearly sixty years of age, and have brought up and educated a family, as you see, thus far. Yet some ingenious gentlemen have recently discovered that I am still an African; that a continent, three thousand miles, and more, from the place where I was born, is my native country. And I am advised to go home. Well, it may be so. Perhaps, if I should only be set on the shore of that distant land, I should recognize all I might see there, and run at once to the old hut where my forefathers lived a hundred years ago." His tone of voice, his whole manner, sharpened the edge of his sarcasm. It was irresistible. And the laugh which it at first awakened soon gave way to an expression, on every countenance, of that ineffable contempt which he evidently felt for the pretence of the Colonization Society. At the table sat his excellent, motherly wife, and his lovely, accomplished daughters, — all with himself somewhat under the ban of that accursed American prejudice, which is the offspring of slavery. I learnt from him that their education, evidently of a superior kind, had cost him very much more than it would have done, if they had not been denied admission into the best schools of the city.

Soon after dinner we all left the house to attend a meeting of the Philadelphia Female Antislavery Society. It was my privilege to escort one of the Misses Forten to the place of meeting. What was my surprise, when, on my return to Boston, I learnt that this action of mine had been noticed and reported at home. "Is it true, Mr. May," said a lady to me, "that you walked in the streets of Philadelphia with a colored girl?" "I did," was my reply, "and should be happy to do it again. And I wish that all the white young ladies of my acquaintance were as sensible, well educated, refined, and handsome withal as Miss Forten." This was too bad, and I was set down as one of the incorrigibles.

MR. ROBERT PURVIS

was then an elegant, a brilliant young gentleman, well educated and wealthy. He was so nearly white that he was generally taken to be so. I first saw and heard him in our Antislavery Convention in Philadelphia. I was attracted to him by his fervid eloquence, and was surprised at the intimation, which fell from his lips, that he belonged to the proscribed, disfranchised class. Away from the neighborhood of his birth he might easily have passed as a white man. Indeed, I was told he had travelled much in stage-coaches, and stopped days and weeks at Saratoga and other fashionable summer resorts, and mingled, without question, among the beaux and belles, regarded by the latter as one of the most attractive of his sex. Robert Purvis, therefore, might have removed to any part of our country, far distant from Philadelphia, and have lived as one of the self-styled superior race. But, rather than forsake his kindred, or try to conceal the secret of his birth, he magnanimously chose to bear the unjust reproach, the cruel wrongs of the colored people, although he has been more annoyed, chafed, exasperated by them than any other one I have ever met with. Indeed, he seems to have grown more impatient and irascible as the heavy burden of his people has been lightened. Because all their rights have not been accorded to them, he sometimes seems to deny that any of their rights have been recognized. Because the *elective franchise* is still meanly withheld from them in some of the States, he will hardly acknowledge that *slavery* has been abolished throughout the land, — a glorious triumph in the cause of humanity, which his own eloquence and pecuniary contributions have helped to achieve. But we must make the largest allowance for Mr. Purvis. No man of conscious power and high spirit, who has not felt the gnawing, rasping, burning of a cruel stigma, can conceive how hard it is to bear.

WILLIAM WELLS BROWN

has distinguished himself as a diligent agent and able antislavery lecturer in this country and throughout Great Britain and Ireland. He has also published books that have been highly creditable to him as an author.

CHARLES LENOX REMOND,

when quite a young man, became a frequent and effective speaker in our meetings. In 1838 or 1839 he was appointed an agent of the Massachusetts Antislavery Society, in which capacity he rendered abundant and very valuable services. He spent the greater part of the year 1841 in Great Britain and Ireland. He lectured in many of the most important places throughout the United Kingdom. Everywhere he drew large audiences, and was much commended and admired for the pertinence of his facts, the cogency of his arguments, and the fire of his eloquence. In *The Liberator* for November 19, 1841, there was copied from a Dublin paper a speech which Mr. Remond had then recently made to a large and most respectable audience in that city. Mr. Garrison commended it to his readers as "a very eloquent production, worthy of careful perusal and high commendation. Let those," he added, "who are ever disposed to deny the possession of genius, talent, and eloquence by the colored man read that speech, and acknowledge their meanness and injustice."

REV. J. W. LOGUEN.

Soon after I removed to Syracuse, in 1845, I became acquainted with the Rev. J. W. Loguen, then a school-teacher, and for several years since minister of the African Methodist Church here. His personal history is a remarkable one, revealing at times no little force of character. He was born in Tennessee, the slave of an ignorant, intemperate, and brutal slaveholder. He witnessed the sale of several of his mother's children, her frantic but unavailing resistance, the horrible scourging she endured without releasing them from her embrace, and her agonizing grief when they were at last violently torn from her. Twice he was himself beaten nearly to death, — left bleeding and senseless, to be comforted and brought back to life by the care of his fond mother. At last he saw his sister (after a terrible fight with the ruffian slave-traders to whom she had been sold) subdued, manacled, and forced away, screaming for her children, imploring at least that she might have her infant. He could endure his bondage no longer. He resolved to escape to the land of the free, and there earn the means and find the way to bring his mother to partake with him of the blessings of liberty. He took his master's best horse, — one that he had trained to do great feats, if required, — and, in company with another young slave of kindred spirit, also well mounted, he started, on the night before Christmas, 1834, from the interior of Tennessee, near Nashville, to go to Canada, — a distance of six hundred miles, half the way through a slaveholding country. They encountered, as they expected to do, fearful perils and exhausting hardships. At last they reached a place of safety, but it was in the dead of a Canadian winter. Their stock of provisions had long since been exhausted; their money was all spent; their clothing utterly insufficient; and thus they had come into a most inhospitable climate, unknowing and unknown, at a season of the year when little employment was to be had. Undaunted by this array of appalling circumstances, Mr. Loguen persevered, made friends, got work, and in the spring of 1837, only three years after his escape from slavery, had so commended himself to the confidence of an employer that he was intrusted with a farm of two hundred acres, near Hamilton, which he was to work on shares. Here, and afterwards by labor in St. Catharine, he laid up several hundred dollars, and then removed to Rochester, N. Y. In that city he obtained a situation as waiter in the best hotel, where, by his aptness and readiness to serve, he so ingratiated himself with all the boarders and transient visitors that his perquisites amounted to more than enough to support him, and being totally abstinent from the use of intoxicating liquors and tobacco, he was able to lay up all his wages, — thirty dollars a month. At the expiration of two years he found that, together with what he had brought from Canada, he was possessed of about nine hundred dollars. As much of this as might be necessary, he resolved to expend in the acquisition of knowledge. Ever since his arrival at the North he had availed himself of all the assistance he could get to learn to read, and had attained to some proficiency in the art. By plying this, whenever opportunity offered him the use of books and newspapers, he had added much to his information. But he longed for more education, — at least sufficient to enable him to be useful as a minister of religion, or as a teacher of the children of his people. So he left his lucrative situation in Rochester, and entered the Oneida Institute, a manual labor school, then under the excellent management of Rev. Beriah Green.

In 1841 Mr. Loguen came to reside in Syracuse, and undertook the duties of pastor of the "African Methodist Church," and of school-teacher to the children of his people. In both these offices he was successful. And not in these alone. With the help of one of the best of wives, he has brought up a family of children, and educated them well. He has established a good, commodious, hospitable home. In it was fitted up an apartment for fugitive slaves, and, for years before the Emancipation Act, scarcely a week passed without some one, in his flight from slavedom to Canada, enjoyed shelter and repose at Elder Loguen's. By industry, frugality, and the skilful investment of his property, he has gained a good estate. He is respected by his fellow-citizens, and has so risen in the esteem of his Methodist brethren, that within the last year he has been made a bishop of their order.

FREDERICK DOUGLASS.

I need give but one more example of a colored man of my acquaintance who has exhibited great intellectual ability as well as moral worth. And he is one extensively known and admired throughout our country, Great Britain, and Ireland. Of course I mean Frederick Douglass. His well-written, intensely interesting autobiography, entitled "My Bondage and My Freedom," has probably been read so generally that I need not attempt any sketch of his life. Suffice it to say he was born a slave in Maryland. He experienced all the indignities, and suffered most of the hardships and cruelties, that passionate slaveholders could inflict upon their bondmen. When about twenty-one years of age he resolved that he would endure them no longer, and in 1838 he found his way from Baltimore to New Bedford, the best place, on the whole, to which he could have gone. There, with his young wife, he commenced the life of a freeman. The severest toil now seemed light. He worked with a will, because the avails of his labor were to be his own. Being, as most colored persons are, religiously inclined, he soon became a member of a Methodist church, and erelong was appointed a class-leader and a local preacher.

While in slavery Mr. Douglass had contrived, in various ingenious ways, to learn to read and write. So soon, therefore, as he came to live in Massachusetts, he diligently improved his enlarged opportunities to acquire knowledge. Erelong he became a subscriber for *The Liberator*, and week after week made himself master of its contents, in which he never found a silly or a worthless line. Of course its doctrines and its purpose were altogether such as his own bitter experience justified. And the exalted spirit of religious faith and hope, at all times inspiring the writings and speeches of Mr. Garrison, awakened in the bosom of Mr. Douglass the assurance that he was "the man, — the Moses raised up by God to deliver his Israel in America from a worse than Egyptian bondage."

In the summer of 1841 there was a large antislavery

convention held in Nantucket. Mr. Douglass attended it. In the midst of the meeting, to his great confusion, he was called upon and urged to address the convention. A number were present from New Bedford who had heard his exhortations in the Methodist church, and they would not allow his plea of inability to speak. After much hesitation he rose, and, notwithstanding his embarrassment, he gave evidence of such intellectual power — wisdom as well as wit — that all present were astonished. Mr. Garrison followed him in one of his sublimest speeches. "Here was a living witness of the justice of the severest condemnation he had ever uttered of slavery. Here was one 'every inch a man,' ay, a man of no common power, who yet had been held at the South as a piece of property, a chattel, and had been treated as if he were a domesticated brute," &c.

At the close of the meeting, Mr. John A. Collins, then the general agent of the Massachusetts Antislavery Society, urgently invited Mr. Douglass to become a lecturing agent. He begged to be excused. He was sure that he was not competent to such an undertaking. But Mr. Garrison and others, who had heard him that day, joined Mr. Collins in pressing him to accept the appointment. He yielded to the pressure. And, in less than three years from the day of his escape from slavery, he was introduced to the people of New England as a suitable person to lecture them upon the subject that was of more moment than any other to which the attention of our Republic had ever been called.

Mr. Douglass henceforth improved rapidly. He applied himself diligently to reading and study. The number and range of his topics in lecturing increased and widened continually. He soon became one of the favorite antislavery speakers. The notoriety which he thus acquired could not be confined to New England or the

Northern States. A murmur of inquiry came up from Maryland who this man could be. A pamphlet which he felt called upon to publish in 1845, in answer to the current assertions that he was an impostor, that he had never been a slave, made it no longer possible to conceal his personality. The danger of his being captured and taken back to Maryland was so great that it was thought advisable he should go to England. Accordingly, he went thither that year in company with James N. Buffum, one of the truest of antislavery men, and with the Hutchinson family, the sweetest of singers.

Although not permitted to go as a cabin passenger, many of the cabin passengers sought to make his acquaintance and visited him in the steerage, and invited him to visit them on the saloon-deck. At length they requested him to give them an antislavery lecture. This he consented and was about to do, when some passengers who were slaveholders chose to consider it an insult to them, and were proceeding to punish him for his insolence; they threatened even to throw him overboard, and would have done so had not the captain of the steamer interposed his absolute authority: called his men, and ordered them to put those disturbers of the peace *in irons* if they did not instantly desist. Of course they at once obeyed, and shrank back in the consciousness that they were under the dominion of a power that had broken the staff of such oppressors as themselves.

This incident of the voyage was reported in the newspapers immediately on the arrival of the vessel at Liverpool, and introduced Mr. Douglass at once to the British public. He was treated with great attention by the Abolitionists of the United Kingdom; was invited to lecture everywhere, and rendered most valuable services to the cause of his oppressed countrymen. So deeply did he interest the philanthropists of that country that they paid seven hundred and fifty dollars to procure from his master a formal, legal certificate of manumission, so that, on his return to these United States, he would be no longer liable to be sent back into slavery. They also presented him with the sum of twenty-five hundred dollars for his own benefit, to be appropriated, if he should see fit, to the establishment of a weekly paper edited by himself, which was then his favorite project.

Soon after his return in 1847 he did establish such a paper at Rochester and conducted it with ability for several years. He has since become one of the popular lecturers of our country, and every season has as many invitations as he cares to accept. He is extensively known and much respected. Many there are who wish to see him a member of Congress; and we confidently predict that, if he shall ever be sent to Washington as a Representative or a Senator, he will soon become a prominent man in either House.

THE UNDERGROUND RAILROAD.

Everybody has heard of the Underground Railroad. Many have read of its operations who have been puzzled to know where it was laid, who were the conductors of it, who kept the stations, and how large were the profits. As the company is dissolved, the rails taken up, the business at an end, I propose now to tell my readers about it.

There have always been scattered throughout the slaveholding States individuals who have abhorred slavery, and have pitied the victims of our American despotism. These persons have known, or have taken pains to find out, others at convenient distances northward from their abodes who sympathized with them in commiserating the slaves. These sympathizers have known or heard of others of like mind still farther North, who again have had acquaintances in the free States that they knew would help the fugitive on his way to liberty. Thus, lines of friends at longer or shorter distances were formed from many parts of the South to the very borders of Canada, — not very straight lines generally, but such as the fleeing bondmen might pass over safely, if they could escape their pursuers until they had come beyond the second or third stage from their starting-point. Furnished at first with written "passes," as from their masters, and afterwards with letters of introduction from one friend to another, we had reason to believe that a large proportion of those who, in this way, attempted to escape from slavery were successful. Twenty thousand at least found homes in Canada, and hundreds ventured to remain this side of the Lakes.

So long ago as 1834, when I was living in the eastern part of Connecticut, I had fugitives addressed to my care. I helped them on to that excellent man, Effingham L. Capron, in Uxbridge, afterwards in Worcester, and he forwarded them to secure retreats.

Ever after I came to reside in Syracuse I had much to do as a station-keeper or conductor on the Underground Railroad, until slavery was abolished by the Proclamation of President Lincoln, and subsequently by the according Acts of Congress. Fugitives came to me from Maryland, Virginia, Kentucky, Tennessee, and Louisiana. They came, too, at all hours of day and night, sometimes comfortably, — yes, and even handsomely clad, but generally in clothes every way unfit to be worn, and in some instances too unclean and loathsome to be admitted into my house. Once in particular, a most squalid mortal came to my back-door with a note that he had been a passenger on the Underground Railroad. "O Massa," said he, "I 'm not fit to come into your house." "No," I replied, "you are not now, but soon shall be." So I stepped in and got a tub of warm water, with towels and soap. He helped me with them into the barn. "There," said I, "give yourself a thorough washing, and throw every bit of your clothing out upon the dung-hill." He set about his task with a hearty good-will. I ran back to the house and brought out to him a complete suit of clean clothes from a deposit which my kind parishioners kept pretty well supplied. He received each article with unspeakable thankfulness. But the clean white shirt, with a collar and stock, delighted him above measure. He tarried with me a couple of days. I found him to be a man of much natural intelligence, but utterly ignorant of letters. He had had a hard master, and he went on his way to Canada exulting in his escape from tyranny.

In contrast with this specimen, my eldest son, late one Saturday night, came up from the city, and as he opened the parlor-door, said, "Here, father, is another living epistle to you from the South," and ushered in a fine-looking, well-dressed young man. I took his hand to make him sure of a welcome. "But this," said I, "is not the hand of one who has been used to doing hard work. It is softer than mine." "No, sir," he replied, "I have not been allowed to do work that would harden my hands. I have been the slave of a very wealthy planter in Kentucky, who kept me only to drive the carriage for mistress and her daughters, to wait upon them at table, and accompany them on their journeys. I was not allowed even to groom the horses, and was required to wear gloves when I drove them." Perceiving that he used good language and pronounced it properly, I said, "You must have received some instruction. I thought the laws of the slave States sternly prohibited the teaching of slaves." "They do, sir," he replied, "but my master was an easy man in that respect. My young mistresses taught me to read, and got me books and papers from their father's library. I have had much leisure time, and I have improved it." In further conversation with him I found that he was quite familiar with a considerable number of the best American and English authors, both in poetry and prose. "If you had such an easy time, and were so much favored, why," I asked, "did you run away?" "O, sir," he replied, "slavery at best is a bitter draught. Under the most favored circumstances it is bondage and degradation still. I often writhed in my chains, though they sat so lightly on me compared with most others. I was often on the point of taking wings for the North, but then the words of Hamlet would come to me, 'Better to bear those ills we have, than fly to others that we know not of,' and I should have remained with my master had it not been that I learned, a few weeks ago, that he was about to sell me to a particular friend of his, then visiting him from New Orleans. I suspected this evil was impending over me from the notice the gentleman took of me and the kind of questions he asked me.

"At length, one of my young mistresses, who knew my dread of being sold, came to me and, bursting into tears, said, 'Harry, father is going to sell you.' She put five dollars into my hand and went weeping away. With that, and with much more money that I had received from time to time, and saved for the hour of need, I started that night and reached the Ohio River before morning. I immediately crossed to Cincinnati and hurried on board a steamer, the steward of which was a black man of my acquaintance. He concealed me until the boat had returned to Pittsburg. There he introduced me to a gentleman that he knew to be a friend of us colored folks. That gentleman sent me to a friend in Meadville, and he directed me to come to you." "Well," said I, "Harry, if you are a good coachman and waiter withal, I can get you an excellent situation in this city, which will enable you to live comfortably until you shall have become acquainted with our Northern manners and customs, and have found some better business." "O," he hastily replied, "thank you, sir, but I should not dare to stop this side of Canada. My master, though he was kind to me, is a proud and very passionate man. He will never forgive me for running away. He has already advertised me, offering a large reward for my apprehension and return to him. I should not be beyond his reach here. I must go to Canada." He tarried with us until Monday afternoon, when I sent him to Oswego with a letter of introduction to a gentleman in Kingston, and a few days afterwards heard of his safe arrival there.

Not long after, I one day saw a young lady, of fine person and handsomely dressed, coming up our front steps. She inquired for me, and was ushered into my study. A blue veil partly concealed her face and a pair of white gloves covered her hands. On being assured that I was Mr. S. J. May she said, "I have come to you, sir, as a friend of colored people and of slaves." "Is it possible," I replied, "that you are one of that class of my fellow-beings?" She removed her veil, and a slight tinge in her complexion revealed the fact that she belonged to the proscribed race, — a beautiful octoroon. "But where were you ever a slave?" I asked. "In New Orleans, sir. My master, who, I believe, was also my father, is concerned in a line of packet steamers that ply between New Orleans and Galveston. He has, for several years past, kept me on board one of his boats as the chamber-maid. This was rather an easy and not a disagreeable situation. I was with the lady passengers most of the time, and by my close attentions to them, especially when they were sea-sick, I conciliated many. They often made me presents of money, clothes, and trinkets. And, what was better than all, they taught me to read. At each end of the route I had hours and days of leisure, which I improved as best I could. The thought that I was a slave often tormented me. But, as in other respects I was comfortable, I might have continued in bondage, had I not found out that my master was about to sell me to a dissolute young man for the vilest of purposes. I at once looked about for a way of escape. Being so much of the time among the shipping at New Orleans, I had learnt to distinguish the vessels of different nations. So I went to one that I saw was an English ship, on board of which I espied a lady, — the captain's wife. I asked if I might come on board. 'Certainly,' she replied. Encouraged by her kind manner, I soon revealed to her my secret and my wish to escape. She could hardly be persuaded that I was a slave. But when all doubt on that point was removed, she readily consented to take me with her to New York. To my unspeakable relief we sailed the next day. The captain was equally kind. I was able to pay as much as he would take for my passage, for I had succeeded in getting all the money I had saved, with much of my clothing, on board the ship the night before she left New Orleans. On our arrival at New York the captain took pains to inquire for the Abolitionists. He was directed to Mr. Lewis Tappan, and took me with him to that good gentleman. Mr. Tappan at once provided for my safety in that city, and the next day sent me to Mr. Myers, at Albany, on my way to you."

I offered to find a place for her in some one of the best families in Syracuse; but she was afraid to remain here. She had seen in New York her master's advertisement, offering five hundred dollars for her restoration to him.

She was sure there were pursuers on her track. Two men in the car between Albany and Syracuse had annoyed and alarmed her by their close observation of her. One had seated himself by her side and tried to engage her in conversation and look through her veil. At length he asked her to take off the glove on her left hand. By this she knew he must have seen the advertisement, that stated, among other marks by which she might be identified, that one finger on her left hand was minus a joint. She at once called to the conductor and asked him to protect her from the impertinent liberties the man was taking with her. So he gave her another seat by a lady, and she reached our city without any further molestation, but in great alarm.

We secreted her several days, until we supposed her pursuers must have gone on. She occupied herself most of the time by reading, and we observed that she often was poring over a French book, and on inquiring learnt that she could read that language about as well as English. So soon as her fears were sufficiently allayed, I committed her to the care of one of my good antislavery parishioners who happened to be going to Oswego. He escorted her thither, saw her safely on board the steamboat for Kingston, and a few days afterwards I received a well-written letter from her informing me of her safe arrival, and that she had obtained a good situation in a pleasant family as children's maid.

I need give my readers but one more specimen of the many passengers I have conducted on the Underground Railroad. At eleven o'clock one Saturday night, in the fall of the year, three stalwart negroes came to my door with "a pass" from a friend in Albany. They were miserably clad for that season of the year and almost famished with hunger. We gave them a good, hearty supper, but could not accommodate them through the night. So at twelve o'clock I sallied forth with them to find a place or places where they could be safely and comfortably kept, until we could forward them to Canada. This was not so easily done as it might have been at an earlier hour. I did not get back to my home until after two in the morning. The next forenoon, after sermon I made known to my congregation their destitute condition, and asked for clothes and money. Before night I received enough of each for the three, and some to spare for other comers. I need only add, that in due time they were safely committed to the protection of the British Queen.

Other friends of the slave in Syracuse were often called upon in like manner, and sometimes put to as great inconvenience as I was in the last instance named above. So we formed an association to raise the means to carry on our operations at this station. And we made an arrangement with Rev. J. W. Loguen to fit up suitably an apartment in his house for the accommodation of all the fugitives, that might come here addressed to either one of us. The charge thus committed to them Mr. Loguen and his excellent wife faithfully and kindly cared for to the last. And I more than suspect that the fugitives they harbored, and helped on their way, often cost them much more than they called upon us to pay.

It was natural that I should feel not a little curious, and sometimes quite anxious, to know how those whom I had helped into Canada were faring there. So I went twice to see; the first time to Toronto and its neighborhood, the second time to that part of Canada which lies between Lake Erie and Lake Huron. I visited Windsor, Sandwich, Chatham, and Buxton. In each of these towns I found many colored people, most of whom had escaped thither from slavery in one or another of the United States. With very few exceptions, I found them living comfortably, and, without an exception, all of them were rejoicing in their liberty.

I was particularly interested in the Buxton settlement, called so in honor of that distinguished English philanthropist, Hon. Fowell Buxton. It was established by the benevolent enterprise and managed by the excellent good sense of Rev. William King. This gentleman was a well-educated Scotch Presbyterian minister. He had come to America and settled in Mississippi. There he married a lady whose parents soon after died, leaving him, with his wife, in possession of a considerable property in slaves. He was ill at ease in such a possession, but, as he held it in the right of his wife, he did not feel at liberty to do with it as he would otherwise have done. A few years afterwards she died. By this dispensation he was made the sole proprietor of the persons of fifteen of his fellow-beings, and he was brought to feel that the great purpose of his life should be to deliver them from slavery, and place them in circumstances under which they might become what God had made them capable of being. With this purpose at heart he went to Canada. He purchased nine thousand acres of government land of good quality and well located, though covered with a dense forest. To this place he transported, from Mississippi, his fifteen slaves, and gave to each of them fifty acres. He then offered to sell farms for two dollars and a half an acre to colored men, who should bring satisfactory testimonials of good moral character and strictly temperate habits. When I was there in 1852, about four years after the beginning of his undertaking, there were ninety families settled in Buxton. Mr. King told me there had not been a single instance of intoxication or of any disorderly conduct, and most of them had nearly paid for their farms.

I spent the whole day with this wise man, this practical philanthropist, in visiting the settlers at their homes in the woods. I found them all contented, happy, enterprising. Several of them confessed to me that they had never suffered such hardships as they had experienced since they came to live in Canada. The severity of the cold had sometimes tried them to the utmost, and clearing up their heavy-timbered lands had been hard work indeed, especially for those who had been house-servants in Southern cities. But not one of them looked back with desiring eyes to the leeks and onions of the Egypt from which they had escaped. They seemed to be sustained and animated by one of the noblest sentiments that can take possession of the human soul, — the love of liberty, the determination to be free. They had cheerfully made sacrifices in this behalf. Like the Pilgrim Fathers of New England, many of them had fled from the abodes of ease, elegance, luxury, and sought homes in a wilderness that they might be free. Like them they counted it all joy to suffer, — perils by land and by water, travels by night, a flight in the winter, and a life in the wilds in an inhospitable climate, if by so suffering they might secure to themselves and their posterity the inestimable boon of liberty.

GEORGE LATIMER.

It must be obvious to my readers that I have not been guided in my narrative by the order of time, so much as by the relation of events and actors to one another. My last article had to do in part with occurrences that happened in 1852. I shall now return to 1842.

Much to my surprise, in 1842, I was nominated by Hon. Horace Mann, and appointed by the Massachusetts Board of Education, to succeed Rev. Cyrus Peirce as Principal of the Normal School then at Lexington.

At once was heard from various quarters murmurs of displeasure, because an *Abolitionist* had been intrusted with the preparation of teachers for our common schools. Mr. Mann was not a little annoyed. He earnestly admonished me to beware of giving occasion to those unfriendly to the school to allege that I was taking advantage of my position to disseminate my antislavery opinions and spirit. I assured him that I should not conceal my sentiments and feelings on a subject of such transcendent importance. But he might depend upon me that I should not give any time that belonged to the school to any other institution or enterprise; that I should conscientiously endeavor to discharge faithfully every one of my duties; but that, as I should not be able to attend antislavery meetings, or co-operate personally with the Abolitionists, except perhaps in vacations, I should contribute to their treasury more money than I had hitherto been able to afford.

Accordingly, I consecrated every day and every evening of every week of term time to my duties, so long as I was principal of that school, excepting only the afternoon and evening of every Saturday. Those hours I always gave up to some kind of recreation. So much as this about myself, the readers will soon perceive, is pertinent to the tale now to be unfolded.

Some time in the month of October, 1842, an interesting young man, calling himself George Latimer, made his appearance in Boston. He was so nearly white that few suspected he belonged to the proscribed class. But soon afterwards a Mr. Gray, of Norfolk, Virginia, arrived in the city, and claimed the young man as his slave. At his instigation a constable arrested Latimer, and the keeper of Leverett Street Jail took him into confinement. Their only warrant for this assault upon the liberty of Latimer was a written order from the said Gray. It was as follows: —

"TO THE JAILER OF THE COUNTY OF SUFFOLK.

"SIR, — George Latimer, a negro slave belonging to me, and a fugitive from my service in Norfolk, in the State of Virginia, who is now committed to your custody by John Wilson, my agent and attorney, I request and DIRECT you to hold on my account, at my costs, until removed by me according to law.

"JAMES B. GRAY.

"BOSTON, October 21, 1842."

To this high-handed assumption of authority was added an indorsement, by a young lawyer of Boston, of which the following is a copy : —

"BOSTON, October 21, 1842.

"I hereby promise to pay to the keeper of the jail any sum due him for keeping the body of said Latimer, on demand.

"E. G. AUSTIN."

With reason were the good people of Boston and the old Commonwealth aroused, excited, almost maddened with indignation and alarm at this insolent, daring assault upon the palladium of their liberty. If such a proceeding should be allowed, no one would be safe, black or white. Here comes a man from a distant part of our country, an utter stranger in our city, and arrests another man about as light-complexioned as himself, claims him as his negro slave, and, without offering any proof that he had ever held the man in that condition, hands him over to a common jailer for safe-keeping. This surely could not be borne with. Some of the colored people to whom Latimer was known first bestirred themselves. They attempted to get him out of prison by a writ of *habeas corpus*. Hon. Samuel E. Sewall, the long-tried friend of the oppressed, always ready to endure obloquy and encounter danger in their service, assisted by his friend, C. M. Ellis, Esq., earnestly endeavored to get that writ allowed. They petitioned for it in the Court at which Chief Justice Shaw was then presiding, and, strange to say, their petition was denied. That eminent jurist, on the authority of the United States Court, in the famous Prigg case, gave it as his opinion, that, by the supreme law of the land, so expounded, the man Gray had permission to come to Boston and seize the man Latimer (as he had done), put him into jail or some other place of confinement, and keep him there until he could have time to bring on proof that he was his property, and then take him off by the assistance of any persons he could get to help him. Accordingly, Judge Shaw refused the writ of *habeas corpus*, and left Latimer in Leverett Street prison. This action of the chief justice aggravated the public excitement.

Mr. Gray, alarmed probably by the outcries of indignation that came to him from so many quarters, brought charges against Latimer of thefts committed upon his property, both in Norfolk and in Boston, as the reason for his arrest. If this were true, it was said, he surely should have proceeded against the criminal, in the ordinary course at common law, and not under the decision in the Prigg case. But by this step he got himself into another and graver difficulty. George Latimer, instructed by his legal advisers, at once commenced the prosecution of Gray for slander and libel. So the biter, finding he was about to be bitten, let go this hold upon poor Latimer, and determined to rely wholly upon the decision of Judge Story of the United States Court, who was soon to hold a session in Boston.

But the excitement of the public had spread far and wide, and the tones of indignation were deeper and louder. An immense meeting was held in Faneuil Hall. Mr. Sewall presided, and made a full, clear statement of the case, exhibiting all its odious features. Mr. Edmund

Quincy addressed the meeting with great force; and Mr. Phillips spoke most effectively. Public meetings on the subject were held in Lynn, Salem, New Bedford, Worcester, Abington, and in many other large towns. And petitions were prepared and extensively signed and sent to Congress, praying that we of the free States might be relieved from such outrages upon the feelings of the people, and such violations of common law, as could be perpetrated under the exposition of United States law, given by the court in the "Prigg case." Petitions were also prepared and extensively signed to the Massachusetts Legislature, praying that the prisons and jails of the Commonwealth might not be used by slaveholders or their agents for the safe-keeping of their fugitive bondmen when retaken; and that all sheriffs, constables, police officers of every grade might be peremptorily forbidden, in any way, to assist in the capture or return of slaves.

The sheriff and the deputy sheriff of Suffolk County and the keeper of Leverett Street Jail were severely censured for the part they had taken in Mr. Gray's service. And the sheriff was about to order the release of Latimer, when negotiations were entered into with Mr. Gray for the purchase of his victim's emancipation. Fearing that he might lose all, he concluded to take a part, and sold him for four hundred dollars, although he had declared he would not let him go for three times that sum.

Wholly engrossed as I was by my duties in the Normal School, I could not help hearing of the great excitement, and sympathizing with those who were determined Massachusetts should not be made a hunting-ground for slaves. At length it was reported that there was to be "*a Latimer meeting*" at Waltham, five or six miles from Lexington. And lo! a few days afterwards there came letters from Rev. Samuel Ripley, then the prominent minister of Waltham, and from his son-in-law, the Rev.

George F. Simmons, who a few years before had been compelled to resign his pastorate of the Unitarian Church of Mobile, and hastily leave the city, because he had dared to speak from his pulpit of the evils of slavery and the duties of those who held their fellow-beings in that condition.

Each of those gentlemen cordially invited me, urgently requested me, to attend the meeting in behalf of George Latimer that was to be held in their meeting-house, adding that it was appointed on the next Saturday evening, so as to accommodate the operatives in the factories, who were not required to work on that evening.

As I have already said, Saturday evening was my *leisure* time. Always on closing school at noon of Saturday, I endeavored to lay aside my cares with my text-books, and if possible think no more of school until Sunday evening, when I never failed to examine the lessons I intended to teach the next day. It seemed to me that nothing would refresh and recreate me so much as attending an antislavery meeting, and giving vent to my pent-up feelings. Then I was the more eager to go to Waltham, because Mr. Ripley was one of those who had been particularly severe and satirical in their remarks upon *my* appointment to the charge of the Normal School. I really wished to see how he would look, and act, and speak, under the inspiration of his new-born zeal in the cause of freedom. So I informed my two devoted assistants, who needed recreation not less than myself, and who I knew were zealous Abolitionists, of my intention, and invited them to accompany me. Almost immediately I received the names of twenty of my pupils who wished to attend the meeting. Accordingly, I procured two double sleighs, and we started for Waltham, as I supposed in good season. But we did not not reach the meeting-house until just as the exercises were to begin. We naturally walked in together without the slightest thought of making a parade. But on opening the door, we found all the pews filled excepting the conspicuous ones, on either side of the pulpit. To these, therefore, we went as quietly as possible, but not without attracting the notice of the audience, and calling out the remark from more than one, "There comes Mr. May with his Normal School!"

Before long I was invited by Rev. Mr. Ripley, who presided, to address the meeting. I did so for twenty minutes or more, and I have no doubt that my words and manner, my accents and emphases, showed plainly enough how deep was my abhorrence of slavery, and how sincerely I sympathized in the public alarm caused by the high-handed procedure of the claimant of Latimer and his abettors.

I returned to Lexington revived, invigorated, knowing that I had neglected no duty to the school, and utterly unconscious that I had violated any obligations, expressed or implied by my words, when I accepted the appointment. But a few days afterwards I received a letter from Mr. Mann, complaining of what I had done, informing me that I had given serious offence to several prominent gentlemen of Waltham, and had lost as a pupil a bright, fine girl who was intending to enter my school at the beginning of the next term. I replied stating the circumstances of the case just as I have done above, — that I had taken no time, withheld no attention, no thought, which was due to the school; adding that I did not believe any concealment of my sentiments, or other unreasonable concessions to the prejudices of the pro-slavery portion of the community, would conciliate them. But, as it seemed my understanding of my duties differed so much from his, I thought it best for me to retire from the position; and therefore I tendered him my resignation. This he would not communicate to the Board, and requested me to withdraw it. I did so. But scarcely a month had elapsed before it was announced in the newspapers that I was to deliver one in a course of antislavery lectures in Boston, without stating, as I had requested, that it would be given *during my vacation.* This brought a still more earnest remonstrance from Mr. Mann, showing how hard pressed he was on every side by the conflicting influences, in the midst of which he was striving so nobly to infuse into our common schools the right spirit, and to establish our system of public instruction upon the true principles of human development and culture. In this instance he was more easily satisfied that I had not departed from even the letter of our agreement, though I have no doubt he wished I would keep my antislavery zeal in abeyance through my vacations, as well as in term time.

I have given this recollection, that my readers may be more fully informed to what extent the so-called free States of our Union, not excepting Massachusetts, were permeated by the spirit of the slaveholders, or rather by the disposition to acquiesce in their most overbearing demands.

Let it not, however, for a moment be inferred, from what I have related, that Horace Mann was ever willing, for any consideration, to abandon the rights of the enslaved to the will of their oppressors, and suffer the dominion of slaveholders to be extended over the whole of our country. Far otherwise. A few years after the arrest of Latimer, Mr. Mann became a member of Congress; and there he uttered some of the boldest words for freedom and humanity ever heard in our Capitol. As he assured his constituents, in convention at Dedham on the 6th November, 1850, "with voice and vote, by expostulation and by remonstrance, by all means in his power, to the full extent of his ability, he resisted the passage of all the laws" proposed in Mr. Clay's Omnibus Bill, especially the one respecting fugitives from slavery. He emphatically declared that "he regarded the question of human freedom, with all the public and private consequences dependent upon it, both now and in all futurity, as first, foremost, chiefest among all the questions that have been before the government, or are likely to be before it."

But in 1842 Mr. Mann could not foresee, nor be persuaded to apprehend, that the senators and representatives of the Southern States would become audacious enough in 1850 to demand that the people of the free States should do for them the work of slave-catchers and bloodhounds. And he was, at that time, so intent upon his great undertaking for the improvement of our common schools, that he thought it our duty to repress our interest in every other reform that was unpopular.

THE ANNEXATION OF TEXAS.

He who knew so well what is in man said: "The children of this world are wiser towards their generation than the children of light." And certainly the slaveholders of our country and their partisans have been incomparably more vigilant in watching for whatever might affect the stability of their "peculiar institution," and far more adroit in devising measures, and resolute in pressing them to the maintenance and extension of *Slavery*, than their opponents have been in behalf of *Liberty*.

Slave labor has ever been found wasteful and exhaustive of the soil from which it has taken the crops. Therefore, it used to be a common saying, "the Southern planter needs all the lands that join his estate."

Ample as was the territory of that portion of the United States in which slavery was established, the "barons of the South" early looked beyond their borders for new acquisitions of land. Partly to gratify their cupidity, the immense tract of land between the Mississippi and the Rocky Mountains, with the valley of the Columbia River, was purchased by our Federal Government in 1803. Sixteen years afterwards Florida was given them. And then they began to turn their desiring eyes upon the rich and fertile plains of Texas. They gained admission to these by an artifice worthy of men who were accustomed to set at naught all the rights of humanity. In 1819 a man named Austin, then living in Missouri, went to Spain, represented to the King that the Roman Catholics in the United States were subjected to grievous persecutions, and supplicated for them an asylum in Mexico. His pious Majesty, deeply moved by this appeal, made a very large and gratuitous grant of land of the finest quality to Austin and his associates on this one condition, that they should introduce within a limited time a certain number of Roman Catholic settlers "of good moral character." This condition was complied with, and thus our Southern slaveholders gained a foothold in Texas. They were diligent to confirm and extend their possession by the sale of immense quantities of land to intended settlers and to land jobbers throughout the Southern States. Thus commenced what erelong became "one of the most stupendous systems of bribery and corruption ever devised by man."

In 1821 Mexico became independent of the Spanish crown, and soon after confirmed the royal grant to the settlers in her province of Texas. In 1824 the Mexican Government adopted some measures preparatory to the manumission of slaves, and in 1829 decreed the complete and immediate emancipation of all in bonds throughout their borders.

The vigilant Southerners were of course alarmed. A nation of freemen adjoining them on the Southwest! A door thrown wide open for the easy escape of fugitives from their tyrannous grasp!! Something must be done to avert the threatened evil. Mr. Benton, of Missouri, in 1829, broached the scheme of the annexation of Texas, and the re-establishment of slavery there. He urged this as obviously necessary: first, in order to prevent the easy and continual escape of their slaves into an adjoining free country, the government of which had persistently refused to return the fugitives; second, to open a new field for slave labor, which was rapidly exhausting the soil of the old States, and a new market for the slaves of those States which, no longer capable of producing large crops, might still be sustained in population and political power by becoming the nurseries of slaves for the immense territory, to be obtained from Mexico by purchase or force; third, by adding to the number of slave States, to provide new securities for the continued ascendency of the slaveholders' influence in the government of the nation.

This last reason was probably the most momentous in the estimation of Southern statesmen. For the Texas, which they aimed to annex to our country, they foresaw might from time to time be divided and subdivided into seven States as large as New York, or into forty-three States as large as Massachusetts. Thus might the majority of the United States Senate be kept always ready to support any measure favorable to the interests of the slaveholding aristocracy, which had assumed the government of our Republic. Mr. Calhoun openly declared that "the measure of annexation is calculated and designed to uphold the institution of slavery, extend its influence, and secure its permanent duration."

The devoted, indefatigable, self-sacrificing, Benjamin Lundy, was living in Missouri at the time when Mr.

Benton first proposed the Texas scheme, and at once gave him battle, so far as he was permitted to do it, in the newspapers of that State. Afterwards on removing to Maryland and establishing there his own paper, *The Genius of Universal Emancipation,* he did all in his power to alarm the country. He went to Texas and, at great personal hazard, traversed that country and gathered a large amount of most important information, revealing the spirit of the settlers there and the designs of the projectors and managers of the scheme.

He did not labor in vain. The leading National Republican papers in the free States seconded his efforts. Especially my good friend and classmate David Lee Child, Esq., as early as 1829, when editor of *The Massachusetts Journal,* emphatically denounced the dismemberment and robbery of Mexico for the protection and perpetuation of slavery in the United States. And he manfully contended against that nefarious, execrable plot until further opposition was made useless, as we shall see, by the perpetration of the great inquity in 1845. In 1835 Mr. Child addressed a number of carefully prepared letters to Mr. Edward S. Abdy, a philanthropic English gentleman, hoping thereby to awaken the attention of British Abolitionists. In 1836 he wrote nine or ten able articles on the impending evil, that were published in a Philadelphia paper. The next year he went to France and England. In Paris he addressed an elaborate memoir to the "Société pour l'Abolition d'Esclavage," and in London he published in the *Eclectic Review* a full exposition of the interest which the British nation ought to take in utterly extinguishing the slave-trade, and preventing the re-establishment of slavery in Texas, and the aggrandizement of the unprincipled slaveholding power in that country, larger than the whole of France. No two persons did so much to prevent the annexation of Texas as did Benjamin Lundy and David L. Child. They undoubtedly furnished the Hon. John Q. Adams with much of the information and some of the weapons that he plied with so much vigor on the floor of Congress; but, alas! as the event proved, with so little effect to prevent the great transgression which the Southern statesmen led our nation to commit. At first the indignation of the people in many of the free States at the proposed extension of the domain of slaveholders, and the confirmation of their ascendency in the government of our nation, seemed to be general, deep, and fervent. In 1838 the legislatures of Massachusetts, Ohio, and Rhode Island, with great unanimity, passed resolutions, earnestly and solemnly protesting against the annexation of Texas to our Union, and declaring that no act done, or compact made for that purpose, by the government of the United States would be binding on the States or the people.

For a while it seemed as if the villany was averted; but it was started again in 1843, and from that time until its consummation the protests of the above-named States were renewed with frequent repetition and, if possible, in still more emphatic language. No party within their borders ventured to take the side of the slaveholders. Connecticut and New Jersey at that time joined in the protest. Massachusetts of course took the lead. Meetings of the people, to declare their opposition to the proposed outrage upon the Union, were held in many of the principal towns of the State. At length, when the resolutions providing for the annexation were pending in both Houses of Congress, a great convention of her citizens met in Faneuil Hall, to make known their displeasure in a still more impressive tone and manner. The call to the meeting was signed by prominent men of all parties. It invited the cities and towns of the Commonwealth to send as many delegates to the Convention as they could legally send representatives to the General Court. This took place in January, 1845, only three months before my removal to Syracuse. I was then living in Lexington. A town-meeting was held there to respond to the call to Faneuil Hall, by the choice of two delegates. To my great surprise I was chosen one of the two, and General Chandler, high sheriff of the county, was the other. But unutterable was my astonishment when, on coming into the Convention, I found William Lloyd Garrison seated among the members, sent thither with other delegates by the votes of a large majority of the Tenth Ward of the city of Boston, where he resided. This did, indeed, betoken a marvellous change in the sentiments and feelings of the community. He, who a few years before had been dragged through the streets with a halter, by a mob of "gentlemen of property and standing," clamoring for his immediate execution, was there in the "Cradle of Liberty," member of a Convention that comprised the men of Massachusetts who were accustomed to represent, on important occasions, the intelligence, the patriotism, and weight of character of the Commonwealth.

Mr. Garrison addressed the Convention, and was listened to with respectful attention. I need not say that he spoke in a manner worthy of the place and the occasion, and in perfect consistency with his avowed principles. The chief business done by the Convention was the issuing of an elaborate, carefully prepared Address to the people of the United States, setting forth the reasons why Texas should not be annexed to our Republic, and why we ought not to submit to such a violation of the Constitution of our Union, and such an outrage upon the territory and institutions of an adjoining nation. Mr. Garrison published the document in his

Liberator of the next week and said, "The Address of the Convention was, as a whole, a most forcible and eloquent document, worthy to be read of all men, and to be preserved to the latest posterity. It was adopted unanimously, after a disclaimer by Samuel J. May and myself of that portion of it which seeks to vindicate the United States Constitution from the charge of guaranteeing protection to slavery." I was irresistibly impelled to ask that that part of the otherwise admirable Address might be omitted, because it would obliterate the most momentous lesson taught in the history of our nation,— namely, that the reluctant, indirect, inferential consent given by the framers of our Republic to the continuance of slavery in the land — not any deliberate explicit guaranty — had countenanced and sustained the friends of that "System of Iniquity," from generation to generation, in violating the inalienable rights of millions of our fellow-beings, and had brought upon us, who are opposed to that system, the evils of political discord, national disgrace, and the fear of national disruption and ruin.

I urged the Convention to acknowledge distinctly that, "under the commonly received interpretation of the Constitution, we have hitherto been giving our countenance and support to the slaveholders in their outrages upon humanity, the fundamental rights of man, — an iniquity of which we will no longer be guilty. We have been roused from our insensibility to the wrongs we have wickedly consented should be inflicted upon others — "the least of the brethren" — by the discovery of the evils we have thereby brought upon ourselves, and the ruin that awaits our nation if we do not stay the iniquity where it is, and commence at once the work "meet for the repentance" that alone can save us,— the extermination of slavery from our borders." "Let this Convention declare, that we certainly will not consent to the extension of slavery,—no, not an inch. And if they urge to its consummation the annexation of Texas, in the way they propose, they will, by so doing, trample the Constitution under foot, set at naught some of its most important provisions, grossly violate the compact of our United States, and therefore absolve us from all obligations to respect it or live under it any longer."

Mr. Garrison urged that the Address should be further amended by adding that, if our protest and remonstrance shall be disregarded, and Texas be annexed, then shall the Committee of the Convention call another at the same place; that then and here Massachusetts shall declare the union of these States dissolved, and invite all the States, that may be disposed, to reunite with her as a Republic based truly upon the grand principles of the Declaration of Independence. Although his motion was not carried by the Convention, it was received with great favor by a large portion of the members and other auditors; and he sat down amidst the most hearty bursts of applause.

It seemed as if the opposition of Massachusetts and other States to annexation was too strong, and the reasons urged against it were too weighty, to be disregarded by the legislators, the guardians of the nation. The contest waxed and waned throughout the whole of the year 1845. A petition signed by fifty thousand persons was sent to Congress at its opening in December of that year. But several prominent Whig members of Congress from the Southern States were found, in the end, to care more for the perpetuation of slavery than for their party or their principles. And certain members from the free States (one even from Massachusetts) were plied by considerations and alarmed by threats, which the Southern statesmen knew so well how to wield, until they gave way, and suffered the nefarious, the abominable, unconstitutional, disastrous deed to be done, — *Texas to be annexed.*

Late in the year 1845, when some of the hitherto opposers were evidently about to yield, Mr. D. L. Child, as a final effort against the consummation of the great iniquity, prepared an admirable article for the *New York Tribune*, under the title, — "Taking Nâboth's Vineyard." But alas! "considerations" had affected Mr. Greeley's mind also, and he refused to publish it. Mr. Child then hired him to publish the article in a supplement to his paper, and paid him sixty dollars for the service. But instead of treating it as a supplement is wont to be treated, instead of distributing it coextensively with the principal issue, my friend tells me that Mr. Greeley, having supplied the members of the two Houses of Congress each with a copy, sent the residue of the edition to him. So strangely have political considerations, particularly those suggested by slaveholding statesmen, influenced the politicians of the North.

Other besides political considerations were no doubt plied to affect the votes of the representatives of the free States. It was reported at the time that no less than forty of them had their pockets stuffed with Texas scrip, which would become very valuable if annexation should be effected.

ABOLITIONISTS IN CENTRAL NEW YORK. — GERRIT SMITH.

In April, 1845, I came to reside in Syracuse. Having visited the place twice before, I was pretty well acquainted with the characters of the people with whom I should be associated, and the rapidly growing importance of the town, owing to its central position and its staple product. During each of my visits I had delivered antislavery lectures to good audiences, and found quite a number of individuals here who had accepted the doctrines of the Immediate Abolitionists. Mr. Garrison, Gerrit Smith, Mr. Douglass, and others, had lectured in Syracuse several times, and, though at first insulted and repulsed, they had convinced so many people of the justice of their demands for the enslaved, and of the disastrous influence of the "peculiar institution" of our Southern States, that the community had come to respect somewhat the right of any who pleased to hold antislavery meetings. The minister and many of the members of the Orthodox Congregational Church, as well as the Unitarian, were decided Abolitionists, and several members of the Presbyterian, Methodist, and Baptist churches openly favored the great reform.

On the first of the following August, at the invitation of a large number of the citizens, I delivered an address on British West India Emancipation from the pulpit of the First Presbyterian Church, and it was published by the request of a large number of the auditors, — half of them members of one or another of the orthodox sects.

On the 10th of the next month a large meeting was held in the Congregational Church to uphold the freedom of the press, and to protest against the alarming assault that had been made upon that palladium of our liberties in Kentucky, by the violent suppression of *The True American*, — a paper established and edited by Hon. Cassius M. Clay, to urge upon his fellow-citizens the self-evident truths of our Declaration of Independence, and their application to the colored population of that State. Our meeting was officered by some of the most prominent and highly respected citizens of Syracuse. And after several excellent speeches, a series of very pertinent, explicit, emphatic antislavery resolutions was unanimously adopted. Thus was my great regret at being removed so far from the New England Abolitionists assuaged by the sympathy and co-operation of many of my new neighbors and fellow-citizens.

On another account I had reason to rejoice in my removal to this place. Here I found myself within a few miles of the residence of Gerrit Smith, and very soon was brought into an intimate acquaintance with that pre-eminent philanthropist. Here I must indulge myself in telling some of the much that I have known of the benefactions of this magnificent giver.

If I have been correctly informed, Mr. Smith obtained by inheritance from his father and by purchase from his fellow-heirs (besides much other property) *seven hundred and fifty thousand acres of land* lying in various parts of New York and of several other States. Erelong he became deeply impressed by a sense of his responsibility to God for the right use of such an immense portion of the earth's surface, — the common heritage of man. He could not believe that it had been given him merely for his own gratification or aggrandizement. He received it as a trust committed to him for the benefit of others. He felt as a steward, who would have to give an account of the estate intrusted to his care. He contrasted his condition with that of others, — he the possessor of an amount of land which no one man could occupy and improve, — millions of his fellow-men, inhabitants of the same country, without a rood that they could call their own and fix upon it the humblest home. He profoundly pitied the landless, and earnestly set himself to consider the best way in which to bestow portions of his estate upon those who needed them most.

The father of Mr. Smith, like most other gentlemen of his day in New York, was a slaveholder until many years after the Revolution. Gerrit was accustomed to slavery through his childhood, and until he was old enough to judge for himself of its essential and terrible iniquity. He has repeatedly assured me that, although the bondage of his father's negroes was of the mildest type, he early saw that slaveholding was egregiously wrong, and sympathized deeply with the enslaved. He rejoiced when the law of the State, in 1827, prohibited utterly its continuance, and immediately felt that all that could be should be done to repair the injuries it had inflicted upon those who had been subjected to it. He longed for the entire, immediate abolition of the great iniquity throughout the land. He early joined the Colonization Society, believing that the tendency of the plan, as well as the intention of many of its Southern patrons, was to effect the subversion and overthrow of that gigantic system of wickedness. Notwithstanding the exposures of its duplicity made by Mr. Garrison and Judge William Jay, he retained his confidence in the Colonization Society, and contributed generously to its funds, until near the close of the year 1835. At that time, as I have stated heretofore, Mr. Smith became fully convinced that the Society was opposed to the emancipation of our enslaved countrymen, unless followed by their expatriation. Thereupon he paid three thousand dollars, the balance due on his subscription to its funds, and withdrew forever from the Colonization Society, to which he had contributed at least *ten thousand* dollars.

This discovery that even these professed friends of our colored people, with whom he had been co-operating, were planning to get them out of the country, and proposed to make their *removal* the condition of their release from slavery, roused Mr. Smith to new efforts and still more generous contributions of money for their relief. He not only joined the American and the New York Antislavery Societies, and gave very largely to the funds of each,—in all not less than *fifty thousand* dollars,—but, he set about endeavoring to get as many free colored men as possible settled upon lands and in homes of their own. Before the middle of 1847 he had given an average of forty acres apiece to three thousand colored men, in all one hundred and twenty thousand acres. He did me the honor to appoint me one of the almoners of this bounty, so I am not left merely to conjecture how much time and caution were put in requisition to insure as far as practicable the judicious bestowment of these parcels of land. The only conditions prescribed by the donor were, that the receivers of his acres should be known to be landless, strictly temperate and honest men.

Mr. Smith exerted himself in various ways to secure the blessings of *education* to those of the proscribed race who were at liberty to receive them. He established and for a number of years maintained a school in Peterboro', to which colored people came from far and near. He was an early and very liberal patron of Oneida Institute, the doors of which were ever open, without any respect to complexion or race. He gave to that school several thousand dollars, and upwards of three thousand acres in Vermont, besides land contracts upon which considerable sums were still due.

Mr. Smith did much more for Oberlin College, because of its hospitality to colored pupils and those of both sexes as well as all complexions. He gave to it outright between five and six thousand dollars, and twenty thousand acres of land in Virginia, from the sales of which the college must have derived more than fifty thousand dollars.

Moreover, the unsuccessful attempt to establish and maintain New York Central College at McGrawville, where colored and white young men and women were well instructed together for a few years, cost Mr. Smith four or five thousand dollars.

But I cannot leave my readers to infer from my silence that his benefactions were confined wholly or mainly to colored persons. His gifts to other needy ones, and to institutions for their benefit, were more numerous and larger than he himself has been careful to record. Many of them have come to my knowledge, and I will so far depart from the main object of my book as to mention two.

In 1850 Mr. Smith called upon me and other friends to assist him in selecting five hundred poor white men, strictly temperate and honest, to each of whom he would give forty acres. And having learnt that some of his colored beneficiaries had been unable to raise means enough to remove with their families to the lands he had given them, he added ten dollars apiece to the portions that he gave to the white men.

Not satisfied with these bestowments, yearning over the poverty of the many who had little or nothing in a world where he had so much, and having given fifty dollars to each of a hundred and forty poor, worthy women, whose wants had been brought to his consideration, he again requested me and others to find out in our neighborhoods five hundred worthy widowed or single poor white women, to whom such a donation would be especially helpful, that he might have the pleasure of bestowing upon them also fifty dollars apiece. I need not say that these unasked, unexpected gifts carried great relief and joy wherever they were sent.

But such labors of love, although so grateful to his benevolent heart, were *labors.* Then Mr. Smith's sympathy with his suffering fellow-beings, whom he could not immediately relieve, and his lively interest and hearty co-operation in all moral and social reforms, were unavoidably wearing. As might have been expected, his health was impaired and at length gave away. In the latter part of 1858 he had a serious attack of typhoid fever, which was followed by months of mental prostration. And after his recovery he was obliged for a long while to be sparing of himself, especially avoiding exciting scenes and subjects.

This incident in the life of my noble friend came upon him when he was planning a magnificent enterprise for the public good. His enlightened benevolence prompted him to devise an institution for the highest education of youths of both sexes, and all complexions and races. It was to be a university based upon the most advanced principles of intellectual and moral culture. He disclosed his intention to his intimate friend and legal adviser, the late Hon. Timothy Jenkins, of Oneida, and to myself, informing us that he meant to appropriate five hundred thousand dollars to its accomplishment. At his request I made known his purpose to the late Hon. Horace Mann, whom we regarded as the best adapted to develop the plan and preside over the execution of it, and who we thought would like to take charge of an educational institution that might from the beginning be ordered so much in accordance with his own enlarged ideas; but he promptly declined the invitation, being, as he said, too far committed to Antioch College.

Mr. Mann's refusal deferred the undertaking, and no other one, who could be had, appearing to Mr. Smith to be just the person to whose conduct he should be willing to commit the university, it was postponed until his alarming sickness and protracted debility, and the threatening aspect of our national affairs, led him to dismiss the project altogether. So he distributed among his nephews and nieces the larger part of the money he had intended to expend as I have stated above.

Shortly after, our awful civil war broke out. Of this he could not be a silent or inactive spectator. He freely gave his money, his influence, himself, to the cause of his country in every way that a private citizen of infirm health could. He not only gave many thousand dollars to promote the enlistment of white soldiers in his town and county, but he offered to equip a whole regiment of *colored* men, if the governor of the State would put one in commission. But, alas! the chief magistrate of New York was not another John A. Andrew.

Mr. Smith contributed largely to the funds of the Sanitary Commission, and not a little to the Christian Commission; and he kindly cared for many families at home that had been called to part with fathers, husbands, or sons, on whom they were dependent.

So soon as the grand project of establishing schools for the freedmen was started, Mr. Smith entered into it with his wonted zeal and generosity. I have heard often of his donations larger or smaller, and have not a doubt that he has contributed as much as any other person in our country.

I need not say that it has indeed been a great benefit, as well as joy, to me to have been brought to know so intimately, and to co-operate so much as I have done, for more than twenty years, with such a philanthropist as Gerrit Smith.

Not alone by his bountiful gifts of land and money has he mightily helped the cause of our cruelly oppressed and despised countrymen. He has spoken often, and written abundantly in their behalf, — always faithfully, sometimes with exceeding power. I am sure there is not an individual in Central New York, I doubt if there be one in our whole country, unless he has been an agent or appointed lecturer of some Antislavery Society, who has attended so many antislavery meetings, has made so many antislavery speeches, and written and published so many antislavery letters, as has our honored and beloved brother of Peterboro', always excepting, of course, those devotees, Mr. Garrison and Mr. Phillips. I shall have occasion hereafter to tell of one or more of his timely and most effective speeches.

Mr. Smith has entertained and freely expressed some opinions that have been peculiar to himself, and has done some things that have appeared eccentric; but I believe that he has never consciously done or said anything unfriendly to an oppressed or despised fellow-being, white or black.

CONDUCT OF THE CLERGY AND CHURCHES.

The most serious obstacle to the progress of the antislavery cause was the conduct of the clergy and churches in our country. Perhaps it would be more proper to say the churches and the clergy, for it was only too obvious that, in the wrong course which they took, the shepherds were driven by the sheep. The influential members of the churches,— "the gentlemen of property and standing," — still more the politicians, who "of course understood better than ministers the Constitution of the United States, and the guaranties that were given to slaveholders by the framers of our Union,"—these gentlemen, too important to be alienated, were permitted to direct the action of the churches, and the preaching of their pastors on this "delicate question," "this exciting topic." Consequently the histories of the several religious denominations in our country (with very small exceptions) evince, from the time of our Revolution, a continual decline of respect for the rights of colored persons, and of disapproval of their enslavement. In the early days of our Republic — until after 1808 — all the religious sects in the land, I believe, gave more or less emphatic testimonies against enslaving fellow-men, especially against the African slave-trade. But after that accursed traffic was nominally abolished, the zeal of its opponents subsided (not very slowly) to acquiescence in the condition of those who had long been enslaved and their descendants. "They are used to it"; "they seem happy enough"; "unconscious of their degradation"; it was said. Then "the labor of slaves is indispensable to their owners, especially on the rich, virgin soils of the Southern States." "It is sad," said the semi-apologists, "but so it is. The condition of laboring people everywhere is hard, and we are by no means sure that the condition of the slaves is worse, if so bad as, that of many laborers elsewhere who are nominally free." "Many masters," it was added, "are very kind to their slaves; feed them and clothe them well, and never overwork them, unless it is absolutely necessary." But the consciences of the doubting were quieted more than all by the plea that "in one respect certainly the condition of the enslaved Africans has been immensely improved by their transportation to our country. Here they are introduced to the knowledge of 'the way of salvation'; here many of them become Christians. As Joseph through his bondage in Egypt was led to the highest position in that empire, next only to the king, so these poor, benighted heathen, by being brought in slavery to our land, may be led to become children of the King of kings, so wonderful are the ways of Divine Providence." By these and similar palliations and apologies, the people of almost every religious sect at the South, and their Methodist or Baptist or Presbyterian or Episcopalian brethren at the North, were led to overlook the *essential* evil, the tremendous wrong of slavery, and to hope and trust that God would, in due time, by his inscrutable method, bring some inestimable good out of this great evil.

Accordingly, we find, on turning to the doings of the great ecclesiastical bodies of our country, that they have descended from their very distinct protests against the enslavement of men, in 1780, 1789, 1794, &c., to palliations of the "sum of all villanies," as Wesley called it, — and apologies for it, and justifications of it, and explicit, biblical defences of it, until at length — after Mr. Garrison and his co-laborers arose, demanding for the slaves their inalienable right to liberty — the churches and ministers of all denominations (excepting the Freewill Baptists and Scotch Covenanters) gathered about the "Peculiar Institution" for its *protection;* and vehemently denounced as incendiaries, disunionists, infidels, all those who insisted upon its abolition.*

This, I repeat, was the most serious obstacle to the progress of our antislavery reform. In 1830, and for several years afterwards, the influence of the clergy and the churches was paramount in our Northern, if not in the Southern communities; certainly it was second only to the love of money. The people generally, then, were wont to take for granted that what the ministers and church-members approved must be morally right, and what they so vehemently denounced must be morally wrong. Accordingly, the most violent conflicts we had, and the most outrageous mobs we encountered, were led on or instigated by persons professing to be religious.

If the clergy and churches have less influence over the people now than they had forty years ago, it must be in a great measure because the people find that they were wofully deceived by them as to the character of slavery, and misled to oppose its abolition, until the slaveholders, encouraged by their Northern abettors, dared to attempt the dissolution of our Union, and so brought on our late

* See "The American Churches the Bulwarks of American Slavery," by J. G. Birney, "Slavery and Antislavery," by W. Goodell, and "The Church and Slavery," by Rev. Albert Barnes.

civil war, in which hundreds of thousands of the people were killed, and an immense debt imposed upon this and succeeding generations.

In justice, however, to the professing Christians of our country, it should be recorded that very much the larger portions of our antislavery host were recruited from the churches of all denominations, though some persons who made no pretensions to a religious character rendered us signal services. It ought also to be stated that more of the antislavery lecturers, agents, and devoted laborers had been of the *ministerial* profession than of any other of the callings of men, in proportion to the numbers of each. Still, it cannot be denied that the most formidable opposition we had to contend against was that which was made by the ministers and churches and ecclesiastical authorities. When the true history of the antislavery conflict shall be fully written, and the sayings and doings of preachers, theological professors, editors of religious periodicals, and of Presbyteries, Associations, Conferences, and General Assemblies, shall be spread before the people in the light of our enlarged liberty, no one will fail to see that, practically, the worst enemies of truth, righteousness, and humanity were of those who professed to be the friends and followers of Christ. Had *they* been generally faithful and fearless in behalf of the oppressed, no other opponents would have dared to withstand the just demand for their immediate emancipation.

Mr. Garrison, who was and is by nature and education an unfeignedly religious man, felt that he ought to look first to the clergy and the professing Christians for sympathy, and should confidently expect their co-operation. Indeed, he knew that if they would heartily espouse the cause of our enslaved countrymen, he might, without unfaithfulness to them, retire to some printing-office, and get his living as he had been trained to do. His disappointment and astonishment were unspeakable when he found how blind and deaf and dumb the preachers of the Gospel were in view of the unparalleled iniquity of our nation, and the inestimable wrongs that were allowed to be inflicted upon millions of the people. It was as painful to him and his associates as it was necessary, to expose to the people the infidelity of their religious teachers and guides; to show them that, not only had the statesmen and politicians of our country become fearfully corrupted by consenting with slaveholders, but also the bishops, priests, ministers of religion. All, with few exceptions, had lost faith in the true and the right, and in the God of truth and righteousness. They were afraid to obey the Divine Law, and bowed rather to the commandments of men. They respected a compromise more than a principle, and trusted to what seemed politic rather than to that which was self-evidently right. "The whole *head* of our nation was sick, and the whole *heart* was faint. From the sole of the foot, even unto the head, there seemed to be no soundness in it." "Except the Lord of hosts had left unto us a very small remnant, we should have been as Sodom; we should have been like unto Gomorrah."

UNITARIAN AND UNIVERSALIST MINISTERS AND CHURCHES.

It must have been observed by my readers that, in speaking above of the sympathy and co-operation of the Northern ministers and churches with their slaveholding brethren in the Southern States, I did not name Universalists and Unitarians among the guilty sects. This was because I reserved them for a separate, and the Unitarians for a more particular notice. Of the course pursued by the Universalists I have known but little. There are very few churches of their denomination in any of the slaveholding States; in most of them, I believe, not one. They claimed the Rev. Theodore Clapp, of New Orleans, a preacher of distinguished ability, and in some respects a very estimable gentleman, but who was one of the most unblushing advocates of slavery in the country. In a sermon preached at New Orleans, April 15, 1838, he said: "The venerable patriarchs Abraham, Isaac, Jacob, and others were all slaveholders. In all probability each possessed a greater number of bondmen and bondwomen than any planter now living in Louisiana or Mississippi." "The same God who gave Abraham sunshine, air, rain, earth, flocks, herds, silver, and gold *blessed him with a donative of slaves.* Here we see God dealing in slaves, giving them to his favorite child, — a man of superlative worth, and as a reward for his eminent goodness." These extracts are not an exaggerated specimen of the whole discourse. A few years afterwards, it was rumored that Mr. Clapp had essentially modified his opinions as above expressed. This rumor brought out an explanation in *The New Orleans Picayune* (probably from himself), to the effect that, "Christian philanthropy does not require the immediate emancipation of slaves." "Whilst one lives in a slave State, he is bound by Christianity to submit to its laws touching slavery." "Christianity does not propose to release the obligations of slaves to their masters." I am not informed that his Universalist brethren at the North ever passed any censure upon him for such misrepresentations of our Heavenly Father, and of the duty of men to their oppressed fellow-beings.

UNITARIANS.

In commencing the discreditable account I must give of the proslavery conduct of the Unitarian denomination, I may as well record the fact, of which the mention of Rev. Theodore Clapp reminds me. Notwithstanding the utterance of such sentiments as I have just now quoted, none of which had been retracted or apologized for, a few years afterwards Mr. Clapp was specially invited by a committee of Boston Unitarians to attend their religious anniversaries; and his letter in reply was read in their principal meeting, where, perhaps, a thousand persons were present, including a large number of ministers and prominent laymen, without any remonstrance or rebuke to those who had invited him.

But before I procceed further with the disagreeable narrative, let me state, to the honor of the sect, that though a very small one in comparison with those called Orthodox (having at this day not more than three hundred and sixty ministers, and in 1853 only two hundred and seven), we Unitarians have given to the antislavery cause more preachers, writers, lecturers, agents, poets, than any other denomination in proportion to our numbers, if not more without that comparison. Of those Unitarian ministers no longer on earth, we hold in most grateful remembrance Dr. N. Worcester, Dr. Follen, Dr. Channing, Dr. S. Willard, Theodore Parker, John Pierpont, Dr. H. Ware, Jr., and A. H. Conant. Others, though less outspoken, were always explicitly on the side of the oppressed, — Dr. Lowell, Dr. C. Francis, Dr. E. B. Hall, G. F. Simmons, E. Q. Sewall, B. Whitman, N. A. Staples, S. Judd, B. Frost. Of those who are still in the body, we gratefully claim as fellow-laborers in the antislavery cause Drs. J. G. Palfrey, W. H. Furness, J.

F. Clarke, T. T. Stone, J. Allen, G. W. Briggs, R. P. Stebbins, O. Stearns, and Rev. Messrs. S. May, Jr., C. Stetson, W. H. Channing, M. D. Conway, O. B. Frothingham, J. Parkman, Jr., J. T. Sargent, N. Hall, A. A. Livermore, J. L. Russell, J. H. Heywood, T. W. Higginson, R. W. Emerson, S. Longfellow, S. Johnson, F. Frothingham, W. H. Knapp, R. F. Wallcut, R. Collyer, E. B. Willson, W. P. Tilden, W. H. Fish, C. G. Ames, John Weiss, R. C. Waterston, T. J. Mumford, C. C. Shackford, F. W. Holland, E. Buckingham, C. C. Sewall, F. Tiffany, R. R. Shippen. All these are or were Unitarian preachers, and did service in the conflict. Many of them suffered obloquy, persecution, loss, because of their fidelity to the principles of impartial liberty. I may have forgotten some whose names should stand in this honored list. I have mentioned all whose services I remember to have witnessed or to have heard of. How small a portion of the whole number of our ministers during the last forty years!

The Unitarians as a body dealt with the question of slavery in any but an impartial, courageous, and Christian way. Continually in their public meetings the question was staved off and driven out, because of technical, formal, verbal difficulties which were of no real importance, and ought not to have caused a moment's hesitation. Avowing among their distinctive doctrines, "The *fatherly character* of God as reflected in his Son Jesus Christ," and "*The brotherhood of man with man everywhere*," we had a right to expect from Unitarians a steadfast and unqualified protest against so unjust, tyrannical, and cruel a system as that of American slavery. And considering their position as a body, not entangled with any proslavery alliances, not hampered by any ecclesiastical organization, it does seem to me that they were *pre-eminently guilty* in reference to the enslavement of the millions in our land with its attendant wrongs, cruelties, horrors. They, of all other sects, ought to have spoken boldly, as one man, for *God our Father*, for *Jesus the all-loving Saviour and Elder Brother*, and for *Humanity*, especially where it was outraged *in the least of the brethren.* But they did not. They refused to speak as a body, and censured, condemned, execrated their members who did speak faithfully for the down-trodden, and who co-operated with him whom a merciful Providence sent as the prophet of the reform, which alone could have saved our country from our late awful civil war. Let no honor be withheld from the individuals who were so prominent and noble exceptions to the general policy of the denomination, — the ministers whom I have named above, together with those faithful laymen, Samuel E. Sewall, Francis Jackson, David L. Child, Ellis Gray Loring, Edmund Quincy, A. Bronson Alcott, Dr. H. I. Bowditch, William I. Bowditch, with others; and those excellent women, Mrs. L. M. Child, Mrs. Maria W. Chapman, Mrs. Follen, Miss Cabot, Mrs. Mary May, Misses Weston, Misses Chapman, Miss Sargent, and more who should be named; let no honor be withheld from these and such as they were. But let the sad truth be plainly told, as a solemn warning to all coming generations, that even the Unitarians, as a body, were corrupted and morally paralyzed by our national consenting with slaveholders, even the Unitarians to whose avowed faith in the paternity of God, the brotherhood of all mankind, and the divinity of human nature, the enslavement of men should have been especially abhorrent. On a subsequent page I shall have occasion to tell of their most glaring dereliction of duty to the enslaved, and those who were ready to help them out of bondage. Meanwhile I must state some facts in support of my allegations against the sect to which I belong and with which I shall labor for the dissemination of our *most precious faith* so long as life and strength remain.

In 1843 the subject of the slavery of millions in our land was brought before the American Unitarian Association by Rev. John Parkman, Jr. But it was not discussed. It was put aside as a matter about which there were serious differences of opinion among the members, and with which that body, therefore, had better not meddle.

Early in 1844 an address on the subject was sent from British Unitarians to their brethren in America. It was an able, affectionate, respectful appeal to us, signed by one hundred and eighty-five ministers. A meeting of the Unitarian clergy was held in Boston to consider and reply to it. But it seemed to be regarded by many, and was spoken of by some, as an *impertinence.* "Our British brethren," it was said, "are interfering in a matter which is beset with peculiar difficulties in this country, about which they know little or nothing." And my cousin, Rev. Samuel May, Jr., of Leicester, who had visited England the year before, was severely censured for having encouraged our brethren there thus to meddle. Here let me say, few have labored so diligently, faithfully, disinterestedly, as Mr. May has in the cause of the slaves. And no one of our denomination has taken so much pains to prevent the Unitarians from committing themselves to the wrong side, or failing to do their duty on the right side, of every question relating to slavery. For this fidelity he has received anything but the thanks of most of the brethren. Here and elsewhere I am bound to tell what I know of him, for owing to the similarity of our names, and the sameness of our connections with the Antislavery Societies, many of *his* good words and deeds have been attributed to *me* by those who do not know both of us.

At the Autumnal Unitarian Conference held at Worcester, Mass., October, 1842, he offered a series of resolutions, setting forth the great extent, the appalling evils, and fearful wickedness of slavery, and endeavored to bring the Conference to resolve: "That, as ministers and disciples of Jesus Christ, we feel bound to declare our solemn opinion, that the institution of slavery is radically and inherently opposite to his religion; that it ought to be immediately abandoned by all who profess to be Christians; and that we do affectionately admonish and entreat all who hold 'the like precious faith' with us, to free themselves at once from the guilt of sustaining this evil thing." There was manifested a great unwillingness to express any opinion upon the subject, and the Conference adjourned without taking action upon it.

When in England, in the summer of 1843, Mr. May attended a large meeting of Unitarians. Having been invited to address them, and to speak particularly upon the subject of slavery in America, and of the attitude of our denomination towards the great iniquity, he did speak at considerable length. But he gave a very truthful and candid statement of the case as it then was. He set before his British hearers the influences which tended to mislead even the most kindly disposed in this country, and the obstacles and difficulties that beset the way of those who were most resolute in the cause of the enslaved. He acknowledged gratefully, generously, the important services which Dr. Follen, Dr. Channing, and other Unitarian ministers and laymen had rendered. But he was obliged, as a man of truth, to confess that our denomination as a whole had been recreant to their duty. And he encouraged our English brethren to address a letter of fraternal counsel and entreaty to us, not doubting that such a communication would be gratefully received by the American Unitarians as coming from those who had had to contend against a similar system of iniquity, and had helped their national government to abolish it. But I have already stated how utterly disappointed he was in the result.

Soon after his return from England, at the annual meeting of the American Unitarian Association in May, 1844, he again brought up the subject, and earnestly endeavored, with others, to induce that body to vote that slaveholding was anti-republican, inhuman, and unchristian. It led to a protracted discussion of two days or more, which resulted in nothing else than a vote of censure passed upon the Unitarian Church in Savannah, Georgia, because they refused to receive the services of the Rev. Mr. Motte, sent to them by the Executive Committee of the Association, having heard that he had protested in a sermon against the wrongs inflicted upon the colored people both at the North and South.

Henry H. Fuller, of Boston, strenuously opposed the introduction of the subject of slavery to the consideration of the Association in any way. "We of the North have nothing to do with it. It is a system of labor established in some of our sister States by their highest legislative authority. It was consented to by the framers of our National Constitution, and guaranties given for its protection," &c., &c. After much more of the same sort, he gave way for Mr. May to offer the following resolutions, instead of those by which he had called up the debate: —

1. "*Resolved*, That the American Unitarian Association, desirous that the pecuniary or other aid rendered by them from time to time to individuals and societies in the slaveholding sections of our country should not be misunderstood or misconstrued, do hereby declare their conviction that the institution of slavery, as existing in this country, is contrary to the will of God, to the Gospel of Christ (especially to the views

which *we* entertain of it), to the rights of man, and to every principle of justice and humanity; and in a spirit not of dictation, but of friendly remonstrance and entreaty, would call upon those whom they may address, as believers in one God and Father of all, to bear a faithful testimony against slavery.

2. "*Resolved*, That the Executive Committee be, and they hereby are, requested to transmit a copy of the preceding resolution to each of our auxiliary Associations, and to such societies in the slaveholding sections of the country as may from time to time receive pecuniary aid from this Association."

Dr. J. H. Morison objected to any action by the meeting. "1st. Because we shall thereby lose our influence at the South. 2d. Because we shall convert the Association into an Abolition Society. 3d. Because it would be a dastardly proceeding, at our distance from the scene of danger, to utter sentiments hostile to slavery, with which the Southern Unitarian societies might be identified."

Dr. E. S. Gannett said that the Association never contemplated any action on slavery. It was contrary to the objects of its formation. It would also be an invasion of the rights of conscience, — being the setting up of a creed with reference to this subject. Moreover, he said, it would be injurious to the slaves. Ten years ago their bondage was much lighter than at present. And then it would be to identify ourselves with the Abolitionists of the free States, whom he most unsparingly and vehemently condemned, and said there was little comparative need for us to go South to rebuke an evil, when we had such a "hellish spirit alive and active here in our very midst, even in New England."

Hon. S. C. Phillips, of Salem, was not in favor of such action as the resolutions proposed, but still thought we should take some action, and very properly in connection with this case of the Savannah church we should present, as we fairly might, our views on the whole subject of slavery. He said there had been great error in our so long silence on the subject. Our leading policy had been to avoid it, and much injury, and the prevention of much good, had been the consequence. "The time has come," said he, "when no man can be silent everywhere, and at all times, on this subject without guilt."

Mr. Phillips offered a series of resolutions instead of Mr. May's.

Rev. Mr. Lunt, of Quincy, opposed any action, and spoke with great severity of the Abolitionists, whom he charged with being bent on the dissolution of our Union and also the subversion of Christianity.

My cousin vindicated the Abolitionists from Mr. Lunt's charges, reminding him and the audience of the ground which Dr. Channing and other true friends of our country had taken respecting disunion, in case of the annexation of Texas. Mr. May showed that the Abolitionists had opposed only a false and corrupt church, not the Church of Christ, and still less Christianity itself, in which they gloried as the basis and impelling principle of their movement.

The resolutions were ably supported by the mover, Mr. Phillips, and four other laymen, and by eleven ministers, and finally passed by a majority of forty to fifteen, and were in part as follows: —

After a preamble, setting forth the offensive conduct of the Savannah church, —

"*Resolved*, That, viewing the institution of slavery in the light of Christianity, we cannot fail to perceive that it conflicts with the natural rights of human beings as the equal children of a common Father, and that it subverts the fundamental principle of human brotherhood.

"*Resolved*, In the necessary effects of slavery upon the personal and social condition, and upon the moral and religious character of all affected by it, we perceive an accumulation of evils over which Christianity must weep, against which Christianity should remonstrate, and for the removal of which Christianity appeals to the hearts and consciences of all disciples of Jesus to do what they can by their prayers, by the indulgence and expression of their sympathy, and by the unremitting and undisguised exertion of whatever moral and religious influence they may possess."

Then follows a resolution that it should not be considered, in any part of our country, a disqualification of any minister or missionary for the performance of the appropriate duties of his office, that he is known to have expressed antislavery sentiments, and approving the course of the Executive Committee in withdrawing their assistance from the church in Savannah because of their rejection of Rev. Mr. Motte.

The discussions at that meeting were seasoned with many vehement denunciations of the Abolitionists, uttered by several prominent Unitarian ministers. William L. Garrison was denounced as one "instigated by a diabolical spirit." "The Abolitionists," it was said, "were aiming to subvert Christianity, to extirpate it from the earth." Dr. Francis Parkman, of Boston, loudly declared that "no letter or resolution condemning slavery should ever go forth from the American Unitarian Association while he was a member of it." And he highly commended a New England captain, of whom we had then recently heard, because "he put his ship about and carried back to the master a slave whom he had found secreted on board the vessel." Dr. Parkman openly and personally denounced those who introduced the subject, as "born to plague the Association." And he, together with Dr. G. Putnam, and other prominent ministers, spoke of Dr. Channing's earnestness in the antislavery cause as a great weakness.

Later in the same year, 1845, at a meeting of Unitarian ministers in Boston, "A Protest against American Slavery," prepared I suppose by Rev. Caleb Stetson, John T. Sargent, and Samuel May, Jr., was adopted and sent out to be circulated for signatures. It received the names of one hundred and seventy-three ministers, of whom one hundred and fifty-three were of New England. It was publicly stated at the time that about eighty, comprising many of the most influential ministers of the denomination, refused to sign the Protest. Among the recusants were the Rev. Drs. Gannett, Dewey, Young, Parkman, Lothrop, G. Putnam, Lamson, N. Frothingham, S. Barrett, E. Peabody, G. E. Ellis, Bartol, Morison, and Lunt.

Of those who did sign the Protest, I am sorry to add not a large proportion can with truth be said to have been faithful to the solemn pledge they therein gave, as follows: "We on our part do hereby pledge ourselves, before God and our brethren, never to be weary in laboring in the cause of human rights and freedom, until slavery shall be abolished and every slave set free."

Once or twice afterwards Mr. May pressed the subject upon the Unitarian Association, but with little better results. Subsequent events, however, have shown, too plainly to be denied or doubted, that it would have been more creditable to themselves, and far better for our country, if "the older and wiser" men of our denomination had listened to his counsels and followed his noble example. Alas, our land is filled with testimonies written in blood, that if the ministers of religion had only been fearless and faithful in declaring the impartial love of the Heavenly Father for the children of men of all complexions, and their equal, inalienable rights, which would assuredly be vindicated by Divine justice, our late civil war would have been averted!

In 1847 Mr. May was appointed *General Agent of the Massachusetts Antislavery Society*, and continued in that responsible and laborious office until after the abolition of slavery in 1865. He was instant in season and out of season, and in co-operation with his devoted assistant, Rev. R. F. Wallcut, rendered services the amount and value of which cannot easily be estimated.

THE FUGITIVE SLAVE LAW.

The awful iniquity of our nation culminated in the enactment of the *Fugitive Slave Law*, which, as Edmund Quincy said at the time, stood, as it now stands, "a piece of diabolical ingenuity, for the accomplishment of a devilish purpose, *without a rival* among all the tyrannical enactments or edicts of servile parliaments or despotic monarchs." It was the essential article of a political conglomerate, prepared by the Arch Compromiser, Henry Clay, which was called the Omnibus Bill; some parts of which, he vainly thought, would conciliate the Northern States to the reception of the whole. It provided for the admission of California into our Union, with an anti-slavery Constitution; for the organization of two other Territories without the prohibition of slavery; the extension of the southwestern boundary of Texas to the Rio Grande; the abolition of the slave-trade in the District of Columbia, with the guaranty of slavery to its inhabitants until they should see fit to abolish it; and the perpetuity of the interstate slave-trade; but infinitely worse than any of these objectionable parts were the stringent measures it proposed for the recovery of fugitives from slavery. Stripped of the verbiage of legal enactments, the provisions of this abominable law were as follows: —

1. The claimant of any person who had escaped, or should escape from slavery in any State or Territory, might apply to any Court of Record or Judge thereof, describe the fugitive and make satisfactory proof that he or she owed service or labor to said claimant. Thereupon the Court, or in vacation the Judge, was required to cause a record to be made of the description of the alleged fugitive, and of the proof of his or her enslavement, and give an attested copy of that record to the claimant; which copy was required to be received by any court, judge, or commissioner in any other State or Territory of the Union, as full and conclusive evidence that the person claimed, and so described, was a fugitive from slavery and owed service to the claimant, and therefore should be delivered up.

Any marshal or deputy who should refuse to arrest such a fugitive was to be fined *one thousand dollars.* And if, after having arrested him or her, the fugitive should in any way escape from his custody, the marshal or deputy should be held liable to pay to the claimant the value of the runaway.

And any person who should in any way prevent the claimant or his agent or assistants from getting possession of the fugitive, by hiding him or helping him to escape, or by open opposition to his would-be captor, — such offender was to be fined *one thousand dollars* for violating this *righteous* law; and be liable to pay another *thousand dollars* to the claimant of the fugitive.

In order that every facility should be afforded to *our slaveholding brethren* to retake their fleeing property, many commissioners were ordered to be appointed in all suitable places (in addition to the courts and judges) whose especial duty it should be to attend to cases that might arise under the Fugitive Slave Law. And each commissioner or judge, who found the accused guilty of having fled from bondage, was to receive a fee of ten dollars. But if the proof adduced by the claimant did not satisfy him that the accused was a fugitive from his service, then the judge or commissioner was to receive only five dollars. Thus bribery was by this law superadded to every other device to enable the American slaveholder to recover his escaped slave, and return him or her to a still more cruel bondage.

Nor was this all that was atrociously wicked in the enactment. It provided further that, while the claimant or his agent might give testimony or make affidavit to the enslavement of the arrested one, "in no trial or hearing under the Act was the testimony of the alleged fugitive to be admitted in evidence" that he was not the one that his claimant called him, or that he had been emancipated by the will of a former owner, or by the purchase of his liberty.

If there be among the laws of any other nation, in any other part and in any other age of the world, an enactment, a decree, a ukase, so profoundly wicked, so ingeniously cruel, as this law which the Congress of the United States passed in 1850, — the very middle of the nineteenth century, — I beg to be informed of it, for I confess at the close of this recital I feel as if, in my shame and misery, I should be relieved for a moment by bad company.

At first it may seem strange that Mr. Clay should have supposed the people of the Northern States would conform to the requirements of such a law; would consent that their States should be made the hunting-grounds, and themselves the bloodhounds of Southern oppressors in pursuit of their fleeing slaves. And yet was he not justified in this low opinion of us by the conduct of many of those who were elected to be representatives of the opinions and wishes of the majority of our communities? The execrable bill could not have become a law, without the concurrence of Northern members in both Houses of Congress; for, in both, the larger number were from the non-slaveholding States. Yet it was enacted by the votes of twenty-seven of the Senators against only twelve; and by one hundred and nine of the Representatives opposed by seventy-five. And many of these recreants to the fundamental principles of justice and humanity had led Mr. Clay, and the Southern politicians generally, to expect such votes as they gave by the sentiments they uttered in the preceding debates.

DANIEL WEBSTER.

The man who did more than any one, if not more than all of the members of Congress from the free States, to procure the passage of the Bill of Abominations, was *Daniel Webster*, who had represented Massachusetts in the United States Senate for twenty-five years; who led her in opposition to the Missouri Compromise in 1819, and for nearly twenty years afterwards was regarded as a leader of the advanced guard of liberty and humanity. But when, in 1838, he went into the Southern States to make his bids for the presidency, he uttered words that foretold his moral declension, though not to so deep a depth as he descended in his advocacy of the Fugitive Slave Law. The infamy of his speech on the 7th of March, 1850, can never be forgotten while he is remembered. He then declared it to be his intention "to support the Bill with all its provisions to the fullest extent."

Another fact which adds a sting of bitterness to the shame of the North was, that this Act, the baseness, meanness, cruelty of which no epithet in my vocabulary can adequately express, became a law by the signature of the President, subscribed by *Millard Fillmore*, a New York man and a Unitarian withal.

Notwithstanding the general expressions of indignation and disgust at Mr. Webster's baseness and treachery in supporting the Fugitive Slave Bill throughout the North, especially from all parts of his own State, Massachusetts, he and other members of the Senate and the House of Representatives persisted until, as we have seen, the Act became a law. The arch-traitor was rewarded with the office of Secretary of State. Such was his gratitude for this small compensation that, on taking leave of the Senate, he pledged himself anew to the infamous principles he had avowed on the 7th of March.*

No sooner was the deed done, the Fugitive Slave Act sent forth to be the law of the land, than outcries of contempt and defiance came from every free State, and pledges of protection were given to the colored population. It is not within the scope of my plan to attempt an account of the indignation-meetings that were held in places too numerous to be even mentioned here. They will make a proud episode in the history of our nation since 1830, whenever it shall be fully written. Meanwhile, let me here refer my readers to the admirable Reports of the Massachusetts Antislavery Society, especially those written by the piquant pen, under the guidance of the astute mind, of Edmund Quincy, for the last ten or fifteen years of our fiery conflict.

I must confine myself to my personal recollections, and in this particular they are most grateful to me, and honorable to the city of Syracuse, where I have resided since 1845.

The Fugitive Slave Act was signed by the President on the 18th of September. Eight days afterwards, a call was issued through our newspapers summoning the citizens of Syracuse and its vicinity, without respect to party, to meet in our City Hall on the 4th of October ensuing, to denounce and take measures to withstand this law. As the time of the meeting approached the

* See Appendix.

popular excitement increased, and at an early hour the hall was crowded to its utmost capacity. Hon. A. H. Hovey, the Mayor of the city, was elected to preside, sustained by eight vice-presidents of the two political parties, three of whom had been then, or have been since, mayors of Syracuse, and the other five, gentlemen of the highest respectability, though only one of them had been active with the Abolitionists, — Hon. E. W. Leavenworth, Hon. Horace Wheaton, John Woodruff, Esq., Captain Oliver Teall, Robert Gere, Esq., Hon. L. Kingsley, Captain Hiram Putnam, Dr. Lyman Clary.

The President addressed the meeting very acceptably, declared himself to be with us in opposition to the law, adding: "The colored man must be protected, — he must be secure among us, come what will of political organizations." A series of thirteen resolutions was read, three of which will make known sufficiently the spirit of them all. The second was: —

1. "*Resolved,* That the Fugitive Slave Law, recently enacted by the Congress of these United States, is a most flagrant outrage upon the inalienable rights of man, and a daring assault upon the palladium of American liberties."

3. "That every intelligent man and woman throughout our country, ought to read attentively, and understand the provisions of this law, in all its details, so that they may be fully aware of its diabolical spirit and cruel ingenuity, and prepare themselves to *oppose* all attempts to enforce it."

13. "*Resolved,* That we recommend the appointment of a Vigilance Committee of thirteen citizens, whose duty it shall be to see that no person is deprived of his liberty without 'due process of law.' And all good citizens are earnestly requested to aid and sustain them in all needed efforts for the security of every person claiming the protection of our laws."

The meeting was addressed in a very spirited strain by two colored gentlemen, — Rev. S. R. Ward and Rev.

J. W. Loguen. They each declared that they and their colored fellow-citizens generally had determined to make the most violent resistance to any attempt that might be made to re-enslave them. They would have their liberty or die in its defence.

Mr. Charles A. Wheaton, Chairman of a Committee, then read an Address to the citizens of the State of New York, setting very plainly before them the degradation to which this law would reduce them. It showed them how the law would nullify all the provisions made in the Constitution for the protection of our dearest rights, as well as the liberties of any amongst us who might have complexions shaded in any measure. And it called upon the citizens of the Empire State to rise in their majesty and put down all attempts to enforce this law.

Hon. Charles B. Sedgwick then rose and advocated the Resolutions and Address in an admirable speech. He exposed the atrocious features of the slave-catching law in detail, demonstrated its unconstitutionality as well as cruelty, and awakened throughout his audience the keenest indignation against it. He said it was the vilest law that tyranny ever devised. He would resist it, and he called on all who heard him to resist it everywhere, in every way, to the utmost of their power. Rev. R. R. Raymond, of the Baptist Church, then spoke stirring words in thrilling tones. "How can we do to others as we would that they should do to us, if we do not resist this law? Citizens of Syracuse! shall a live man ever be taken out of our city by force of this law?" "No! No!!" was the response loud as thunder. "Let us tell the Southerners, then, that it will not be safe for them to come or send their agents here to attempt to take away a fugitive slave. [Great applause.] I will take the hunted man to my own house, and he shall not be torn away, and I be left alive. [Tremendous and long cheering.]"

I was then called up. But I shall leave my readers to imagine what I said, if they will only let it be in very strong opposition to the law.

The Report of the Committee on Resolutions, and an Address, was then put to vote, and adopted with only one dissenting voice. The Vigilance Committee of thirteen was appointed, and the meeting was adjourned to the evening of the 12th.

Our second meeting was, if possible, more enthusiastic than the first. All the seats in the hall were filled, and the aisles crowded before the hour to which the meeting was adjourned. The Mayor called to order precisely at seven o'clock. It devolved upon me, as Chairman of the Committee, to report Resolutions. There were too many of them to be repeated here. Two or three must suffice.

1. "*Resolved*, That we solemnly reiterate our abhorrence of the Fugitive Slave Law, which in effect is nothing less than a license for *kidnapping*, under the protection and at the expense of our Federal Government, which has become the tool of oppressors."

6. "*Resolved*, That now is the day and now the hour to take our stand for liberty and humanity. If we now refuse to assert our independency of the tyrants who aspire to absolute power in our Republic, we may hope for nothing better than entire subjugation to their will, and shall leave our children in a condition little better than that of the creatures of absolute despots."

10. "*Resolved*, That as all of us are liable at any moment to be summoned to assist in kidnapping such persons as anybody may claim to be his slaves, and to be fined one thousand dollars if we refuse to do the bidding of the land-pirates, whom this law would encourage to prowl through our country, it is the dictate of prudence as well as good fellowship in a righteous cause, that we should unite ourselves in an Association, pledged to stand by its members in opposing this law,

and to share with any of them the pecuniary losses they may incur, under the operation of this law."

11. "*Resolved,* That such an Association be now formed, so that Southern oppressors may know that the people of Syracuse and its vicinity are prepared to sustain one another in resisting the encroachments of despotism."

William H. Burleigh first spoke in support of the resolutions. One of the newspapers the next day said: "We can do no justice to the ability and surpassing eloquence of Mr. Burleigh's speech; the deep feelings of his soul were poured out in terms of consuming oratory." Judge Nye, then of Madison County, was present, and being called to address the meeting, said, among many other good things: "I am an officer of the law. I am not sure that I am not one of those officers who are clothed with anomalous and terrible powers by this Bill of Abominations. If I am, I will tell my constituency that I will trample that law in the dust, and they must find another man, if there be one who will degrade himself, to do this dirty work." "Be assured, Syracusians, there is not a man among the hills and valleys of Madison County who would take my office on condition of obedience to this statute." These sentences, and other good things that Judge Nye said, were received with great applause.

Hon. C. B. Sedgwick then presented a petition to Congress for the repeal of the Act, and called upon his fellow-citizens to sign it. He enforced this call by a very impressive speech, declaring again and again his fixed determination to oppose to the utmost any attempt to carry back from Syracuse a fugitive slave. "A man (no, a dog) may come here scenting blood on the track of our brother Loguen; shall we let him drag him off to slavery again? No! never!! Loguen has been driven and stricken from childhood to manhood. He has been literally a man of sorrows. His soul was trodden upon by oppression. But he rose in the might of his manhood, and made his way across rivers, through swamps, over mountains, to our city. And it shall be a place of safety to him. We will not give him up. He is a husband and a father on our free soil, and will you give him back to the hell of slavery? No! never!!

'Dear as freedom is,
And in my soul's just estimation prized above all price, I had rather be myself the slave,
And wear the bonds, than fasten them on him.'"

I wish I could convey to the ears of my readers the hearty, deep-toned notes of applause that welcomed these declarations.

I then presented a pledge, binding those who might sign it to stand by one another, and share equally all pecuniary penalties they might be made to suffer because of their opposition to this oppressive and cruel Act.

Rev. Mr. Raymond was afterwards called up, and he spoke in a manner that was very affecting. I have room for only a brief extract from the report of it.

"Oh! the hardships this law has brought upon the fugitives from slavery that have sought an asylum with us! I attended the other day a meeting of Baptist ministers in Rochester. There was a colored brother there in the depths of distress. He arose in our midst and gave voice to the agonies of his soul. A few years since he escaped from one of the richest slaveholders in Kentucky. With him, he had been brought up in ignorance. Since coming among us he had learnt to read, and had become so well educated as to be able to teach others. In the course of two years he had gathered a church in a meeting-house that had been built mainly by his instrumentality. He had a comfortable homestead in Rochester, and a happy family about him. But now his master had sent for him, declaring he would have him under this law. 'Oh!' he cried, 'what have I done? what is my crime? All the power and cunning and sagacity of this great nation are moving to drag me back again into slavery, — worse than death.' His head fell upon his bosom, he sobbed aloud, and we wept with him, and a deep groan of execration went up from the souls of us all to the God of mercy against this law." This recital awakened intense feeling throughout our meeting and murmurs of indignation. "And now," Mr. Raymond continued, "suppose that while we were glowing with sympathy for that brother and abhorrence of the law, — suppose the man-thief had come into that meeting and put his hand upon that brother to bear him off to the South. What would have been the result? I tell you we would have defended him, if we had had to tear that man-thief in pieces." This was received with great applause. "What," continued Mr. Raymond, "what if the officers should come here and put their hand on me as one claimed to be the property of another man, would you let me go?" "No! No!! No!!!" from every quarter was the hearty response. "And yet why not me as readily as a man of darker skin? If ever there was a law which it was right to trample upon, it is this. You are counselling revolution, some may say. Revolution indeed! O, my fellow-citizens, blood has been flowing, not in battle-fields, but from the backs of our enslaved countrymen ever since 1776, and is flowing now. [Deep sensation.] Yes, and that blood has gone up to Heaven and provoked God against us. Yes, and blood will flow profusely on the battle-fields of a civil war if we carry out this accursed law, — if we do not proclaim freedom throughout the land."

Several other gentlemen addressed the meeting in a

similar strain; among them, Colonel Titus, who said: "With all my heart I concur in the sentiments and spirit of the resolutions and in the speech of Mr. Raymond. I am for suspending the operation of the bill until it shall be repealed. If the Southerners or their Northern minions undertake to enforce its provisions, and attempt to carry off our friend Loguen, or any other citizens, I am prepared to fight in their defence. I would advise our colored neighbors not to remove to Canada, but to rely on the patriotism of the citizens of Syracuse for protection. The Assistant United States Marshal is in the hall, and it is well to have him understand what are the real sentiments of his fellow-citizens, which I trust will be found to be almost unanimous in favor of resistance to this execrable law."

Such was the very general uprising of the people of Syracuse in opposition to the rendition of fugitives from slavery.

My own sentiments and feelings were very fully declared, a few days afterwards, from my own pulpit, and subsequently in Rochester and Oswego. I trust my readers will bear with a somewhat extended abstract of my sermon.

"If there be a God, almighty, perfectly wise, and impartially just and good, his will ought to be supreme with all moral beings throughout his universe. To teach otherwise,— to teach that we or any of his moral offspring are bound or can be bound by any earthly power to do what is contrary to *divine law*, is virtually Atheism; it is to enthrone Baal or Mammon in the place of Jehovah. *And this is just what the people of this country are now called upon by our Federal Government to do.* The legislators of this Republic have enacted a law which offends every feeling of humanity, sets at naught every precept of the Christian religion, outrages our highest sense of right. And now they and their political and priestly abettors demand that we shall conform to the requirements of this law, because it was enacted by the government under which we live.

"Brethren, are any of you ready to bow and take this yoke upon your necks, and do the biddings of these wicked men? I hope not. You shall not be, if I can convince you that you ought not. The iniquity of our country has culminated in the passage of this infernal law. Fearful encroachments have successively been made upon our liberties. This last is the worst, the most daring. If we yield to it, all will be lost. Our country will be given up to oppressors. There can be no insult, no outrage upon our moral sense, which we shall be able to withstand; no spot on which we can raise a barrier to the tide of political and personal pollution that must ever follow in the wake of slavery. Our government will become a despotism or a cruel oligarchy, and our religion will be in effect, if not in name, the worship of Baal, which means 'him that subdues.' . . . .

"This horrible law, which in the middle of the nineteenth century of the Christian era the legislators of the most highly favored nation on earth have had the effrontery to enact, — this law peremptorily, under heavy fines and penalties, forbids us to give assistance and comfort to a certain class of our fellow-men in the utmost need of help, — those who have fled and are longing to be saved from the greatest wrongs that can be inflicted upon human beings, — *the wrongs of slavery*. And yet we are told by many — many who profess to be Christians, even teachers of Christianity, ah! Doctors of Divinity — that the pulpit may not remonstrate against this tremendous iniquity, because, forsooth, it has passed into a law. What, are we, then, to allow that there is no authority higher than that of the earthly government under which we live, — a government framed by our revered but fallible fathers, and which we administer by agents of our own election, who are by no means incorruptible? Has it come to this? Is this the best lesson our Republican and Christian wisdom can teach the suffering nations of earth? Nay, are we to submit to this human authority without question? May we not so much as discuss the justice of its demands upon us? Must even those men be silent who were set in our midst for the defence of the Gospel, — the Gospel of Him who was 'anointed to preach to the poor, who was sent to heal the broken-hearted, to preach deliverance to the captives, to set at liberty them that are bruised?' Such is the doctrine of our politicians and of our politico-religious ministers. But a more heartless, demoralizing, base, antidemocrat, and antichristian doctrine could not be preached. I repudiate it utterly. . . . . *The pulpit has no higher function than to expound, assert, and maintain the rights of man.* The assumption of Mr. Webster and his abettors — that there is no higher law than an enactment of our Congress or the Constitution of the United States — is glaringly *atheistical*, inasmuch as it denies the supremacy of the Divine Author of the *moral constitution* of man. . . . .

"It is a matter of great interest to me personally, that my attention was first powerfully called to the subject of slavery, and my resolution to do my duty regarding it, was first roused by Daniel Webster, when he was a *man*, and not a mere self-seeking politician. The first antislavery meeting I ever attended was one in which Mr. Webster took a conspicuous part. It was on the 3d of December, 1819, in the State House at Boston, called to oppose the Missouri Compromise. Then and there generous, humane, Christian sentiments respecting slavery were uttered by him and others that kindled in my bosom a warmth of interest in the cause of the oppressed that has never cooled. But the next year, on the 22d of December, 1820, a few days before I entered the pulpit as a preacher, Mr. Webster delivered his famous oration at Plymouth. It was an admirable exposition of the rise, characteristics, and spirit of our free political and religious institutions. Towards the close, having alluded to slavery and the slave-trade, he said, with deep solemnity: '*I invoke the ministers of our religion, that they proclaim its denunciation of these crimes. If the pulpit be silent wherever or whenever there may be a sin bloody with this guilt within the hearing of its voice, the pulpit is false to its trust.*'

"Thus solemnly charged by one whom I *then* revered as a good man, no less than as a great statesman, the following Sunday I commenced preaching. Tremblingly alive to the weighty responsibilities I was about to incur, I fully resolved that the pulpit which might be committed to my charge should not be silent respecting slavery or any other great public wrong. . . . .

"And now, that same Daniel Webster, who first roused me to feel somewhat as I ought for the enslaved, has done more than any other man to procure the enactment of a law, under the provisions of which, if I do my duty, and by my preaching incite others to do their duty, to those who are in danger of being enslaved, I and they may be subjected to unusually heavy fines, or may be thrown into prison as malefactors. Have I not, then, a personal controversy with that distinguished man, — distinguished now, alas! for something else than splendid talents and exalted virtues? If I have gone wrong, did not Mr. Webster misdirect me? If I have done no more than he solemnly charged all preachers to do, has he not basely deserted and betrayed me? Verily, verily I say unto you, he bound the burden of this antislavery reform, and laid it upon the shoulders of others, but he himself has not helped to bear it, — no, not with one of his fingers. Nay, worse, he has done all he could to prepare the prison, and to whet the sword of vengeance for those sons of New England who shall obey the injunction he gave them from Plymouth Rock, that spot hallowed by all who truly love liberty and hate oppression. . . . .

"Tell me, then, no more that the pulpit has nothing to do, — that I as a Christian minister have nothing to do with politics, when I see how politics have corrupted, yes, utterly spoiled the once noble (we used in our admiration to say), godlike Daniel Webster! If that man, with his surpassing strength of intellect and once enlarged, generous views of the right and the good, — if he has not been able to withstand the demoralizing influences of political partyism, but has been shrivelled up into a mere aspirant for office, basely consenting to any and every sacrifice of humanity demanded by the oppressors of our country, and at last pledging himself to sustain all the provisions of a law more ingeniously wicked than the stimulated fears of the most cowardly tyrants ever before devised, — I repeat, if such a man as Daniel Webster once was has been corrupted and ruined by politics, shall I, a minister of the

Christian religion, fail to point out as plainly as I may, and proclaim as earnestly as I can, the moral dangers that beset those who engage in the strife for political preferment? . . . .

"For one, I will not help to uphold our nation in its iniquity, — no, not for an hour. If it cannot be reclaimed, let it be dissolved. The declaration so often made by the professed friends of our Union, that it cannot be preserved unless this horrible law can be enforced, is unwittingly a declaration that it is the implacable enemy of liberty, — an obstacle in the way of human progress. If it really be so, it must be, it will be removed. And he who attempts to prevent its dissolution will find himself fighting against God. If such a law as this for the recapture of fugitive slaves be essential to our Republic as now constituted, let it be broken up, and some new form of government arise in its stead. A better one would doubtless succeed. A worse one it could not be, if the enslavement, continued degradation and outlawry of more than three millions of our people, be indeed the bond of our present Union. . . . .

"Suppose that a considerable proportion of the States in this Union were, or should become, idolatrous heathen. Suppose that they worshipped Moloch, or some other false deity who delighted in human sacrifices. And suppose that, to propitiate the people of those States, and to secure the pecuniary and political advantages of a continued Union with them, Congress should enact that the people of the Christian States should allow those idolaters to come here when they pleased and offer human sacrifices in our midst, or carry away our children to be burnt on their altars at the South; would Mr. Webster or Mr. Clay, or the editors of *The New York Observer*, or *The Journal of Commerce*, or the Doctors of Divinity who have endeavored to array the public on the side of wrong, — would even they call upon us to obey such a law? I am sure they would not. And yet I fain would know wherein such a law as I have supposed would be any worse than this law which they are laboring to enforce. . . . . Why, then, if it would be reasonable and proper, in the view of Mr. Webster and his reverend abettors, to nullify a law requiring us to permit human beings to be offered as burnt sacrifices, — why is it not equally reasonable and proper for us to set at naught this law which commands us to do something worse, — that is, to assist in reducing human beings to the condition of domesticated brutes? . . . . Nay, further, I insisted that the Fugitive Slave Law violates the religious liberty, interferes with the faith and worship of Christians, just as much as the law I have supposed would do. . . . . A law of the land requiring you, as this Fugitive Slave Law does, to disobey the Golden Rule is, indeed, a far more grievous encroachment upon your liberty of conscience than a law prescribing to your faith any creed, or any rites and ceremonies by which you must worship God. . . . .

"Fellow-citizens! Christian brethren! the time has come that is to test our principles, to try our souls. I would not that any one in this emergency should trust to his own unaided strength. Let us fervently pray for wisdom to direct us, and for fortitude to do whatever may be demanded at our hands, by the Royal Law, — the Golden Rule. . . . .

"I would counsel prudence, although this evil day demands of us courage and self-sacrifice. . . . . We should spare no pains through the press, by conversation, and by public addresses, particularly by faithful discourses from the pulpits, to cherish and quicken the sense of right and the love of liberty in the hearts of the people. A correct public sentiment is our surest safeguard. . . . .

"Do you inquire of me by what means you ought to withstand the execution of this diabolical law? It is not for me to determine the action of any one but myself. 'Thou shalt love thy neighbor as thyself,' is the second great command which all should faithfully try to obey. Every man and woman among you is bound, as I am, to do for the protection or rescue of a fugitive from slavery what, in your hearts before God, you believe it would be right for you to do in behalf of your own life or liberty, or that of a member of your family. If you are fully persuaded that it would be right for you to maim or kill the kidnapper who had laid hands upon your wife, son, or daughter, or should be attempting to drag yourself away to be enslaved, I see not how you can excuse yourself from helping, by the same degree of violence, to rescue the fugitive slave from the like outrage. . . . .

"Before all men, I declare that you are, every one of you,

under the highest obligation to disobey this law, — nay, oppose to the utmost the execution of it. If you know of no better way to do this than by force and arms, then are you bound to use force and arms to prevent a fellow-being from being enslaved. There never was, there cannot be, a more righteous cause for revolution than the demands made upon us by this law. It would make you kidnappers, men-stealers, bloodhounds. . . . .

"It is known that I have been and am a preacher of the 'doctrine of non-resistance.' I believe it to be one of the distinctive doctrines of Christianity. But I have never presumed to affirm that I possessed enough of the spirit of Christ, — enough confidence in God and man, — enough moral courage and self-command to act in accordance with the Gospel precept in the treatment of enemies. But there is not a doubt in my heart that, if I should be enabled to speak and act as Jesus would, I should produce a far greater and better effect than could be wrought by clubs, or swords, or any deadly weapons. . . . . I shall go to the rescue of any one I may hear is in danger, not intending to harm the cruel men who may be attempting to kidnap him. I shall take no weapon of violence along with me, not even the cane that I usually wear. I shall go, praying that I may say and do what will smite the hearts rather than the bodies of the impious claimants of property in human beings, — pierce their consciences rather than their flesh. . . . .

"Fellow-citizens, fellow-men, fellow-Christians! the hour is come! A stand must be taken against the ruthless oppressors of our country. Resistants and non-resistants have now a work to do that may task to the utmost the energies of their souls. We owe it to the millions who are wearing out a miserable existence under the yoke of slavery; we owe it to the memory of our fathers who solemnly pledged their lives, their fortunes, and their sacred honor to the cause of liberty; we owe it to the expectations, the claims of oppressed and suffering men the world over; we owe it to ourselves, if we would be true men and not the menials of tyrants, to trample this Fugitive Slave Law under foot, and throw it indignantly back at the wicked legislators who had the hardihood to enact it."

It was obvious enough that some parts of the discourse were not relished by quite a number of my auditors. Several seemed to be seriously offended. It is therefore to be cherished among my many grateful recollections that, as I was coming down from the pulpit the late Major James E. Heron, of the United States Army, then one of the prominent members of our society, came up to me glowing with emotion, gave me his hand, and said, quite audibly: "Mr. May, I thank you. I was once a slaveholder. I know all about the Southern system of domestic servitude. I am intimately acquainted with the principles of the slaveholders, and the condition of their bondmen. You have never in my hearing exaggerated the wrongs and the vices inherent in the system. You cannot overstate them. And the bold attempt which is now making to subjugate the people of the Northern States to the will and service of the slaveholders ought to be resisted to the last." He must have been heard by many. His words were repeated about the city, and his full indorsement of my antislavery fanaticism helped to make it much more tolerable, in the regards of some who were ready to revolt from it.

The Vigilance Committee appointed on the 4th of October, and the Association we formed on the 12th, to co-operate with that committee, and to bear mutually the expenses that might be incurred in resisting the law, kept the attention of our citizens alive to the subject. And their interest was quickened and their determination confirmed by the reports that came to us from Boston, New York, Philadelphia, and many other places, of the preparations that were making to protect the colored people, and set at defiance the plan for their re-enslavement. The historian of our country, if he be one worthy of the task, will linger with delight over the pages on which he shall narrate the uprising of the people generally, in 1850 and 1851, throughout the Northern States, in opposition to the Fugitive Slave Law. There were not wanting fearless preachers who took up the arms of the Gospel and faithfully fought against the great unrighteousness. Only a few days after the infamous speech of Mr. Webster on the 7th of March, Theodore Parker addressed a crowded audience in Faneuil Hall, and exposed to their deeper abhorrence the atrocious provisions of the Bill which the Massachusetts senator had had the effrontery to advocate and pledge himself to maintain. On the 22d of September following he preached to his hearers in the Melodeon a thrilling discourse on "The Function and Place of Conscience in Relation to the Laws of Men," which must have fired them all the more to stand to the death in defence of any human being who had sought, or should seek, an asylum in Massachusetts. And again on the 28th of November, 1850, the day of annual Thanksgiving, he delivered his comprehensive, deep-searching discourse on "The State of the Nation," showing the reckless impiety of rulers who could frame such unrighteousness into law, and the folly of the people who could suppose themselves bound to obey such a law. Oh! if the ministers of religion generally, throughout our country, had said and done, before and after that date, a tithe as much as Mr. Parker said and did against the "great iniquity" of our nation, the slaveholders could never have gained such an ascendency in our Government, nor have become so inflated with the idea of their power, as to have attempted the dissolution of the Union, which it cost all the blood and treasure expended in our awful civil war to preserve. Mr. Parker was not indeed left alone to fight the battle of the Lord. Rev. Dr. Storrs, of Brooklyn, N. Y., Rev. G. W. Perkins, of Guilford, Conn., Rev. J. G. Forman, of West Bridgewater, Rev. Charles Beecher, Rev. William C. Whitcomb, of Stoneham, Rev. Nathaniel West, of Pittsburg, each spoke and wrote words of sound truth and great power, as well as those whose services I have acknowledged in another place, and others no doubt whose names have escaped my memory. But of the thirty thousand ministers of all the denominations in the United States, I believe not one in a hundred ever raised his voice against the enslavement of millions of our countrymen, nor lifted a finger to protect one who had escaped from bondage. And many, very many of the clergy openly and vehemently espoused the cause of the oppressors. Not only did the preachers in the slaveholding States, with scarcely an exception, justify and defend the institution of slavery, but there were many ministers in the free States who took sides with them. The most distinguished in this bad company were Professor Stuart, of Andover, Dr. Lord, President of Dartmouth College, New Hampshire, Bishop Hopkins, of Burlington, Vt., and Rev. Dr. Nehemiah Adams, of Boston. But I must refer my readers to the books mentioned at the bottom of page 349, if they would know how "the orthodox and evangelical" ministers of the free States contributed their influence to uphold "the peculiar institution of the South." And it must be left for the future historian of our Republic in the nineteenth century to tell to posterity how fearfully the American Church and ninety-nine hundredths of the ministers were subjugated to the will and behest of our slaveholding oligarchy. My purpose is to give, for the most part, only my personal recollections. And on this point, I am sorry to say, they are numerous and mortifying enough.

THE UNITARIANS AND THEIR MINISTERS.

When the Fugitive Slave Law was first promulgated, there was, as I have stated, a very general outburst of indignation throughout the North,— a feeling of dreadful shame, a sense of a most bitter insult. The first impulse of the Unitarians, as of others, was to denounce it. At their autumnal convention in Springfield, October, 1850, they did so, though not without strong opposition to any vote or action on the subject. Probably the opposers would have prevailed, and the law have been left unrebuked, had not that venerable man, the late Rev. Dr. Willard, of Deerfield, risen and earnestly —yes, solemnly — protested against passing lightly over a matter of such fearful importance. Dr. Willard was old, and had long been blind. Would to God that the moral sight of many of his younger ministerial brethren had been half as clear and pure as his! With tremulous eloquence he called upon them to reconsider their motion. He appealed to their pity for men and women over whom was impending the greatest calamity that could befall human beings. He appealed to their regard for the honor of their country, and besought them to avert her shame, by doing what they might to show the world, that it was the statesmen and politicians, not the people of the Northern States, who approved of this wicked, cruel law. His words roused others, who spoke to the same effect; and so that Convention was persuaded to adopt resolutions condemning the law. But quite a number of the prominent ministers of the denomination soon after gave strong utterance to an opposite opinion. I need mention but three. Rev. Dr. Lunt, of Quincy, preached a discourse on the "Divine Right of Government," in which he endeavored to bring his hearers to the conclusion that, "wise, practical men would allow the laws of the land, which have been enacted in due form, to have their course and be executed, until we can so far change the current of public opinion that what is objectionable in those laws may be corrected." He conceded, indeed, that "there are cases when rulers may be rightfully resisted, and when revolution is a duty; yet these are extreme cases, and require for their justification the most imperative necessity." He said this all unconscious, it would seem, that such an extreme case was upon us; unconscious, and leaving his hearers unconscious, that the Fugitive Slave Law must be resisted, or the people of Massachusetts would consent to become menials of the slaveholders, kidnappers, robbers of men, bloodhounds.

The excellent Dr. E. S. Gannett, of Boston, was heard to say, more than once, very emphatically, and to justify it, "that he should feel it to be his duty to turn away from his door a fugitive slave, — unfed, unaided in any way, rather than set at naught the law of the land."

And Rev. Dr. Dewey, whom we accounted one of the ablest expounders and most eloquent defenders of our Unitarian faith, — Dr. Dewey was reported to have said at two different times, in public lectures or speeches during the fall of 1850 and the winter of 1851, that "he would send his *mother* into slavery, rather than endanger the Union, by resisting this law enacted by the constituted government of the nation." He has often denied that he spoke thus of his "maternal relative," and therefore I allow that he was misunderstood. But he has repeatedly acknowledged that he did say, "I would consent that my own brother, my own son, should go, *ten times rather* would I go myself into slavery, than that this Union should be sacrificed." The rhetoric of this sentence may be less shocking, but the principle that underlies it is equally immoral and demoralizing. It is, that the inalienable, God-given rights of man ought to be violated, outraged, rather than overturn or seriously endanger a human institution called a government.

Although our denomination at that time was numerically a very small one, yet it was so prominent, not only in Boston and its immediate vicinity, but before the whole nation, and in view of all the world, that it seemed to me to be a matter of great moral consequence that it should take and maintain a truly Christian stand respecting this high-handed, glaring attempt to bring our Northern free States into entire subjection to the slaveholding oligarchy. Therefore, at the next annual meeting of the American Unitarian Association, in May, 1851, I offered the following Preamble and Resolution : —

"Whereas, his Excellency, Millard Fillmore, whose official signature made the Fugitive Slave Bill a law, is a *Unitarian;* and the Hon. Daniel Webster, who exerted all his official and personal influence to procure the passage of that bill, has been until recently, if he is not now, a member of a Unitarian church; and whereas, one of the only three Representatives from New England, who voted for that bill, is the Hon. S. A. Eliot, a distinguished Unitarian of Boston, known to have been educated for the Unitarian ministry; and whereas, the present representative of the United States Government at the Court of the British Empire is a Unitarian, and his two immediate predecessors were once preachers of this Gospel, and one of them, Hon. Edward Everett, has publicly declared his approval of Mr. Webster's course touching this most wicked law; and whereas, the Hon. Jared Sparks, President of Harvard College, and President of the Divinity School at Cambridge, formerly a distinguished minister, and a very elaborate and able expounder of our distinctive doctrines, is one of the number who addressed a letter to Mr. Webster, commending him for what he had said and done in behalf of the Fugitive Slave Law; and still more, because the late President of this American Unitarian Association (Dr. Dewey), one of the most popular preachers, expounders, and champions of the Unitarian faith, has been more earnest and emphatic than any man in his asseveration that this law, infernal as it is, ought nevertheless to be obeyed; and because the gentleman who this day retires from the highest position in our ecclesiastical body, the Rev. Dr. Gannett, is understood to have given his adhesion to this lowest of all laws, and several of the distinguished, titled ministers of our denomination in and near Boston, the head-quarters of Unitarians, have preached obedience to *this law*, —

"We, therefore, feel especially called upon by the highest considerations, at this, the first general gathering of our body, since the above-named exposures of the unsoundness of our members, to declare in the most public and emphatic manner that we consider the Fugitive Slave Law a most fearful violation of the law of God, as taught by Jesus Christ and his apostles, and, therefore, all obedience to it is practical infidelity to the Author and Finisher of the Christian faith, and to the impartial Father of the whole human family.

"*Resolved*, Therefore, that we, the American Unitarian Association, earnestly exhort all who would honor the Christian name, but especially all who have embraced with us views of human nature similar to those held up by our revered Channing, — to remember those in bonds as bound with them; ever to attempt to do for them, as we would that the now enslaved or fugitive should do for us in an exchange of circumstances, — to comfort and aid them in all their attempts to escape from their oppressors, and by no means to betray the fugitives, or in any way assist or give the least countenance to the cruel men who would return them to slavery."

Both the Preamble and Resolutions were cordially seconded by Rev. Theodore Parker, and their adoption urged in a brief but most significant speech. The moment he had ceased speaking Henry Fuller, Esq., of Boston, sprang to his feet, and, in an impassioned manner, moved that the paper just read by the Rev. Mr. May, of Syracuse, be not even received by the Association. "This ecclesiastical body had nothing to do with such a political matter. The entertaining of the subject here would be indecorous, and only help to increase the alienation of feeling between the South and the North." With equal warmth of manner and speech Rev. Joseph Richardson, of Hingham, seconded Mr. Fuller's motion, and cut off all debate by calling for the "previous question." So the motion not to receive my paper was put, and carried by twenty-seven to twenty-two.

The next day, at a meeting of the "Ministerial Conference," which comprised all the clerical members of the American Unitarian Association, I proposed for adoption the same Preamble and Resolution, and am happy to add, with a much more gratifying result. The following is a very brief report of the discussion and action of that body, taken from *The Commonwealth* of June 2, 1851: —

"Rev. Mr. Judd, of Augusta, Me., thought it the duty of the clergy to speak freely upon the question of slavery, but with perfect plainness to all parties. He approved of the sentiment of the resolve, but disliked the preamble, as too personal in its language.

Rev. Mr. May, of Syracuse, N. Y., said reference was made in the resolve to those only whom the Conference had a right to mention, namely, prominent Unitarians who had sustained the Fugitive Slave Law.

"Rev. Dr. Hall, of Providence, R. I., thought that, as citizens, as Unitarians, and as Christians, they were called upon to speak in opposition to the law, but the right place should be selected, in order that no false impression should be given in case the topic should not be acted upon. For himself, he should not obey the law, though the country went to pieces.

"Rev. Mr. Parker, of Boston, read extracts from an English paper, showing the action of an ecclesiastical body abroad that had resolved not to countenance or admit to its pulpits any of the American clergy who uphold the Fugitive Slave Law or slavery.

"Rev. Mr. Holland, of Rochester, N. Y., deemed obedience to the law a violation of conscience and duty. His voice and prayer were for progress and liberty.

"Rev. Mr. Frost, of Concord, Mass., had had a committee of his society ask him to abstain from preaching on slavery thenceforth. He replied, that when the slave power had taken possession of the departments of Government, controlled the decisions of our courts, and influenced the moral position of the Church itself, glossing over all the iniquities of the system, he should not keep silence. Obedience to the Fugitive Law was treason to God; he preferred to be disloyal to man.

"Rev. William H. Channing, of New York City, thought the Church should take common ground against this national sin. But to the slaveholder he would be fair and candid. He would meet him in conclave, show him the evils of slavery, the worth of freedom, and join with him in removing the willing free colored population to the lands of the West, and as a remuneration give them the blessings of free labor and social prosperity.

"Rev. Mr. Osgood, of New York City, admitted the iniquity of the Fugitive Slave Law, and the sin of slavery, and thought them proper subjects for pulpit discussion; but he wanted a moral influence to be exerted, without a violation of Christian gentleness. He said Rev. Mr. Furness, of Philadelphia, and Rev. Dr. Dewey, of New York, had had a correspondence in reference to the latter's position on political questions, and he (Mr. Osgood) honestly believed, from the results of that correspondence, and from conversations he himself had held with the Doctor, that, in his support of the Slave Law, he was making self-sacrifice to what he conceived his duty.

"Rev. Mr. Pierpont, of Medford, proclaimed the superiority of God's law to man's law. He would not obey the latter when it interfered with the former. The government might fine and imprison, but it could do no more; he was mindful of the penalty, but he would not obey. If all would act with him the law would fail of being executed.

"Rev. Dr. Gannett, of Boston, was impressed with the immensity of this question, the terrible awfulness that lay behind it, and he would discuss it with all solemnity and seriousness in view of the impending evil. He believed in his heart the maintenance of government, the comfort of the people, *and the perpetuity of our Union depended on the support of the Fugitive Law.* He would not have the subject treated lightly, but prayerfully, fearfully, in view of the great responsibilities resting upon it. We should respect private convictions, and allow the integrity of motives of those who differ with us.

"Rev. Mr. Ellis, of Charlestown, hailed that day as the first when these differences had been rightly discussed. But if the Conference, comprising members of different though honest views, should take ground on this question, he should leave it. As an organized body we have nothing to do with it. No action could be binding, and he was unwilling to have the Conference interfere with the question. He had himself ever entertained ultra-abolition views, and did now; but he had no such fears for the Union as Brother Gannett. If the Union was held together by so feeble a tenure as here presented, he thought it was not worth saving; and further, if our Northern land is to be the scouring-ground of slave-hunters, the sooner the Union was sundered the better. But our sphere of action did not allow interference with the question.

"Dr. Gannett spoke of the character of that parishioner of his who returned a slave (Curtis). He had done so from convictions of his constitutional obligations as an upholder of law and as a good citizen, and he esteemed that a wrong was done him in stigmatizing him as a 'cruel' man, because of that return, as the resolution expressed it.

"On motion of Mr. Pierpont, the word 'cruel' was stricken out, and the resolution having been previously altered so as to make it a proposition for discussion rather than as a test for votes, it was entered upon the records.

"The debate (of which I have given a very limited sketch) here terminated by general consent, the feeling being almost unanimous as expressed by the majority of the speakers."

But the Unitarians as a body were by no means redeemed from the moral thraldom in which the whole nation was held. There was still among them so little heartfelt abhorrence of slavery and the Fugitive Slave Law, that the year after Mr. Fillmore was dropped from the presidency of the nation, which he had so dishonored, he was specially invited to preside at the Annual Festival of the Unitarians, to be given, if I remember correctly, in Faneuil Hall. He declined the honor proffered him, but our denomination was left to bear the shame of having asked him to receive an expression of our respect, as there was no protest against the action of the Committee.

THE RESCUE OF JERRY.

I should love to tell of the generous, daring, self-sacrificing conflicts with the abettors and minions of the slaveholders in different parts of our country. But I must leave those bright pages to be written by the historian of those times, and confine myself to that part of the field where I saw and was engaged in the fight.

In the early part of the summer of 1851 Mr. Webster travelled quite extensively about the country, exerting all his personal and official influence, and the remnants of his eloquence, to persuade the people to yield themselves to the requirements of the Fugitive Slave Law. On the 5th or 6th of June he came to Syracuse. He stood in a small balcony overlooking the yard in front of our City Hall and the intervening street. Of course he had a large audience. But his hearers generally were disappointed in his appearance and speech, and those who were not already members of the proslavery party were much offended at his authoritative, dictatorial, commanding tones and language. There is no need that I should give an abstract of what he said. It was but a rehash of his infamous speech in Congress on the 7th of March, 1850. At or near the close he said, in his severest manner, "Those persons in this city who mean to oppose the execution of the Fugitive Slave Law are traitors! traitors!! traitors!!! This law ought to be obeyed, and it will be enforced, — yes, it shall be enforced; in the city of Syracuse it shall be enforced, and that, too, in the midst of the next antislavery Convention, if then there shall be any occasion to enforce it." Indignation flashed from many eyes in that assembly, and one might almost hear the gritting of teeth in defiance of the threat.

I stated on page 354 that at the meeting on the 12th of October, 1850, we commenced an association to co-operate and to bear one another's burdens in defence of any among us who should be arrested as slaves. Many came into our agreement. We fixed upon a rendezvous, and agreed that any one of our number, who might know or hear of a person in danger, should toll the bell of an adjoining meeting-house in a particular manner, and that, on hearing that signal, we would all repair at once to the spot, ready to do and to dare whatever might seem to be necessary. Two or three times in the ensuing twelve months the alarm was given, but the cause for action was removed by the time we reached our rendezvous, excepting in one case, when it was thought advisable to send a guard to protect a threatened man to Auburn or Rochester.

But on the first day of October, 1851, a real and, as it proved to be, a signal case was given us. Whether it was given on that day intentionally to fulfil Mr. Webster's prediction is known only to those who have not yet divulged the secret. There was, however, on that day an antislavery convention in Syracuse, and, moreover, a meeting of the County Agricultural Society, so that our city was unusually full of people, which proved to be favorable to our enterprise.

Just as I was about to rise from my dinner on that day I heard the signal-bell, and hurried towards the appointed place, nearly a mile from my home. But I had not gone half-way before I met the report that Jerry McHenry had been claimed as a slave, arrested by the police, and taken to the office of the Commissioner. So I turned my steps thither. The nearer I got to the place, the more persons I met, all excited, many of them infuriated by the thought that a man among us was to be carried away into slavery.

Jerry was an athletic mulatto, who had been residing in Syracuse for a number of years, and working quite expertly, it was said, as a cooper. I found him in the presence of the Commissioner with the District Attorney, who was conducting the trial, — a one-sided process, in which the agent of the claimant alone was to be heard in proof, that the prisoner was an escaped slave belonging to a Mr. Reynolds, of Missouri. The doomed man was not to be allowed to state his own case, nor refute the testimony of his adversary, however false it might be. While we were attending to the novel proceedings, Jerry, not being closely guarded, slipped out of the room under the guidance of a young man of more zeal than discretion, and in a moment was in the street below. The crowd cheered and made way for him, but no vehicle having been provided to help his escape, he was left to depend upon his agility as a runner. Being manacled, he could not do his best; but he had got off nearly half a mile, before the police officers and their partisans overtook him. I was not there to witness the meeting; but it was said the rencounter was a furious one. Jerry fought like a tiger, but fought against overwhelming odds. He was attacked behind and before and soon subdued. He was battered and bruised, his clothes sadly torn and bloody, and one rib cracked, if not broken. In this plight he was thrown upon a carman's wagon, two policemen sat upon him, one across his legs, the other across his body, and thus confined he was brought down through the centre of the city, and put into a back room of the police office, the whole *posse* being gathered there to guard him. The people, citizens and strangers, were alike indignant. As I passed amongst them I heard nothing but execrations and threats of release. Two or three times men came to me and said, "Mr. May, speak the word, and we'll have Jerry out." "And what will you do with him," I replied, "when you get him out? You have just seen the bad effect of one ill-advised attempt to rescue him. Wait until proper arrangements are made. Stay near here to help at the right moment and in the right way. In a little while it will be quite dark, and then the poor fellow can be easily disposed of."

Presently the Chief of the Police came to me, and said, "Jerry is in a perfect rage, a fury of passion; do come in and see if you can quiet him." So I followed into the little room where he was confined. He was indeed a horrible object. I was left alone with him, and sat down by his side. So soon as I could get him to hear me, I said, "Jerry, do try to be calm." "Would you be calm," he roared out, "with these irons on you? What have I done to be treated so? Take off these handcuffs, and then if I do not fight my way through these fellows that have got me here, — then you may make me a slave." Thus he raved on, until in a momentary interval I whispered, "Jerry, we are going to rescue you; do be more quiet!" "Who are you?" he cried. "How do I know you can or will rescue me?" After a while I told him by snatches what we meant to do, who I was, and how many there were who had come resolved to save him from slavery. At length he seemed to believe me, became more tranquil, and consented to lie down, so I left him. Immediately after I went to the office of the late Dr. Hiram Hoyt, where I found twenty or thirty picked men laying a plan for the rescue. Among them was Gerrit Smith, who happened to be in town attending the Liberty Party Convention. It was agreed that a skilful and bold driver in a strong buggy, with the fleetest horse to be got in the city, should be stationed not far off to receive Jerry, when he should be brought out. Then to drive hither and thither about the city until he saw no one pursuing him; not to attempt to get out of town, because it was reported that every exit was well guarded, but to return to a certain point near the centre of the city, where he would find two men waiting to receive his charge. With them he was to leave Jerry, and know nothing about the place of his retreat.

At a given signal the doors and windows of the police office were to be demolished at once, and the rescuers to rush in and fill the room, press around and upon the officers, overwhelming them by their numbers, not by blows, and so soon as they were confined and powerless by the pressure of bodies about them, several men were to take up Jerry and bear him to the buggy aforesaid. Strict injunctions were given, and it was agreed not intentionally to injure the policemen. Gerrit Smith and several others pressed this caution very urgently upon those who were gathered in Dr. Hoyt's office. And the last thing I said as we were coming away was, " If any one is to be injured in this fray, I hope it may be one of our own party."

The plan laid down as I have sketched it was well and quickly executed, about eight o'clock in the evening. The police office was soon in our possession. One officer in a fright jumped out of a window and seriously injured himself. Another officer fired a pistol and slightly wounded one of the rescuers. With these exceptions there were no personal injuries. The driver of the buggy managed adroitly, escaped all pursuers, and about nine o'clock delivered Jerry into the hands of Mr. Jason S. Hoyt and Mr. James Davis. They led him not many steps to the house of the late Caleb Davis, who with his wife promptly consented to give the poor fellow a shelter in their house, at the corner of Genesee and Orange Streets. Here they at once cut off his shackles, and after some refreshing food put him to bed. Now the excitement was over, Jerry was utterly exhausted, and soon became very feverish. A physician was called, who dressed his wounds and administered such medicine as was applicable. But rest, sleep, was what he needed, and he enjoyed them undisturbed for five days,—only four or five persons, besides Mr. and Mrs. Davis, knowing what had become of Jerry. It was generally supposed he had gone to Canada. But the next Sunday evening, just after dark, a covered wagon with a span of very fleet horses was seen standing for a few minutes near the door of Mr. Caleb Davis's house. Mr. Jason S. Hoyt and Mr. James Davis were seen to help a somewhat infirm man into the vehicle, jump in themselves, and start off at a rapid rate. Suspicion was awakened, and several of the "patriots" of our city set off in pursuit of the "traitors." The chase was a hot one for eight or ten miles, but Jerry's deliverers had the advantage on the start, and in the speed of the horses that were bearing him to liberty. They took him that night about twenty miles to the house of a Mr. Ames, a Quaker, in the town of Mexico. There he was kept concealed several days, and then conveyed to the house of a Mr. Clarke, on the confines of the city of Oswego. This gentleman searched diligently nearly a week for a vessel that would take Jerry across to the dominions of the British Queen. He dared not trust a Yankee captain, and the English vessels were so narrowly watched, that it was not until several days had elapsed that he was able to find one who would undertake to transport a fugitive slave over the lake. At length the captain of a small craft agreed to set sail after dark, and when well off on the lake to hoist a light to the top of his mast, that his whereabouts might be known. Mr. Clarke took Jerry to a less frequented part of the shore, embarked with him in a small boat, and rowed him to the little schooner of the friendly captain. By him he was taken to Kingston, where he soon was established again in the business of a cooper. Not many days after his arrival there we received a letter from him, expressing in the warmest terms his gratitude for what the Abolitionists in Syracuse had done in his behalf. After pouring out a heartful of thanks to us, he assured us that he had been led to think more than ever before of his indebtedness to God, — the ultimate Source of all goodness, — and had been brought to the resolution to lead a purer, better life than he had ever done. We heard afterwards that he was well married, and was living comfortably and respectably. But, ere the fourth year of his deliverance had closed, he was borne away to that world where there never was and never will be a slaveholder nor a slave.

Foiled in their attempt to lay a tribute at the feet of the Southern oligarchy, the officers of the United States Government set about to punish us "traitors," who had evinced so much more regard for "the rights of man conferred by God" than for a wicked law enacted by Congress. Eighteen of us were indicted. The accusation was brought before Judge Conkling at Auburn. Thither, therefore, the accused were taken. But we went accompanied by nearly a hundred of our fellow-citizens, many of them the most prominent men of Syracuse, with not a few ladies. So soon as the indictment was granted, and bailors called for, Hon. William H. Seward stepped forward and put his name first upon the bond. His good example was promptly followed, and the required amount was quickly pledged, by a number of our most responsible gentlemen. Mr. Seward then invited the rescuers of Jerry and their friends, especially the ladies, to his house, where all were hospitably entertained until it was time for us to return to Syracuse.

But the hand of law was not laid upon the friends of Jerry alone. James Lear, the agent of his claimant, and the Deputy Marshal who assisted him, were arrested on warrants for attempting to kidnap a citizen of Syracuse. They, however, easily escaped conviction on the plea that they were acting under a law of the United States.

Many of the political newspapers were emphatic in their condemnation of our resistance to the law, and only a few ventured to justify it. *The Advertiser* and *The American* of Rochester, *The Gazette* and *Observer* of Utica, *The Oneida Whig*, *The Register*, *The Argus*, and *The Express* of Albany, *The Courier and Inquirer* and *The Express* of New York, although of opposite political parties, were agreed in pronouncing "the rescue of Jerry a disgraceful, demoralizing, and alarming act."

A mass convention of the citizens of Onondaga County, called to consider the propriety of the rescue, met in our City Hall on the 15th of October, and with entire unanimity passed a series of resolutions fully justifying and applauding the deed.

Ten days afterwards, an opposing convention of the city and county was held in the same place, and sent forth an opposite opinion, but not without dissent.

In one of our city papers I was called out by three of my fellow-citizens as the one more responsible than any other for the rescue of Jerry, and was challenged to justify such an open defiance of a law of my country. Thus was the subject kept before the public, and the questions involved in it were pretty thoroughly discussed.

Meanwhile the United States District Attorney was not neglectful of his official duty. He summoned several of the indicted ones to trial at Buffalo, at Albany, and at Canandaigua. But he did not obtain a conviction in either case. Gerrit Smith, Charles A. Wheaton, and myself published in the papers an acknowledgment that we had assisted all we could in the rescue of Jerry; that we were ready for trial; would give the Court no trouble as to the fact, and should rest our defence upon the unconstitutionality and extreme wickedness of the Fugitive Slave Law. The Attorney did not, however, see fit to bring the matter to that test. He brought a poor colored man — Enoch Reed — to trial at Albany, and summoned me as one of the witnesses against him. When called to the stand to tell the jury all that I knew of Mr. Reed's participation in the rescue, I testified that I saw him doing what hundreds of others did or attempted to do, and that he was not particularly conspicuous in that good work. The Attorney was much offended. He assured the Judge that I knew much more about the matter than I had told the jury, and requested him to remind me of my oath to tell the whole truth. When the Court had so admonished me, I bowed and said: "May it please your Honor, I do know all about the rescue of Jerry; and if the prosecuting officer will arraign Gerrit Smith Charles A. Wheaton or myself, I shall have occasion to tell the jury all about the transaction. I have now truly given the jury all the testimony I have to give respecting the prisoner at the bar."

Of course Enoch Reed was acquitted, and no other one of those indicted was convicted. The last attempt to procure a conviction was made at Canandaigua, before Judge Hall, of the United States District Court, in the autumn of 1852. A few days before the setting of that Court, Mr. Gerrit Smith sent copies of a handbill to be distributed in that village and the surrounding country, announcing that he would be in Canandaigua at the time of the Court, and speak to the people who might assemble to hear him, on the atrocious wickedness of the Fugitive Slave Law.

On his arrival at Canandaigua, Mr. Smith found all the public buildings closed against him. He therefore requested that a wagon might be drawn into an adjoining pasture, and notice given that he would speak there. At the appointed hour a large assembly had gathered to hear him. He addressed them in his most impressive manner. He exposed fully the great iniquity that was about to be attempted in the court-room hard by, — the iniquity of sentencing a man as guilty of a crime for doing that which, in the sight of God, was innocent, praiseworthy, — yes, required by the Golden Rule. He argued to the jurors, who might be in the crowd surrounding him, that, whatever might be the testimony given them to prove that Jerry was a slave; whatever words might be quoted from statutes or constitutions to show that a man can be by law turned into a slave, a chattel, the property of another man, they nevertheless might, with a good conscience, bring in a verdict acquitting any one of crime, who should be accused before them of having helped to rescue a fellow-man from those who would make him a slave. "If," said he, "the ablest lawyer should argue before you, and quote authorities to prove that an article which you know to be wood is stone or iron, would you consent to regard it as stone or iron, and bring in a verdict based upon such a supposition, even though the judge in his charge should instruct you so to do? I trust not. So neither should any argument or amount of testimony or weight of authorities satisfy you that a man is a chattel. Jurors cannot be bound more than other persons to believe an absurdity."

The United States Attorney, Mr. Garvin, found that he could not empanel a jury upon which there were not several who had formed an opinion against the law. So he let all the "Jerry Rescue Causes" fall to the ground forever.

At the time of this his boldest, most defiant act, Mr. Smith was a member of Congress. For this reason, "his contempt of the Court," "his disrespect for the forms of law, the precedents of judicial decisions, and the authority of the constitution," was pronounced by "the wise and prudent" to be the more shameful, mischievous, and alarming. But "the common people" could not be easily convinced that any wrong could be so great as enslaving a man, nor that it was criminal to help him escape from servile bondage.

My readers will readily believe that we exulted not a little in the triumph of our exploit. For several years afterwards we celebrated the 1st of October as the anniversary of the greatest event in the history of Syracuse. Either because, in 1852, there was no hall in our city capacious enough to accommodate so large a meeting as we expected, or else because we could not obtain the most capacious hall, — for one or the other of these reasons, — the first anniversary of the Rescue of Jerry was celebrated in the rotunda of the New York Central Railroad, just then completed for the accommodation of the engines. John Wilkinson, Esq., at that time President of the road, promptly, and without our solicitation, proffered the use of the building, large enough to hold thousands. It was well filled. Gerrit Smith presided, and the speeches made by him, by Mr. Garrison, and other prominent Abolitionists, together with the letters of congratulation received from Hon. Charles Sumner, Rev. Theodore

Parker, and others, would fill a volume, half the size of this, with the most exalted political and moral sentiments, and not a few passages of sublime eloquence.

After our triumph over the Fugitive Slave Law, we Abolitionists in Central New York enjoyed for several years a season of comparative peace. We held our regular and our occasional antislavery meetings without molestation, and were encouraged in the belief that our sentiments were coming to be more generally received. The Republican party was evidently bound to become an abolition party. Hon. Charles Sumner was doing excellent service in the Senate of the United States, and Hon. Henry Wilson and others in Congress were seconding his efforts, to bring the legislators of our nation to see and own that the institution of slavery was utterly incompatible with a free, democratic government, and irreconcilable with the Christian religion.

Still we could perceive no signs of repentance in the slaveholding States, and had despaired of a *peaceful* settlement of the great controversy. How soon the appeal to the arbitrament of war would come we could not predict; but we saw it to be inevitable. All, therefore, that remained for the friends of our country and of humanity to do, was diligently to disseminate throughout the non-slaveholding States a just appreciation of the great question at issue between the North and the South; a true respect for the God-given rights of man, which our nation had so impiously dared to trample upon; and the sincere belief that nothing less than the extermination of slavery from our borders could insure the true union of the States and the prosperity of our Republic. To this work of patriotism, as well as benevolence, therefore, we addressed ourselves so long as the terrible chastisement which our nation had incurred was delayed.

Wellnigh exhausted by my unremitted attention to

the duties of my profession, and to the several great reforms that have signalized the last fifty years, I was persuaded to go to Europe for recreation and the recovery of my health. I spent six months of the year 1859 on the Continent, and three months in England, Scotland, and Ireland.

Numerous as are the interesting places and persons to be seen in each of these last-named countries, I must confess that my greatest attraction to them was the expectation of seeing many of the friends of liberty, who had coöperated so generously with us for the abolition of slavery. And in this respect I was not disappointed. I lectured by request to large audiences in several of the chief cities of the kingdom. But, what was much better, I had meetings for conversation with the prominent Abolitionists, especially in London, Glasgow, and Dublin. These were numerously attended, and the intelligent questions put to me, by those who were so well informed and so deeply interested in the cause of my enslaved countrymen, saved me from misspending a minute on the commonplaces of the subject, and led me to give our friends the most recent information of the kinds they craved.

I remember particularly the conversations that I had in Glasgow and Dublin. The former was held in the ample, well-stored library room of Professor Nichol of the University of that city. His wife was, a few years before, Miss Elizabeth Pease, one of the earliest, best-informed, and most liberal of our English fellow-laborers. He promptly concurred with her in cordially inviting me to his home. And on my second or third visit, he had gathered there to meet me the prominent Abolitionists of the city and immediate neighborhood. He presided at the meeting, and introduced me in a most comprehensive and impressive speech on human freedom, — the paramount right of man, — of all men, — demanding protection wherever it was denied or endangered from all who can give it aid, without consideration of distance or nationality. That well-spent evening I shall never forget, especially his and his wife's contributions of wise thought and elevated sentiment. But my too brief personal acquaintance with them is kept more sacred in my memory by his death, which happened soon after, and an intensely interesting incident connected with it.

At Dublin and its vicinity I spent a fortnight, — too short a time. But I had the happiness, while there, of seeing face to face several of our warm-hearted sympathizers and active co-laborers, especially James Haughton, Esq., and Richard D. Webb. The former I found to be more engaged in the cause of Peace, and much more of Temperance, than in the antislavery cause. Indeed, in the cause of Temperance he had done then, and has done since, more than any other man in Ireland, excepting Father Matthew. Still, he had always been, and was then, heartily in earnest for the abolition of slavery everywhere.

But Richard D. Webb could hardly have taken a more active part with American Abolitionists, or have rendered us much more valuable services, if he had been a countryman of ours, and living in our midst. The readers of *The Liberator* cannot have forgotten how often communications from his pen appeared in its columns, nor how thorough an acquaintance they evinced with whatever pertained to our conflict with "the peculiar institution," that great anomaly in our democracy. Mr. Webb was afterwards the author of an excellent memoir of John Brown, whose "soul is still marching on," — the spirit of whose hatred of oppression, and sympathy with the down-trodden, is spreading wider and descending deeper into the hearts of our people, and will continue so to spread, until every vestige of slavery shall be effaced from our land, and all the inhabitants thereof shall enjoy equal rights and privileges on the same conditions. Mr. Webb's memoir shows how justly he appreciated and how heartily he admired the intentions of John Brown, whatever he thought of the expediency of his plan of operations. For a week I enjoyed the hospitality of Mrs. Edmundson, and at her house met one evening many of the moral *élite* of Dublin, for conversation respecting the conflict with slavery in our country. Their inquiries showed them to be very well informed on the subject, and alive to whatever then seemed likely to affect the issue favorably or unfavorably.

Lord Morpeth, who was at that time Lord Lieutenant of Ireland, graciously invited me to lunch with him. He had visited our country a few years before, and had manifested while here the deepest interest in the principles and purposes of the Abolitionists. I was delighted to find that he and his sister, Lady Howard, continued to be as much concerned as ever for our success.

On my return from Europe, early in November, 1859, the steamer stopped as usual at Halifax. There we first received the tidings of John Brown's raid, and the failure of his enterprise. I felt at once that it was "the beginning of the end" of our conflict with slavery. There were several Southern gentlemen and ladies among our fellow-passengers, and Northern sympathizers with them, as well as others of opposite opinions. During our short passage from Halifax to Boston there was evidently a deep excitement in many bosoms. Occasionally words of bitter execration escaped the lips of one and another of the proslavery party. But there was no dispute or general conversation upon the subject. The event, of which we had just heard, was a portent of too much magnitude to be hastily estimated, and the consequences thereof flippantly foretold.

On my arrival in Boston, and the next day in Syracuse, I found the public in a state of high excitement; and for two or three months the case of John Brown was the subject of continual debate in private circles as well as public meetings. The murmurs and threats that came daily from the South, intimated plainly enough that the slaveholding oligarchy were preparing for something harsher than a war of words. They were gathering themselves to rule or ruin our Republic. Under the imbecile administration of Mr. Buchanan, the Secretary of War, John B. Floyd, could do as he saw fit in his department. It was observed that the arms and ammunition of the nation, with the greater part of the small army needed in times of peace, were removed and disposed of in such places as would make them most available to the Southerners, if the emergency for which they were preparing should come. They awaited only the issue of the next presidential contest. The first ten months of the year 1860 were given to that contest. All the strength of the two political parties was put in requisition, drawn out, and fully tested and compared. And when victory crowned the friends of freedom and human rights, — when the election of Mr. Lincoln was proclaimed, — then came forth from the South the fierce cry of disunion, and the standard of a new Confederacy was set up. It is not my intention to enter upon the period of our Civil War. These Recollections will close with occurrences before the fall of Fort Sumter.

In pursuance of a plan adopted several years before, by the American Antislavery Society, arrangements were made early in December, 1860, to hold our annual conventions during the months of January and February, in Buffalo, Syracuse, Albany, and in a dozen other of the principal cities and villages between the two extremes. We who had devoted ourselves so assiduously for a quarter of a century or more to the subversion of the slavery in our land, of course had many thoughts and feelings upon the subject at that time, which pressed for utterance. We were the last persons who could be indifferent to the state of our country in 1860, or be silent in view of it. Nor had we any reason then to suppose that our counsels and admonitions would be particularly unacceptable to the people, as we were then frequently assured that the public sentiment of New York, as well as New England, had become quite antislavery.

We were not a little surprised, therefore, at the new outbreak of violent opposition in Boston, and afterwards in Buffalo and other places. About the middle of January I attended the convention at Rochester, where we were rudely treated and grossly insulted. I could no longer doubt that there was a concerted plan, among the Democrats everywhere, to evince a revival of their zeal in behalf of their Southern partisans by breaking up our meetings. And it appeared that the Republicans were afraid to take the responsibility, and incur the new odium of protecting our conventions in their constitutional rights. Still I hoped better things of Syracuse.

But a few days before the time appointed for our Convention, I was earnestly requested by the Mayor of the city to prevent the holding of such a meeting. I replied I would do so, if there was indeed so little respect for the liberty of speech in Syracuse that the assembly would be violently dispersed. In answer to this, his Honor assured me that, much as he wished we would forbear to exercise our undoubted right, still, if we felt it to be our duty to hold the convention, "he would fearlessly use every means at his command to secure order, and to prevent any interference with our proceedings." Thus he took from me the only apology I could offer to our Committee of Arrangements for interposing to prevent the assembling of a meeting, which they had called in accordance with the duty assigned them.

A day or two afterwards I received a letter, written probably at the solicitation of the Mayor, and signed by twenty of the most respectable gentlemen of Syracuse (ten of them prominent members of my church), urging me to prevent the holding of the convention, as "they were credibly informed that an organized and forcible effort would be made to oppose us, and a collision might ensue between the police force of the city and a lawless mob." Still, they assured me that they recognized our right to hold such a convention, and "that they should be in duty bound to aid in protecting us if we did assemble." I felt obliged to answer them very much as I had answered the Mayor, and added what follows: —

"In common with my associates, I am very sincere in believing that the principles we inculcate, and the measures we advise, are the only ones that can (without war) extirpate from our country the root of that evil which now overshadows us, and threatens our ruin. We have much to say to the people, much that we deem it very important that they should hear and believe, lest they bow themselves to another compromise with the slaveholding oligarchy, which for many years has really ruled our Republic, and which nothing will satisfy but the entire subjugation of our liberties to their supposed interests.

"We perceive that the 'strong' men of the Republican party are trembling, and concession and compromise are coming to be their policy. We deprecate their fears, their want of confidence in moral principle and in God. We therefore feel deeply urged to cry aloud, and warn the people of the snare into which politicians would lead them. We are bound at least to *offer* to them the word of truth, whether they will hear or whether they will forbear.

"If, gentlemen, you had assured me that our proposed meeting will be violently assaulted; that those who may assemble peacefully to listen will not be allowed to hear us; that they will be dispersed with insult if not with personal injury; and that you, gentlemen of influence as you are, shall stand aside and let the violent have their way; then I should have felt it to be incumbent on me to advertise the friends of liberty and humanity that it would not be worth their while to convene here, as it would be only to be dispersed.

"But, gentlemen, as you generously 'affirm,' in the letter before me, 'that your duties as citizens will require you to aid in extending protection to our convention, in case it shall be convened, in the exercise of all the rights which all deliberative bodies may claim,' and as the Mayor of our city has assured me that 'he shall fearlessly use every means at his command to secure order and to prevent any interference with our proceedings,' I should not be justified in assuming the responsibility of postponing the convention. For, gentlemen, if you will do what you acknowledge to be your duty, and if the Mayor will fulfil his generous promise, I am confident the rioters will be overawed, the liberty of speech will be vindicated, and our city rescued from a deep disgrace.

"Yours, gentlemen, in great haste, but very respectfully,

"Samuel J. May."

Just before the hour appointed for the opening of the convention, on the 29th of January, 1861, I went to the hall which I had hired for its accommodation. It was already fully occupied by the rioters. A meeting had been organized, and the chairman was making his introductory speech. So soon as he had finished it, I addressed him:

"Mr. Chairman, there is some mistake here, or a greater wrong. More than a week ago I engaged this hall for our Annual Antislavery Convention to be held at this hour." Immediately, several rough men turned violently upon me, touched my head and face with their doubled fists, and swore they would knock me down, and thrust me out of the hall, if I said another word. Meanwhile, the Rev. Mr. Strieby, of the Plymouth Church, had succeeded in getting upon the platform, and had commenced a remonstrance, when he was set upon in like manner, and threatened with being thrown down and put out, if he did not desist at once.

The only police officer that I saw in the hall soon after rose, addressed the chairman and said: "I came here, Sir, by order of the Mayor, who had heard that there was to be a disturbance, and that the liberty of speech would be outraged here. But I see no indications of such an intended wrong. The meeting seems to me to be an orderly one, properly organized. I approve the objects of the meeting as set forth in your introductory speech, and trust you will have a quiet time."

Thus dispossessed, we of course retired, and, after consultation, agreed to gather as many of the members of the intended convention, as could be found, at the dwelling-house of Dr. R. W. Pease, who generously proffered us the use of it. A large number of ladies and gentlemen assembled there early in the evening, and were duly organized. Pertinent and impressive addresses were made by Beriah Green, Aaron M. Powell, Susan B. Anthony, C. D. B. Mills, and others, after which a series of resolutions was passed, of which the following were the most important: —

"*Resolved*, That the only escape for nations, as well as individuals, from sin and its consequences, is by the way of unfeigned repentance; and that our proud Republic must go down in ruin, unless the people shall be brought to repentance, — shall be persuaded to 'cease to do evil, and learn to do well; to seek justice, relieve the oppressed.' Compromises with the wrong-doers will only plunge us deeper in their iniquity. Civil war will not settle the difficulty, but complicate it all the more, and superadd rapine and murder to the sin of slaveholding. The dissolution of the Union, even, may not relieve us; for if slavery still remains in the land, it will be a perpetual trouble to the inhabitants thereof, whether they be separate or whether they be united; slavery must be abolished, or there can be no peace within these borders.

"*Resolved*, That our General Government ought to abolish all Fugitive Slave Laws; for, unless they can dethrone God, the people will ever be under higher obligations to obey him than to obey any laws, any constitutions that men may have framed and enacted. And the law of God requires us to befriend the friendless, to succor the distressed, to hide the outcast, to deliver the oppressed.

"*Resolved*, That as the people of the free States have from the beginning been partakers in the iniquity of slavery, — accomplices of the oppressors of the poor laborers at the South, — therefore we ought to join hands with them in any well-devised measures for the emancipation of their bondmen. Our wealth and the wealth of the nation ought to be put in requisition, to relieve those who may impoverish themselves by setting their captives free; to furnish the freed men with such comforts, conveniences, implements of labor as they may need; and to establish such educational and religious institutions as will be indispensable everywhere, to enable them, and, yet more, their children and children's children, to become what the free people, the citizens of self-governing states, ought to be, — *intelligent, moral, religious.*

"*Resolved*, That the abolition of slavery is the great concern of the American people,— 'the one thing needful' for them, — without which there can be no union, no peace, no political virtue, no real, lasting prosperity in all these once United States.

"*Resolved*, That, so far from its being untimely or inappropriate to stand forth for unpopular truths, in seasons of great popular excitement, apprehension, and wide passionate denial of them, it is then pre-eminently timely, appropriate, and all vitally important, whether regarded in view of the paramount obligations of fealty to the Supreme King, or the sacred considerations of the redemption and welfare of mankind; and as it behooved then most of all to speak for Jesus, when Jesus was arraigned for condemnation and crucifixion, as it has ever been the bounden and, sooner or later, the well-acknowledged duty of every friend of the truth in past history to stand firm, and ever firmer in its behalf, amid whatever wave of passion, malignity, and madness, even though the multitude all shout, Crucify! and devils be gathered thick as tiles on the house-tops of Worms to devour; so at the present hour it sacredly behooves Abolitionists to abide fast by their principles, and in the very midst of the present storm of passion and insane folly, in face of every assault, whether of threat or infliction, to speak for the slave and for man; and, with an earnestness and pointed emphasis unknown before, to press home upon their countrymen the question daily becoming more imminent and vital, whether the few vestiges of freedom yet remaining shall be blotted out, and this entire land overswept with tyranny, violence, and blood."

The members of the Convention refused to make any further attempt to hold a public meeting, but the citizens who were present at Dr. Pease's house resolved to attempt a meeting the next forenoon in the hall from which the convention had been expelled, for the express purpose of testing the faithfulness of the city authorities, and manifesting a just indignation at the outrage which had been perpetrated in our midst upon some of the fundamental rights of a free people. But the attempt was frustrated by the same rioters that had ruled the day before.

And the following night the mob celebrated their too successful onslaught upon popular liberty by a procession led by a band of music, with transparent banners, bearing these inscriptions: —

"FREEDOM OF SPEECH, BUT NOT TREASON."

"THE RIGHTS OF THE SOUTH MUST BE PROTECTED."

"ABOLITIONISM NO LONGER IN SYRACUSE."

"THE JERRY RESCUERS PLAYED OUT."

Prominently in the procession there were carried two large-sized effigies, — one of a man the other of a woman, — the former bearing my name, the latter Miss Anthony's. After parading through some of the principal streets, the procession repaired to Hanover Square, the centre of the business part of our city, and there amid shouts, hootings, mingled with disgusting profanity and ribaldry, the effigies were burned up; but not the great realities for which we were contending.

For more than thirty years the Abolitionists had been endeavoring to rouse the people to exterminate slavery by moral, ecclesiastical, and political instrumentalities, urging them to their duty by every religious consideration, and by reiterating the solemn admonition of Thomas Jefferson, that "If they would not liberate the enslaved in the land by the generous energies of their own minds and hearts, the slaves would be liberated by the awful processes of civil and servile war." But the counsels of the Abolitionists were spurned, their sentiments and purposes were shamelessly misrepresented, their characters traduced, their property destroyed, their persons maltreated. And lo! our country, favored of Heaven above all others, was given up to fratricidal, parricidal, and for a while we feared it would be suicidal war.

God be praised! the threatened dissolution of our Union was averted. But discord still reigns in the land. Our country is not surely saved. It was right that our Federal Government should be forbearing in their treatment of the Southern Rebels, because the people of the North had been, to so great an extent, their partners in the enslavement of our fellow-men, that it would have ill become us to have punished them condignly. But our Government has been guilty of great injustice to the colored population of the South, who were all loyal throughout the war. These should not have been left as they have been, in a great measure, at the mercy of their former masters. Homes and adequate portions of the land (they so long had cultivated without compensation) ought to have been secured to every family of the Freedmen, and some provision for their education should have been made. With these and the elective franchise conferred upon them, the Freedmen might safely have been left to maintain themselves in their new condition, and work themselves out of the evils that were enforced upon them by their long enslavement.

May the sad experience of the past prompt and impel our nation, before it be too late, to do all for the colored population of our country, South and North, that righteousness demands at our hands.

APPENDIX.

Appendix I.

On page 137 I have alluded to Hon. J. G. Palfrey. He evinced his respect for the rights of man by an act which was incomparably more significant and convincing than the most eloquent words could have been. On the death of his father, who was a slaveholder in Louisiana, he became heir to one third of the estate, comprising about fifty slaves. His co-heirs would readily have taken his share of these chattels and have given him an equivalent in land or money. But he was too conscientious to consent to such a bargain. If his portion of his father's bondmen should thereafter continue in slavery, it must be by an act of his own will, and involve him in the crime of making merchandise of men. From this his whole soul revolted. Accordingly, he requested that such a division of the slaves might be made as would put the largest number of them into his share. The money value of the women, children, and old men being much less than that of the able-bodied men, twenty-two of the slaves were assigned to him. I presume their market value could not have been less than nine thousand dollars. All of them were brought on, at Mr. Palfrey's expense, from Louisiana to Massachusetts.

Assisted by his Abolitionist friends, especially Mrs. L. M. Child, Mrs. E. G. Loring, and the Hathaways of Farmington, N. Y., and their Quaker friends, he succeeded after a while in getting them all well situated in good families, where the old were kindly cared for, the able-bodied adults were employed and duly remunerated for their labors, and the young were brought up to be worthy and useful. It has been my happiness to be personally acquainted with some of them and their friends, and to know that what I have stated above is true. Their transportation from Louisiana to Massachusetts; their maintenance here until places were found for them; and their removal to their several homes, must have cost Mr. Palfrey several hundred dollars, — I suppose eight or ten hundred. If so, he nobly sacrificed ten thousand dollars' worth of his patrimony to his sense of right and his love of liberty.

In 1847 this excellent man was elected a Representative of Massachusetts in the Congress of the United States. As those who knew him best confidently expected, he early took high antislavery ground there.

The following are extracts from his first speech in Congress: "The question is not at all between North and South, but between the many millions of non-slaveholding Americans, North, South, East, and West, and the very few hundreds of thousands of their fellow-citizens who hold slaves. It is time that this idea of a geographical distinction of parties, with relation to this subject, was abandoned. It has no substantial foundation. Freedom, with its fair train of boundless blessings for white and black, — slavery, with its untold miseries for both, — these are the two parties in the field. . . . . I will now only express my deliberate and undoubting conviction, that the time has quite gone by when the friends of slavery might hope anything from an attempt to move the South to disunion for its defence. . . . . I do not believe it is good policy for the slaveholders to let their neighbors hear them talk of disunion. Unless I read very stupidly the signs of the times, *it will not be the Union they will thus endanger, but the interest to which they would sacrifice it.* If they insist that the Union and slavery cannot live together, they may be taken at their word, but IT IS THE UNION THAT MUST STAND."

At its close, the Hon. J. Q. Adams is reported to have exclaimed: "Thank God the seal is broken! Lord, now lettest thou thy servant depart in peace." And "the old man eloquent" died at his post a month afterwards.

Appendix II.

On page 147 I have named, among other members of the Society of Friends who gave us efficient support in the day when we most needed help, Nathaniel Barney, then of Nantucket. He was one of the earliest of the immediate Abolitionists, was most explicit and fearless in the avowal of his sentiments, most consistent and conscientious in acting accordingly with them. He denounced "the prejudice against color as opposed to every precept and principle of the Gospel," and said, "It betrays a littleness of soul to which, when it is rightly considered, an honorable mind can never descend." Therefore, he would not ride in a stage-coach or other public conveyance, from which an applicant for a seat was excluded *because of his complexion.*

He was a stockholder in the New Bedford and Taunton Railroad. In 1842 he learned that *colored* persons were excluded from the cars on that road. Immediately he sent an admirable letter, dated April 14, 1842, to the New Bedford *Mercury* for publication, condemning such proscription. It was refused. He then offered it to the *Bulletin,* where it was likewise rejected. At length it appeared in the New Bedford *Morning Register*, and was worthy of being republished in every respectable newspaper in our country. In it he said: "The thought never entered my mind, when I advocated a liberal subscription to that railroad among our citizens, that I was contributing to a structure where, in coming years, should be exhibited a cowardice and despotism which I know the better feelings of the proprietors would, on reflection, repudiate. . . . . I cannot conscientiously withdraw the little I invested, neither can I sell my share of the stock of this road, while the existing proscriptive character attaches to it; and with my present views and feelings, so long as the privileges of the traveller are suspended on one of the accidents of humanity, I should be recreant to every principle of propriety and justice, *were I to receive aught of the price* which the directors attach to them. In the exclusion, therefore, by the established rules of one equally entitled with myself to a seat,

I am excluded from any share of the money, — the profit of said infraction of right."

Surely, the name of such a man ought to be handed down to our posterity to be duly honored, when the great and mean iniquity of our nation shall be abhorred.

Appendix III.

Speech of Gerrit Smith, referred to on page 169. I have omitted a few passages for want of room.

"On returning home from Utica last night, my mind was so much excited with the horrid scenes of the day, and the frightful encroachments made on the right of free discussion, that I could not sleep, and at three o'clock I left my bed and drafted this resolution: —

"'*Resolved,* That the right of free discussion, given to us by God, and asserted and guarded by the laws of our country, is a right so vital to man's freedom and dignity and usefulness, that we can never be guilty of its surrender, without consenting to exchange that freedom for slavery, and that dignity and usefulness for debasement and worthlessness.'

"I love our free and happy government, but not because it confers any new rights upon us. Our rights spring from a nobler source than human constitutions and governments, — from the favor of Almighty God.

"We are not indebted to the Constitution of the United States, or of this State, for the right of free discussion. We are thankful that they have hedged it about with so noble a defence. We are thankful, I say, that they have neither restrained nor abridged it; but we owe them no thanks for our possession of rights which God gave us. And the proof that he gave them is in the fact that he requires us to exercise them.

"When, then, this right of free discussion is invaded, this home-bred right, which is yours, and is mine, and belongs to every member of the human family, it is an invasion of something which was not obtained by human concession, something as old as our own being, a part of the original man, a component portion of our own identity, something which we cannot be deprived of without dismemberment, something which we never can deprive ourselves of without ceasing to be MEN.

"This right, so sacred and essential, is now sought to be trammelled, and is in fact virtually denied. . . . . Men in denying this right are not only guilty of violating the Constitution, and destroying the blessings bought by the blood and toil of our fathers, but guilty of making war with God himself. I want to see this right placed on this true, this infinitely high ground, as a DIVINE right. I want to see men defend it and exercise it with that belief. I want to see men determined to maintain, to their extremest boundaries, all the rights which God has given them for their enjoyment, their dignity, and their usefulness.

. . . . .

"We are even now threatened with legislative restrictions on this right. Let us tell our legislators, in advance, that we cannot bear any. The man who attempts to interpose such restrictions does a grievous wrong to God and man, which we cannot bear. Submit to this, and we are no longer what God made us to be, — MEN. Laws to gag men's mouths, to seal up their lips, to freeze up the warm gushings of the heart, are laws which the free spirit cannot brook; they are laws contrary alike to the nature of man and the commands of God; laws destructive of human happiness and the divine constitution; and before God and man they are null and void. They defeat the very purposes for which God made man, and throw him mindless, helpless, and worthless at the feet of the oppressor.

"And for what purpose are we called to throw down our pens, and seal up our lips, and sacrifice our influence over our fellow-men by the use of free discussion? If it were for an object of benevolence that we are called to renounce that freedom of speech with which God made us, there would be some color of fitness in the demand; but such a sacrifice the cause of truth and mercy never calls us to make. That cause requires the exertion, not the suppression, of our noblest powers. But here we are called on to degrade and unman ourselves, and to withhold from our fellow-men that influence which we ought to exercise for their good. And for what? I will tell you for what. That the oppressed may lie more passive at the feet of the oppressor; that one sixth of our American people may never know their rights; that two and a half millions of our countrymen, crushed in the cruel folds of slavery, may remain in all their misery and despair, without pity and without hope.

"For such a purpose, so wicked, so inexpressibly mean, the Southern slaveholder calls on us to lie down like whipped and trembling spaniels at his feet. Our reply is this: Our republican spirits cannot submit to such conditions. God did not make us, Jesus did not redeem us, for such vile and sinful uses.

"I knew before that slavery would not survive free discussion. But the demands recently put forth by the South for our surrender of the right of discussion, and the avowed reasons of that demand, involve a full concession of this fact, that free discussion is incompatible with slavery. The South, by her own showing, admits that slavery cannot live unless the North is tongue-tied. Now you, and I, and all these Abolitionists, have two objections to this: One is, we desire and purpose to employ all our influence lawfully and kindly and temperately to deliver our Southern brethren from bondage, and never to give rest to our lips or our pens till it is accomplished. The other objection is that we are not willing to be slaves ourselves. The enormous and insolent demands put forth by the South show us that the question is now, not only whether the blacks shall continue to be slaves, but whether our necks shall come under the yoke. While we are trying to break it off from others, we are called to see to it that it is not fastened on our own necks also.

"It is said: 'The South will not molest our liberty if we will not molest their slavery; they do not wish to restrict us if we will cease to speak of their peculiar institution.' Our liberty is not our *ex gratia* privilege, conceded to us by the South, and which we are to have more or less, as they please to allow. No, sir! The liberty which the South proffers us, to speak and write and print, if we do not touch that subject, is a liberty we do not ask, a liberty which we do not accept, but which we scornfully reject.

"It is not to be disguised, sir, that war has broken out between the South and the North, not easily to be terminated. Political and commercial men, for their own purposes, are industriously striving to restore peace; but the peace which they may accomplish will be superficial and hollow. True and permanent peace can only be restored by removing the cause of the war, — that is, *slavery*. It can never be established on any other terms. The sword now drawn will not be sheathed until that deep and damning stain is washed out from our nation. It is idle, criminal, to speak of peace on any other terms.

. . . . .

"Whom shall we muster on our side in this great battle between liberty and slavery? The many never will muster in such a cause, until they first see unequivocal signs of its triumph. We don't want the many, but the true-hearted, who are not skilled in the weapons of carnal warfare. We don't want the politicians, who, to secure the votes of the South, care not if slavery is perpetual. We don't want the merchant, who, to secure the custom of the South, is willing to applaud slavery, and leave his countrymen, and their children, and their children's children to the tender mercies of slavery forever.

"We want only one class of men for this warfare. Be that class ever so small, we want only those who will stand on the rock of Christian principle. We want men who can defend the right of free discussion on the ground that God gave it. We want men who will act with unyielding honesty and firmness. We have room for all such, but no room for the time-serving and selfish."

Appendix IV.

Notwithstanding the caution I have given my readers in the Preface and elsewhere, not to expect in this volume anything like a complete history of our antislavery conflict, many may be disappointed in not finding any acknowledgment of the services of some whom they have known as efficient, brave, self-sacrificing laborers in our cause. I was reproached, accused of ingratitude and injustice, because I did not give in my articles in *The Christian Register* any account of the labors of certain persons, whose names stand high on the roll of antislavery philanthropists. The following is a copy of a part of one of the letters that I received:—

BOSTON, April, 1868.

DEAR SIR,—The writer of this is a subscriber to *The Christian Register*, and has there read your "Reminiscences of the Antislavery Reformers." The numbers thus far (including the thirty-eighth) contain no notice of, or allusion to, our late lamented friend, Nathaniel P. Rogers, editor of *The Herald of Freedom*. His numerous friends in New England have been waiting and wondering that his name did not appear in your papers. Mr. Rogers gave up a lucrative profession, in which he had attained a high rank, and devoted himself *soul, body, and estate*, to the service of the antislavery cause, in which he labored conscientiously during the rest of his life, and left his family impoverished in consequence. That Mr. Rogers was one of the few most talented Abolitionists no one will deny who knew them; and that he was the intimate friend and fellow-laborer of Mr. Garrison was equally well known. He went to Europe with Mr. Garrison, and together they visited the most distinguished Abolitionists in England and Scotland; and, after his return, George Thompson, on his first visit to this country, was received by him in his family, and passed several days with him.

You have mentioned many names in your papers quite obscure, and of very little account in this movement, and why you have thus far omitted one of such prominence has puzzled many of your readers.

Notwithstanding, the writer will not allow himself to doubt that it is your intention in the end to do to all equal and exact JUSTICE.

I cordially indorse my unknown correspondent's eulogium of Nathaniel P. Rogers. I remember hearing much of his faithfulness and fearlessness in the cause of our enslaved countrymen, and of liberty of speech and of the press. Between the years 1836 and 1846 he wrote much, and so well that his articles in the *Herald of Freedom* were often republished in the *Antislavery Standard* and *Liberator.* I generally read them with great satisfaction. They were racy, spicy, and unsparing of anything he deemed wrong. Mr. Rogers, I have no doubt, rendered very important services to the antislavery cause, especially in New Hampshire, and was held in the highest esteem by the Abolitionists of that State. But it was not my good fortune to know much of him personally. I seldom saw him, and never heard him speak in any of our meetings more than two or three times. The only reason why I have only named him is that I really have no personal recollections of him. A volume of his writings, prefaced by a sketch of his life and character from the pen of Rev. John Pierpont, was published in 1847 and republished in 1849. It will repay any one for an attentive perusal, and help not a little to a knowledge of the temper of the times, — the spirit of the State and the Church, — when N. P. Rogers labored, sacrificed, and suffered for impartial liberty, for personal, civil, and religious freedom. The fact that he was a lineal descendant of the never-to-be-forgotten Rev. John Rogers — the martyr of Smithfield — and also one of the Peabody race, will add to the interest with which his writings will be read.

Appendix V.

An intimation is given on page 272 that I have known some remarkable colored women. I wish my readers had seen, in her best days, *Sojourner Truth.* She was a tall, gaunt, very black person, who made her appearance in our meetings at an early period. Though then advanced in life, she was very vigorous in body and mind. She was a slave in New York State, from her birth in 1787 until the abolition of slavery in that State in 1827, and had never been taught to read. But she was deeply religious. She had a glowing faith in the power, wisdom, and goodness of God. She had had such a full experience of the wrongs of slavery, that she could not believe they were permitted by God. She was sure He must hate them, and would destroy those who persisted in perpetrating them. She often spoke in our meetings, never uttering many sentences, but always such as were pertinent, impressive, and sometimes thrilling.

Appendix VI.

On page 283 I have spoken of Harriet Tubman. She deserves to be placed first on the list of American heroines. Having escaped from slavery twenty-two years ago, she set about devising ways and means to help her kindred and acquaintances out of bondage. She first succeeded in leading off her brother, with his wife and several children. Then she helped her aged parents from slavery in Virginia to a free and comfortable home in Auburn, N. Y. Thus encouraged she continued for several years her semi-annual raids into the Southern plantations. Twelve or fifteen times she went. Most adroitly did she evade the patrols and the pursuers. Very large sums of money were offered for her capture, but in vain. She succeeded in assisting nearly two hundred persons to escape from slavery.

When the war broke out she felt, as she said, that "the good Lord has come down to deliver my people, and I must go and help him." She went into Georgia and Florida, attached herself to the army, performed an incredible amount of labor as a cook, a laundress, and a nurse, still more as the leader of soldiers in scouting parties and raids. She seemed to know no fear and scarcely ever fatigue. They called her their *Moses.* And several of the officers testified that her services were of so great value, that she was entitled to a pension from the Government. The life of this remarkable woman has been written by a lady, — Mrs. Bradford, — and published in Auburn, N. Y. I hope many of my readers will procure copies of it, that they may know more about Harriet Tubman.

Appendix VII.

The saddest, most astounding evidence of the demoralization of our Northern citizens in respect to slavery, and of Mr. Webster's depraving influence upon them, is given in the following letter addressed to him soon after the delivery of his speech on the 7th of March, — signed by eight hundred of the prominent citizens of Massachusetts. I have given the names of a few as specimens of the whole.

From the Boston Daily Advertiser of April 2, 1850.

To the Hon. Daniel Webster:

Sir, — Impressed with the magnitude and importance of the service to the Constitution and the Union which you have rendered by your recent speech in the Senate of the United States on the subject of slavery, we desire to express to you our deep obligation for what this speech has done and is doing to enlighten the public mind, and to bring the present crisis in our national affairs to a fortunate and peaceful termination. As citizens of the United States, we wish to thank you for recalling us to our duties under the Constitution, and for the broad, national, and patriotic views which you have sent with the weight of your great authority, and with the power of your unanswerable reasoning into every corner of the Union.

It is, permit us to say, sir, no common good which you have thus done for the country. In a time of almost unprecedented excitement, when the minds of men have been bewildered by an apparent conflict of duties, and when multitudes have been unable to find solid ground on which to rest with security and peace, you have pointed out to a whole people the path of duty, have convinced the understanding and touched the conscience of a nation. You have met this great exigency as a patriot and a statesman, and although the debt of gratitude which the people of this country owe to you was large before, you have increased it by a peculiar service, which is felt throughout the land.

We desire, therefore, to express to you our entire concurrence in the sentiments of your speech, and our heartfelt thanks for the inestimable aid it has afforded towards the preservation and perpetuation of the Union. For this purpose, we respectfully present to you this, our Address of thanks and congratulation, in reference to this most interesting and important occasion in your public life.

We have the honor to be, with the highest respect,

Your obedient servants,

T. H. PERKINS,
CHARLES C. PARSONS,
THOMAS B. WALES,
CALEB LORING,
WM. APPLETON,
JAMES SAVAGE,
CHARLES P. CURTIS,
CHARLES JACKSON,
GEORGE TICKNOR,
BENJ. R. CURTIS,
RUFUS CHOATE,
JOSIAH BRADLEE,
EDWARD G. LORING,
THOMAS B. CURTIS,
FRANCIS J. OLIVER,
J. A. LOWELL,
J. W. PAGE,
THOMAS C. AMORY,
BENJ. LORING,
GILES LODGE,
WM. P. MASON,
WM. STURGIS,
W. H. PRESCOTT,
SAMUEL T. ARMSTRONG,
SAMUEL A. ELIOT,
JAMES JACKSON,
MOSES STUART,*
LEONARD WOODS,*
RALPH EMERSON,*
JARED SPARKS,†
C. C FELTON,‡

And over seven hundred others.

* Of the Theological Institution at Andover.
† President of Harvard University.
‡ Professor of Greek in Harvard University.

THE END.

Cambridge: Electrotyped and Printed by Welch, Bigelow, & Co.

www.ingramcontent.com/pod-product-compliance
Lightning Source LLC
LaVergne TN
LVHW020058110826
845151LV00001B/10
9781425544881